PRODUCTION MANAGEMENT AND MATERIALS MANAGEMENT

TEXT AND CASES

[Suitable for BBA(H), MBA and PGDM Programmes of Indian Universities and B-Schools]

Prof. S.K. Sarangi

B. Tech (Hons-IIT Kgp) PGDM (Eqv. MBA) M. Phill (Mgmt),
C. Engg. MACS (USA) MIMA AMT (AIMA) FIE FIV.
Head, Deptt. of Business Administration

&

VICE-PRINCIPAL

B.P. Poddar Institute of Management and Technology

Salt Lake, Kolkata (India)

Asian Books Private Limited

7/28, Mahavir Lane, Vardan House, Ansari Road,
Darya Ganj, New Delhi - 110 002.

Production and Materials Management
S. K. Sarangi

Asian Books Private Limited

Registered and Editorial Office
7/28, Mahavir Lane, Vardan House, Ansari Road, Darya Ganj, New Delhi - 110 002.
E-Mail : asian@asianbooksindia.com
World Wide Web : http://www.asianbooksindia.com
Phones : 23287577, 23282098, 23271887, 23259161
Fax : 91 11 23262021

First Published : 2011
ISBN: 978-81-8412-148-3

Published by **Kamal Jagasia** for Asian Books Pvt. Ltd., 7/28, Mahavir Lane, Vardan House, Darya Ganj, New Delhi - 110 002.

Typeseting at **ADD Computers,** B-49, Joshi Colony Patpar Ganj I.P. Extn. New Delhi-1100092

Printed at **Yash Printograph's,** Delhi

Sales Offices

Bangalore 103, Swiss Complex No. 33, Race Course Road, Bangalore - 560 001
Ph.: 080-22200438, 32942173 Fax : 91 80 22256583
Email : asianblr@blr.vsnl.net.in

Chennai 17, Mezzanine Floor, Pycrofts Road, 1st street, Royapettah, Chennai-600014
Ph. : 044-28601927/28, 32979058
Fax : +91-44-28486927
Email : asianchennai@asianbooksindia.com

Delhi 7/28, Mahavir Lane, Vardan House, Ansari Road, Darya Ganj, New Delhi - 110 002
Phones : 011-23287577, 23282098, 23271887, 23259161, Fax : 91 11 23262021
E-Mail : asian@asianbooksindia.com

Guwahati 6, G.N.B. Road, Panbazar, Guwahati, Assam - 781 001
Ph. : 0361-2513020, 2635729
Email : asianghy1@sancharnet.in

Hyderabad 3-5-315, Street No. 7, Narayanguda, Vittalwadi, Hyderabad - 500 029
Phones : 040-23220112, 23220113, 32927534 Fax : 91 40 24751152
Email : hydasianbooks@gmail.com

Kolkata 10 A, Hospital Street, 700 072
Ph. : 033-22153040, 32506706 Fax : 91 33 22159899
Email : calasian@vsnl.net.in

Mumbai (wadala) Shop No. 3 & 4 Ground Floor Shilpin Centre
40, GD. Ambekar Marg, Sewree Wadala Estate, Wadala, Mumbai - 400031
Ph. : 022-32510689, 24157611-12 Fax 91-22-24157613
Email : asianbk@mtnl.net.in

Mumbai (VT) 103, Blackie House, walchand marg, opp. GPO, Mumbai - 400001
Ph : 022-22657807, 32037931, 32047807
Email : asianbooksvt@asianbooksindia.com

Pune Shop No. 5-8, Ground Floor Shaan Brahma Complex, Near Ratan Theatre,
Budhwar Peth, Pune - 02
Ph. : 020-32304554, 24497208 Fax : 91-20-24497207
Email : asianpune@asianbooksindia.com

Dedicated To The Divine Mother

Preface

Production Management and Materials Management are part of syllabi of BBA and MBA/PGDM of all Indian Universities and B-Schools.

For W.B. University of Technology, Production Management and Materials Management are studied under two separate papers for BBA (H) fourth semester and for MBA second semester these two subjects are combined under one paper "Production and Operations Management".

Quality Management aspects consisting of Inspections and Quality Control, TQM and Six Sigma etc. are also studied under above papers

Having taught these subjects for more than a decade in UG and PG levels of Management, I felt the urge of writing a textbook covering above Programmes and hence the new book under the title "Production Management and Materials Management".

The book has been written in simple language and style with large number of solved numericals. Interesting case studies are provided on Plant Location, Production system, Customer Demand Planning, Aggregate Planning, Inventory Management and MRPII (Resource Planning) to help students gain in-depth knowledge about the subjects.

In addition to the Probable questions for each chapter, a comprehensive "Question Bank" is given at the end of the book to facilitate students prepare for the examination.

I am thankful to Ms. Purobi Biswas, Production Manager, Asian Books Pvt. Ltd. for her keen interest and sincere efforts in publishing this book.

Prof. S. K. Sarangi
Author

Contents

UNIT-I

Production Management

1

Production Management System

• Production and Operations Management Systems • Manufacturing and Services—Differences and Similarities • Production Function and its Interrelation with other Functions with an Organisation • Probable Questions

1.1 PRODUCTION AND OPERATIONS MANAGEMENT SYSTEMS

1.1.1 Introduction

Production implies the creation of goods and services to satisfy human wants. It involves the transformation of inputs (resources) into outputs (products).

Production is the process of transforming raw materials or purchased components into finished products for sale.

In a wide sense, production is the process of producing something useful with the object of satisfying human wants.

The activities of universities, transportation agencies, hospitals, insurance companies etc. also involve production function. Production function takes place in all profit and non-profit making organisations including public agencies e.g. factories, offices, hospitals, banks, stores etc.

Operations management refers to the planning, co-ordination and control of all the activities concerned with the conversion of inputs into outputs. Operations management is found in all types of organizations which are involved in producing services and goods.

1.1.2 Examples of Operations Systems

Operations management in a wider term is a production arrangement, Operations management covers service organizations like Banks, Hotels, Air-lines, Insurance companies and Hospitals etc. On the other hand, production management covers only the manufacturing organizations.

Few examples of application of operations management are given as under:

Operation Function in various Enterprises

System Organization	*Inputs*	*Transformation Process*	*Outputs*
Sugar Mill	Sugar Cane	Chemical and Mechanical	Sugar, Molases buggase
Steel Plant	Iron Ore, Flaxes	Chemical	Pig Iron, Steel Slag
Cement Plant	Lime Stones, Gypsum	Chemical	Cement, Clinker
Automobile Plant	Steel Plates components	Fabrication and assembly	Motor vehicles

Contd....

System Organization	*Inputs*	*Transformation Process*	*Outputs*
Hotel	Customers	Boarding and lodging	Food and rests for customers
Hospitals	Patients	Health	Cured Patients
Bank	Customers	Banking	Receipt and lending

1.1.3 Planning and Operating the Production System

Production management implies planning, organising directing and controlling the activities of the production function which is concerned with the conversion of raw materials into finished products.

Production system is the framework within which the production activities of an organization are carried out. Production system is sub-system of the economic system.

The production system is composed of the following sub-systems.

(*a*) **Inputs:** Inputs are the physical and human resources utilised in the production process.

(*b*) **Conversion Process:** Conversion processes refer to a series of operations which are performed on materials, equipment, human effort etc. Inputs constitute the variable costs of production.

(*c*) **Output:** Outputs are the products or completed parts resulting from the conversion process. Outputs generate revenues.

(*d*) **Storage:** Storage takes place after the receipt of inputs, between one operation and other and after the output.

(*e*) **Transportation:** Inputs are transported from one operation to another in the production processes.

(*f*) **Information:** The information sub-system of production system interconnects all physical activities and serves as a basis for managerial decision making.

It provides system control through measurement, comparison, feedback and corrective action.

1.1.4 Controlling Operations with Emphasis on Information System

(*a*) **Production information system:** can be sub-divided into four categories which are given below:

1. **Transaction Processing System:** This sub-system is designed for processing day to day transactions occurring in the production department. It involves large volume of data and mainly helps in the operation of production control function.
2. **Information Providing System:** This sub-system generates information relevant to decision making in production. Production reports are created to provide information concerning manufacturing operations.
3. **Decision Support System:** It is designed to improve the analytical capability of the decision maker.
4. **Programmed Decision System:** An attempt is made here to create systems for programmed decisions. The procedure used in the decision making area is clearly specified.

(*b*) Information Needs of Production Function: A large manufacturing organization requires information regarding the following:

(*i*) Products to be manufactured, relationship with market demand.

(*ii*) Plant Capacity and its utilisation.

(*iii*) Manufacturing system and technology.

(*iv*) Machines and equipment.

(*v*) Product specifications and bill of materials.

(*vi*) Operating costs.

(*vii*) Degree of scrap, spoilage and rework etc.

(*viii*) Alternative materials and their sources.

(*ix*) Materials control, quality control and inventory control system.

(*x*) Cost-volume-profit relationship.

(*xi*) Future market demand and capacity.

(*c*) Production Manager requires information reports concerning following:

(*i*) Production levels achieved.

(*ii*) Variation between budgeted production and actual production.

(*iii*) Orders in hand.

(*iv*) Abnormal production losses of materials, labour and idle facilities.

(*v*) Report of idle labour time due to want of materials or power or broken-down equipment.

(*vi*) Report on machine utilization.

(*d*) Advantages of Information System: The main advantages are as follows:

(*i*) Developing a comprehensive production planning and control system.

(*ii*) Better allocation and management of resources.

(*iii*) Better co-ordination between marketing and production.

(*iv*) Efficient utilisation of Production facilities.

(*v*) Cost effective management inventory.

(*vi*) Flexibility in a manufacturing system to respond quickly to changes in market conditions.

1.3 FACTORS OF PRODUCTION

Production is an organised activity in a manufacturing organization.

The primary responsibility of the Production activity is to produce a product or products at (1) Pre-established Cost (2) according to the specified quality and (3) within the stipulated time schedule.

Main factors of Production are shown as under:

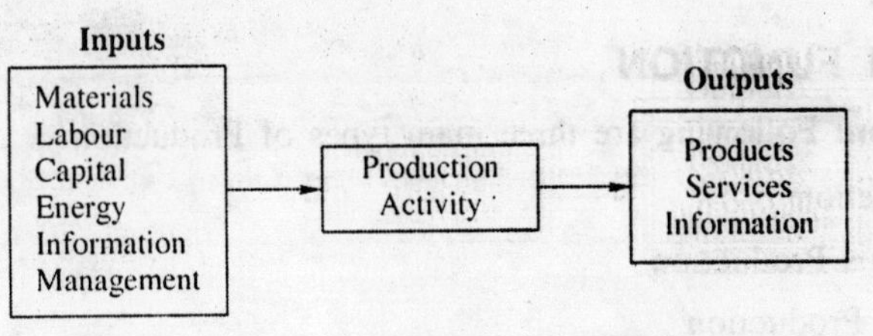

Figure 1.1

Input Factors

Materials: Raw materials and auxiliary items are supplied in proper quantities and qualities.

Labour: Skilled, semi-skilled and un-skilled varieties are necessarily required in production function. Labour efficiency or Labour productivity is very important for efficient Production function.

Capital: Fixed capital is used for acquiring land, constructing building, procuring and installing equipment and machinery and working capital or floating capital is used for day-to-day production activities.

Energy: Electric power and fuels such as coal, diesel or furnace oil are usually the sources of energy in production function. Optimum consumption of energy can keep the cost of production low and results in higher profitability.

Information: Information regarding correct sources, qualities and prices of all materials and energy and about other factors of production is very vital and this helps in controlling the production function and in maintaining high productivity and low cost of Production.

Management: Management is the systematic process of planning, organising, directing, controlling and co-ordinating the activities of production function.

For the production function, Management consists of The Head of Manufacturing unit and his/her subordinate executives and supervisors involved directly or indirectly in the production activity.

Products/Services: These are outputs of the Production Function. Output products are produced in specified quantities and in proper qualities.

Theory of Production and Cost

Production is the basic activity of all industrial units. The production activity is the step-by-step conversion of input materials into a finished product or products.

A production activity produces a product of correct quality, correct quantity, at right time and place and at optimum cost.

Thus, ***Production management is the process of planning, organising, directing, controlling and co-ordinating the activities of production function for the conversion of raw materials into finished products.***

Mass Production

Mass production aims at producing a standardised product on a large scale. The various parts or components of an automobile are produced on large scales as per their standards. These components go through sub-assembly and final assembly for making a car.

Mass production results in uniform quality and low unit cost of production.

1.4 PRODUCTION FUNCTION

1. **Production Function:** Following are three main types of Production:

   (*a*) Job or Unit Production

   (*b*) Mass or Continuous Production

   (*c*) Batch or Quantity Production

Most important task of the Production management is to deal with decision making related to Production processes so that the goods manufactured are according to the specifications in the required quantity, at minimum cost and as per Schedule.

The production function can be represented by the simple mathematical equation:

$$Y = f(X_1, X_2 \text{ etc.})$$

where Y = Units of outputs, which is a function of the quantity of two or more inputs with X_1 indicating units of labour and X_2 units of machinery.

The Cobb-Douglas function (of USA) is given by

$$P = 1.01L^{0.75} \quad C^{0.26} \quad R_2^{0.9409}$$

where P = Total output

L = Index of Labour employed in manufacturing

C = Index of fixed capital in manufacturing

R_2 = Coefficient of determination

The above function shows that by 1% change in labour input (L) is associated by 0.75% change in output when Capital (C) is fixed. Likewise, by 1% change in Capital (C) when labour (L) is constant, there is change of 0.26% in output. The coefficient of determination R_2 shows that 94% of the variations on the dependent variable (P) were accounted for by the variations in the independent variable (L and C).

1.5 TYPES OF PRODUCTION

A. Basis of Batch or Continuous types

1. Batch or Intermittent Production: If a production facility is set up only for a short time and then changed for some other product, this is known as batch or intermittent production method.

Usually, Paints are produced in the batch process in a particular vessel using vehicle and specific pigments.

A particular job is processed in various machines in a workshop, using the batch or intermittent production method. Ministeel plants' foundries use batch production for steel castings.

2. Characteristics of Batch Production:

- Most of the products adopted are made in small quantities.
- Similar types of equipment are grouped at one place *i.e.*, Process Layout.
- Work load is different in different departments.
- General purpose-types of machines are used.
- Raw material inventories are high.
- Requires more floor space and storage space etc.

3. Advantages of Batch Production:

- Best advantage is flexibility.
- Small quantities of numerous orders for production are acceptable.
- Cost of Production is usually high due to change in production set up.
- Plant layout is flexible.
- Emergency rush orders can be pushed effectively.
- There is less risk due to sudden change in market demand.
- Initial investment is less.

4. Disadvantages:

- Product quality may be non uniform.
- Consumption of utilities may be varying per unit product.
- Unit cost of Production may be higher compared to continuous Production.
- Requires more labour, man-hours per unit product compared to continuous production.

5. Continuous Production: Crude Oil Refining is an example of continuous production.

Important factors for Continuous Production:

- Large quantity and small variety is essential.
- Product layout should be adopted.
- Machine capacity and workloads are balanced.
- Operators' high skill is not necessary.
- Raw materials inventories are low.
- Requires less floor space and storage space etc.
- Products of uniform quality are produced.
- Lower unit lost of Production is the main advantage.
- Labour cost per unit of Product is low.

6. Disadvantages of continuous production:

- Product changes are difficult.
- Power failure and machine breakdown result in more wastage and production loss.
- Less flexibility compared to Batch Production.

B. Basis of goods produced

(*i*) Production of capital goods such as Machineries, Equipment, Diesel Generator Sets, Automobiles, Pump & Motor Sets etc. need production of various parts/items which go through the process of sub-assemblies and assemblies to transform into a whole capital item. They use both batch and continuous types of production.

(*ii*) Production of consumer-durable goods such as Refrigerators, TV Sets, Washing Machines and Personal-Computers etc. uses sub-assemblies and final assemblies for production. They too use both batch and continuous production methods.

(*iii*) Production of consumer goods such as Soaps and Detergents, Shampoo and Talcum Powder, Tooth Paste, Ice-cream and Soft-drink etc. which are produced normally using continuous production process.

C. Basis of Technology used

(*a*) High-Technology Production System: This uses patented and well guarded technology such as Micro Soft Technology for Word Processing, and many Pharmaceutical technologies also are patented and proprietorial. Duplication is not easy for these items.

(*b*) Low-Technology Production System: Such as production of Confectioneries, Cornflex and Jeans etc. Examples are KELLOG'S Cornflex and Levi Strauss's Jeans trousers which are easy to duplicate.

1.6 MANUFACTURING AND SERVICES—DIFFERENCES AND SIMILARITIES

(*a*) Differences: The differences between manufacturing and services operation may be described in the following tabular form:

Manufacturing	*Services*
Physical and durable product	Intangible and perishable product
Output can be stored	Output cannot stored
Low degree of customer contact for the organisation	High degree of customer contact for the organisation

Contd....

Manufacturing	*Services*
Long response time	Short response time
Regional, national or international market	Mostly local market
Large infrastructure	Small infrastructure
Capital intensive	Labour intensive
Quality easily measured	Quality not easily measured

(*b*) Similarities between manufacturing and service operations:

- Both the manufacturing and service organisations concerned about quality and timely deliveries to customers.
- Even though service can not be inventoried, the service organisations like Hospitals should store the inputs like medicines etc. which transform in the form of service when necessary.
- So far as customer contact is concerned, the back room of a bank or a back room of a courier service has little contact with customers. This is similar to manufacturing organisation.

Presently, contributions of manufacturing and services for India's GDP are 25% and 55% respectively. The balance 20% contribution to GDP comes from Agriculture.

1.7 PRODUCTION FUNCTION AND ITS INTERRELATION WITH OTHER FUNCTIONS WITHIN AN ORGANISATION

Let us consider a manufacturing unit producing consumer goods is located in a suburban area or a village with its corporate office located in a city or large town in India.

The various functioning departments of the manufacturing unit are shown below with the help of a structured format.

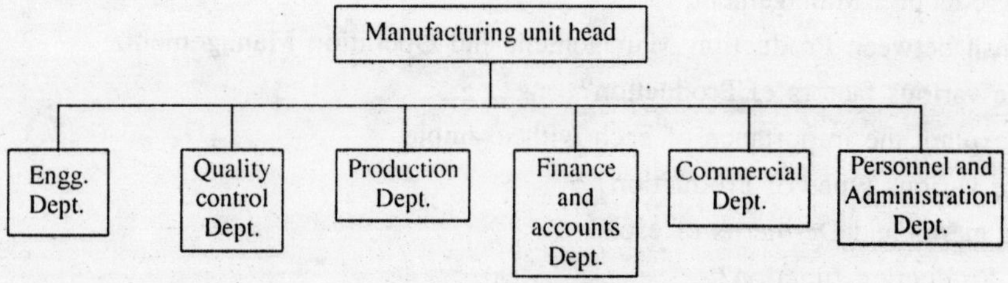

Figure 1.2 Various Departments of a Manufacturing Unit.

While the Manufacturing Unit Head is designated as General Manager (Works), the departments shown above are all headed by respective managers.

Thus the head of Production department is Production Manager and the head of Commercial department is Manager (Commercial) and so on.

Marketing department which renders a vital function is headed by Marketing Manager and is located at the Corporate office.

Every month's manufacturing programme is given by Marketing department indicating type of goods, quantities with dates and the respective quality parameters.

The production department prepares the necessary bill of materials showing types, quantities, dates and quality specifications. This bill of materials is sent to purchase section in the form of materials requisition.

The Commercial department has two sections *i.e.*, Purchase and General Stores and Finished Product Ware-house.

Similarly, the General Stores verify the stock position and takes action for the procurement of general items and spare parts.

The Production bill of materials is also the guiding document for the Engineering department which performs various Engineering functions *i.e.*, Mechanical maintenance, Electrical maintenance, Building and Civil maintenance and Instrumentation repair and maintenance activities.

The quality control department helps the production department in the inspection and quality control functions and finally grading the day production into acceptable and rejected varieties. It also checks the quality of all input items used in the manufacturing system.

The personnel and administration department is responsible for keeping the attendance, leave records, performance appraisals including manpower planning, selection recruitment and training and development functions of various categories of personnel for the Production and interrelated departments of the manufacturing unit.

The finance and accounts department makes payment of wages and salaries of the personnel and also helps the production department in the cost control and cost accounting activities.

The Finished Product warehouse records are maintained by the commercial department which also arranges transport and despatches finished products as per advice of the Marketing department located in the Corporate office.

The General Manager (Works) as the head of the manufacturing unit co-ordinates all the inter departmental activities and reports to the Managing Director in the Corporate office and is responsible for smooth and economic functioning of the unit.

1.8 PROBABLE QUESTIONS

1. Define Production Management.
   Distinguish between Production Management and Operation Management.
2. What are various factors of Production?
   Briefly explain the importance of each with example.
3. What are various types of Production?
   Describe merits and De-merits of each.
4. What is Production function?
   Illustrate the significance of Cobb-Douglas Production function.
5. Briefly describe the inter-relationship of Production function with other important functions in an organisation.

2

Physical Facilities of Production

• Organisation of Physical Facilities for Production • Factory Organisations • Probable Questions.

2.1 ORGANISATION OF PHYSICAL FACILITIES FOR PRODUCTION SYSTEM

Physical facilities imply all the auxiliary and support facilities required to operate the plant and machinery. The facilities play a vital role in the smooth and efficient running of the Production System.

The main utilities required in industry are illustrated below:

***(i)* Land:** Requirement of land has been further described under factory location.

***(ii)* Building:** Requirement of buildings depends on type of industries. Pharmaceutical and Iron & Steel plants require more buildings, whereas oil refineries require less buildings and more storage tanks.

Buildings should be designed to facilitate gravity flow of materials, use of sunlight in the day time and utilise natural ventilation as much as possible.

***(iii)* Water:** Water is required in industry for several puposes *i.e.*, process, steam generation, cooling, fire fighting, drinking etc. in Pulp and Paper, Chemicals, and Power Plants, efficient water management is essential for the very functioning of the unit. Water has to be pumped to different sections of the plant and recovered water has to be brought back, treated and recycled.

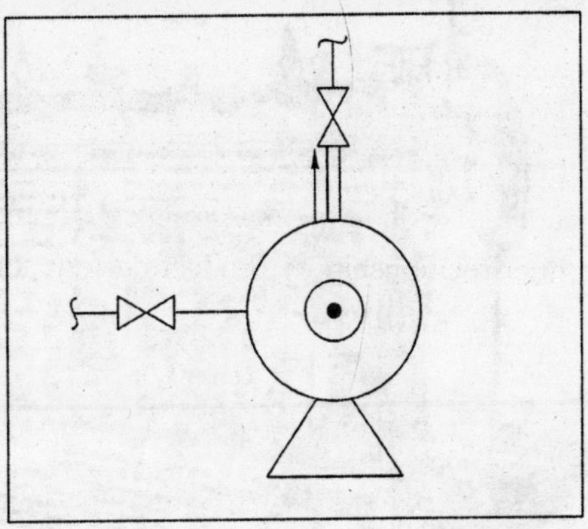

Figure 2.1 A centrifugal Pump for pumping water.

***(iv)* Steam Generation:** In a manufacturing process, steam may be used for heating and for generating power. Boilers and steam turbines are installed to generate steam and electrical power.

The capacities of boilers are in terms of quantity of steam generated per hour at a particular pressure and temperature. The type of boiler to be installed depends on the fuels to be used, their mix and availability etc.

The following figures illustrate a fire-tube and water-tube boilers.

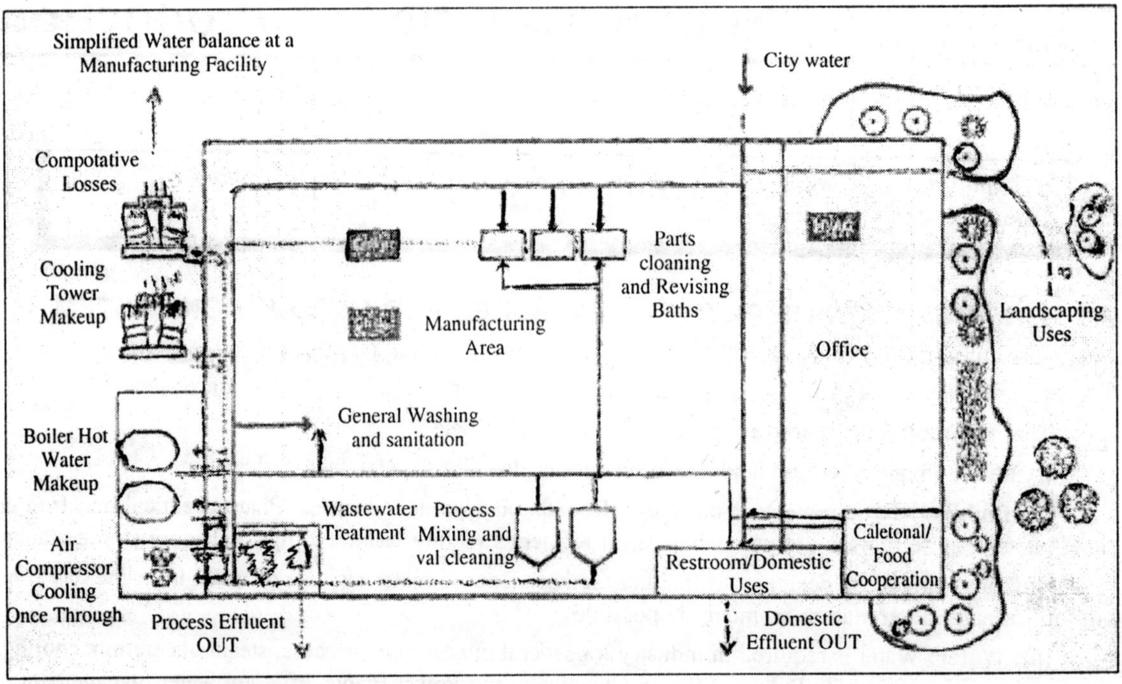

Figure 2.2 Water Supply and Distribution System for Manufacturing Unit.

Figure 2.3 Sectional view of a Fire-Tube boiler for steam generation.

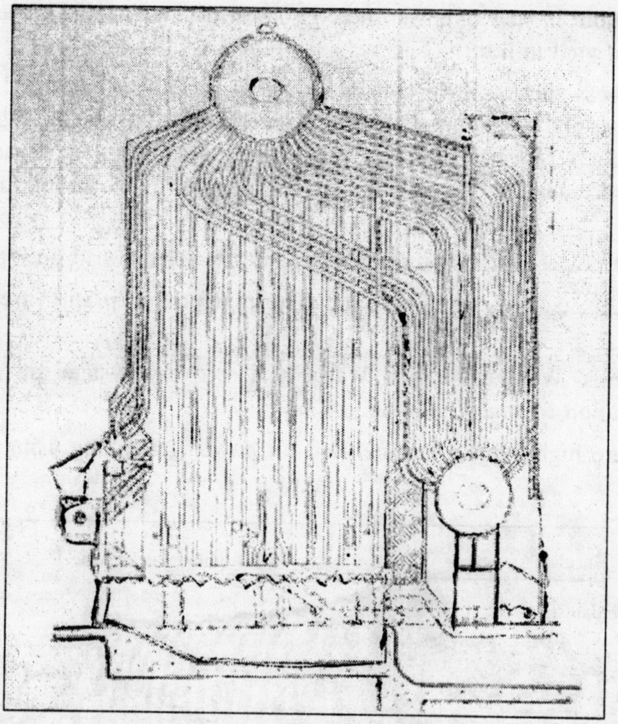

Figure 2.4 Sectional view of a vertical Water-Tube Boiler for steam generation.

(*v*) Compressed Air: This utility is necessary for pneumatic transport of granular materials, operation of knife-gate valves for process control and operation of pneumatic instrumentation systems. Several compressors are installed to supply compressed air to the plant.

The following figure illustrates a two-stage Air Compressor.

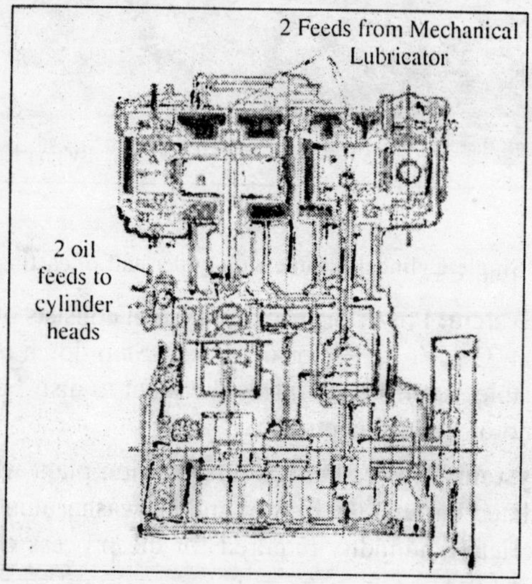

Figure 2.5 Double acting two-stage compressor.

***(vi)* Power Generation:** In view of power shortage and critical nature of a process in the manufacturing system, power becomes a vital utility.

Manufacturing process such as Pulp and Paper Mills, Pharmaceuticals and Soaps and Detergents etc. which use steam at low and medium pressures find it economical to install co-generation power plants for minimising their unit cost of production and to gain competitive advantage over small and medium scale units who are unable to install co-generation power plants owing to low economy scale of operation.

Other plants install power generation system as stand-by for the grid power.

Diesel generating sets, Gas turbines and Thermal-power plants are installed for power generation.

Solar energy systems, Wind Mills, and Waste heat recovery system are some non-conventional sources for power generation for many plants.

The following figure high-lights a turbine used for power generation using steam from boilers.

Figure 2.6 Single-Cylinder turbine with upper half of casting removed.

***(vii)* Power Distribution System:** Power distribution system consists of sub-station where grid power is received at high voltage *i.e.*, at 33 KV, 11 KV or 6 KV etc. Step down transformers, Switch gears and Circuit breakers and necessary cables are installed inside the plant to distribute the power to all the motors in the plant through sectional motor control centres.

***(viii)* Air Conditioning System:** This contains a refrigeration plant which produces chilled water at 7–8°C. This child water is circulated through the blower and air washer unit for producing the conditioned air at desired temperature and relative humidity required for the process of manufacturing.

Figure 2.7 indicates a refrigeration unit for the above system.

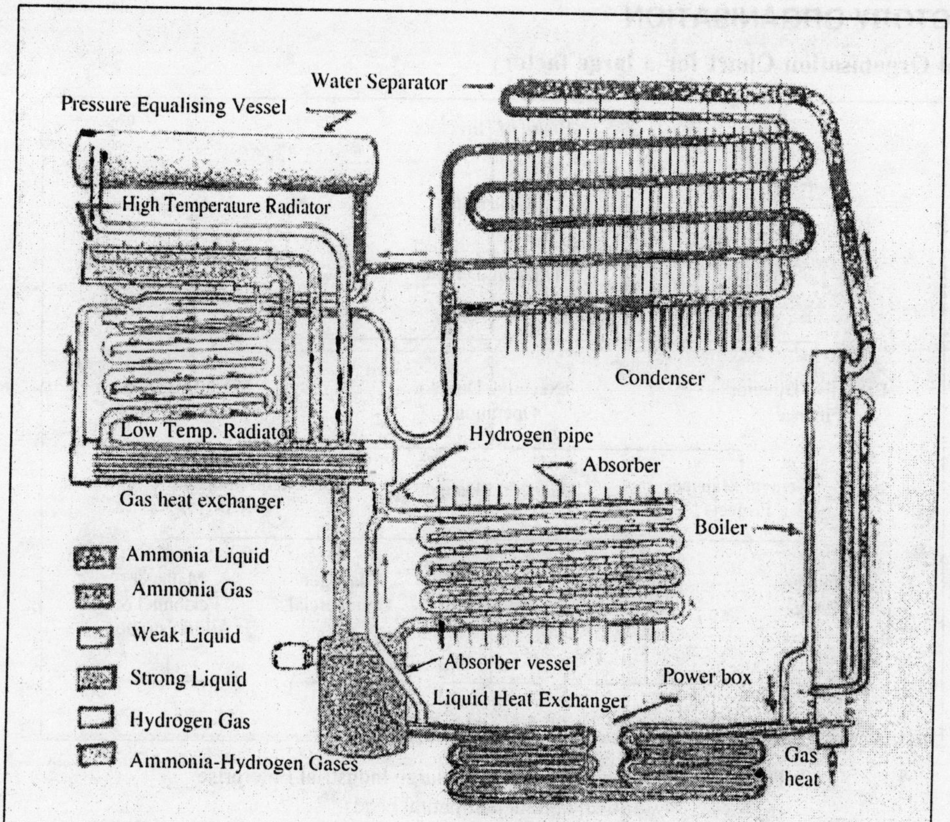

Figure 2.7 A Refrigeration Unit.

***(ix)* Protection of Environment:** Due to existence of the green bench at the Supreme Court and at ıe High Courts and due to growing concern of the people for clean environment, the Pollution Control oards at the Centre and the State levels have prescribed "The Minimal National Standards" for the waste-ıatters of the manufacturing unit for disposal to the surface water, land and atmosphere.

The Effluent Treatment Plants consist of Sump tank, Primary clari flocculater, Aeration Pond, econdary Clarifier and Vacuum-filters etc. for treating the toxic effluent from a manufacturing unit using e activated sludge process for final disposal to land or surface water source.

Similarly, the smoke or flue gas from the plant is treated through Mechanical Dust Collector, Bag lter or Electrostatic Precipitators before discharging through chimney to atmosphere.

***(x)* Miscellaneous:** Other utilities used in a manufacturing unit may be as follows:

- Nitrogen Plant
- Oxygen Plant
- Ventilation System
- Cooling Tower Plant
- Humidification Unit
- Fire Fighting System, etc.

2.2 FACTORY ORGANISATION

(*i*) Typical Organisation Chart for a large factory

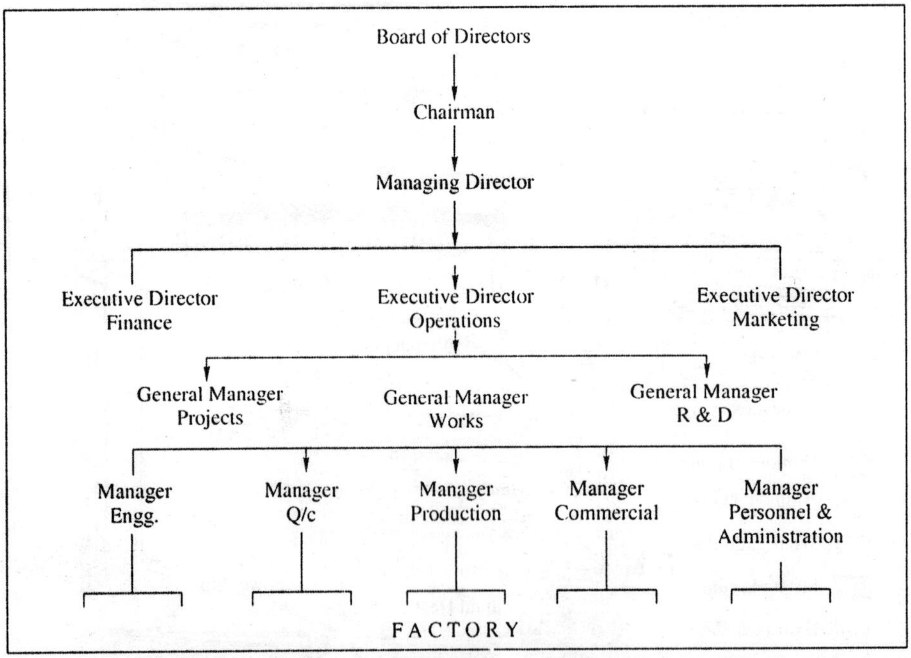

Figure 2.8 Organisation Chart for large Industrial Enterprise Shown upto departmental heads.

(*ii*) Various functional heads in factory: Description of the Organisation Chart.

The chart has shown Corporate office and Factory organisation levels separately. Normally, for a large company, the corporate office is situated in town/city and the day-to-day operational management is handled at the factory level.

For the factory level, General Manager (Works) is the administrative in-charge and so far as administration is concerned GM (Projects) and GM (R & D) have to consult him or taken his concurrence.

Manager (Production) is responsible for all production functions starting from use of raw materials, chemicals upon production of finished products.

For a continuous process the operations are carried out in continuous three shifts throughout the year.

Manager (Engineering) is responsible for maintenance of plant and machineries, generation and supply of power and utilities for production.

Manager (Q/C) is responsible for Quality Control and Quality Assurance.

Manager (Commercial) is responsible for all Commercial matters such as Purchase, General Stores, Inventory Control, Central Excise, Finished Product, Ware-house and despatches of finished products as per instructions from the marketing department. He is also responsible for all receipts including raw materials, coal/fuels and auxiliary materials etc.

Manager (Personnel & Administration) is responsible for all personnel matters starting from time office, recruitment, factory discipline, security and safety etc. Welfare and recreational activities and factory transport also are managed by him.

***(iii)* Factory Administration:** General Manager (Works) administrates the factory matters through all departmental heads.

Once in a day he calls for a meeting in which all functional heads are present. Matters relating to Production, raw materials, auxiliary materials, Power and fuels consumed and quantities of finished products produced in the previous day are reported in the meeting. Quality aspects including productivity, shifts attendance, absenteeism etc. are also discussed and recorded. Also reported are purchases and despatches for the day.

General Manager (Works) sends out a comprehensive statement concerning above matters to the corporate office through Fax, E-mail or Courier.

For the sake of efficient administration, General Manager (Works) gives due importance in maintaining and improving material productivity, labour productivity, Quality of finished products and personnel discipline in the factory.

***(iv)* Corporate Office:** In a public sector unit, the Chairman and Managing Director are the same person, but in many private organizations, Chairman is a non-executive person and Managing Director becomes responsible for all day-to-day matters.

Managing Director conducts the business through functional heads such s Executive Directors (Operations), Executive Directors (Finance) and Executive Director (Marketing).

For efficient running of organisation, Managing Director takes policy decisions in consultation with Executive Directors.

Chairman presides over the meeting of Board of Directors, where overall policy decisions are taken in relation to investments, expansions, diversification, and dividends etc.

2.3 PROBABLE QUESTIONS

1. Briefly describe the importance of various physical facilities for a Production System.
2. Draw the organisation chart for a large industrial enterprise illustrating the "Authority" and "Responsibility".
3. Write about the Line and Staff related activities taking place in day-to-day administration of a large manufacturing unit.

3

Production Planning

• *Production Planning* • *Supply-chain Management* • *Process Re-engineering* • *Probable Questions.*

3.1 PRE PLANNING

3.2 PRODUCTION PLANNING

Proper Planning and Control of the production system is essential for efficient and economical production. Economy and Productivity are to a large extent directly proportional to the thoroughness with which the Planning and Control functions are performed.

(*i*) Concept and need of Production Planning: Production Planning involves management decisions relating to how much to produce, what materials, parts and tools will be needed, what steps should be followed in the production process, within what time limit the production is to be completed and how much work is to be done by each work station.

Production Planning is a production activity involving arranging facilities and designing the production system. It is based on Sales commitments as to quantity, delivery dates, price, quality etc.

Production Planning is the 'thinking' phase of the production process.

The main decisions required in production planning are:

(*a*) Designing the Product
(*b*) Choice of technology
(*c*) Determining capacity and equipment requirement
(*d*) Planning the layout of physical facilities
(*e*) Designing the materials handling system
(*f*) Routing and scheduling of operations
(*g*) Installing quality assurance system

Complex production operations, wide range of products, pressure for higher quality, growing number of suppliers, technological progress etc. have made Production Planning the certain necessity.

There is no substitute for Production Planning as lack of Planning means chaos in industry.

3.3 ELEMENTS OF PRODUCTION PLANNING

The main elements of Production Planning are as follows:

(*a*) **Estimating:** The volume of Production is decided through capacity planning. The product to be produced is decided on the basis of market requirements. The Product design is analysed to determine the materials, tools, parts and labour requirements. A bill of materials is prepared to specify the nature and amount of materials required. Inventory levels for materials are decided and purchase requisitions are issued.

(*b*) **Routing:** Routing is the process of determining the sequence of operations to be performed in the Production Process. The methods of techniques of Production are decided. Routing determines what work will be done on a Product or part as well as where and how it will be done. It specifies the operations to be performed, their sequence and proper types of machines and personnel required. The objective of routing is selecting the best and the cheapest method of work.

Routing depends on the nature of machines, the efficiency of employees, the availability of physical facilities and the type of manufacturing process.

In a continuous Process Industry, route is standardised and fixed.

Route is the path over which materials will travel in course of their conversion into finished product.

A route sheet or Route chart is a written specification of the sequence of operations. Route sheets are very helpful in guiding operations for each part.

(*c*) **Sequencing:** Sequencing decides the operations to be performed, their order and machines on which they will be performed. Proper sequencing ensures smooths and uninterrupted flow of work.

Proper routing and sequencing also helps in minimising delays, wastage and materials handling costs. With the help of proper plant layout, sound materials handling system and an integrated routing plan, the firm can avoid multiple handling, delays, criss-crossing and bottlenecks etc.

3.4 FACTORS INFLUENCING PRODUCTION PLANNING

The main factors that influence the Production Planning are as under:

(*a*) **Volume of Production:** Volume of Production depends upon market forecast and customer orders. Volume determines the degree of production planning and serves as the basis for loading and scheduling.

(*b*) **Nature of Production:** Complex and sophisticated products require more thorough Production Planning than simple products.

(*c*) **Type of Production Process:** In continuous manufacturing system, line balancing is necessary to avoid shutdown. On the other hand, in batch production process, effective use of installed facilities is a more significant problem.

3.5 MANUFACTURING LEAD TIME

It is the time interval required from the date of receiving a customer order upto the date of despatch of finished products. It can be determined by estimating in detail the time involved in processing of order, preparing the work order, communicating to the shop floor, withdrawal of materials from stores, processing of materials and allowances for any unexpected interruptions etc.

Accurate estimation of lead time is very essential for just in time (JIT–Japanese System) manufacturing. PERT/CPM network planning technique can be used where the order represents, a long duration manufacturing spread over several months.

(*d*) **Scheduling:** Scheduling involves fixing priorities for different jobs and laying down the starting and finishing dates for each job. It involves the preparation of a time table which would indicate the total time needed for the manufacture of a product as also the time expected to be spent on each machine or operation.

A Production Schedule specifies when each operation is to be carried out. The objective of scheduling is to issue co-ordinated schedules to the plant so that product is manufactured by the delivery date planned by the sales department. Lack of information regarding existing workload, lead time, manufacturing time is the main obstacle in goods scheduling.

Scheduling begins with the preparation of master schedule which represents the overall production programme of the plant for a given period of time. It indicates the dates on which the various jobs have to be completed. Master Schedule is prepared on the basis of sales forecast, route sheet, loading chart and promised delivery schedule.

The Gantt chart type master schedule is very popular as it facilitates both planning and follow-up of the progress of work.

A sample master schedule is given below:

Production Planning Department Master Schedule

Product M-170 — Date of Issue : 10.10.2007

Dept. – Assembly — Schedule No. – M/1

Type	Line	Required for week ending						
		14/10	21/10	28/10	4/11	11/11	18/11	25/11
M170	A	50	55	45	58			
M171	B	45	50	55				
M172	B			50	45	55		
M173						56	58	

From the master schedule, detailed shop. departmental and daily operation schedules are prepared. These schedules are prepared. These schedules help to implement the master schedule. Shop and departmental schedule should be integrated into the master schedule as planned.

In order to ensure co-ordination, controls must be established at critical points. These controls are accomplished in the detailed schedules for shops and departments.

Thus, three types of schedules are required for scheduling:

- **Master Schedule.** It is the aggregate schedule indicating the dates on which various jobs are to be completed.
- **Department Schedule.** It fixes the time period within which a particular work or operation is to be completed.
- **Daily Operation Schedule.** It indicates the time required to perform each detailed operation on a given job.

Preparation of Production schedule takes into account several factors:

- Various job schedules.
- Production capacities and operating efficiencies of various departments.
- Maintenance schedule.
- Orders already in progress.
- Possible holidays, interruptions and absenteeism.

- Availability of raw materials.

Effective Scheduling is essential for efficient production. It helps to meet delivery commitments, to balance production loads, to minimise inventory level and to maximise utilisation of man and machines. Master Production Schedule serves the basis of manufacturing plan.

(*e*) **Facility Loading:** Loading means the assignment of specific jobs to specific machines for the purpose of completing each operation by the specified date. Loading is the process of converting operation schedule into practice.

Scheduling gives the estimated date for completion of work whereas loading determines the feasibility of these dates.

Available capacity should be fully utilised in loading. Steps involved in loading a machine or other facility are as follows:

- Find out the estimated time to perform each operation.
- Find out the availability of various machines.
- Identify the earliest date when the required hours can be utilised on a given machine.
- Schedule bottleneck operation and schedule subsequent operations as early as possible consistent with route sheet.

3.6 TYPES OF PRODUCTION PLANNING

There are two types of Production Planning:

(*a*) **Long Range Planning:** It focuses on the utilisation of Production facilities in the longrun to achieve organisational objectives. It is strategic in nature. It takes into account the investment capacity product life cycles, technology level, market requirement etc. It is technically called **Capacity planning**.

Crude Petroleum Refining Plants use long range planning technique, since the products demand is uniform throughout the year and do not vary from seasons to seasons.

It lays down the following objectives:

- Product volume
- Operating capacities
- Inventory policies
- Delivery policy and programme
- Maintenance Policy and Programme
- Level of manufacturing cost

(*b*) **Short Term Planning:** It is operational planning concerned with the utilisation of existing facilities rather than with the creation of new facilities. It is tactical in nature.

Usually, small scale plants use short term planning technique, due to their resources constraints, non uniform product demand etc.

Cement Producing Plants also sometimes resort to this type of Planning due to large fluctuations in demand from season to season. Short term planning is designed to respond quickly to changes in Production levels, market condition etc.

3.7 PRODUCTION SCHEDULING

Scheduling determines the programme for operations. In scheduling, order of sequence of each operation and their starting and finishing time is decided so that the required materials machines etc. may be kept ready as per schedule.

Scheduling is fixation of time and date for each operation.

(a) Uses of Scheduling

- It helps in planning the manufacturing, purchase and sale which is also helpful for planning by ancillary and other use industries.
- It helps the production department to find out if there is need for cope up the backlog.
- It helps in planning personnel, extra shift, overtime etc.

(b) Information required for scheduling

- Sequence of operations for manufacture.
- Time required for each operation.
- Machine capacity and its availability per day.
- Availability of materials and components.

(c) Master Scheduling: The Master Schedule shows the quantity of each product to be completed each day, week or month during the period covered.

The Sequential steps in master schedule are as under:

- Completion of design.
- Completion of bill of materials.
- Completion of operation analysis.
- Completion of requisition for essential tools.
- Completion of raw material procurement.
- Completion of sub-assembly.
- Completion of final test and inspection.
- Completion of packing and shipping.

(d) Manufacturing Time: In scheduling process, manufacturing time is an important element. Manufacturing Time is total time for direct labour plus the total time for natural setups plus the total dispatch lag.

Dispatch lag is the normal delay at each machine plus the machine handling time.

Following formula is used for finding the manufacturing time:

$$\text{MT} = \frac{N + D + \left(\dfrac{OL+S}{AE}\right)}{7}$$

MT = Manufacturing time,

N = Number of operations

D = Number of Departments

L = Direct Labour Cost in Rupees/Piece,

S = Total Cost of Set up in Rupees/Piece.

AE = Average Earning per hour per man.

7 = Effective working man-hours/day.

O = Order Quantity

Master Production Schedule (MPS)

Master Production Schedule is an important input for material requirement plan. MPS details how many end items will be produced within specified periods of time. It breaks the aggregate production plan into specific production schedules.

Figure below shows how an aggregate plan for colour TV production breaks down into the weekly master production schedule for each specific type of TV.

	April				May			
Colour TV	1	2	3	4	5	6	7	8
14″	150					150		
21″				120			120	
29″		200	200		200			200
Aggregate Production Plan for Colour TV	670				670			

Figure 3.1 Master Production Schedule for Colour TV sets.

The sums of the quantities in the MPS must equal those in the aggregate production plan.

The aggregate production quantities must be allocated efficiently over time. Capacity limitation such as machine, labour storage space and working capital etc. may determine the time and size of MPS quantities.

***(ix)* Capacity Requirement Planning (CRP):** The purpose of capacity requirement planning is to match the material requirement plan with the plant's production capacity.

Thus the technique for projecting time-phased capacity requirements for workstations is capacity requirements planning CRP).

This technique is used to calculate workload according to work required to complete the scheduled receipts already in the shop and to complete the planned order releases not yet released.

Using the MRP dates for arrival of replenishment orders for an item to avoid shortages, CRP traces back through the item's routing to estimate when the scheduled receipt or planned order will reach each workstation.

The system uses the processing and set up times to estimate the load that the item will impose on each station for each planned order and scheduled receipt of an item.

The adjustment in capacity requirement plan helps in smooth working and remove bottlenecks.

Other options would be to use over time or off-load to another work-station.

***(x)* Finite Capacity Scheduling (FCS):** In large production facilities thousands of orders may be in progress at any time. Manually adjusting the timing of these orders with the use of spreadsheets or wall mounted magnetic schedule boards is virtually impossible.

The best solutions - those that meet the MRP schedule due dates and do not violate any constraints. A useful tool for these situations is Finite Capacity Scheduling (FCS), which is an algorithm designed to schedule a group of orders approximately across an entire shop.

The system utilises routings for the items manufactured, resource constraints, available capacity, shift patterns, and a scheduling rule to be used at each work station to determine the priorities for orders.

To be effective, the FCS system needs to be integrated with MRP. An FCS system operates at a finer level of detail than MRP and needs to know the status of each machine and when the current order will finish processing, the maintenance schedule, the routing, the set up times, machine speeds and capabilities etc. The FCS system uses that information to determine actual, realistic start and end times of jobs and uploads the results to MRP for subsequent replanning.

The FCS system provides a more accurate picture than MRP of when the orders will be completed.

3.8 INTEGRATED PRODUCTION PLANNING SYSTEM

It is desirable for every plant to design and develop an integrated production planning system. In such a system, all the components of production system are properly interlinked. Such a system focuses on aggregate level on a selective basis and does not interfere with detailed planning and scheduling.

The main elements of integrated production planning system are shown in Figure 3.2.

(*vi*) Japanese Production System:

(*a*) **Just In Time Manufacturing (JIT):** It is a Production System developed by Taiichi Ohno at Toyota Motor Co., Japan. Under this system goods are manufactured only at the time and in quantity required. As a result, work in progress inventory and inventory of finished goods are almost nil. Production schedule and supply schedules of materials are perfectly matched to have virtually no inventory of raw materials.

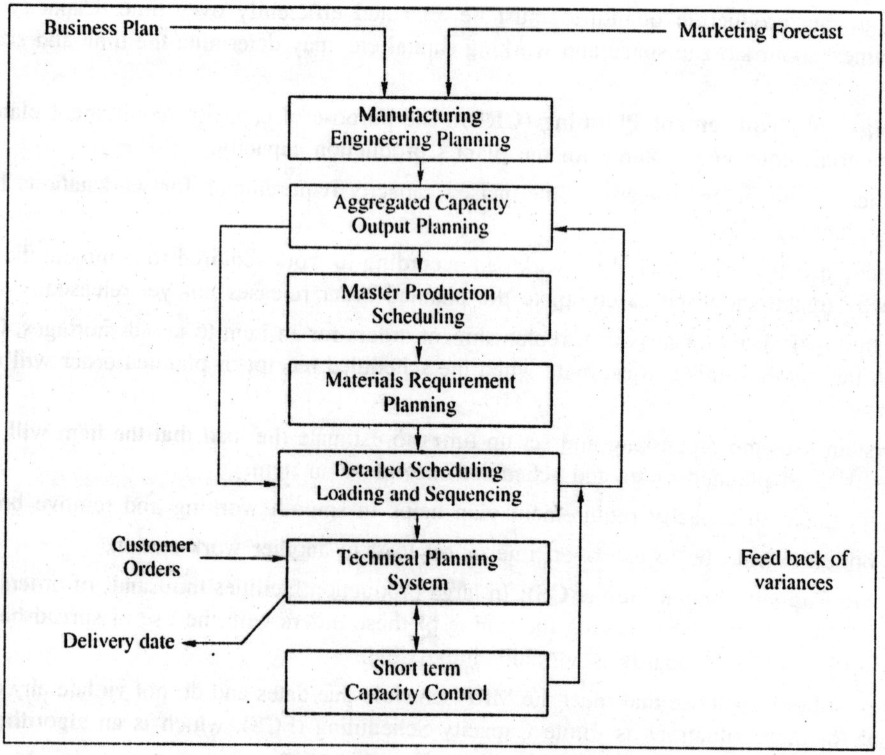

Figure 3.2 Integrated Production Planning System.

JIT is a production and materials planning system wherein procurement and production and production operations are fully synchronised with actual demand so that no waiting is involved.

JIT system helps to reduce wastes caused by waiting, transportation, processing, stocks, defective output and over production. It also helps to improve quality, reduce costs and increase return on investment.

JIT production system can be successful only when the following conditions are satisfied:

- Customer Orientation
- Focus on long term objective
- Common company objective
- All departments work as a team

(*b*) **Kanban: Kanban** is a visual physical control system used in JIT Production System. Transfer of materials from a supply centre to a work centre is authorised with the help of cards. Flow of materials through various stages of production is visually controlled.

The **Kanban** system connects consecutive work centres to realise a conveyor line effect.

Kanban system ensures strict control on the production system in following ways:

- No inventory moves without authorisation by a card.
- Each bin contains only fixed quantity of inventory.
- There is a separate card for each bin.
- As soon as materials are removed from a bin its card also moves out.

3.9 MATERIALS REQUIREMENT PLANNING (MRP)

The system of calculating the requirements of input materials at different points of time on the basis of Production plan is called material requirement planning.

The basis objective of MRP is to ensure the supply of right quantity of parts at the right time.

MRP is used for dependent demand items. Requirement of finished product is calculated on the basis of demand/customer order.

Main steps in MRP are as follows:

Advantage of MRP

- It will avoid both overstocking and stock outs.
- It helps in rescheduling due to unforeseen events such as changes in orders, quantity, delays in delivery of materials.
- It enables managers to check deviations on capacity.
- MRP can generate reports on load, capacity, net requirements and inventory status.

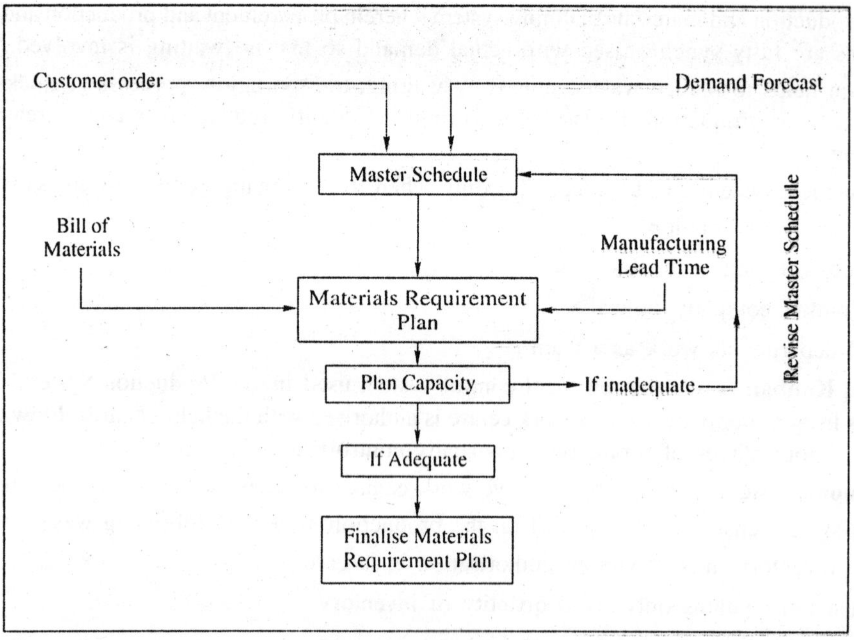

Figure 3.2 Process of MRP.

MRP versus JIT Systems

MRP is useful as overall materials planning and data management and can be used to support the informational needs of various functional areas in the firm. MRP systems can be used effectively to understand the implications of lot sizing decisions and master scheduling changes on overall inventories and capacity. In contrast, JIT systems are a less expensive, more effective way to control material flows on the shop floor. A Kanban system as described earlier can be used to maintain low levels of inventory and to adjust product rates over time.

The nature of the production process determines the appropriate system. For line flows, order releases don't change from week to week, so a rate-based system such as JIT works well. MRP is an effective technique for scheduling production on a weekly basis.

In a repetitive manufacturing operation, a hybrid system such as JIT MRP is more useful.

Any production and inventory system by itself will not set things right, but significant improvements in performance can be achieved by shaping manufacturing environment properly.

3.10 ENTERPRISE RESOURCE PLANNING (ERP)

The on set of supply-chain management, E-commerce, and global operations has created a need to provide and exchange information directly with other companies and customers.

ERP is a system that has additional capabilities for quantity management, fields service, maintenance management, distribution marketing, and supplier management.

In addition, these systems have databases structured for ease of external access and the ability to access the information system of other companies.

ERP systems are responding to the need for a more comprehensive view of manufacturing.

ERP enables a firm to deal directly with suppliers to assess the availability of their resources. It can even enable the firm to manage suppliers as if they were an internal process to the firm.

ERP enables the firm to access information at each supplier's site, and inventories. Use of internet will be the source of data interchange for the system. ERP links the firm's manufacturing planning and control system to its customers and suppliers through Electronic Data Interchange (EDI) and the internet. Customers can query the schedule directly to find out when the firm can fill a new order, thereby providing the firm a competitive edge over other manufacturers.

An ERP system collects, processes and provides information about an organisation's entire enterprise, including orders, product design production, purchasing, inventory, distribution, and forecasting of future demand.

Such a system links these areas of activity into a network as shown in Figure 3.3.

(*xii*) Supply-Chain Management: Supply chain management is the term for managing the sequence of suppliers and purchasers, covering all stages of procuring from obtaining raw materials to distributing finished goods to final consumers.

An important component of supply chain management is managing relationships with suppliers. Managers set up procedures for identifying desirable supplies and other purchases.

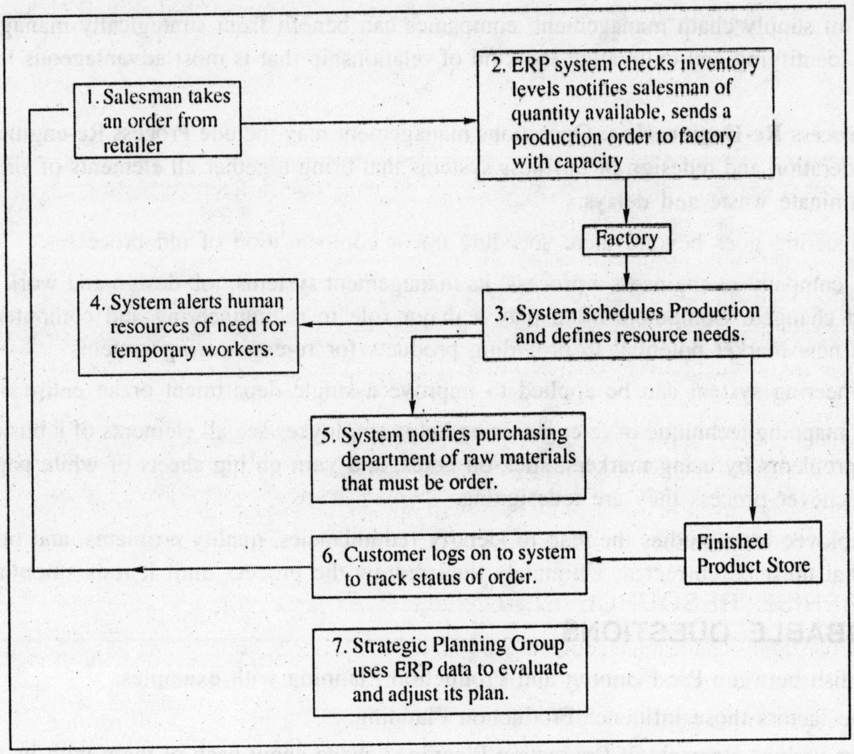

Figure 3.3 Illustrates an ERP system.

The Toyota Motor Co. of Japan for buying the exhaust system and suspension components for its car from Arvin Industries in USA, had sent two engineers to Arvin's works to help the latter in process improvement, materials management and quality production.

Mahindra and Mahindra Ltd. in India similarly had entered into long-time supply agreement with some suppliers of auto-components for production of its popular passenger motor car "Scorpio". These suppliers have been supported by Mahindras in R & D Programmes and quality production of vital auto components.

Because supply chain management involves supplies relationships, it relies heavily on the activities known as logistics. Logistics involve the activities required to physically move materials into the companies operation facility and to move finished products to customers.

Logistic is not merely a matter of transporting goods, but includes those activities along with managing the relationships needed to move goods in a timely and efficient fashion consistent with the company strategy.

The supplier relationships of many organisations involve an arm's length approach, in which an organisation spreads purchases among many suppliers, encouraging them to compete with one another to provide the best qualities at the lowest price.

Other organisations use partnering, cultivating relationship with selected suppliers and collaborators with them to co-ordinate tasks and help the suppliers meet organisations unique needs.

Many automobile manufacturers in India enjoy the strategic benefits of collaboration with suppliers of batteries, spark plugs, stearing wheel and gear-boxes etc.

As part of supply chain management, companies can benefit from strategically managing supplier relationships, identifying and cultivating the kind of relationship that is most advantageous for each kind of purchase.

***(xiii)* Process Re-Engineering:** Operations management may include Process Re-engineering which is the reconsideration and redesign of business systems that bring together all elements of single business process to eliminate waste and delays.

Re-engineering goes beyond mere speeding up or compensation of old processes.

When a company re-engineers a process, its management systems, job design and work flow are re-evaluated and changed. Computers often play a major role in re-engineering and computer companies recognise the new market potential in providing products for re-engineering systems.

Re-engineering system can be applied to improve a single department or an entire organisation.

Process mapping technique of re-engineering helps employees see all elements of a business process and identify problems by using markers, stick-on notes, and yarn on big sheets of white paper to create a map of whichever process they are redesigning.

The employee team studies the map to identify redundancies, quality problems, and other snags in the process that must be corrected. Ultimately they redraw the process until it runs smoothly.

3.11 PROBABLE QUESTIONS

1. Distinguish between Pre-Planning and Production Planning with examples.
2. Describe factors those influence Production Planning.
3. What are various elements of Production Planning? Write about each of them with its significance.
4. What are various types of Production Planning? Provide names of industries for which they are adopted.

5. Write notes on:

(*a*) Integrated Production Planning System.

(*b*) Materials Requirement Planning.

(*c*) JIT Manufacturing.

6. What is Production Planning Scheduling?

Describe the method of preparing a Master Schedule.

7. What is Capacity Planning?

How is Capacity requirement planned?

8. Write notes on:

(*a*) Enterprise Resource Planning.

(*b*) Supply-chain Management.

(*c*) Process Re-engineering.

4

Production Control

• *Production Control* • *Probable Questions.*

4.1 PRODUCTION CONTROL

While the product is being manufactured, the production must be controlled to ensure that the planned output is constantly maintained. This function is known as production control.

Production Planning and Production Control are two different kinds of activities but are the responsibility of the Production Department.

Meaning and Objectives of Production Control: Production control involves implementation of production plans or schedules by co-ordinating different activities.

Production Planning serves as the basis for Production control which in turn ensures that Production Plans are converted into performance.

Production Planning & Production Control

Production Planning (Plan your work)	Production Control (Work your plan)
• Estimating	• Dispatching
• Routing	• Expediting
• Scheduling	
• Loading	• Corrective action

4.2 ELEMENTS OF PRODUCTION CONTROL

(*a*) **Dispatching:** In dispatching orders are issued in terms of their priority and work is assigned to operations. Dispatching in effect determines by whom the work shall be done. Dispatching involves giving the necessary authority to start the work as per schedule. The dispatching department issues requisitions for materials and tools on the production order and checks to see that the materials, parts and tools are available in time.

The dispatch section of the Production Planning and Control department is responsible for the following:

1. Collecting and then issuing to supervisors the drawings specifications, materials lists, route cards, requisitions etc.
2. Ensuring that materials, parts, tools and other aids are made available to the manufacturing department at the right time.
3. Obtaining inspection schedules and issuing them to the inspection section.
4. Releasing work orders for the start of manufacturing operations.

5. At the end of manufacture, ensuring that all the drawings, layouts and tools are returned to their appropriate places.

(*b*) **Progressing or Expediting Follow Up:** Progressing is ensuring that work is carried out as planned and delivery dates are met. Progressing ensures that production is proceeding according to plans. Progressing ensures that production is proceeding according to monitor progress of work and to expedite the work centres falling behind schedule.

Need for expediting may arise due to several reasons e.g. delay in supply of materials, excessive absenteeism on the part of workers, changes in specification or delivery dates by customers, breakdown of machines or tools, errors in drawings etc.

(*c*) **Corrective Action:** After the causes of delays and deviation are identified, necessary action is to be taken to rectify the problems. It is by corrective action that control over manufacturing operations is maintained. Jobs may be shifted to other machines or work stations, overtime for workers may be authorised and steps may be taken to work back on the original schedule.

When the work schedules are upset due to indisciplines or poor performance training, transfer and motivation of staff may be required.

Benefits of Production Control: The main benefits of Production Planning and Control (PPC) are as follows:

1. **Lower investment:** PPC helps to minimise capital investment in inventories and equipment.
2. **Reduce Unit Cost:** An efficient PPC system results in minimum wastage of materials, time and other resources and results in lower unit cost.
3. **Customer Satisfaction:** Proper scheduling and follow up to work helps in meeting the promised delivery dates. Goods of proper quality and in right quantity are supplied to customers on promised delivery date. This results in customer satisfaction.

Limitation of Production Control: The Production Planning and Control or PPC suffers from the following draw backs:

1. PPC is based on certain assumptions or forecasts about customer's orders, plant capacity, availability of materials and power. If these assumptions or forecasts go wrong, PPC becomes ineffective.
2. PPC is a time consuming process. For urgent delivery of goods, it may not be possible to practise PPC process.
3. PPC is a costly device. Small firms cannot employ experts for practising PPC system.
4. External factors like power failures, changes in technology, natural calamities and Govt. controls etc. may make PPC ineffective.

4.3 PRODUCTION MANNING & CONTROL IN DIFFERENT PRODUCTION SYSTEMS

No one Production control system is good for all types of industries. The nature and scope of PPC differs from one Production system to another.

(*a*) **PPC in Process Industry:** PPC in continues process industry is relatively simple. Routing is almost automatic and uniform because standard techniques and specialised equipment are used. Departmental schedule are prepared from the master schedule on a continuous basis. Dispatching involves repetitive orders issued to ensure a steady flow of materials.

(*b*) **PPC in Job Production Industry:** PPC is relatively difficult in Job Production Industry. There is no standardised route plan and a new route is prepared for every order.

Production schedules are drawn up according to relative urgency of order. Dispatching and follow up are also order oriented.

(*c*) **PPC in Batch Production Industry:** In batch production system, raw materials are converted into components or parts for stock but they are combined according to the customer's orders.

Every batch differs from others but all units within a batch are identical.

PPC in batch production unit is a mixture of those used in process industry and job order production.

(*d*) **PPC in Assembly Industry:** In an assembly industry, there is a uniform sequence of repetitive operation but the number of components and their proportion to be assembled differ from one product to another.

Production schedules are drawn up for each product so as to achieve the targets of production.

Follow up measures need to be taken to ensure that every product is being assembled as per the specifications and schedules laid down in advance.

Requirement of Effective Production Control: PPC system becomes effective when the following requirements are met:

(*a*) **Organisation Set-up:** A sound organisation set up can only derive full benefits of PPC system. There should be proper delegation of authority and fixation of responsibility at all levels.

Both the top operating management must realise the importance of PPC system.

(*b*) **Information feed back system:** Reliable and up-to-date information must be available to all concerned persons implementing PPC system. Information about order quantity, quality, delivery date, materials and machines availability and other relevant conditions should be within the knowledge of the concerned persons.

(*c*) **Trained Personnel:** The concerned personnel must be properly trained in the use of specified tools, operating particular machines and taking correction actions whenever and wherever needed.

(*d*) **Flexibility:** PPC system should be flexible enough to accommodate changes and bottlenecks like shortages of materials, power failures, breakdown of machinery and absence of some personnel etc.

(*e*) **Periodic Follow up:** PPC is a continuous process. A periodic review of various activities should be made to identify and remove the redundant measures.

Continuous checking will help to keep the system effective.

4.4 DOCUMENTATION FOR PRODUCTION CONTROL

1. Work Order: A work order is issued to authorise the plant to commence production.

A typical work order is as follows:

<table>
<tr><th colspan="8">Work Order Specification</th></tr>
<tr><td colspan="5">Date
Description
Code Number</td><td colspan="3">Department
Material
Drawing No.</td></tr>
<tr><td colspan="8">Process</td></tr>
<tr><td rowspan="2">Process</td><td rowspan="2">Code</td><td rowspan="2">Dept.</td><td rowspan="2">Charge No.</td><td rowspan="2">Eqpt.</td><td colspan="3">Charges</td></tr>
<tr><td>Materials</td><td>Machine</td><td>Labour</td></tr>
<tr><td colspan="8">Special Instructions:
Inspection details
Special Treatment or Processes</td></tr>
</table>

2. Material Requisition: This document is used to draw materials mentioned in it.

Material Requisition

Description	Code Number
Required by (Dept.)	Quantity required ....
Job Number	
Date	
	Signature of Foreman
Quantity Issued	Date ....
	Signature of Stores Incharge
....	Date ....

3. Control Sheet: This sheet is prepared for each batch of work.

It may be as an internal delivery note at the final stage when the finished parts are kept into stores.

Control Sheet

	1	2	3	4	5	
Operation Code Quantity received Quantity rejected Quantity delivered						
Description:				Delivered to: Job No. .... Stores............... Part No. .... Date		

4. Progress Note: A progress note is prepared after the completion of each operation. It informs the production planning and control dept. that the batch has progressed to the next operation. It also states the number of good items and rejected items forwarded.

5. Machine Load Chart: It displays the available capacity of a machine or work station and whether it is overloaded or underloaded.

6. Gantt Chart: A Gantt Chart or bar chart indicates graphically the volume of work ahead of equipment and the amount of capacity still available for processing the additional work. It is an effective chart.

Gantt Charts are described in details in Chapter 20.

4.5 EFFICIENCY OF PRODUCTION PLANNING AND CONTROL

Efficiency of Production Planning and Control will depend on the decision making with respect to the following factors:

(*a*) Frequency of inventory taking to decide on few or many breaks in production for buffer stocks.

(*b*) Size of the inventories to decide on high inventory or low inventory or no inventory.

(*c*) Degree of inventory control to decide on greater or lesser details of control on input stage, work-in progress stage and finished product stage.

(*d*) Identify the items to be controlled to decide on controls designed to minimise machine downtime, labour cost, progressing time, maximising output of particular products or minimising usage of certain materials.

(*e*) Implementation of quality control for high-reliability and quality or for lowering the cost of production.

(*f*) Use of ISO 9000 standards and ISO 14,000 standards pertaining to the "International Quality Standards" for obtaining benefits of ISO certification.

ISO 9,000 and ISO 14,000 are described in a Chapter 17 in this book.

4.6 PROBABLE QUESTIONS

1. What are objectives of Production Control?

   Describe various elements of Production Control.
2. What are benefits and limitation for Production control?
3. Write notes on:

   (*a*) Efficiency of Production Planning and control.

   (*b*) Production Controls in various production systems.

5

Production Economics

• *Production Function and Cobb-Douglas Method* • *Isoquant* • *Marginal Rate of Technical Substitution (MRTS)* • *Leontief Static Open Model (LSOM)* • *Leontief Production Function* • *Production Economics* • *Return to Scale* • *Economies of Scale* • *Production Process-Short Run and Long Run-Concept* • *Production and Supply* • *Capacity and Cost of Production* • *Probable Questions.*

5.1 PRODUCTION FUNCTION AND COBB-DOUGLAS METHOD

The production function is a purely technical relation which connects factor inputs and outputs. It describes the lower of proportions, that is, the transformation of factor inputs into products (outputs) at any particular time period.

The Production function represents the technology of a firm of an industry, or of the economy as a whole. The production function includes all the technically efficient methods of production.

A method of production (process, activity) is a combination of factor inputs required for the production of one unit of output. Usually a commodity may be produced by various methods of production.

For example, a unit of commodity x may be produced by the following processes:

	Process P_1	Process P_2	Process P_3
Labour units	2	3	1
Capital units	3	2	4

Figure 5.1

Activities may be presented graphically as follows (Figure 5.2):

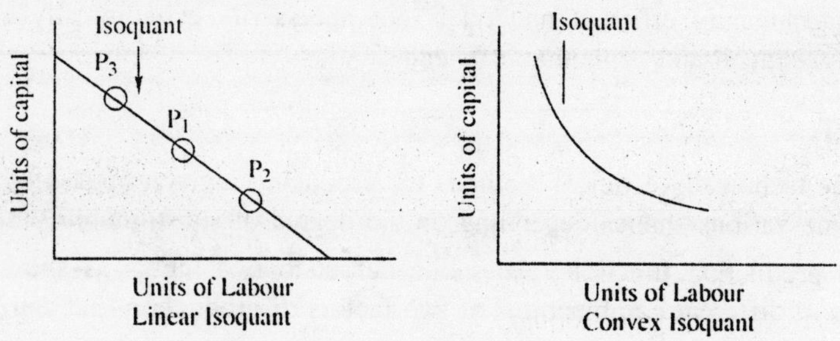

Figure 5.2

Along the Isoquant Curve, same quantity of output with varying combinations of labour and capital.

If a process uses less of some factor and more of some other factor, compared to other process, then these two processes can be directly compared on the criterion of technical efficiency.

The type of process to be chosen for production depends upon the prices of factors. The Theory of Production describes the laws of Production.

Higher is the economic efficiency, greater can be the profitability of the manufacturing unit.

The efficiency of production also depends upon long term changes like (*a*) technical progress or improvements in technology (*b*) economics of large scale production and (*c*) capital labour substitution or the degree of mechanisation.

The basic analytical device for analysing all the above ingredients of economic efficiency is the concept of production function which gives the systematic relationship between inputs and outputs.

Production function along with the related analytic concept of isoquant is used to find the least cost (most efficient) combination of inputs.

The study of the production function is concerned with establishing the maximum output from a given set of inputs and with a given state of technology.

The Production function can be stated in the general form of an equation:

$$Y = f(x_1, x_2, \text{etc.})$$

where Y = the units of output, a function of two or more inputs, say labour and capital

x_1 = Units of labour and x_2 = Units of capital.

The method of estimating the production function is the method of least square. A popular production function derived by Mr. Cobb and Mr. Douglas (Cobb – Douglas method) is as follows:

$P = BL^a C^{1-a}$ P = Total output, L = Index of labour employment in manufacturing unit.

C = Index of fixed Capital in mfg. unit a & $(1 - a)$ an elasticities of Production in percentages.

Typically in a place, this eqn. becomes

$$P = 1.01L^{0.75}\ C^{0.26}\ R_2^{\ 0.94}$$

This shows that by 1% change in labour input (L) is associated by 0.75% change in output when capital (c) is fixed. Likewise, by 1% change in capital (c) when labour (L) is constant there is change of 0.25% in output. Coefficient of determination R_2, shows that 94% of the variations on the dependent variable (P) were accounted for by the variations in the independent variable (L and C).

The choice of any particular technique is an economic one, based on prices, and not a technical one.

Therefore, a technically efficient method is not necessarily economically efficient, and there is difference between technical and economic efficiency.

5.2 ISOQUANT

This includes all the technically efficient methods for producing a given level of output. The production Isoquant may assume various shapes depending on the degree of substitutability of factors.

The simplest production function relates one output to two inputs as shown in Figure 5.3. The alternative methods of different combinations of two factors of production that can yield the same output and the resulting curve is called an isoquant. It shows that a given quantity of output can be produced with the varying proportion of labour and capital.

Isoquant: This type assumes perfect substitutability of factors of production, a given commodity may be produced by using only capital, or only labour, or by an infinite combination of Labour and Capital.

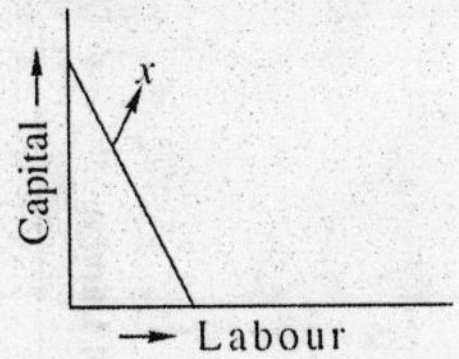

Figure 5.3

Definition of Isoquant

Various alternative methods using different combinations of two factors of production that can yield same output are represented in a curve known as "Isoquant". All points on the curve represent the same quantity of output.

So, Isoquant represents all the combination of the two factors of the Production that yield the same output.

(*a*) **ISOQUANTS:** Isoquants are a geometric representation of the production function. The same level of output can be produced by various combinations of factor inputs.

The curve which is the locus of all possible combination is called **Isoquant** or **Iso-product Curve.**

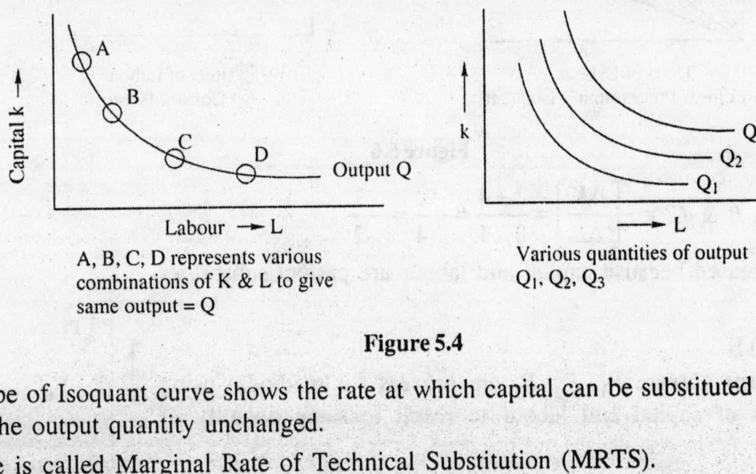

A, B, C, D represents various combinations of K & L to give same output = Q

Various quantities of output Q_1, Q_2, Q_3

Figure 5.4

The slope of Isoquant curve shows the rate at which capital can be substituted for labour and vice-versa, while the output quantity unchanged.

The rate is called Marginal Rate of Technical Substitution (MRTS).

5.3 MARGINAL RATE OF TECHNICAL SUBSTITUTION (MRTS)

Marginal Rate of "Technical Substitution (MRTS) is defined as the rate at which factors (K & L) are substituted for each other.

Say 10 pairs of shoes can be produced in following ways:

Q	K	L
10	8	2
10	4	4
10	2	8

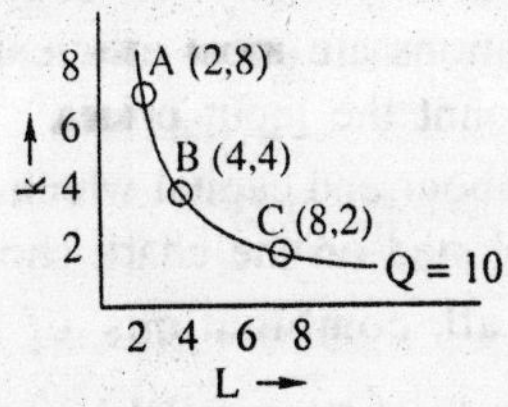

Figure 5.5

The MRTS of labour for capital between points *A* and *B*

$$= -\left[\frac{\Delta K}{\Delta L}\right] = \frac{4}{2} = 2\ (-)\ \text{ve, since it is diminishing downwards.}$$

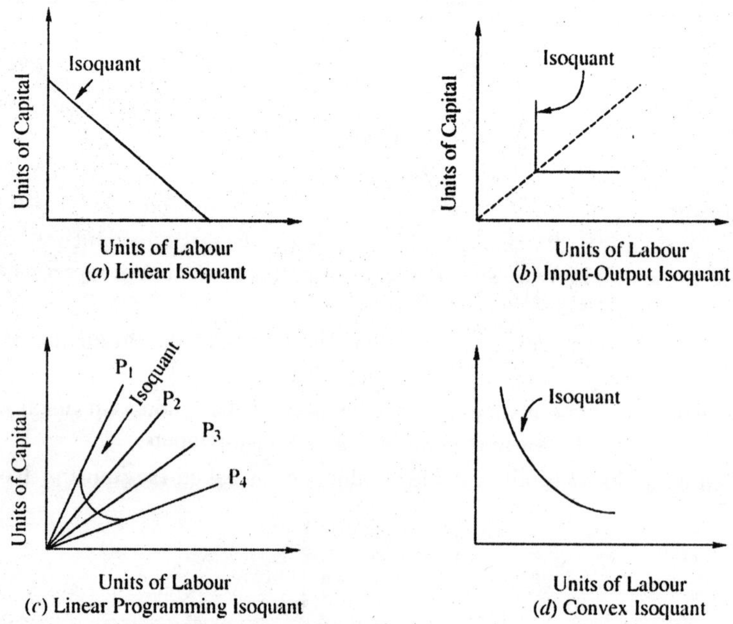

(*a*) Linear Isoquant (*b*) Input-Output Isoquant (*c*) Linear Programming Isoquant (*d*) Convex Isoquant

Figure 5.6

$$\text{MRTS between } B \,\&\, C = -\left[\frac{\Delta K}{\Delta L}\right] = \frac{2-4}{8-4} = -\frac{2}{4} = -\frac{1}{2}$$

MRTS has decreased because capital and labour are perfect substitutes for each other.

Isoquant and MRTS

The Slope of Isoquant Curve: P_1, P_2, P_3 are process (or methods) using various combinations of capital and labour to result in same quantity of output.

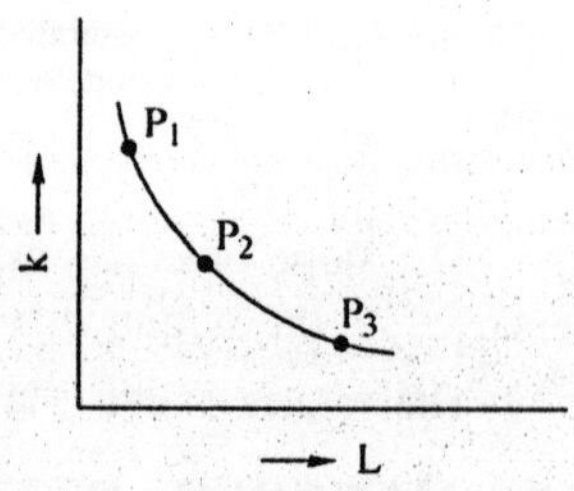

Figure 5.7

The slope of the isoquant curve shows the rate at which capital can be substituted for labour and vice-versa, keeping the level of output unchanged.

This rate is called Marginal rate of technical substitution (MRTS).

The point at which this rate is equal to ratio between the prices of inputs represents the optimum combination of inputs.

Isocost-Curves: Isoquants deal with physical combination of inputs and do not tell which input combinations are most efficient or optimal. For this purpose, we must take into account the input prices.

The various quantities of labour and capital which can be obtained from a given amount of money are plotted on the chart, showing Isocost Curves.

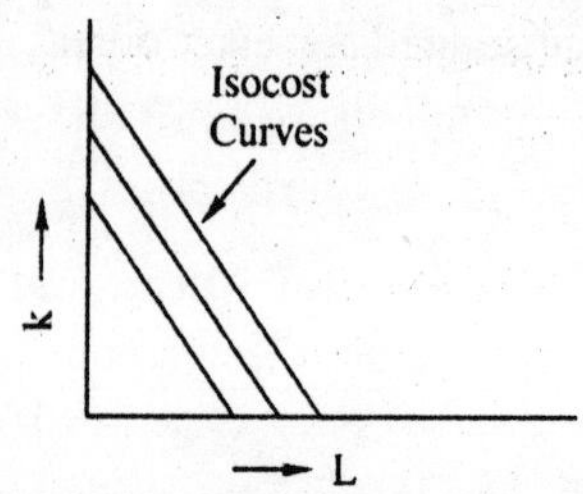

Figure 5.8

An isocost line shows all combinations of inputs that can be employed for a given cost. Isocost lines are parallel *i.e.*, slope of each line $\frac{PL}{PK}$

since that represent the rate at which input L can be substituted by input K while output is unchanged.

5.4 LEONTIEF STATIC OPEN MODEL

Input-Output Isoquant: This assumes strict complementarity (that is, zero substitutability of the factors of production).

There is only one method of production for any one commodity. The isoquant takes the shape of a right angle. This type of Isoquant is also called 'Leontief Isoquant' after Leontief, who invented the input output analysis.

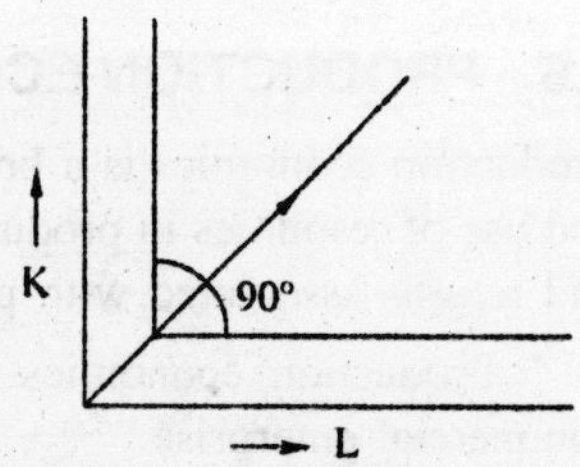

Figure 5.9

In this case K & L are not substitutive

K stand for Capital and L stands for Labour.

5.5 LEONTIEF PRODUCTION FUNCTION OR FIXED PROPORTION FUNCTION

This production function is based on the condition that there is a **fixed proportion in which the various** factors are to be used in the production process.

If an input is available in a greater quantity than required by this **proportion, the additional quantity will be redundant, while it is available in lesser quantity than needed by the proportion, then the other input** will be rendered redundant.

For example, if for a particular process 10 labour and 4 **capital units are required, and if the firm** has 12 labour and 4 capital units, it will find 2 units of labour **unused, while if it had 9 units of labour** it can use only 3 units of capital with it, *i.e.*, its 1 unit each **of capital and labour will be rendered** unemployed. ($3K = 7.5L = 8L$).

This function has the following general form:

X = minimum $\left(\frac{K}{a}, \frac{L}{b}\right)$ K and L are capital and labour, a and b are constants. **Minimum words** implies that output X depends on the smaller of two ratios $\frac{K}{a}, \frac{L}{b}$.

(*a*) Utility of Production Function for Managers

The usefulness of production function is very easily **under-standable.**

It is helpful in making **decisions because they can give guidance in two directions.**

(*i*) How to obtain **maximum output from the given input.**

(*ii*) How to obtain a **given output from the minimum input.**

From a given production function, for a certain output, **one can derive all the combinations of the** two factors of production **that will produce the same output.**

Using Linear programming method, **the production function can be easily estimated.**

(*b*) Production Management

Production management implies planning, organising, directing and controlling the activities of the production function which is concerned with the conversion of raw materials into finished products.

Production management deals with **decision making related to production processes so that the** resulting good or service is produced **according to specifications in the amounts and by the schedule** demanded and at minimum cost.

Production management covers only the manufacturing organisations while operations management has a much wider scope consisting of both manufacturing and service organisations such as Banks, Insurance, Hospitals and Transport Companies etc.

5.6 PRODUCTION ECONOMICS

Production economics is a branch of micro-economics. It is concerned with the analysis of the allocation and use of resources in production processes within individual business firm. It involves the study of costs and returns associated with production functions.

Production economics is defined as "the application of the principles of micro-economics in a commercial enterprise."

Production economics clarifies the concepts of costs, returns, input output relationship and resource allocation for cost reduction or profit maximisation. Production economics enables the business manager to respond correctly to change in wage rates, interest rates, prices and other such variables.

Production economics is helpful in finding correct answers to the following questions:

(*i*) What is efficient production?

(*ii*) What is optimum level of output?

(*iii*) How to determine the most economical amount of input?

(*iv*) How should a business firm respond to a change in the price of its product?

(*v*) How should a firm respond to a change in wage rate or interest rate?

(*vi*) How does technological change influence cost and output?

(*a*) Scope of Production Economics

The economics of production deals with vital issues that influence the viability and profitability of a manufacturing concern. Some of these issues are as follows:

(*a*) determination of plant capacity.

(*b*) location of physical facilities.

(*c*) layout of physical facilities.

(*d*) decision of product and product mix.

(*e*) process design.

(*f*) number of shifts working.

(*g*) material handling facilities.

(*h*) maintenance practicises (*i*) control of quantity etc.

(*b*) Economic Efficiency, Unit Total Cost

Production economics is mainly concerned with the firm's problem of attaining and maintaining unit costs of production at the minimum level.

It explains the effect of technological change, economics of scale, and unit costs of production etc. Production economics is concerned with the problem of economic efficiency or cost of effectiveness of production.

The goal of production economics is effective design and operation of production system so as to maximise economic efficiency or to minimise cost of production per unit.

Economic efficiency or cost effectiveness depends upon two factors:

(*a*) quantities inputs and outputs and

(*b*) prices of inputs and outputs.

Suppose, a factory produces 1,20,000 wrist watches per annum (Q = 1,20,000). The cost of labour is Rs. 60,000 per annum (*i.e.*, the annual wage Ci = Rs. 60,000) and the factory uses 100 men years (it employs 100 workers throughout the year *i.e.*, Ni = 100). Then we get

$$\text{Unit labour cost} = \frac{60{,}000}{1{,}20{,}000/100} = \text{Rs.}50/-$$

Similarly, we can calculate the unit cost for every other input and then add them to obtain the unit total cost *i.e.*

$$\text{Unit total cost} = \frac{\sum CiNi}{Q}$$

The lower is the unit total cost, higher is the economic efficiency or more cost effective is the production.

5.7 THE LAW OF VARIABLE PROPORTIONS

The laws of production describe the technically possible ways of increasing the level of production. Output may increase in various ways.

Output can be increased by changing all factors of production. Clearly this is possible only in the long run. Thus the laws of return to scale refer to the long-run analysis of production.

In the short run output may be increased by using more of the variable factor(s), while capital (and possibly other factor as well) is kept constant.

The marginal product of the variable factor(s) will decline eventually as more quantities of this factor are combined with the other constant factors.

The expansion of output with one factor (at least) constant is described by the (eventually) diminishing return of the variable factor, which is often referred to as the law of variable proportions.

This law states that as more and more of one factor input is employed, all other input quantities constant, a point will eventually be reached where additional quantities of varying input will yield diminishing marginal contributions to total product.

This is the law of variable proportions and this is a familiar economic assumption which underlies the short-run production function.

Example Production Function with one variable input.

Nos. of Labour Units	*Total Physical Product*	*Average Physical Product*	*Marginal Physical Product*
(1)	(2)	(3) = (2) ÷ (1)	(4)
1	100	100	100
2	210	105	110
3	330	110	120
4	430	107.5	100
5	520	104	90
6	600	100	80
7	670	95.7	70
8	720	90	50
9	750	83.3	30
10	760	76	10

In the above table, it is assumed labour is the only variable input.

5.8 LAW OF DIMINISHING RETURN

The law of diminishing return states that as more and more of the variable input is added to the fixed factor base, the increment to total output after some point will decline progressively with each additional unit of variable factor.

The law of diminishing return is also referred to as the "law of variable proportion" which implies that as additional units of variable factors are added to a given quantity of all other factors, the increment to output attributable to each of the additional units of the variable factor will increase at first, decrease later, and eventually become negative.

The law of diminishing returns is strictly a short run phenomenon.

5.9 RETURNS TO SCALE

Returns to scale is a long-run phenomenon where we can change all inputs simultaneously. Under this concept, the behaviour of output is studied when all factors of products are changed in the same direction and in the same proportion.

(*a*) **Increasing return to scale:** If output increases more than proportionate to the increase in all inputs.

(*b*) **Constant returns to scale:** If all inputs are increased by the same proportion, output will also increase by the same proportion.

(*c*) **Decreasing returns to scale:** If increase in output is less than proportionate to the increase in all inputs.

The three kinds of returns to scale can be illustrated with the help of following example:

Units of Labour	*Units of Capital (Rs. 000)*	*Percentage increase in labour and capital*	*Total Product ('00 units)*	*Percentage increase in total product*	*Return to scale*
(1)	(2)	(3)			
1	100	—	100	—	—
2	200	100%	220	120%	
3	300	50%	350	59%	Increasing
4	400	33.33%	500	42.9&	
5	500	25%	625	25%	Constant
6	600	20%	750	20%	
7	700	16.66%	860	16.66%	
8	800	14.29%	940	9.3%	Decreasing
9	900	12.5%	1,000	6.4%	

When output increases in the same proportion as the increase in the amounts of the factors of production, we have what is known as 'Constant return to Scale', when output increases in a greater proportion as compared to the increase in the amounts the factors of production, we have increasing return to scale.

When output increases in a smaller proportion as compared to the increase in the amounts of the factors of production, we have diminishing return to scale.

It is often observed that when a firm increases all the factors of production in a fixed proportion, output increases in three distinct phases:

1. Increasing returns to scale.

2. Constant returns to scale.
3. Diminishing returns to scale.

The concept of returns to scale is associated with the tendency of production that is observed when the ratio between the factors is kept constant but the scale is expended.

The most important reason of increasing returns to scale is the 'technical and managerial indivisibilities'. The meaning or an indivisible factor of production is that there is certain minimum size of the factor and even if it is large in relation to the size of the output, it has to be used and it can not be divided.

Other reasons for increasing returns to scale are specialization and efficiency.

When the quantity of other factors is increased and the scale of production expanded in a bid to boost up production, the proportion of other factors in relation to enterprise increases. Beyond a certain point, this results in diminishing returns as enterprise becomes scarce in relation to other factors.

Main reason for the operation of diminishing returns to scale is managerial difficulties.

In case of law of variable proportions some of the inputs are held constant while in the case of returns to scale all the inputs are changed in the same proportion. This means that the former explains the behaviour of output when the proportion in which different factors are all used changes, while the latter explains the behaviour of output when all inputs change simultaneously in the same proportion.

5.10 ECONOMIES OF SCALE

(*i*) **Meaning and Analysis of Economies of Scale:** Economies of Scale means economies which arise from the firm increasing its plan size.

Economies of Scale may also arise from an increase in the number of plants of a firm, irrespective of whether the firm continues to produce the same product in the new plants of a firm, irrespective of whether the firm continues to produce the same product in the new plants or diversifies.

In general, such inter-plant economies of scale are of the same nature as the single-plants (intra-plant) economies, although the importance of each type of scale economies may be different with an increase of the scale of operation of the firm via the installation of additional plants.

Pecuniary (concerning) economies are economies realised from paying lower prices for the factors used in the production and distribution of the product, due to bulk-buying by the firm as its size increases.

Such monetary economics do not imply an actual decrease in the quantity of inputs used but accrue to the firm from lower prices paid for raw materials (bought at a distant due to large volume of the purchase), lower interest rates (and lower cost of finance in general) as the size of the firm increases.

Real economies are those associated with a reduction in the physical quantity of inputs, raw materials, various types of labour and various types of capital (fixed or working capital).

(*ii*) **We may distinguish the following main type of real economies:**

(*a*) production economies

(*b*) selling or marketing economies

(*c*) managerial economies

(*d*) transport and storage economies

(*e*) pecuniary Economies.

(*a*) Production economies of Scale

Production economies may arise from:

- **Labour Economies:** These are achieved as the scale of output increases due to specialization, time-saving, automation of the production process and cumulative volume.

- **Technical Economies:** These are associated with the fixed capital which includes all types of machinery and other equipment.

  The main technical economies arise from:

  - Specialization of capital equipment and high degree of mechanisation for large scale of output.
  - Set-up Costs.
  - Initial fixed costs.
- **Reserve Capacity Requirement:** This means stand by equipment necessary to avoid disruption of production in case of break-down.
- **Inventory Economies:** Stocks of raw materials do increase with scale but not proportionately. Random fluctuations in the supply of such inputs are smoothed out with stocks whose size need change by less than the size of the firm.

(*b*) Selling or Marketing Economies

Selling economies are associated with the distribution of the product of a firm. The main types of economies arise from the following:

- Advertising economies.
- Special arrangements with exclusive dealers and distributors.

Large firms can enter exclusive agreements with distributors, who undertake the obligation of maintaining good service department.

This is usual for motor-car and two-wheeler and household goods (Refrigerator, TVs etc.)

(*c*) Managerial Economies

Managerial costs are partly production costs and partly selling costs.

Managerial economies arise from the following:

- **Specialisation of Management:** *i.e.*, each managerial function is specialized, production, finance, marketing, personal etc. are specialised.
- **Decentralisation of Decision-making Process:** The decentralisation of decision-making in large firms has been found very effective in the increase of efficiency of management. With decentralisation the flow of information within the firm is reduced and thus distortions and delays of this information in the various sections of the firm is to a large extent avoided.

  Decentralisation of the decision-making process is one of the main means of increasing the efficiency of management in large scale plants and of avoiding managerial dis-economies in still larger plants.
- **Mechanisation of Managerial Functions:** Large Scale firms are able to achieve high degree of mechanisation in managerial functions by telephones, telex, fax, dictaphone, e-mail, video-conferencing, internets, voice mails etc. and computers with various softwares etc.

(*d*) Transport and Storage Economies

Transport and storage costs are incurred partly on the production side and partly on the selling side of the firm.

Costs of constructing larger tanks, warehouses become less as the size increases.

Similarly, large firms are capable of maintaining their own transports for transport of raw materials and finished products and thus may be able to reduce costs.

Also, large firms may adopt cheaper modes of transport such as cable trolleys, conveyors, trolleys on rails, water ways transport using ships, steamers and barges etc. and these methods of transport will reduce the transportation costs.

(*e*) Pecuniary Economies of Scale

These are economies accruing to a large firm due to discounts that it can obtain due to its large scale operations.

The larger firm may achieve:

- Lower prices of its materials, bought at special discounts from its suppliers.
- Lower costs of external finance-banks usually offer loans to large companies at a lower rate of interest and other favourable terms.
- Lower advertising prices may be granted to larger firms if they advertise at large scales.

Transport rates are often lower if the bulk transportation is resorted by the large companies.

The total average cost is the summation of all costs (of production, marketing, managerial, transport etc.) and it is generally accepted that the total LAC Curve falls as the Scale of plant increases, at least upto a certain point.

5.11 PRODUCTION PROCESS—SHORT-RUN AND LONG-RUN CONCEPTS

"Short-run" and "Long-run" are an economist's terms and actually they do not refer to any fixed time period.

The short-run refers to a period of time in which the supply of certain inputs like plant, building, equipment etc. is fixed or inelastic. In the short-run therefore, production of a good may be increased by increasing the use of only variable inputs like labour and raw materials.

The long-run refers to a period of time in which supply of all inputs may vary and elastic, except a change in technology.

Therefore, in the long-run, production of a good may be increased by employing more of both variable and fixed inputs. In other words, in a production process, in the short-run only the variable costs (*i.e.*, cost due to variable inputs of labour and raw materials) can be changed. Whereas, in the long-run period both the fixed and variable costs (*i.e.*, costs due to fixed and variable inputs) can be altered.

In business economies, inputs of a production process are taken as land, capital, labour raw materials and time.

Production process involves physical conversion of raw materials (*i.e.*, Iron ore) or intangible input (*i.e.*, legal or consultancy service) into tangible products (*i.e.*, steal) or intangible output respectively.

5.12 PRODUCTION AND SUPPLY

Often we assume that the volume of supply is equal to the volume production *i.e.*, whatever is produced is offered for sale. This however is not necessary. One important reason for the difference between the amount produced and amount supplied in the market is that the producers may also be consumers often. For example, the Indian farmers grows rice, wheat, and cereals essential for his own consumption. He sells in the market only the surplus above his own consumption. How much will be his marketable surplus will depend upon the price of the good and the general level of income of the farmer.

Many durable and semi-durable goods may be stored if producers anticipate higher prices, or, past stocks may be sold in the market alongwith current production, if producers anticipate fall in price in the near future. The market supply can, therefore, be more or less than the current production—more if past accumulated stocks are unloaded and less if part of the current production is hoarded.

(*a*) Supply Curve

According to the law of supply larger quantities of products will be supplied at higher prices, other things being equal. The higher the price, the greater is the inducement to the producer to produce and sell more. An imaginary supply schedule of match-boxes is given in the table as follows.

Supply Schedule of Match-Boxes

Price per dozen of Match-Boxes Rs.	*No. of Dozens of Boxes Supplied*
2.00	25,000
2.50	30,000
3.00	35,000
3.50	40,000

The above supply schedule is illustrated in Figure 5.10. The supply schedule as well as the supply curve shows clearly that other things being equal, the supply of a commodity will expand at higher prices and contract at lower prices. This is known as expansion and contraction of supply in relation to prices.

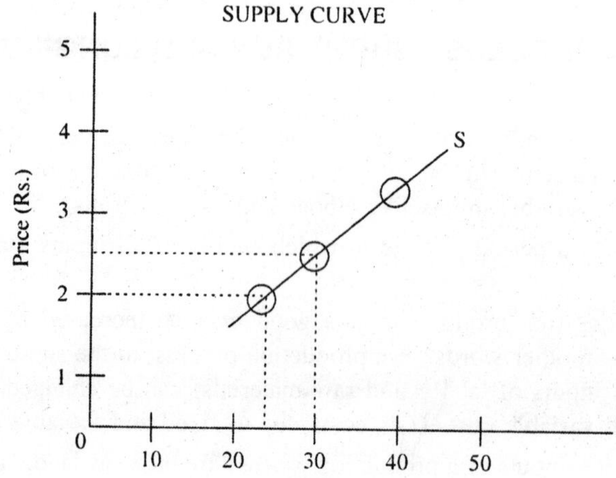

Figure 5.10

(*b*) Determinants of Supply

The supply of a product depends upon the number of firms and scale and rate of production. The larger the number of firms the bigger the size of firms in an industry, the more will be the supply of the product. Every industry supply schedule is therefore prepared on the assumption of a given number of firms, certain scale of productions and a given rate of production. Any change in this assumption will raise or lower the supply schedule.

Secondly, the supply schedule of the product is prepared on the assumption of a given production technology. An improvement in technology will reduce cost of production and increase the supply.

Thirdly, the cost of production influences the supply of a product. Now cost of production is based on the price of factors of production, viz. wages, rate of interest on funds borrowed, hire of machinery, equipment, raw materials etc. If cost of production goes up, there would be a decrease in supply and the supply curve is pushed upwards and vice-versa.

Fourthly, we assume that the supply of a product depends upon the price of that commodity only and not of other commodities. The supply of commodities and prices at which it is offered will obviously depend upon the supply of other commodities which are produced together with it. For instance the amount of butter which a dairy farm can supply will depend upon the amount of milk which the farm is supplying in the market.

Finally, the supply of commodity depends upon such general conditions, as weather conditions (for agricultural goods as example), war, government policies regarding taxation (raise the cost and reduces the supply) subsidies etc.

It is assumed that at any given time all the determinants are given and that there are no changes which will upset a supply curve. The moment these conditions change, the supply curve will not hold good any more, a new supply curve will come into existence.

(c) Measure of Elasticity of Supply

Elasticity of supply is defined as the degree of responsiveness of supply to a given change in price. The formula for elasticity of supply is:

$$e_s = \frac{\text{Percentage change in supply}}{\text{Percentage change in price}}$$

Elasticity of supply can be elaborated as

$$e_s = \frac{\frac{\text{change in supply}}{\text{original supply}} \times 100}{\frac{\text{change in price}}{\text{original price}} \times 100}$$

Using symbols, the formula for elasticity of supply can be written as:

$$e_s = \frac{\frac{\Delta q}{Q}}{\frac{\Delta P}{P}} = \frac{\Delta q}{Q} \times \frac{p}{\Delta p} = \frac{\Delta q}{\Delta p} \times \frac{P}{Q}$$

$$\therefore \quad e_s = \frac{\Delta q}{\Delta P} \times \frac{P}{Q}$$

Let us use a numerical example to calculate elasticity of supply. Suppose that 1000 fountain pens are supplied at a price of Rs. 4.00 and that 1,500 pens are offered at Rs. 5 per pen the elasticity of supply is

$$e = \frac{500}{1} \times \frac{4}{1,000} = 2$$

We can also illustrate the measurement of elasticity of supply with the help of Figure 5.11. In Figure 5.11, the supply curve is SS, NT is the line drawn to be tangent to the supply curve at points *A* & *C* (These two points are assumed to be close to each other, so close that they can be taken as one point). Between these two points the slope of the supply curve SS and slope of NT are exactly same. In this figure.

Original Price = OP (= QA)

Original Supply = OQ (= PA)

Change in Price = PP_1 (= BC)

Change in Supply = QR (= AB)

We know the formula for elasticity of supply is:

$$e_s = \frac{\Delta q}{\Delta p} \times \frac{P}{Q}$$

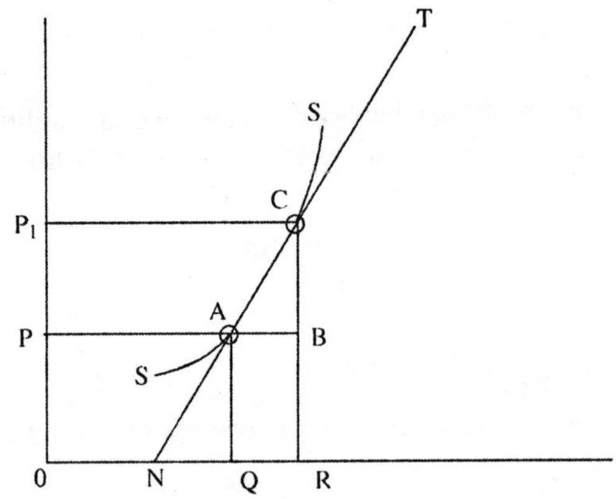

Figure 5.11 Elasticity of Supply

Substituting by the symbols of Figure 5.11

$$e = \frac{AB}{BC} \times \frac{QA}{OQ}$$

(Taking change in quantity and change in price in the small triangle *ABC*).

It may be observed that *ABC* and *NQA* are similar triangles and the ratio of their sides are equal. In other words *AB*/*BC* can be substituted by *NQ*/*QA*. In that case

$$e_s = \frac{AB}{BC} \times \frac{QA}{OQ}$$

$$e_s = \frac{NQ}{QA} \times \frac{QA}{OQ}$$

$$e_s = \frac{NQ}{OQ}$$

If we assume that *A* & *C* are close to each other so that they may be taken as one point (viz. point *A*) elasticity of supply is given by the formula *NQ*/*OQ*. In Figure 5.11, *NQ*/*OQ* is less than one for *NQ* is smaller than *OQ*. This means that elasticity of supply at point *A* is less than 1.

On the other hand if *NT* passes through the origin of the axes and is tangent to the supply curve then elasticity of supply will be equal to 1. If finally *NT* line which is tangent to the supply curve passes through the *y*-axis, then elasticity of supply will be more than one.

5.13 CAPACITY AND COST OF PRODUCTION

(*i*) **Capacity of Production:** The determinants of production and supply affects the cost of production. Broadly the determinants of cost of production are: the size of the plant, the level of production *i.e.*, the utilisation of the plant, the nature of technology used, prices of various inputs like raw materials, labour, power etc. managerial and labour efficiency etc. For instance, larger the size of the plant, the greater are the internal economies of production, and consequently, the large form will experience increasing returns or decreasing cost. In other words, the average cost will decline. Likewise better utilisation of plant, the use of better technology and increasing managerial and labour efficiency will bring about rise in production and fall in the cost of production. In the same manner a fall in the prices of inputs like raw materials or a fall in transport charges will also reduce the average cost of production.

(*ii*) **Variable Cost of Production:** Variable cost of production are cost incurred by a firm on the variable factors of the production processes. Such costs can be increased or decreased according to the volume of production, as for example, labour, raw material, fuel, power etc. If the output is zero, the total variable cost will also be zero, but with every increase in production the total variable costs will also increase. Variable cost are also called as direct cost of production or prime cost.

(*iii*) **Fixed Cost:** Fixed cost relate to the expenses incurred by the firm on fixed factors in the start period viz. buildings and business premises, managerial and technical labour. These costs are fixed in the short period in the sense that they do not change with output or, they are independent of output. By defination total fixed cost will be a given amount weather the output is zero, or it is small or large. Fixed costs are also called general costs, overhead cost or indirect cost. Marshall called fixed cost as supplementary cost.

Fixed cost are associated with fixed factors of production in the short period, for in the long-run, all factors are variable and all long period costs are variable cost.

5.14 PROBABLE QUESTIONS

1. Define Isoquant and Iso-cost.

What is the significance of Marginal Rate of Technical Substitution?

2. Describe the following:

(*a*) Leontief Static Open Model

(*b*) Leontief Production Function.

3. Define law of variable proportions. What are various Returns to Scale?

4. State with examples various Economies of Scale.

5. Describe Short-Run and Long-Run concepts of Production Process.

6

Factory Management

• *Factory Locations* • *Plant Layout Planning* • *Principles for Plant Layout* • *Flexibility of Layout* • *Factory Layout* • *Factors Affecting Plant Layout* • *Layout Engineering* • *Plant Design* • *Probable Questions.*

6.1 FACTORY LOCATION

(*i*) Definition of Factory

A factory is involved in manufacturing activities utilising man, material, machines, land and management. Precious resources like men, materials and machines are systematically deployed by management for producing finished goods for sale.

A factory is a Plant for producing necessary goods required by customers.

A factory or a Plant is built on a plot of land which is effectively utilised.

There are small scale factories producing Hosiery goods, Writing pens or Stationery Exercise books, which require much less quantity of resources of men, materials, machines, and land. These plants may be located on a small piece of land measuring may be 1000 sq. feet or less in area. These plants may produce goods worth few lacs of rupees or even less. Compared to above, large factories which may be Oil Refineries, Fertilizer plants, Steel plants, Automobile units or Petrochemicals plants which deploy huge quantity of resources and produce goods worth few billions of rupees.

(*ii*) Importance of Location

Location of a Factory is an important managerial decision. It involves a heavy commitment of resources for a long time. A mistake in location may result in a disaster.

The ideal location is the site at which the cost of gathering materials and processing them plus the cost of distributing the finished products to the customers will be minimum per unit. In actual practice such a location may not be possible and a compromise may have to be made.

Location determines the operating and capital costs of a Factory Location is an important element in the design of a Production system due to following reasons:

1. Location affects the layout of physical facilities.
2. Location has an impact on the efficiency of distribution of product or service.
3. Location is an important determination of the efficiency and cost of Production Process. Location and distribution plans represent the basic strategy of the firm for getting access to markets. They may exercise important influence on sales revenues and customer services.

(*iii*) Factors Influencing Location

Plant location is the function of deciding where the Plant should be located so as to maximise operating efficiency and to minimise costs. The need for location decision may arise both at the time of setting up a new plant and at the time of expansion.

While deciding the location for a Production Unit, four main factors should be considered:

(*a*) **Input Costs:** Inputs are economic resources used in a process production e.g. land, labour, capital, raw materials, power etc.

Land exercises have little influence in location except in terms of land costs, access roads, sewers etc.

Power and water exercise some amount of influence on location. But for large production units, own power generation facility may be installed depending type of fuel is available in the proximity.

Water supply facility is important for production unit like paper, jute, etc. which require large quantities of water for the manufacturing process.

Raw materials availability in the proximity is an important factor for a plant location. Industries like cement and steel using bulky and heavy materials are located near the sources of lime stone etc. and iron ore etc.

Sugar and paper and other industries for which transportation cost is significant are also located near point of raw materials supply.

But industries using light and heavy weight costly materials are located near markets. Location of an Automobile Unit is such an example.

Labour costs depend largely on the prevailing wage rates in the area. But differences in labour productivity may more than off set any apparent gain in lower wage rates. Industries tend to be localised in areas which have abundant supply of cheap/skilled labour.

(*b*) **Location of the Output Market:** In many cases, plants tend to be located near the market for their products. In recent years the output market has been exerting an increasing "pull" on industrial location. The reasons for this trend are:

- The relatively higher costs of transporting bulky and heavy finished goods than the cost of moving raw materials.
- The advantage of being close to customers for service purposes is particularly in high technology and services industries.
- Units producing perishable and fragile products such as bread, ice-cream, glasses etc. to tend to be located near the market.
- Units producing bulky or heavy goods also tend to locate near the market so as minimise transport costs. For example, Automobile and furniture making units are located near the users.
- Soft drink units also tend to be located near the market, because soft drinks increase in weight when water is added to the syrup and this can easily be done at customers' location.

(*c*) **Transportation Costs:** Transportation costs play a significant role in locational decisions. An industry which uses considerably more than a ton of materials to make a ton of output will tend to be located near the place of supply of materials, provided that its products are fairly easy to transport.

Transportation costs depend mainly on the weight to be carried and the distance to be covered.

In some industries the weight of raw materials is much higher than that of the finished products *i.e.*, weight losing industries such as sugar (4 to 5 tons sugarcane give one ton sugar), Paper (2.5-3 ton bamboo give one ton paper) and steel plants (2 tons iron ore give one ton pig iron) are located proximity to the sources of raw materials in order to minimise transportation costs.

Whereas, in the case of weight gaining industries, such as Soft Drinks, Ice-Creams and Furniture etc. these are normally located near to the market *i.e.*, near the cities or large towns.

(*d*) **Agglomeration economies and other factors:** Alfred Weber's theory on plant location is based on an analysis of transportation costs, labour costs and the economies and diseconomies arising from the concentration of industries.

These are the savings in costs arising from the concentration of industries in a particular region. These savings could accrue from developed infrastructure (roads, railways etc.), skilled labour, banking services, common research facilities, ancillary firms etc.

There are three main type of costs savings open to a firm as a result of agglomeration or clustering of industries:

(*i*) **Internal economies:** With increase in market size, the long-run average cost per unit of product decreases.

(*ii*) **Localisation economies:** Which are external to the firm but internal to the industry *i.e.*, if several closely related firms are located together common facilities become available to each. Common research facilities, ancillary units, consultancy services are examples of such facilities.

(*iii*) **External economies:** Which are gains to all firms in all industries which result from locating together, *i.e.*, they include the presence of highly developed infrastructure of roads, railways, ports banking and capital markets, and market research facilities etc.

Miscellaneous factors like climate, Government policies, Political interference etc. also influence industrial location.

(*e*) **Locational Break-even Analysis:** Break-even analysis can be usefully employed to compare costs of alternative locations. Many of these may vary with the volume of production. When the expected volume for a new plant is likely to fluctuate, the economic comparison can be made by identifying the fixed costs and variable costs and by plotting them on a graph. This graphic method is some times called locational break-even analysis.

This approach is superior to the tabular approach as we can easily identify ranges over which one location is preferable to another.

Locational break-even analysis consists of following steps:

1. Determine all relevant costs that vary with the locations under consideration.
2. Classify these costs into fixed and variable costs.
3. Plot the costs associated with each location on a single chart of annual cost versus annual volume.
4. Select the location with the lowest total annual cost (Tc) at the expected production volume (V).

Locational break-even analysis is a means of comparing all relevant costs for several alternative locations and selecting a plant location that will minimise costs for a given plant. When transportation/distribution costs vary from one location to another they should be included in the relevant costs.

Example 6.1 A sugar mill has to choose from three alternative locations with the following cost data:

Site	*Fixed Costs per annum (Rs.)*	*Variable Costs per unit (Rs.)*
X	20,000	50
Y	40,000	30
Z	80,000	10

Find the most economical location for 1,850 units.

Solution. Let us calculate total costs for 3 sites at a volume of 2,000 units.

Site $X = 20{,}000 + 2{,}000 \times 50 =$ Rs. 1,20,000

Site $Y = 40{,}000 + 2{,}000 \times 30 =$ Rs. 1,00,000

Site $Z = 80{,}000 + 2{,}000 \times 10 =$ Rs. 1,00,000.

Now Plot these on a graph,

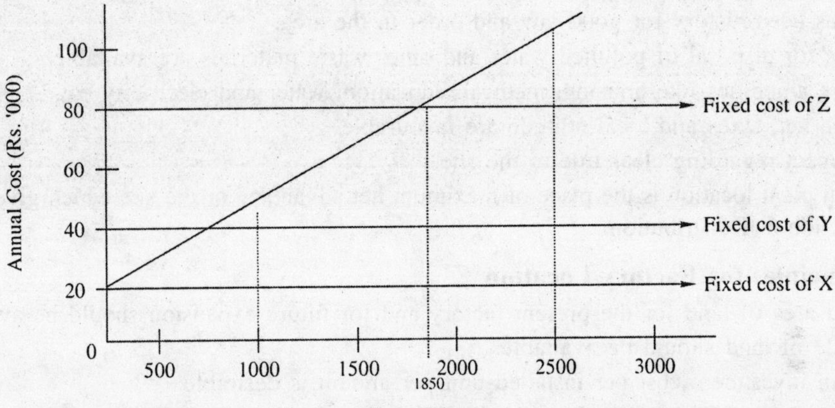

Figure 6.1

From the graph, we find that the most economical location for 1850 units is Site *Y*. Note that for volume less than 1000 units Site *X* is preferable, while for volume exceeding 2,500 units, Site *Z* is preferable.

Choice of factory site

Once the region in which the plant is to be located is decided, the next step in plant location is to choose the site.

City versus Village Site

Three types of location are available for a plant, namely, village (Country side), City and Suburbs. The last is a combination of the earlier two.

Village or country site offers advantages of abundant supply of chap land, abundant supply of cheap unskilled labour, healthy surroundings, incentives and subsidies, minimum municipal and other regulations, absence of traffic congestion and overcrowding and low rents and taxes. Also sufficient land is available for expansion of business operations. But there is lack of adequate supply of skilled labour, and absence of housing, education, medical, banking and such other facilities.

On the other hand, city site provides skilled labour, auxiliary service like repairs etc., banking and credit facilities, large market, better transport and public services. But land and buildings are costly in cities. Rents and taxes are high, municipal restrictions are stringent and wage rates high, moreover overcrowding, congestion of traffic and pollution are common in the cities.

A suburb seems to offer the advantages of both. Recent trends indicate that industrial estates have been developed on the outskirts of big cities. For example, Okhla, Faridabad, Ghaziabad, Noida and Bahadurgarh near Delhi, Falta, Dankuni, Uluberia and Ganganagar near Kolkata and Patalganga, Santacruz near Mumbai etc. have become important industrial centres around big cities.

In all cases, the guiding principle in the fixation of the exact optimum location for the Plant is that it must result in the lowest unit cost in producing and distributing the product to the consumer.

Determination of Plant Site location

After the city/village is selected, the specific site at which the plant will be located has to be decided. In this choice, the following factors should be considered.

1. The site should be well connected by different modes of transport.
2. Availability of sufficient land at reasonable cost. The size of the plot should have scope for expansion.
3. Labour is available and attitude of labour is positive.
4. There has been history for good law and order in the area.
5. Facilities for disposal of polluted water and other waste materials are available.
6. There are amenities like housing, medical, education, water and electricity etc.
7. Local market, taxes and local attitude are favourable.
8. Legal aspect regarding clear title to the site.

The ideal plant location is the place of maximum net advantage or the site which gives lowest unit cost of production and distribution.

Guiding Principles for Factory Location

1. Required area of land for the present factory and for future expansion should be available.
2. Clear title of land should be available.
3. Minimum investment cost per installed unit per annum is desirable.
4. Minimum unit cost of production and distribution should be obtained.

Comparative Factors for various location sites with examples:

Sl. No.	*Factors*	*City/Town*	*Village Site*	*Suburbs*
1.	Cost of Land	High	Low	Medium
2.	Availability of land	Large Plot may not be available	Available	May be available
3.	Tax and Rent	High	Low	Medium
4.	Polluting type industries	Cannot be located	Can be located	Can not be located
5.	Availability large quantity of water	May not be available	Available	May be available
6.	Availability of Electricity	Available	Not Available/ To be installed	Facility may have to be installed
7.	Social infra-structure like housing, to be installed schools, shopping complex Health care facilities and recreation centres	Available	Not Available but may have to be installed	May be available
8.	Skilled labour and professionals	Available	Not available but to be appointed with suitable terms.	May be available

Examples of some large and small plants locations.

1. Tata Steel at Jamshedpur, Reliance Petro-Chemicals at Hazira and Haldia Petro-Chemicals at Haldia, 130 Kms. from Kolkata are some good locations for large industries which meet the necessary conditions of Plant locational economies.
2. Noida, Faridabad, Dankuni, Ganganagar, Bantala, Santacruz etc. are example of goods suburban areas as available locations for clusters of medium scale and small-scale industries.
3. As per high court orders the polluting industries in and around Delhi were relocated at distant places in 2000 A.D., similarly, large numbers of Tannery Units in the east part of Kolkata are being distantly relocated at Bantala complex.
4. Present location of automobile manufacturing plants at Gurgaon near Delhi, Hind Motor near Kolkata and Bajaj Auto in Pune, Maharashtra also justify the plant locational economies.
5. Locations of non-polluting electronic industries, computer and IT units and software companies requiring large numbers highly qualified and experienced professionals are suitably located in cities of Bangalore, New Delhi, Hyderabad, Pune and Kolkata etc.

Factors affecting plant location

The following factors need to be considered for suitable plant locations:

1. Input Factors

(*i*) **Land:** Availability of sufficient land, cost, free title and Government regulations, cost of construction of a factory etc.

(*ii*) **Availability of input materials:** Quantity and quality cost and regularity supply etc.

(*iii*) **Plant Utilities:** Water, Electricity, coal etc. Availability and costs etc.

(*iv*) **Labour:** Skills types, availability, wage rates, attitude towards trade-unionism etc.

(*v*) **Capital:** Debt and Equity characteristics, availability of working capital etc.

(*vi*) **Availability of infra structural facilities for working staff and executives with their families:** Schools, markets, hospitals, recreation centres, near-by towns/cities with road connectivities etc.

2. Processing factors for consideration

(*i*) **Presence of auxiliary industries:** Repair works, development of spare parts, work shops etc.

(*ii*) **Maintenance:** Service and repair facilities.

3. Output Consideration

(*i*) **Distribution:** Distribution and storage facilities.

(*ii*) **Transportation:** Facilities, speed and cost etc.

(*iii*) **Local taxes and rates:** etc.

(*iv*) **Present and future market potential.**

4. Other factors for consideration

(*i*) **Attitude of local residents, societies towards the industry.**

(*ii*) **Environmental standards:** Water, Land air pollution control norms, building codes etc.

(*iii*) **Political factor:** Political situation, Political stability and attitudes.

(*iv*) **Law and orders situation:** Peaceful situation, absence of any attitudes.

(*v*) **Law and orders situation:** Peaceful situation, absence of any turmoil condition in future etc.

Examples: of Plants locations with proximity of main raw materials are as follows:

1.	Tata Steel at Jamshedpur and Indian Iron and Steel at Durgapur	Near Deposits of Iron Ore and Coal.
2.	Cement Plants at Rajasthan and Madhya Pradesh	Proximity of lime-stone and Gypsum deposits.
3.	Hindustan Aluminium at Hira Kud, Orissa and National Aluminium Co. Ltd. near Paradip, Orissa.	Hydroelectricity from Hirakud, dam and Aluminium Ore (Bauxite) deposits are abundantly available.
4.	Coca-Cola and Pepsi Co.'s bottling plants near the market	In metro cities for speeds in distribution and involving least cost.

Table 6.1 Operating parameters with weightages for Plant Locations

Sr. No.	*Factors*	*Relative Weightage*	*Other influencing factors*
1.	Labour	40	Skilled, Semiskilled unskilled, supply, wages and strikes etc.
2.	Supplies of Raw Materials	20	Source and cost.
3.	(*a*) Power	6	Govt. agency or private cost service.
	(*b*) Fuel	3	Cost and quality, oil gas, coal etc.
	(*c*) Water supply	1	Quality, Quantity and Cost.
4.	Transportation	10	Modes of transportation and cost.
5.	Taxes and Law	10	Government and local.
6.	(*a*) Climate	2	Maximum and minimum temperatures, average rainfall, snowfall etc.
	(*b*) Living conditions	3	Cost of living, sanitation, health-care and housing facilities.
7.	Other facilities like		
	(*a*) Cost of construction	3	Provision for expansion, material supply, property and soil etc.
	(*b*) Location of site	2	Railway connection, provision for drainage, water and labour supply etc.
	Total	100	

Use of OR in determining the most economical location for an industrial project:

The following table illustrate the weighing method for selection of local site and other influencing factors.

While doing weighing we establish a percentage to represent the relative importance.

It may be important that better the technique for getting the weighing the better may be the decision.

In this aspect a questionnaire survey or a consensus can be used in making the optimal choice of location with the help of OR.

(*a*) Method for making decision by OR

Step I Find the important factors. First to all find the factors which are considered important. For finding this, statistical analysis or questionnaire survey may be employed.

The important factors can be written down in the following table in order of importance.

Step II Putting the relative weightages for each important factor. This is done the best way when all the factors are considered according to the same scale desirability.

There may be many methods to get these evaluations like cost studies, statistical analysis, work sampling, questionnaire and all other tools of OR.

Step III Weighing the factors with relative economic importance. In this we establish a percentage (100) to represent the relative importance.

The following Table 6.2 shows the factors are weighed in putting them in the middle column. It may be important that better the technique for getting the weightages, the better the decision.

Step IV Calculating weighed scores for alternatives.

For this, multiply each unweighed point rating with the appropriate weight.

In the example, for factor 1 *i.e.*, availability of labour for site-1, multiply 10 by 40 to get 400. In this way the following Table 6.2 is completed. Finally, add the weighed points to find the best site to choose.

Now observe that how the choice is reversed by weighing. At site 1, with 825 becomes the first choice instead of the third.

Table 6.2

Sr. No.	*Important factors*	*Unweighed site evaluation*			*Weighing*	*Weighed site evaluation*		
		Site-I	*Site-II*	*Site-III*		*Site-I*	*Site-II*	*Site-III*
1.	Availability of labour	10	8	7	40	400	320	280
2.	Availability of raw material	8	7	6	20	160	140	120
3.	Availability of power etc.	8	7	10	10	80	70	100
4.	Availability of Transport	7	9	8	10	70	90	80
5.	Local taxes and other cost	6	10	9	10	60	100	90
6.	Climate conditions	5	9	10	5	25	45	50
7.	Other facilities	6	5	10	5	30	25	50
	Total evaluation score	50	55	60	100%	825	790	770
	Relative desirability site	3rd	2nd	1st		1st	2nd	3rd

(*b*) The best location for the small scale industry

Following are the points which are to be considered in addition to main factors while considering location for small plant:

1. Select the area where the entrepreneur has an idea about the local people, their habits customs and need.
2. Preferably, the entrepreneur should meet the local people, panchayat or MLA and/or the law enforcing authority.
3. Location in rented premises is better because of its higher flexibility.
4. Other factors are similar to large industrial site location as discussed earlier.

Factory Site location on the basis of Rate of Return (in percentage)

For 3 locations *A*, *B* and *C* the parameters mentioned as follows are considered:

Sr. No.	*Factors*	*Site-A*	*Site-B*	*Site-C*
1.	Total Investments required for the Plant (Rs. '000)	250	315	250
2.	Total annual projected Sales income (Rs. '000)	340	390	350
3.	Expenses (annual) on raw materials (Rs. '000)	85	100	120
4.	Expenses (annual) on distribution (Rs. '000)	50	50	80
5.	Expenses (annual) Power and utilities (Rs. '000)	50	40	25
6.	Salaried wages per annum (Rs. '000)	25	30	25
7.	Community facilities	Poor	Good	Bad
8.	Community attitude	Indifferent	Good	Indifferent
9.	Total expenses (3 to 6)	Rs. 2,10,000	Rs. 2,20,000	Rs. 2,50,000
10.	Rate of Return (%)	52	54	40

It is seen that site *B* is advantageous as it gives the highest rate of return and community facilities and community attitudes are also good.

6.2 PLANT LAYOUT PLANNING

Layout Planning involves decisions about the physical arrangement of economics activity centres within a facility. An economic activity centre can be anything that consumer expects.

The goal of layout planning is to allow workers and equipment to operate most effectively.

The following four questions should be addressed before making decision regarding physical arrangement.

(*i*) What centres should the layout include? Centres should reflect process decisions and maximise productivity.

(*ii*) How much space and capacity does each centre need?

Inadequate space can reduce productivity, create health hazards and safety hazards. However, excessive space is wasteful and must be avoided.

(*iii*) How should each centre's space be configured?

The amount of space, its shape and the elements in a centre are introduced.

Providing a favourable atmosphere should be considered as part of the configuration.

(*iv*) Where should each centre be located?

Location can significantly affect productivity. Interrelationship between centre for smooth production/ operation should be considered carefully.

It should be borne in mind that the location of a centre has two considerations *i.e.*, (1) relative location and (2) absolute location.

Both the above affect the centre's actual performance.

6.3 PRINCIPLES FOR PLANT LAYOUT

The following factors are guiding principles for designing a Plant layout.

1. **Principle of minimum movement:** Both materials and labour should make movement over minimum distances.
2. **Principle of flow:** The operation area should be such arranged that there is continuous flow of materials without any reverse flow or congestion.
3. **Principle of space:** All the available three dimensional area for operation should be utilised in the optimum way both horizontally and vertically.
4. **Principle of safety:** For designing the layout due consideration should be given for the safety of workers, machines and otherwise.
5. **Principle of flexibility:** Layout should be so designed that Production facilities can easily be rearranged when it becomes necessary for expansion or installation of improved technology in future.
6. **Principle of interdependence:** Interdependent operations and processes should be located in close proximity to each other. For example, materials should be stored near the area of requirement; transport etc.
7. **Principle of minimum investment:** The layout should yield savings in fixed capital investment through optimum utilisation of available facilities.
8. **A Sound Plant Layout** must ensure the following:
   (*a*) Steady and uninterrupted flow of work.
   (*b*) Absence of reverse or congested flow of materials/process.
   (*c*) Full utilisation of equipment and plant capacity.
   (*d*) Flexibility to meet technological changes and increased production facility.
   (*e*) Easy control of production.
   (*f*) Effective and less expensive supervision.
   (*g*) Unit list of production the lowest.

6.4 FLEXIBILITY OF LAYOUT

As far as possible certain amount of flexibility of arrangement and operation is essentially desired in a plant layout. Economy should be the prime consideration in layout.

When changes are affected in the product design, methods of operation the type of product or the production quantities then the machines, or departments may also have to be arranged. Therefore, it is necessary to design layouts in such a way so as to minimise the affect of subsequent alteration on the production process.

Flexibility in layout can be secured in the following ways:

(*i*) Keep enough unobstructed floor space.

(*ii*) Separate electric motor for each machine instead of line shaft drive arrangement is preferable.
(*iii*) Portable conveyor units may be employed.
(*iv*) Make use of portable jigs and fixures.
(*v*) Equipment may be placed on rubber footings instead of being mounted permanently.

6.5 FACTORY LAYOUT

(*i*) Objectives of Layout: Plant layout implies the physical arrangement of machines, equipment and other industrial facilities on the factory floor in such a manner that they may be handled efficiently. It may be defined as a technique of locating machines, processes and plant services within the factory so as to achieve the right quantity and quality of output at the lowest possible cost of manufacturing.

As a floor plan of production facilities, plant layout indicates the space allotted for material movement, storage and all supporting facilities for overall economy in production.

It involves a judicious arrangement of production facilities so that work flows in as direct a path as possible.

The various objectives of a good plant layout are as follows:

(*a*) to minimise handling and transportation of materials.
(*b*) to ensure economic utilisation of available floor space.
(*c*) to minimise work-in-progress inventory by eliminating bottlenecks.
(*d*) to ensure efficient control over the various processes of production.
(*e*) to maximise convenience and safety of workers.
(*f*) to obtain more efficient utilisation of machinery, equipment and other facilities.
(*g*) to minimise cost of production.

The basic objective of factory layout is to develop a production system that meets requirements of quantity and quality in the most economical way.

(*ii*) Advantages of good layout: An efficient plant layout facilitates the best possible use of plant, equipment, materials, labour and space.

Some of the main benefits of good layout are as follows:

(*a*) economical use of production; storage and service space.
(*b*) reduction in material handling cost and the amount of work in progress due to minimum movement of materials between processes.
(*c*) efficient utilisation of machinery and labour by avoiding delays and bottlenecks.
(*d*) effective planning, supervision and control of manufacturing operations.
(*e*) higher safety and improved work conditions for workers.
(*f*) lesser capital investment in plant, equipment, tooling and other physical facilities.
(*g*) reduction in installation and maintenance costs due to efficient routing of services.
(*h*) improvement in the production process as a whole on account of less energy consumption, less inspection costs, less fatigue and high worker morale.
(*i*) improvement in the quality of output.

(*iii*) Types of Layout: There are four broad categories of factory layout:

1. **Product or Line Layout:** In this layout, machines and equipment are arranged in the sequence of the manufacturing operations required for the product. The materials move from one work station to another sequentially without any back tracking or deviation of material.

It is called line layout because machines are arranged in a straight line. The raw materials are fed at one end and taken out as the finished product on the other.

A straight line type of product layout is shown below:

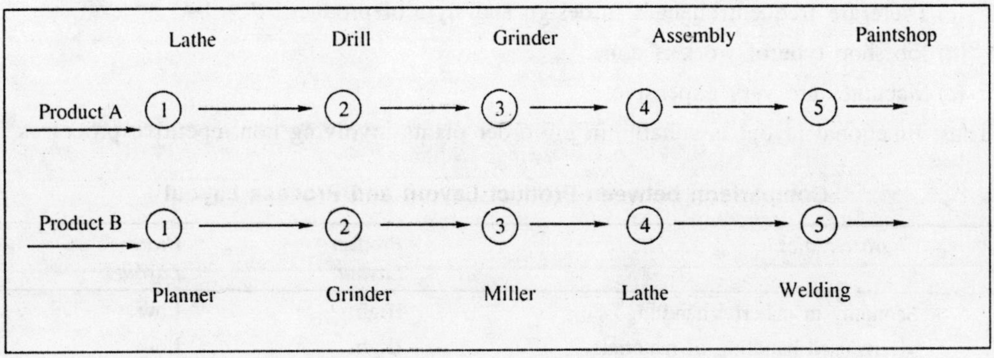

Figure 6.2 Product Layout showing movement of two products.

Product layout is useful under the following conditions:

(*a*) Mass Production of standardised products.

(*b*) Simple and repetitive manufacturing process.

(*c*) Operation time for different processes is more or less equal.

(*d*) Reasonably stable demand for product.

(*e*) Inter changeability of parts.

(*f*) Continuous supply of materials.

Large Automobile assembly plants, food-processing chains and continuous process industries use line layout system.

In other words, line layout best suits those industries which manufacture a large volume of standard products involving repetitive processes. In these industries, line layout reduces inventory handling and supervision costs.

2. **Process or Functional Layout:** In this type of layout, machines of similar type are located together according to their functions. Products move between the groups of equipments in order of the operations required. For examples, all the lathe machines are placed in the lathe department, all the drilling machines in the drilling department, all the welding equipment in welding department and so on.

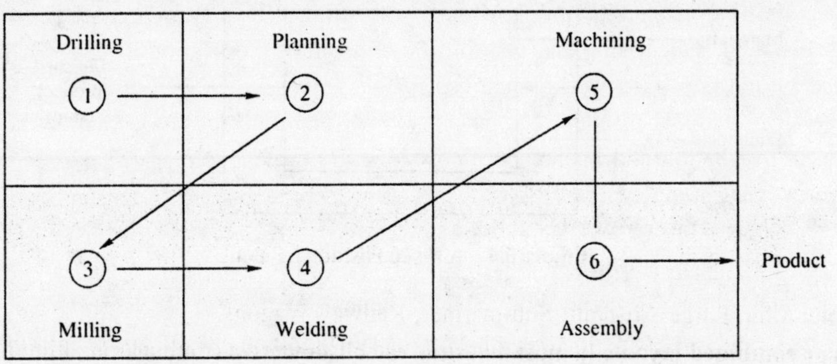

Figure 6.3 Process Layout showing movement of a product.

Process layout is useful when:

(*a*) Products are not standardised

(*b*) Quantity produced is small

(*c*) There are frequent changes in design and style of product

(*d*) Job shop type of work is done.

(*e*) Machines are very expensive.

Thus, functional layout is suitable in job order plants involving non-repetitive processes.

Comparison between Product Layout and Process Layout

	Characteristics	*Product Layout*	*Process Layout*
1.	Economy in material handling	High	Low
2.	Mechanised handling of materials	High	Low
3.	Bottlenecks in flow of work	Low	High
4.	Economy in manufacturing time	High	Low
5.	Production Control	Simple	Difficulty
6.	Costs of Inspection	Low	High
7.	Accumulation of work-in-progress	Low	High
8.	Flexibility	Low	High
9.	Scope for expansion	Low	High
10.	Utilisation of equipment	Low	High
11.	Utilisation of labour	Low	High
12.	Adaptability in case of break down	No	Yes

3. **Fixed Position Layout:** In this type of layout, the major product being produced is fixed at a location. Equipment, labour and components are moved to that location. This layout is used when materials being processed are large, very heavy and difficult to move.

Shipbuilding, locomotive manufacturing, wagon building, aircraft manufacturing, etc. employ fixed position layout. All facilities are brought and arranged around one work centre.

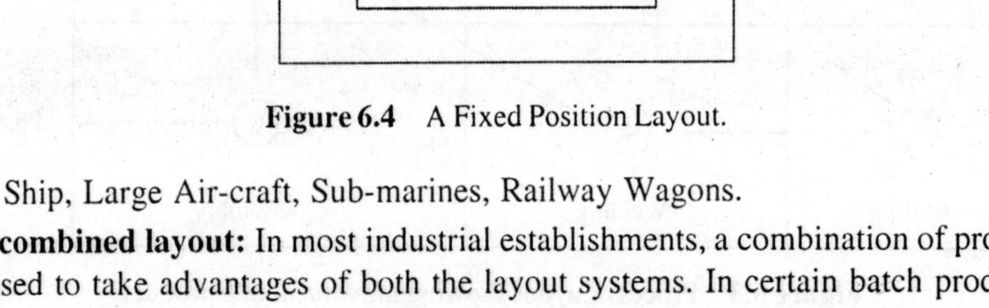

Figure 6.4 A Fixed Position Layout.

Example: Ship, Large Air-craft, Sub-marines, Railway Wagons.

4. **Group or combined layout:** In most industrial establishments, a combination of product and process layout is used to take advantages of both the layout systems. In certain batch production industries

a variety of products are assembled. Product layout is employed for mass production of common components. In addition, process layout is used for assembling the standard components in batches of products.

For example, in Automobile manufacturing plants, the machinery for assembly shop is laid out in a straight line. But ancillary facilities like casting, forging, machining, welding, grinding etc. are arranged on a functional basis.

Thus it is a blending of product based and process oriented layouts. Thus, a combination that produces the desired volume of products at minimum cost per unit is selected.

***(iv)* Typical Layout for an Automobile Plant:** Layout has been designed keeping in mind for maximum utilisation of land available and keeping provision.for future expansion (*see* next page).

Manufacturing and services sections are laid out in a manner that flow path takes course from one end to the other and there is no reverse path for the intermediate product.

Gate 1 is the main gate for entry of Raw materials and visitors including entry and exists of factory personnel.

Gate 2 is only reserved for the exit of finished cars after testing, painting, inspection and completion of Central Excise formalities.

For Car Automobile, Assembly shop is a large building equipped with overhead travelling cranes, hoist, fork lift trucks, mobile crane. The size of the building depends on capacity of the plant.

Raw material store and General Store have been kept at a most Central location from the various activity shops.

Building for Welfare Services consists of canteen, toilets, rest rooms, first aid/dispensary.

Administrative Building contains offices from Chairman, M.D., and all functional heads including manufacturing, finance, marketing and administration.

6.6 FACTORS AFFECTING PLANT LAYOUT

The following factors should be considered while planning the layout of a plant:

(*a*) Plant Location: Plant layout is intimately connected with plant location. As a matter of fact the size and shape of the site and its topography influence the general pattern of layout. Plant site also influences the type of building, mode of transport and scope of expansion which in turn influence layout. Plant layout is generally a compromise between the ideal layout and the limitations of plant site and building.

(*b*) Nature of Product: Standardised products require a product layout whereas custom-made products may need process layout. A fixed position layout would be required for heavy and bulky products. Products involving hazardous and dangerous operations would require isolation of processes. Similarly, value, fragility, volume and quality of product are important considerations in plant layout.

(*c*) Type of Industry: The nature and type of production process exerts considerable influence on plant layout. Generally product layout is more appropriate in continuous process industry, whereas intermittent production requires process layout.

Production Process influences plant layout to a large extent. A continuous process requires a line layout so that various materials and parts merge into the completed assembly in a flow. On the other hand, an analytic process takes the form of a tree as it starts out with a single material and spreads out into a variety of resultant materials.

A conditioning process requires a layout to accommodate lot or batch manufacture. In such a layout the material undergoes no merging or separation but it is simply subjected to physical conditioning as it flows in separate lots through the variety of operations and processes.

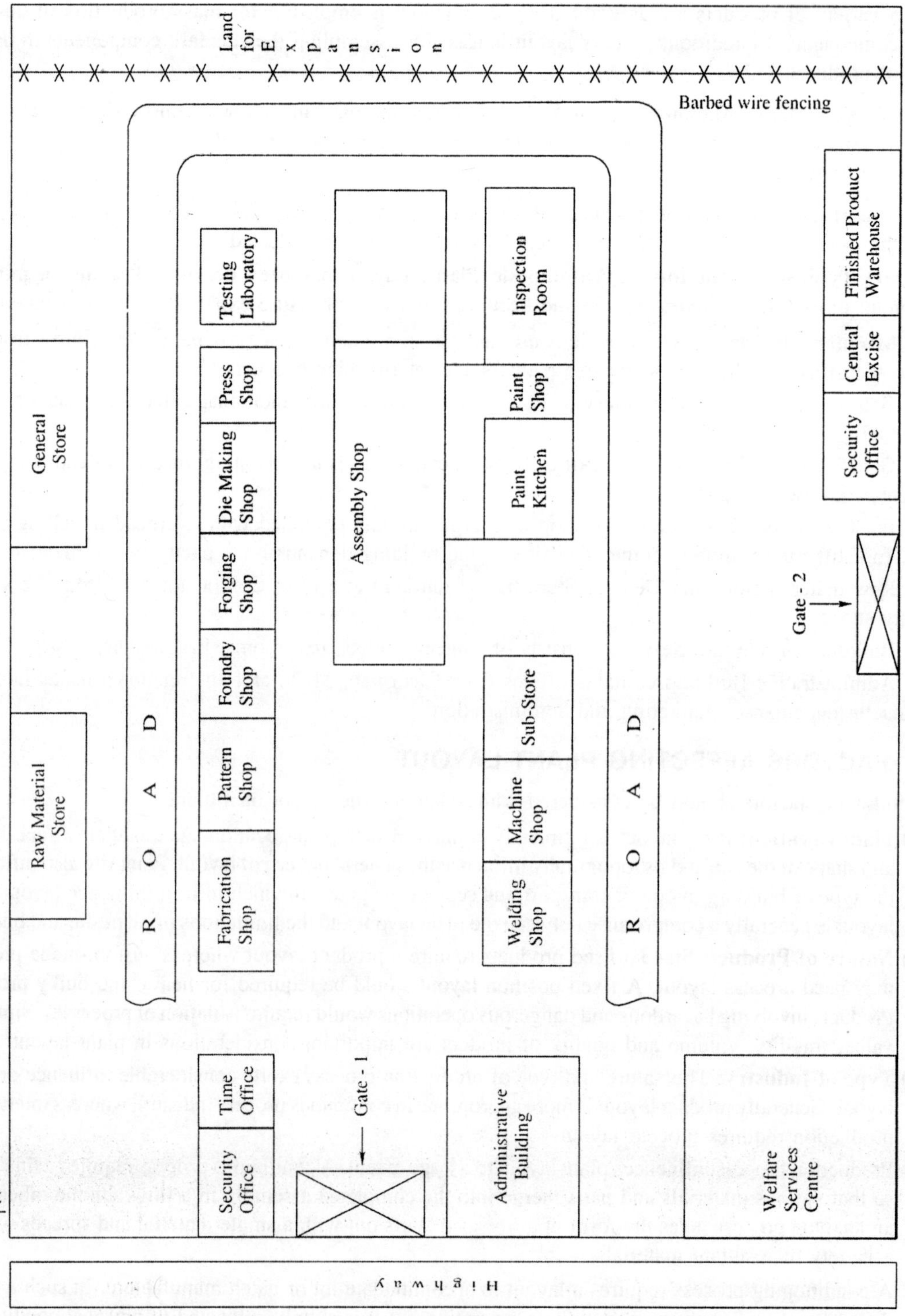

A TYPICAL LAYOUT FOR AUTOMOBILE MANUFACTURING FACTORY FOR LIGHT COMMERCIAL VEHICLES

Thus, the layout designer should keep in mind the type of industry and nature of manufacturing process while planning a layout.

(*d*) **Plant Environment:** In planning factory layout, heat, light, noise, ventilation and other aspects of plant climate should be given due consideration.

For example, Paint shops and plating sections should be located beside an outside wall so that dangerous fumes may be removed through proper ventilation.

(*e*) **Repairs and Maintenance:** Machines and equipment should not be fixed so close to each other that it may create problems in repairs, maintenance and replacement. Access to machine parts for repairs and maintenance should be provided.

(*f*) **Balance:** Proper balance between processes helps to avoid bottlenecks. The arrangement of machine capacity should be such as to ensure a uniform flow of work. At the same time the layout should be designed in such a manner that there is minimum possible movement materials and men.

(*g*) **Management Policy:** Management Policies regarding size, quality, employee facilities and delivery schedules should be considered while deciding plant layout.

For example, size (demand forecast) will determine the size of work stations. Need for flexibility should also be considered. The layout designer must have a complete understanding of management policies that have a bearing on plant layout.

6.7 LAYOUT ENGINEERING

Layout Engineering gives systematic procedure for Plant Layout. The procedure consists of the following steps:

(*a*) Study all the factors affecting plant layout. These factors have been enumerated earlier.

(*b*) Prepare suitable flow charts, models, process charts, templates, diagrams etc. for the proposed layout scheme.

(*c*) Determine routing, space requirement for each work station, service departments, employee facilities etc.

(*d*) Draw building specifications to fit the requirements of the layout.

(*e*) Prepare a floor plan indicating location of doors, windows, stairways, lifts and other facilities.

(*f*) Prepare a draft layout indicating the sequence of operations. Templates or models are used to determine space requirements for each piece of equipment.

(*g*) Give a trial run to the tentative layout. Recheck proposed layout with all concerned departments.

(*h*) For large plants, scale models which are replicas of various equipment and machines in three-dimensions are used and this involves some expenditure. There are specialised companies who prepare such three-dimensional scale modes of different items of equipment.

(*i*) Generally, now-a-days, Auto-CAD is largely used for preparing plant layout and many changes as per suggestions from various departments and corporate executives are incorporated easily before a final layout is adopted.

6.8 PLANT DESIGN

Following factors are to be considered for Plant Design:

(*i*) Products/specifications and capacity determination.

(*ii*) Choice of Technology.

(*iii*) Selection of Plant and equipment (major) and selection of Auxiliary machineries.

(*iv*) Design of Layout.

(*v*) Design of Civil structures, equipment, foundations, buildings, roads/drainage concerning civil/ structural engineering and architectural items.

(*vi*) Design of HT/LT systems including cables and layouts.

(*vii*) Design of off-sites facilities as per process requirement like water supply and distribution, effluent treatment and disposal and refrigeration, steam, compressed air facilities as necessary.

(*viii*) Design of raw materials and F.P. Stores and warehouses.

(*ix*) Design of Q.C. System, Testing and inspection centres.

(*x*) Design of suitable material handling system.

(*xi*) Design of administration building, time office, basic amenities for working man power such as potable cool water, toilets, bath rooms, rest rooms and recreation centres. Health care/first aid facilities etc. including vehicles/transport parking facilities etc.

(*xii*) Man-Power planning and design of organisation structure.

Plant design involves corporate policies and operation group's plans and policies to incorporate such activities which would aim at producing desired quantity of a product/products of specified quality at the most optimum cost and to result in smooth operation of the plant.

6.9 PROBABLE QUESTIONS

1. Explain the factors to be considered in deciding the location of a manufacturing unit.

2. What are the various cost factors to be considered for the selection of a site for production facilities?

3. Compare various factors for different site locations with examples.

4. What is layout of a production unit?
What are various types of layout?
Describe their merits and de-merits.

5. Describe various factors affecting the layout of a manufacturing unit. What are the advantages of a good layout?

6. Write about the system of Plant Design.
What is Layout Engineering?

7

Cost Analysis

> *• Significance of Cost Analysis • Role of Cost in Managerial Decision Making • Cost Concepts • Relevant for Managerial Decisions and Corporate Planning • Standard Costing • Standard Costing & Budgetary Control • Variable Costing System • Differential Accounting and Differential Costs • Cost and Output Relations • Cost and Size of Plant • Optimum Plant Size • Economies of large plant size • Pecuniary Economies of Scale • Economic of Batch Production • Economic Run Lengths • Break-Even Analysis • Revenue Analysis • Following Table gives the Relationship of Output • Probable Questions.*

7.1 SIGNIFICANCE OF COST ANALYSIS

Cost Analysis helps the Management to:

- Draw a distinction between those cost elements that are relevant for managerial decision making and those elements which are not useful for this purpose.
- Understand the basic difference between the various cost concepts.
- Analyse the behaviour of cost.
- Comprehend the difference sources of economics of scale.
- Specify the appropriate method of measuring cost-output relation in specific cases.

7.2 ROLE OF COST IN MANAGERIAL DECISION-MAKING

Study of costs is essential for making a choice among the competing production plans. Production decisions are not possible without their respective cost considerations. Since the productive resources are scarce with any firm and also since these have alternative uses, the use of these resources involves sacrifice and cost. The management will have to analyse these sacrifices or costs whenever it decides to use the resources.

Secondly, no estimate of profit is possible without the knowledge of costs involved.

An useful cost analysis requires the management to:

- Anticipate future condition as precisely as possible.
- Have clarity about the various cost concepts.
- Have a clear understanding of alternative plans and the type of costs involved.
- Decide about the valuation of an asset.
- Ascertain at the outset whether the cost-analysis is being done for the control or appraisal purposes.
- Decide about the method of cost-estimation.

Each Management, in addition to above, has to identify the following determinants important for its business.

- Plant size

- Percentage utilisation of the Plant.
- Technology.
- Prices of various inputs like raw materials, auxiliary materials, labour and power etc.
- Lot size.
- Stability of Production level.
- Management and labour efficiency.

The management must look at the impact of above factors on cost and also supplement its cost function by adding other determinants that are relevant for the particular situation.

Further, Management is vitally concerned with future costs for the simple reason that they are the only costs over which managers can exercise any control. Historical costs are of no interest to management except as basis for evaluating past operations.

7.3 COST CONCEPTS RELEVANT FOR MANAGERIAL DECISIONS AND CORPORATE PLANNING

Managerial decisions involve a selection between alternative course of action. Costs play a very prominent role in such decisions as it helps in specifying various alternatives in terms of their quantitative values. These quantitative values provide indication to the management about the economically most desirable choice, because non-quantitative factors, like labour relations, goodwill etc. may also influence the decisions. Yet, information on quantified costs is necessary for taking a final decision.

Following cost concepts are relevant for managerial decisions and corporate planning:

- **Future Costs:** Managerial decisions are concerned with future. Historical costs provide a basis for predictions, but for decision making and corporate planning only those costs which are expected to be incurred in future are relevant.
- **Incremental Costs:** These are added costs and thus are avoidable costs.

  They are costs which would not be incurred if a particular project is not undertaken.
- **Imputed Costs:** These are theoretical costs which are not recognised by the accounting system, but are of practical relevance for decision making.

  For example, a firm by using its own capital within the business is foregoing the income it would have received had it put the capital to an outside agency. Whereas, in accounting system interest is recognised as a cost only if it is actually paid, but in managerial decision making this cost is to be taken into account.
- **Opportunity Costs:** An opportunity cost is a cost resulting from an alternative opportunity that has been foresaken. The opportunity cost of a good or service is measured in terms of revenue which could have been earned by employing it in some other alternative use.

  For example, the land of a dilapidated and fully depreciated building, if used for the expansion of an existing plant, the rental value of the land should be included to its opportunity cost.
- **Sunk Cost:** A "Sunk Cost" is defined as the one for which the expenditure has been incurred in the past and which will not be affected by the particular decisions under consideration now. The opposite of the sunk costs are the "incremental costs" which require an additional outlay of cash if new decisions are implemented.

  Since sunk costs do not change, they are irrelevant for decision making; while incremental costs are the relevant ones.

- **Common costs or costs of multiple products (or joint costs):** Multiple Product output is the normal pattern of production and for determining the Production cost of individual items allocation of common overhead expenses are made by adopting proper statistical methods which reveal the relationship between overhead expenses and output of various products. In operating Railway Services, the cost of station, track, equipment and staff etc. are common costs (or/indirect cost).

  Common costs are indirect costs.

  In the case of joint product, whose product mix can not be changed, separate costs of products can not be determined and the products have to be considered together. But then the pricing of separate products would be on the basis of market conditions.

- **Marginal Costs and Incremental Costs:** Marginal costs are closely related with incremental costs. Marginal cost deals with unit-by-unit changes in output, whereas incremental cost is not restricted to 'a unit change'.

  Marginal cost is the amount added to total cost by a unit increase in output. Incremental cost is related to change in any number of units of output or even change in its quality.

  Marginal cost as a concept is particularly superior to incremental cost when dealing with decisions like:

  (*a*) Selecting optimum level of output.

  (*b*) Selecting optimum combination of inputs.

  Incremental costs are superior to marginal costs in case if discrete alternatives are to be compared.

  For example, one can compare two technical processes through incremental cost.

- **Marginal Cost and Elasticity of Demand:**

  (*a*) When elasticity of demand is greater than one, the marginal cost is (+) ve and total cost rises as price falls.

  (*b*) When elasticity of demand is equal to one, the marginal cost is zero and a change in price will not change the total cost.

  (*c*) When elasticity of demand is less than one, marginal cost is (–) ve and total cost falls as price falls.

  Marginal cost is earned by selling an additional (marginal) unit of production.

$$\text{Avg. Cost} = \text{Marginal cost} \times \left(\frac{e}{e-1}\right) \qquad \therefore \text{AC} = M \cdot C \cdot \left(\frac{e}{e-1}\right)$$

$$\text{\& M. C.} = \text{AC} \times \left(\frac{e-1}{e}\right) \qquad \text{MC} = \text{AC} \times \left(e - \frac{1}{e}\right)$$

$$e = \left(\frac{\text{AC}}{\text{AC} - \text{MC}}\right)$$

e = elasticity of demand.
AC = Average Cost.
MC = Marginal Cost.

- **Total Costs:**

  TC = TFC + TVC

  TC = Total Costs

  TFC = Total Fixed Costs

  TVC = Total Variable Costs

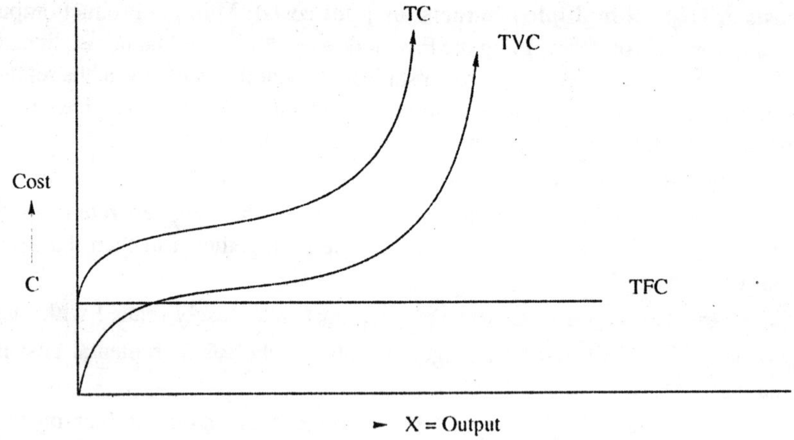

Figure 7.1

The Fixed Costs include:

(*a*) Salaries of staff and executives

(*b*) depreciation of Plant and equipment

(*c*) expenses for building depreciation and repair

(*d*) Interest on Capital borrowed

(*e*) Overhead expenses.

The Variable Costs include:

(*a*) Cost of raw materials

(*b*) Cost of auxiliary items

(*c*) Cost of labour

(*d*) Cost of power

(*e*) Cost of packing materials

(*f*) Cost of maintenance and spares.

Social Costs: Costs due to pollution and congestion on the parts of society are the social costs. Social cost is the total cost to the society on account of production of a good.

Standard Costs: Standard costs are broken down into following categories:

(*a*) Standard direct material costs

(*b*) Standard direct labour costs

(*c*) Standard direct expenses

(*d*) Standard fixed overheads (which do not vary with amount of output)

(*e*) Standard variable overhead cost (which vary with output)

(*f*) Standard selling and distribution costs.

After establishing standard costs, actual product cost figures are collected and compared with corresponding standard costs.

Adverse variances *i.e.*, excess of actual costs over standard costs, are analysed to determine their causes.

Such cost variances may arise due to following reasons:

(*a*) Excess use of materials per unit

(*b*) Higher material prices

(*c*) Lower efficiency of labour

(*d*) Higher wage rates

(*e*) Excess overhead cost

(*f*) Less than the planned output.

Standard costing identifies which of above causes have created the cost variances and who in the organisation is responsible for this.

Standard costing helps in isolating controllable costs and in fixing responsibility for higher than standard costs. Standard costs direct attention on areas where control action is needed and they generate greater cost consciousness among employees. In this way costs are controlled by people who incur and the point of occurrence.

7.4 STANDARD COSTING

Standard costing may be defined as the preparations and use of standard costs, their comparison with actual costs and the analysis of variances to their causes and points of incidence.

Standard costs are scientifically predetermined costs of material, labour and overheads chargeable to a product or service.

The meaning of variances between standard costs and actual costs will be dependent upon the kind of costs with which actual costs are compared. Variances resulting from careless standards will not have the same significance as variances from tight standards.

An ideal standard which is attainable only under the most favourable conditions would be impossible to achieve. An ideal standard may not be able to motivate employees to improve their performance. An expected standard which can be attained during a future specific period is usually set. Such a standard takes into account human, normal machine break downs, and other unavoidable inefficiencies. A reliable standard should provide an incentive to improve performance.

Assuming the existence of proper standard costs, the management can concentrate upon the discrepancies between actual and standard costs. The usefulness of this comparison between actual and standard costs is based, upon the principle of 'management by exception'. According to this principle, management is not concerned with the mass of data which is equivalent to standard cost or standard performance, but only with the exceptional variations.

The following steps are involved in the operation of the technique of standard costing:

(*a*) Set up standard costs for each product.

(*b*) Calculate and record actual costs incurred.

(*c*) Compare actual costs with the predetermined standards in order to ascertain the deviation from the standards, known as cost variance.

(*d*) Investigate the reasons for the differences and bring to the attention of management in the form of a variance analysis.

(*e*) Action by management, where appropriate, to ensure that adverse variances are not repeated in the future and company objectives are achieved.

7.5 STANDARD COSTING AND BUDGETARY CONTROL

The systems of standard costing and budgetary control have the common objective of controlling business operations.

Both the techniques involve accounting for variances between actual results and a predetermined plan.

In both the cases, variances are investigated and corrective action taken.

The two systems are inter-related and complementary to each other but they are not inter-dependent. It is possible to operate one without the other.

However, the control system of an organisation would be most effective if the two systems are operated together.

Although the two systems are similar in principle, the main points of difference between the two are that while Budgeted cost is a total concept, the standard cost is a unit concept. Budgets are periodically revised, normally annually while standards are revised only when they are inappropriate for the current operating conditions.

(*a*) Advantage of Standard Costing: The main advantages of standard costing are:

- Actual performance may be compared with predetermined standard revealing favourable or adverse variances.
- Variances due to external or internal influences can be identified.
- Standard Costing is an example of "management by exception" in that by studying.
- Variances managements attention is directed towards these items that are not performing according to plan.
- Cost control is more effective under standard costing system as variances will be reported.
- Standard costs provide a better guide to pricing than historical costs.
- A more accurate and effective budget can be prepared for the coming years since information of deviations of actual costs from standard costs is continuously provided.
- Standard costs provide a simple basis for stock valuation.
- A properly developed standard costing system will create a positive, cost effective attitude through all levels of management.

(*b*) By-Product and Joint Costs: In modern business, a firm is a multi-product producer. The multiplicity of products by a firm creates cost relationship.

When multiple products are produced with the help of the same production facilities, some costs remain directly chargeable to each product, but other costs (like rent, taxes *i.e.,* fixed costs) are common to all.

A joint product firm which produces a main product and a by-product which is saleable e.g. soap factories producing soap as the main product and glycerine as a by-product.

(*c*) Joint Products Costs: For a multiproduct firm, the costing for products are done on the basis of:

- Fixed proportions, (like meat and hides) or
- Variable proportions

  The basic problem in case of joint products is the allocation of cost to each individual output. Most of costs are common to all the products (like rent, interests, administration).

- **Fixed Proportion Case:** Joint products of fixed proportions variety are one package so far as their production is concerned, but are separate items from the point of pricing.

A firm facing a situation where it has to with-hold a part of the supply or one product from the market, generally resorts to either (*a*) shift in its demand curve through product differentiation or (*b*) tries to adjust its production process so that the surplus output is not produced.

- **Varying Proportion Case:** When a firm can vary proportion in which the joint products are produced, it faces a more normal situation that the one when its cannot do so. In case of varying proportions, the total cost has to be apportioned to each product, and linear programming method is used for products costs estimation.

7.6 VARIABLE COSTING SYSTEM

Variable costing (or marginal costing) may be defined as "the ascertainment of variable costs (marginal costs) and of the effect of changes in volume or type of output on profit, by differentiating between fixed costs and variable costs.

Under variable costing, fixed costs are excluded from the cost computations. The difference between the variable costs of activities and the revenues arising from these activities is known as contribution. It may relate to one unit or to total sales.

A typical formal for variable costing statement is as follows:

Product types or Departments	*A*	*B*	*C*	Total
Sales Revenue	*X*	*X*	*X*	*X*
Less: Variable Costs	*X*	*X*	*X*	*X*
Contribution	*X*	*X*	*X*	*X*
				X
Less: Total Fixed Costs			......	*X*
Total Profit			.....	*X*

Under variable costing system, no attempt is made to calculate profits for individual products or departments—it is individual contributions that are calculated.

The fixed costs are not allocated to the individual products or departments.

Thus decisions based on variable costing statements will not influenced by accounting technicalities relating to the treatment of fixed costs.

(*i*) Features of variable costing:

- Costs are classified into fixed and variable costs.
- Only variable elements of costs are attached to products.
- Price is fixed after taking into consideration the variable cost and marginal contribution.
- Marginal contribution decides the profitability of a product.
- Fixed costs of any period are deducted from total contribution for the period.
- Work-in-progress and finished stock are valued in variable production cost.
- Variable costing is easy to understand and operate, because it involves the computation of variable costs only.
- It avoids any arbitrary appointment of fixed costs among different products.
- A variable costing system leads to contribution analysis, break-even charts and cost-volume-profit analysis, all of which are useful for short-term decision making.

- Responsibility for control is more easily apportioned, since only variable costs over which they have control are presented to each level of management.
- All levels of management are more readily able to see the effects of their decisions-sometimes before an action is taken.

7.7 DIFFERENTIAL ACCOUNTING AND DIFFERENTIAL COSTS

Differential Accounting is concerned with the effect on costs and revenues if a certain course of action is undertaken. An accountant uses the term differential cost to describe the same costs that an economist calls incremental costs.

Differential costs may be defined as the increase or decrease in total cost, or the change in specific elements of cost, that result from any variation in operations.

Incremental Costs are defined as the additional costs of a change in the level or nature of activities.

Any cost that changes as a result of a contemplated decision is a differential cost or incremental cost relating to that decision.

Differential costing eliminates the residual costs which are the same under each alternative, and therefore irrelevant to the analysis.

Differential costs and incremental costs include many costs that are normally classified as fixed or semi fixed and may be regarded as a general class.

Variable costing (marginal costing) is essentially a short-run concept, while differential costing and incremental costing deal with short-run problem (*i.e.,* tactical decision) as well as long term problems (investment decision).

7.8 COST AND OUTPUT RELATIONS

- Total cost of a firm is the sum-total of all the explicit plus implicit expenditures incurred for producing a given level of output.
- It represents the money value of the total resources required for production of goods and services by the firm.
- Average cost is the cost per unit of output, assuming the production of each unit of output incurs the same cost.
- Average cost equals the total cost divided by the number of units produced.
- Total cost equals the total fixed costs and total variable costs.
- Description of fixed and variable costs have been given before.
- Management control is exercised to keep the variable costs lower.

$$\text{Productivity } (P) = \left(\frac{\text{Output } (O)}{\text{Input } (I)}\right)$$

- Productivity is the ratio between the output of goods and services and the input of resources consumed in the process of production.
- Output implies total production while input means land, labour, capital and management.
- Productivity is a measure of how efficiently an organisation has used its resources.
- Productivity is all about the efficient use of inputs, producing more output with the same resources or produce the same output with less resources.
- High productivitv results in low unit cost for good or services.

- Productivity is not only the rate of production of material goods, but its concept is extended to services also e.g. banking, transportation, insurance firms.
- The performance aspects of quality and effectiveness have also been integrated into productivity.
- Optimisation of inputs, process and output requires modern technologies of both production and quality.
- The efficiency of the production system also depends upon marketing.
- Therefore, productivity of the business system embraces marketing also.
- Efficient design, development, transfer of products and services and cost control measures etc. call for involvement of both management and labour throughout the organisation.
- Productivity can be viewed from different perspectives. We may refer to the productivity of a nation, of an industry, of an enterprise or of an individual employee. A nation can be productive only when its Institutions and people are productive.
- Higher productivity leads to economic growth and social progress. It is only by improving productivity that employees can get better wages and working conditions and more employment opportunity.
- Higher productivity brings lower prices for consumers and higher dividend for shareholders. It improves the exports and foreign exchange reserves of a country. Thus, productivity is the key to prosperity.
- Higher productivity is of special significance in a developing country like India.
- Mass poverty and unemployment can not be eliminated without increasing productivity in agriculture, industry and all other areas of human activity.

Cost And Output: Cost comprises of the (*i*) money value represented by the material used to make the product (*ii*) wages of the workers and (*iii*) other indirect costs attributable to its manufacture.

The excess value or market price over the costs incurred in producing the product represents the margin of profit.

In order to make the product more profitable, there should be a constant search for reducing the output costs. Reduced output costs means one or more of the following advantages:

- Increase the margin of profit
- Reduce the wastage
- Enable a reduction in selling price and thus achieve a greater demand for the product.

7.9 COST AND SIZE OF THE PLANT

The long run cost-output relationship can be shown with the help of a long run cost curve. The long run average cost curve is derived from short run cost curves.

Each point on the long run average cost curve corresponds to a point on a short run cost curve, which is tangent to the long run curve at that point.

For example:

A firm faces a choice of three methods of production, each with a different plantsizes; small, medium and large.

These points operate with the average costs SA C_1, SA C_2 AND SA C_3 respectively as shown in the figure.

If the firm plans to produce X_1 output, it will choose the small plant. It will choose the medium size plant if it plans to produce output X_2 and for X_3 output it will choose the large size plant.

Now, if the firm starts with the small plant and faces a gradually increasing demand, it will increase its output. For the small plant, the firms lowest cost output level is X_1, beyond which average cost starts

X sign. But it will continue producing with small plant even beyond X_1, as average cost for these levels of output on the small plant is still lower than that on the medium plant.

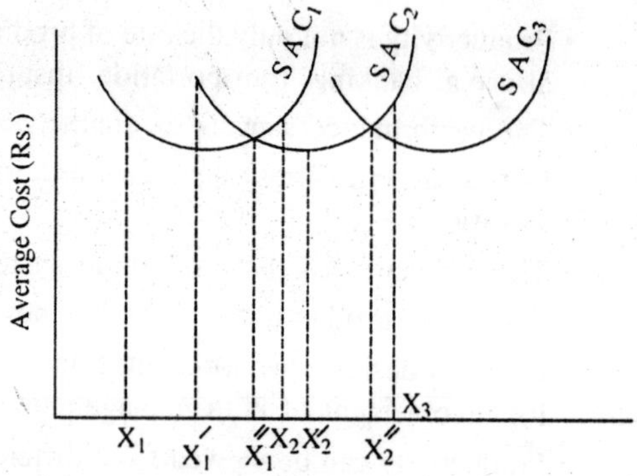

Figure 7.2 Units of output

It is only when the demand for its product reaches the level X_1'' (*i.e.*, point of inter section of SAC_1 and SAC_2) the firm has a choice to either continue producing with small plant or use the medium size plant.

The decision of the firm at this point depends not on the cost but on the firm's expectations about its future demand.

If the firm expects demand to increase beyond X_1'', in future it will choose the medium size plant, because this plant will produce outputs larger than X_1'' at lower average cost than that of the small plant.

The firm will face the similar decision problem when it reaches the level X_2''.

Thus from the above example, we can assume that there are many plant sizes, each suitable for a certain level of output, we will get as many SAC curves intersecting each other. As the number of plant sizes increases, the points of intersection of SAC curves will come closer.

And, if we assume that there are a large number of plant sizes the intersection points will be so near to each other that we get almost a continuous curve known as Long-run Average Cost Curve **(LAC curve).**

This is also known as **Envelope Curve** as it envelopes the short run Average Cost Curves.

This is further shown in the Figure 7.3.

7.10 (*a*) OPTIMUM PLANT SIZE

An optimum size of plant may be defined as the one that leads to the most efficient utilisation of resources. Given technology, there has to be one level of output and the size of plant which results in the least cost output.

Graphically, this unique least-cost plant size can be shown below:

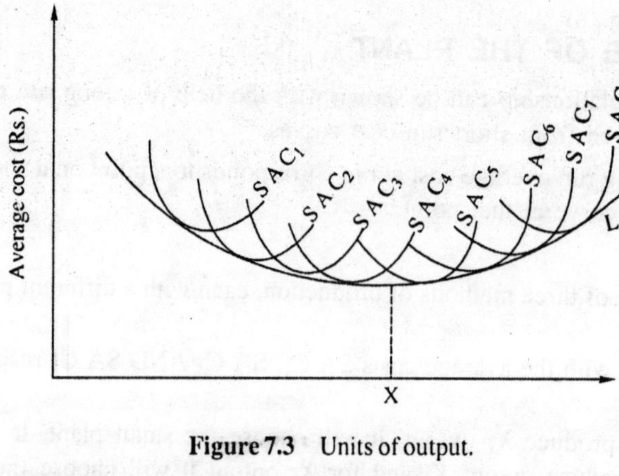

Figure 7.3 Units of output.

The *U*-shapedness of the LAC Curve reflects the laws of returns to scale.

According to these laws, the cost per unit of production decreases as plant size increases due to the economics of scale, which the larger plant sizes make possible.

But the economies of scale exist only upto a certain size of plant known as the optimum plant size, where all possible economies of scale are fully exploited.

Beyond the optimum plant size, diseconomies of scale arise due to managerial inefficiencies.

As plant size increases beyond a limit, the control, the feed-back of information at different levels and decision-making process becomes less efficient.

This makes the **LAC** Curve turn upwards.

In the above graph, "X" is the point of optimum output and the corresponding plant size is the optimum plant size.

7.10 (*b*) ECONOMIES OF LARGE PLANT SIZE

Large corporate houses take the advantage of economies of large plant size and set up large size plant to obtain economies of scale of operation.

For many types of equipment both initial and running costs increase less rapidly than capacity. Tanks, Blast Furnaces and other static and mobile containers are examples of this form of economy.

Any container whose external dimensions are doubled has its volume increased eight times, but the area of its surface walls would have increased only four times. This reduces material costs and, where appropriate, heat loss is the minimum.

Moreover, the management and labour inputs required to operate a large plant are seldom proportionately greater than that required for a smaller size plant. Also, costs incured for R & D market research, development of product design etc. are shared for a large size plant and the unit output costs are the least compared to its competitors with smaller size plants.

7.10 (*c*) PECUNIARY ECONOMIES OF SCALE

These economies include the discounts that a firm can obtain due to its large size. These discounts may be in the nature of:

- Lower raw material prices due to bulk buying.
- Lower cost of capital, as banks usually place greater faith in the large firms, and, therefore charge lower rate of interest.
- Offers of lower rates for advertising to large firms because of their large scale advertising.
- Lower transportation rates due to bulk transportation.
- A large scale firm can easily create good public image and goodwill which form valuable intangible assets for the organisation.
- Due to above benefits, it is able to attract highly qualified and competent professionals and skilled personnel for the over-all benefit of the organisation.

7.11 ECONOMIC BATCH PRODUCTION

One important decision the Production Manager has to take is the quantity of output to be produced at a certain time. This is because goods are produced in anticipation of demands. The quantity produced by a certain equipment may be less than the demand on a particular day.

The optimum of the production lot is called economic production lot or economic batch production.

The deciding parameter for the economic batch production is the unit cost of production.

Thus, the economic batch quantity is the amount of output in one batch which is the most economical to produce and which is the lowest unit cost of production.

The following factors are to be mentioned for resulting in the economic batch production.

(*i*) **Rate of Usage:** The rate of usage or the rate of consumption should be either equal to the rate of supply or little less than the latter.

(*ii*) **Cost of Manufacturing:** As has been seen in the earlier chapter, the larger is the lot size the lesser is the cost of production.

The economic production lot is also known as "Economic Manufacturing Quantity" (EMQ).

The following graph depicts the EMQ.

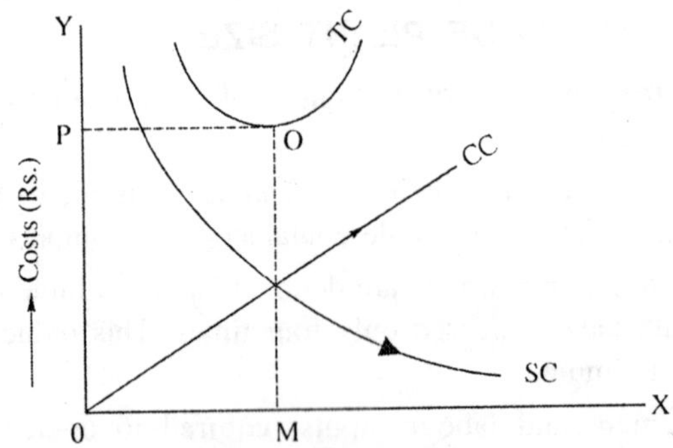

Figure 7.4 Economic Batch Production.

CC = Carrying cost *i.e.,* inventory carrying cost and interest cost etc.

SC = Set up Cost *i.e.,* cost of facility which produces economic lot size production.

TC = Total cost *i.e.,* CC + SC for any quantity

OM is the economic lot size at which total cost is '*P*', the lowest.

Thus, $$\text{EMQ} = \sqrt{\frac{2\,A \times S}{C}}$$

where EMQ = Economic Manufacturing Quantity

A = Average Annual Demand in Units

S = Set up Cost per batch

C = Annual Carrying Cost per unit

The concept of Economic Manufacturing Quantity is similar to Economic Ordering Quantity (EOQ).

7.12 ECONOMIC RUN LENGTHS

Economic Run Length (ERL) is the number of units per production set up used.

ERL is given by,

$$\text{ERL} = \sqrt{\frac{2 \times (\text{Set up cost} \times \text{Average annual demand})}{\text{Carrying Cost}\left[1 - \dfrac{\text{Annual Demand}}{\text{Annual Production}}\right]}}$$

Thus, if a plant produces and uses 24000 bearing units, and the cost of production set up Rs. 85, weekly production rate 1000 units and the production cost is Rs. 5.50 per unit and the annual inventory and carrying cost is Rs. 0.50 per unit the ERL or the number of units the plant should produce for each production run *i.e.,*

$$\text{ERL} = \sqrt{\frac{2 \times 85 \times 24{,}000}{0.50\left[1 - \frac{24{,}000}{52{,}000}\right]}}$$

i.e., Annual production = 1000 units/week × 52 weeks in a year or ERL = 3,890 units **Ans.**

7.13 BREAK-EVEN ANALYSIS

***(i)* Break Even Point:** The break-even point means the level of output or sales at which no profit or loss is achieved.

It indicates the position at which marginal profit or contribution is just sufficient to cover fixed over heads.

In other words, a business is said to break-even when its income equal its expenditure.

When production exceeds the "Break Even Point" the business makes a profit and when it is below the "Break Even Point," the business makes losses.

This is shown as follows:

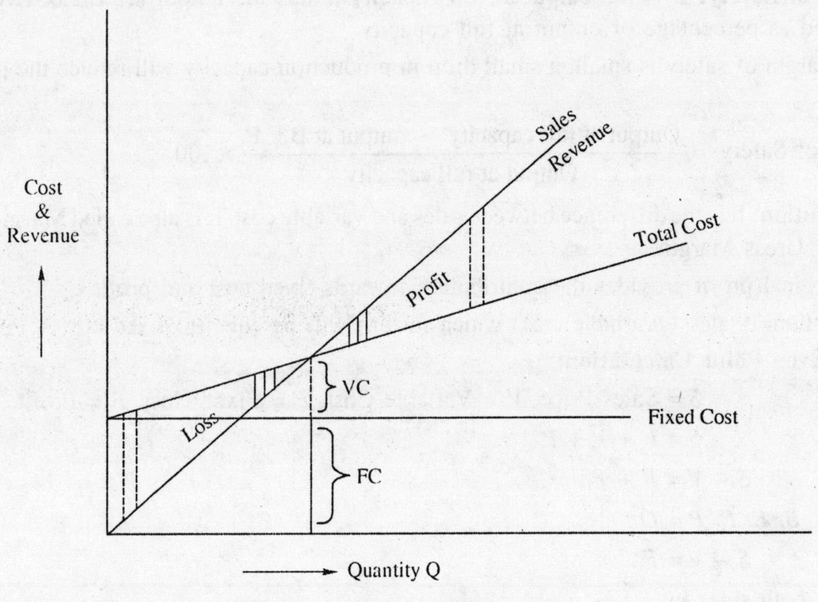

Figure 7.5 → Graphical Method.

***(ii)* Break Even Point Theory:** The break-even point of any two variable situations is the point or the value at which they become equal as the result of a common variable.

There are following two methods to obtain break-even point:

(*a*) Mathematical Method

(*b*) Graphical Method.

(*a*) **Mathematical Method:** Let cost be the common variables in two situation 1 & 2, then cost equation will be:

$$C_1 = f_1\,(X) \text{ .... a function of } (X) \qquad \text{...(1)}$$

$$C_2 = f_2\,(X) \text{ .... another function of } (X) \qquad \text{...(2)}$$

C_1—may be as total cost, annual cost, cost per item or cost per day etc. for situation 1.

C_2—same as C_1 but application to situation 2

X—variable affecting C_1 and C_2

To solve for the value of X, let $C_1 = C_2$

i.e., $$f_1\,(X) = f_2\,(X) \qquad \text{...(3)}$$

Equation (3) can be solved for obtaining value of X.

The value of X making the cost equal in both the situations, is called "Break Even Value."

Below this value of X one situation will be uneconomical while above it another situation will be economical.

(*iii*) Some Important Features on Break Even Analysis

(*a*) **Angle of Incidence:** It is the angle at which income line (sales line) cuts the total cost line. If the angle is large, it is an indication that profits are being made at a high rate, on the other hand, if the angle is small it indicates that less profits are being made and are achieved under less favourable condition.

(*b*) **Margin of Safety:** It is the output at full capacity minus the output at "Break Even Point." It is expressed as percentage of output at full capacity.

If the margin of safety is small, a small drop in production capacity will reduce the profit to a great extent.

$$\text{Margin of Safety} = \frac{\text{Output at full capacity} - \text{output at B.E.P.}}{\text{Output at full capacity}} \times 100$$

(*c*) **Contribution:** It is the difference between sales and variable cost. It is also called Marginal as Marginal Profit or Gross Margin.

The marginal profit provides the contribution towards fixed cost and profit.

Contribution= (sales – variable cost) which in turn will be equal to fixed cost + Profit.

(*d*) **Break Even Point Calculation:**

S = Sales Price, V = Variable Cost, F = Fixed Cost, P = Profit.

Now $S = F + V + P$

or $S - V = F + P$

At $B.\,E.\,P.\ P = O$

and $S - V = F$

Multiply both sides by S

$$S\,(S - V) = FS$$

$$\therefore \quad S = \frac{FS}{S - V} = \frac{F}{\frac{S - V}{S}} = \frac{\text{Fixed Cost}}{\text{Contribution per unit}}$$

and Sales at $B.\,E.\,P.$ $= \left(\text{Rs.}\frac{FS}{S - V}\right)$

and Nos. of Units at B. E. P. $= \left(\dfrac{\text{Fixed Cost}}{\text{Contribution/Unit}}\right)$

$= \left(\dfrac{\text{Fixed Cost}}{\text{Marginal Profit Unit}}\right)$

(*e*) **Assumption in Break Even Analysis:** The various assumptions that underline in this technique are given as under:

(*i*) It is assumed that over the entire range of volume of production all costs are perfectly variable.

(*ii*) It is assumed that over the entire range of volume of production all costs are Dissolutely fixed.

(*iii*) It is assumed that with the physical volume of Production all revenues are perfectly variable.

(*iv*) The volumes of sales and Production are equal.

(*v*) It is assumed that for multi-product output, the product-mix should be stable.

(*vi*) Application or uses of B. E. P.

It can be used to determine the following:

(*a*) **Safety Margin with Proposed Volume:** It refers to the extent which the firm can afford to decline in sales upto the B. E. P. It is expressed by percentage ratio of sales over BEP volume to the sales volume.

$$\therefore \text{ Safety Margin} = \frac{\text{Sales Volume} - \text{Sales at BEP}}{\text{Sales Volume}} \times 100$$

(*b*) **Quantity needed to have desired profit:** It is given by

$$\text{Target Quantity} = \frac{\text{Fixed Cost} + \text{Target Profit}}{\text{Contribution per unit}}$$

(*c*) **Effect of Change in Price:** Sometimes, management/marketing Manager is required to consider whether to reduce price of a product or for selling bulk quantity of product. Management/Marketing Manager has to consider the following facts in this regard.

If the sale price is reduced, then contribution margin will reduce and this will increase the sales volume. But this increased volume may or may not receive increase in demand because it depends on elasticity of demand.

As the sale price is reduced, BEP shifts towards right side *i.e.,* towards larger quantity side.

$$\text{At BEP} \quad Q = \frac{F+P}{S-V}$$

for reduced sale price S_1, Quantity is Q_1

$$Q_1 = \frac{F+P}{S_1 - V}$$

Therefore, Marketing Manager has to obtain a supply order for Q_1 quantity at reduced price level S_1 where $S_1 < S$.

(*d*) **Effect of Change in Costs:** (*i*) Change in Variable cost, (*ii*) Change in Fixed cost.

(*i*) **Change in V.C.:** Variable costs may change due to change in prices of input materials/energy or due to higher losses.

$$\text{At BEP } Q = \frac{F+P}{S-V}$$

for change in $V \longrightarrow V_1$ & $Q \longrightarrow Q_1$, also $S \longrightarrow S_1$

$$Q_1 = \frac{F+P}{S_1 - V_1} (S_1 - V_1) - \text{Change is contribution}$$

If the sales volume remains same, *i.e.*, $Q_1 = Q$

$$\therefore \quad \frac{F+P}{S_1 - V_1} = \frac{F+P}{S-V} \text{ or } S_1 - V_1 = S - V$$

or $\quad S_1 = S + (V_1 - V)$

S_1 is new selling price to maintain present profit.

Due to increase in variable cost *i.e.*, increase in VC will shift BEP right to give higher Q.

Thus higher quantity is to be sold to maintain the present profit with no change in price of product.

***(ii)* Change in Fixed Cost:** Fixed cost may change due to an increase in staff/executive remuneration, taxes, insurance and building rent etc. or overhead expenses.

This in turn will bring change in B.E.P., if the sale price is unchanged.

At BEP $\quad Q = \dfrac{F+P}{S-V} \quad$ ...(*i*)

for $F \longrightarrow F_1 \quad Q \longrightarrow Q_1$

$$Q_1 = \frac{F_1 + P}{S - V} \quad \text{...}(ii)$$

$$\therefore \quad Q_1 - Q = \frac{(F_1 + P) - (F + P)}{S - V}$$

$$= \frac{F_1 - F}{S - V}$$

or $\quad Q_1 = Q\dfrac{F_1 - F}{S - V}$

If Q is unchanged then there is change in Sales price, then $S_1 = S + \dfrac{F_1 - F}{Q}$.

***(e)* Whether To Accept An Order or Not:** If extra capacity to produce a product is variable then some times management has to decide whether to accept another order at a price which less than the initial selling price.

For example, a plant is operating on its 50% full capacity. A, buyer offered to buy 4000 units at Rs. 5.00 per unit while the average cost Rs. 6.00. Now the problem is whether to accept this order or not. The other details of the product are:

Total capacity	= 20,000 units
Present output	= 10,000 units
Direct Materials Cost	= Rs. 10,000 – Rs. 1/pc. Direct cost
Direct Labour	= Rs. 10,000 – Rs. 1/pc. Rs. 2/pc
Fixed costs	= Rs. 40,000

In this question, one can find that additional cost of making these 4000 units is Rs. 4000 for material cost and Rs. 4000 for labour cost (total Rs. 8000) and the revenue from sales would be 4000 × Rs. 5 = Rs. 20,000. Thus, the concern will same = Rs. 20,000 – Rs. 8,000 = Rs. 12,000.

So, it would be profitable to accept anything more than Rs.2 per unit, which is the direct cost per unit.

There is only danger that, if other consumers come to know that this product is being sold at a lower price, they may also demand supply at the lower price.

Therefore, in such case acceptance of order should be kept secret.

(*f*) Whether to Make or Buy:

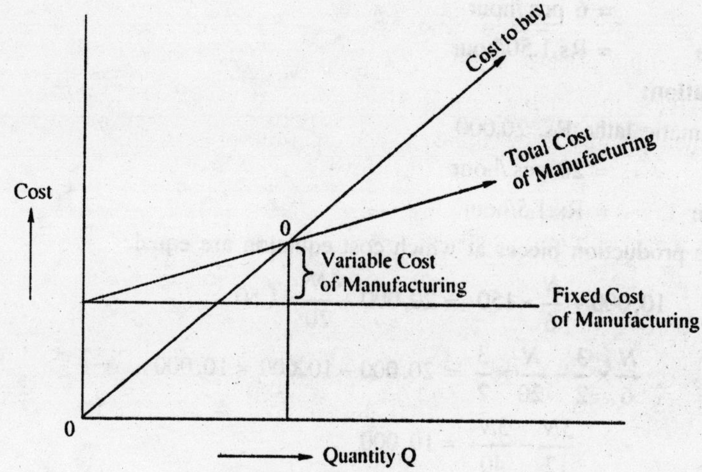

Figure 7.6

$$Q = \frac{\text{Fixed Cost}}{\text{Purchase Cost} - \text{Variable Cost}}$$

Upto Q quantity—it is economical to buy the product.

Beyond Q quantity—it is economical to manufacture item in house.

Example 7.1 The fixed costs of a company are Rs. 3,50,000. The net sales amount to Rs. 6,00,000 annually. The direct costs are 35% of sales in rupees. Determine the following:

(*i*) The Break Even Point in terms of Sales Rupees.

(*ii*) The Sales required to earn a profit of Rs. 80,000.

Solution. (*i*)

$$\text{BEP} = \frac{F}{\left(1 - \frac{V}{S}\right)} = \frac{3,50,000}{\left(1 - \frac{0.35 \times 6,00,000}{6,00,000}\right)}$$

$$= \left(\frac{3,50,000}{0.65}\right) = \text{Rs. } 538,461.53 \textbf{ Ans.}$$

(*ii*) Profit Rs. 80,000

Sales = ?

$$\text{Sales} = \left(\frac{F+P}{1 - \frac{V}{S}}\right) = \left(\frac{3,50,000 + 80,000}{1 - 0.35}\right)$$

$$= \frac{4,30,000}{0.65} = \text{Rs. } 661,538.46 \textbf{ Ans.}$$

Example 7.2 A lathe machine costing Rs. 10,000 can produce components at the rate of 6 pieces per hour and another automatic lathe costing Rs. 20,000 can produce 20 pieces per hour. The operator on either of the machine is to be paid at the rate of Rs. 1.50 per hour. Determine the minimum number of pieces which will change the cost situation in favour of the automatic machine.

Solution. First situation:

Cost of lathe machine Rs. 10,000

Production = 6 pcs./hour

Operator rate = Rs.1.50/hour

Second situation:

Cost of automatic lathe Rs. 20,000

Production = 20 pcs./hour

Operator rate = Rs.1.5/hour

Let N be the production pieces at which cost equation are equal.

Thus, $$10{,}000 + \frac{N}{6} \times 150 = 20{,}000 + \frac{N}{20} \times 1.50$$

or, $$\frac{N}{6} \times \frac{3}{2} - \frac{N}{20} \times \frac{3}{2} = 20{,}000 - 10{,}000 = 10{,}000$$

or, $$\frac{3N}{12} - \frac{3N}{40} = 10{,}000$$

or, $$\frac{3N}{4}\left(\frac{1}{3} - \frac{1}{10}\right) \text{ or } \frac{3N}{4}\left(\frac{10-3}{30}\right)$$

or, $$\frac{3N}{4} \times \frac{7}{30} = \frac{7N}{4} \times \frac{1}{10} = 10{,}000$$

or, $$7N = 10{,}000 \times 40$$

$\therefore$ $$N = \frac{10{,}000 \times 40}{7} = 57{,}142.86 \text{ or } 57{,}143 \text{ pieces.}$$

It means if production is more than 57,143 pieces then automatic lathe machine will be economical.

Example 7.3 The fixed costs for the year 2000 are Rs. 50,000 and variable cost per unit is Rs. 25. The estimated sales for the period are valued at Rs. 15,00,000. Each unit sells at Rs. 150. Determine:

(*i*) BEP.

(*ii*) Rs. 12,00,000 will be the likely sales turnover for the next budget period, calculate the estimate contribution and profit.

(*iii*) If a profit target of Rs. 6,50,000 has been budgeted, compute the sales turnover required.

(*i*) Break Even Point $$= \left(\frac{F}{1 - \frac{V}{S}}\right)$$

F = Fixed cost = 5,00,000

V = Variable cost Rs. 25/unit

S = Selling cost = Rs. 150/unit

$$= \left(\frac{50{,}000}{1 - \frac{\cancel{25}}{\cancel{150}_{6}}}\right) = \left(\frac{5{,}00{,}000}{1 - \frac{1}{6}}\right) = \frac{5{,}00{,}000 \times 6}{5}$$

= Rs. 6,00,000 **Ans.**

(*ii*) Sales Turnover $= \dfrac{\text{Fixed Cost} + \text{Profit}}{1 - \dfrac{V}{S}}$ $\left[\because \left(1 - \dfrac{V}{S}\right) = \dfrac{5}{6}. \text{ From } (i)\right]$

$= (\text{Fixed Cost} + \text{Profit}) \times \dfrac{6}{5}$

or Sales Turnover $\times \dfrac{5}{6} - \text{Fixed Cost} = \text{Profit}$

$$12,00,000 \times \frac{5}{6} - 5,00,000 = \text{Profit}$$

or $10,00,000 - 5,00,000 = \text{Profit}$

$\therefore$ Profit = Rs. 5,00,000.

Now estimated contribution

$$S = \frac{F + P}{\dfrac{S - V}{S}} \quad \text{or} \quad \frac{F + P}{S - V} \times S$$

or $S - V = F + P$

or Contribution $= F + P = 5,00,000 + 5,00,000$
$= \text{Rs. } 10,00,000$ **Ans.**

(*iii*) If Profit is Rs. 6,50,000 then sales = ?

$$\text{Sales} = \frac{F + P}{1 - \dfrac{V}{S}} = \frac{5,00,000 + 6,50,000}{5} \times 6 \quad \left[\because \left(1 - \frac{V}{S}\right) = \frac{5}{6}. \text{ From } (i)\right]$$

$= 13,80,000$ **Ans.**

Problem The fixed costs for the financial year 2000 – 2001 are Rs. 40,000. The sales for this period are Rs. 1,00,000. The variable cost per unit Rs. 2.00. Selling price of each product is Rs. 10 and the number of units involved coincides with the expected volume of output.

Construct the Break Even Chart and determine:

(*a*) Break-Even Point.

(*b*) How many minimum product should be sold to earn profit?

(*c*) Profit earned at a turnover of Rs. 80,000.

(*d*) Margin of Safety.

(*e*) Angle of incidence.

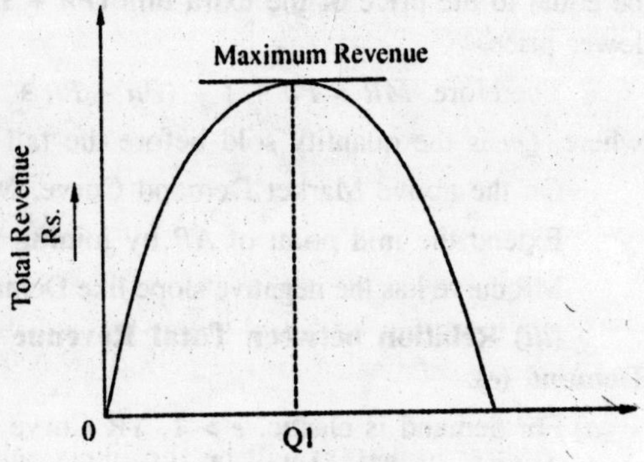

Figure 7.7 *TR* Vs. *Q*.

7.14 REVENUE ANALYSIS: Total Revenue, Marginal Revenue, Average Revenue

(*i*) **Revenue Analysis:** Revenue is the money a seller receives by selling a product to a customer. Total revenue (*TR*) is the amount money a seller receives from a customer by selling a Product quantity (*Q*) at price (*P*).

Therefore $TR = P.Q$.

For a Market Demand Curve linear TR curve also will be linear and initially slopes upwards, reaches the maximum point and then starts falling as shown in Figure 7.8, *TR* versus *Q*.

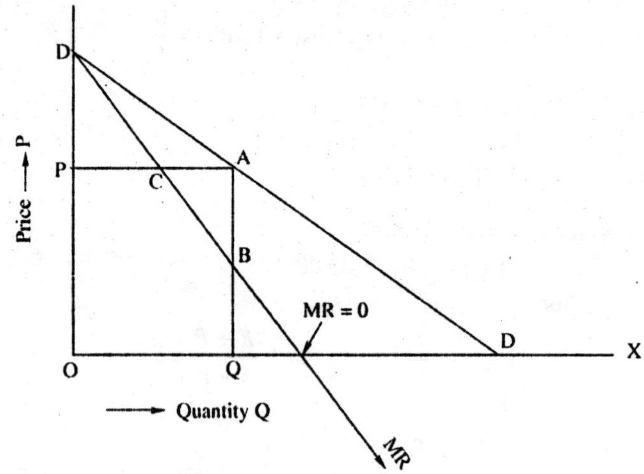

Figure 7.8 Market Demand Curve.

For a Price *P* on Market Demand Curve and Quantity *Q*, total revenue *TR* = Area of rectangle *OPAQ*.

***(ii)* Marginal Revenue (MR):** Marginal Revenue is the change in total revenue resulting from selling an additional unit of the product.

Marginal Revenue is the slope of the total revenue curve at any level of quantity.

In order to sell an additional quantity of product, its price must fall, and the Marginal revenue will be equal to the price of the extra unit ($Pn + 1$) minus the loss from selling all previous units at the new lower price.

Therefore, $MR = Pn + 1 - (Pn - Pn + 1)\, Qn$

where, Qn is the quantity sold before the fall in price.

On the above Market Demand Curve, MR Curve is drawn as follows:

Extend the mid point of *AP* by joining with *D* till it touches the *X*-axis quantity line.

MR curve has the negative slope like Demand Curve and is also a straight line like Demand Curve (*DD*).

***(iii)* Relation between Total Revenue (TR), Marginal Revenue (MR) and Price Elasticity of Demand (*e*).**

(*a*) For demand is elastic, $e > 1$, TR Curve has a positive slope and an increase in price will result in decrease in TR while a decrease in price will result in an increase in TR.

(*b*) For demand is inelastic, $e < 1$, an increase in price leads to an increase in TR and a decrease in price leads to a decrease in TR.

(*c*) For demand has price elasticity $e = 1$, TR is not affected by an change in price and MR = 0.

(*d*) $MR = P\left(1 - \frac{1}{e}\right)$

Usefulness of Elasticity of Demand concept in Business.

The concept of elasticity of demand is useful for the business in the following ways:

(*a*) Elasticity measures help the management in fixing the prices of goods.

(*b*) The concept is also important for a multi product unit for fixing the production target for various goods by estimating likely demands and income elasticity in a market segment.

(*c*) The price elasticity of demand as well as cross elasticity would determine the substitution between goods and hence are useful in fixing the output mix for production plan.

7.15 FOLLOWING TABLE GIVES THE RELATIONSHIP OF OUTPUT WITH TOTAL COST, AVERAGE COST AND MARGINAL COST

Unit of output	*Fixed cost*	*Variable cost - Rs.*	*Total Cost Rs.*	*Marginal Cost - Rs.*	*Ave. Cost 4, 1 Rs.*	*Avg. Fixed Cost 2, 1*	*Ave. Variable Cost 3, 1 Rs.*
(1)	(2)	(3)	(4)	(5)	(6)	(7)	(8)
0	176	0	176	–	–	–	–
1	176	75	251	75	251	176	75
2	176	130	306	55	153	88	65
3	176	175	351	45	117	59	58
4	176	209	385	34	96	44	52
5	176	238	414	29	83	33	48
6	176	265	441	27	74	29	44
7	176	289	465	24	66	25	41
8	176	312	488	23	61	22	39
9	176	328	504	16	56	20	36
10	176	344	520	16	52	18	34

Values in the above table are arbitrary. On studying the above table, following points are note worthy:

(*i*) Average cost is equal to total cost divided by number of units output.

(*ii*) The total cost is equal to the sum of fixed cost and all the marginal cost. For example, for 4 units output, Total cost is Rs. 385 = 176 + 75 + 55 + 45 + 34.

(*iii*) When marginal cost is falling, total cost will rise at a declining rate, but on other side; where marginal cost is rising, total cost will also rise at an increasing rate.

(*iv*) When marginal cost is lower than average cost, average cost will be falling. For example, upto the 10 units output as above, for an output of 11 and 12 units, the marginal cost is rising, but the average cost is falling:

This will be so irrespective of the fact whether the marginal cost is rising or falling.

Let us have the following additional figures added to the above table.

(1)	*(2) Rs.*	*(3) Rs.*	*(4) Rs.*	*(5) Rs.*	*(6) Rs.*	*(7) Rs.*	*(8) Rs.*
11	176	367	543	23	49	16	33
12	176	400	576	33	48	15	33
13	176	448	624	48	48	14	34
14	176	510	686	62	49	13	36
15	176	600	776	90	52	12	40

(*v*) When the marginal cost first falls and then rises, *i.e.*, the marginal cost curve is U-shaped, the marginal cost will be equal to the average cost at a point where the average cost is the minimum. For example, at an output of 13 units, the cost is lowest at Rs. 48 where the marginal cost is also Rs. 48.

(*vi*) When the marginal cost is greater than the average cost, the average cost will rise, for example, for output of 14 and 15 units.

(*vii*) If the marginal cost is below the average variable cost latter must be falling. This can be verified for 11 units output.

(*viii*) If the marginal cost is higher than the average variable cost, the latter must be rising. This can be verified for output levels of 13, 14 and 15 units.

(*ix*) If marginal cost first falls, and then rises, it will be equal to the average variable cost at a point, where the average variable cost is minimum. This is seen for an output of 12 units where marginal cost and average variable are equal to Rs. 33.

The above analysis can easily be given graphically as follows:

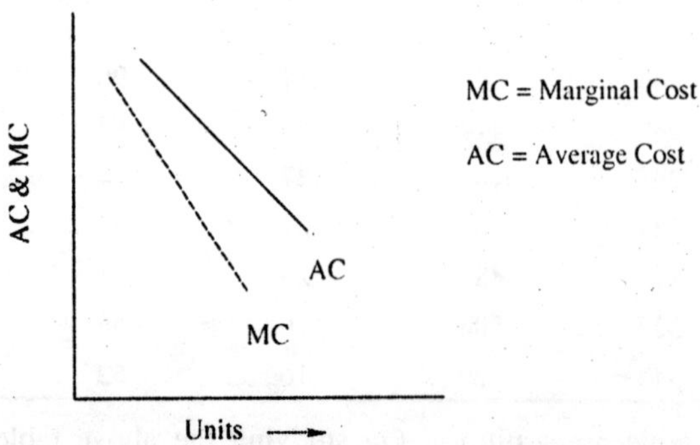

Figure 7.9

(*a*) When M. C. falls, A. C. also falls. Table shows from 5 to 10 units.

(*b*) When M. C. and A. C. are constant. Table gives it for 13 output units.

(*c*) When A. C. increases M. C. also increases. For example, from 13 to 15 units output.

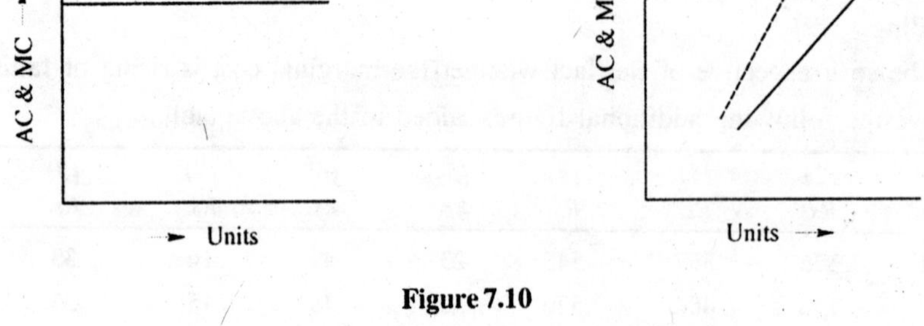

Figure 7.10

(*d*) If we plot a graph between units of output and AC and MC, we get a *U*-shaped curve, both curves intersecting at the lower AC value and the value for MC must be equal to AC at this point. Point *O* is the point of intersection and MC is equal to AC at this point.

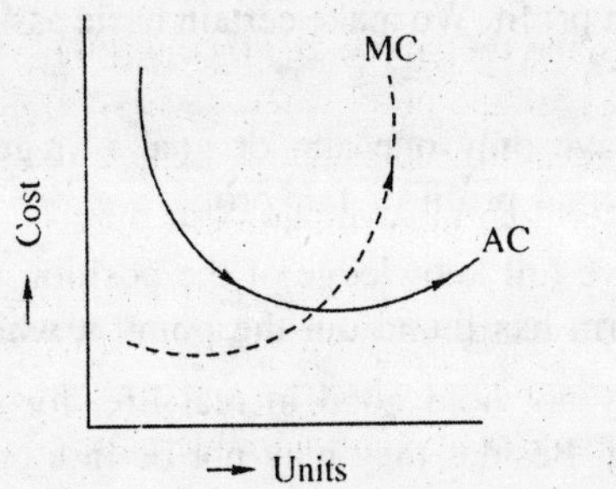

Figure 7.11

(*e*) **Product Cost:** Cost is the price. Cost of a product or finished item reflects the overall expenditure on its manufacture plus profit. Unit cost is the cost of unit item.

The cost of a Product should reflect—

— Its quality
— The volume of material it contains
— The production technology used for manufacture
— The quality of workmanship
— The use of Product.

1. Elements of Cost:

(*i*) **Direct Cost:** It is also called Prime Cost, which varies almost proportionately with the volume of production.

Direct cost includes direct material cost plus direct labour cost plus direct expenses (fuels, electricity and packaging etc.).

(*ii*) **Indirect Cost:** It is also called overhead costs, overhead expenditures are expenses other than direct expenses.

Indirect cost includes indirect material cost (*i.e.*, tools and fixtures used for production) plus indirect labour cost plus indirect expenses (such as advertisement, telephone, rent and insurance and travelling expenses etc.)

We shall write down all costs in the following ways:

Prime Cost = Direct labour + Direct material + other Direct Expenses

Manufacturing cost (Factory Cost) = Prime Cost + Factory Overhead.

Production cost or Unit cost = Manufacturing cost + Establishment cost.

Establishment cost = Office administration + Advertisement and Distribution

Selling Price = Production cost + Profit

Factory overhead = Indirect labour + Indirect material + Other Indirect expenses (all in the factory)

(*f*) **Equilibrium of a Firm:** A consumer is said to be in equilibrium when he spends his limited income on different goods in such a way that he gets maximum satisfaction. Likewise a producer is said to reach equilibrium when he combines the different factors of production so that he produces maximum output of minimum cost. Just as the consumer attempts to maximise his satisfaction and the producer attempts to maximise his outputs, similarly a firm while selling the products attempts to maximise its profit. A firm is said to be in equilibrium when a firm produces that output and fixes that price at which it secures maximum profit. We make certain basic assumption for explaining the equilibrium of the firm.

(*i*) The firm is said to have only one aim or goal *i.e.*, get maximum possible profit, it is not satisfied with only normal profit or fair profit.

(*ii*) The firm is said to have full knowledge of the position where profit is maximum. By a series of experiments, the firm has found out the point at which it can secure maximum profit.

These two assumptions may not hold good in real life, for business firms may be satisfied with whatever profits they are securing. Besides they may not be in a position to change the output and their prices continuously and find out the position of maximum profit.

If a firm goes for maximum profit it will not produce even a single unit of product at a loss. To maximise profit a firm should produce and sell up to the point at which the revenue from the last unit (marginal revenue) is equal to the cost of the last unit (marginal cost). Beyond this point of equality of marginal revenue and marginal cost, the firm will experience losses because additional cost will be more than additional revenue received. Thus the basic condition of a firm's equilibrium is that the firm should stop at the point of equality of marginal cost and marginal revenue (MC = MR).

In case of a monopoly firm marginal revenue is at a lower level than the price. Therefore, marginal cost is lower than the price. In summary form, it is

MC = MR (in equilibrium)

MR < Price (for monopoly firm).

MC < Price or Price > MC

In graphical representation it is as shown in Figure 7.12.

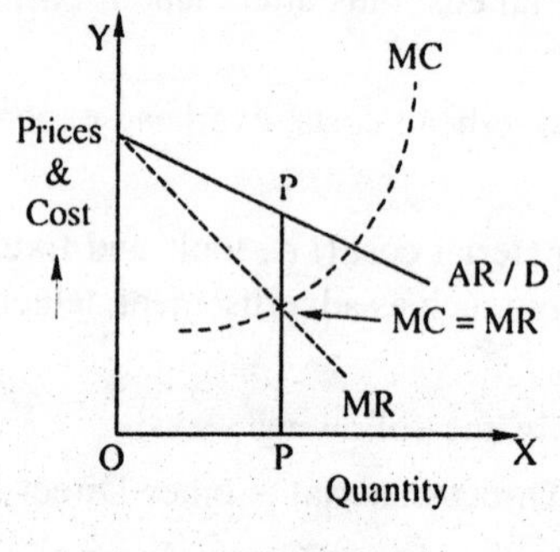

Figure 7.12

7.16 PROBABLE QUESTIONS

1. Describe the importance of cost analysis in managerial decision-making.

2. Write about following:

(*a*) Fixed Cost

(*b*) Variable Cost

(*c*) Opportunity Cost

(*d*) Implicit and Explicit Costs

(*e*) Marginal Cost

(*f*) Social Cost

(*g*) Standard Cost.

3. Prove that Long Run Average Cost Curve (LAC) is derived from Short-Run Average Cost Curves (SAC).

4. What is optimum size of a plant?

5. What is Economic Manufacturing Quantity?

6. Describe the significance of Break Even Point for a Production Unit.

7. Write notes on:

(*a*) Break-Even Sales

(*b*) Angle of Incidence

(*c*) Margin of Safety.

8. Provide the mathematical treatment for "Make or Buy" decision.

9. Show the relationships of Elasticity of Demand with Total Revenue and Marginal Revenue.

10. What is Equilibrium of a firm?

8

Plant Maintenance

• *Maintenance Management* • *Maintenance and Productivity* • *Maintenance Cost and Illustration* • *Maintenance Organisation* • *Maintenance Programme* • *Relative Advantages and Disadvantages* • *Condition Monitoring* • *Overhaul* • *Spares for Overhaul* • *Measuring Effectiveness of Maintenance Programme* • *Probable Questions.*

8.1 MAINTENANCE MANAGEMENT

8.1.1 Introduction

What is Maintenance?

Maintenance is part of Production Management. Keeping the fixed assets like Plant, Machinery, Building and other fixed assets on good physical condition.

Maintenance is upkeep and protection of above items in good working condition. A stationary item like a 'table' needs less maintenance where as a moving item like a Ceiling Fan needs more maintenance.

After running or use for some time, there is wear and tear, stress or strain in the machinery. So, for maintaining quantity and quality of products, maintenance is necessary.

8.1.2 Objective of Maintenance

(*i*) To preserve and prolong the utility of plant and equipment

(*ii*) To minimise idle time and loss of production

(*iii*) To maintain quantity and quality to products

(*iv*) To minimise industrial accidents

(*v*) To minimise machinery up keep costs.

8.1.3 Need For Maintenance

Production function in an organisation largly depends on the maintenance of plant.

The organisation of maintenance department should be such that a proper maintenance and overhauls etc. can be done economically and effectively.

A maintenance department helps in maintaining the machines suitable for quantity and quality production. More and more maintenance is required when a machine becomes old and older.

In the absence of timely upkeep, even the best machine will ultimately breakdown. Regular use over a period of time causes wear and tear. Gears become loose, bolts tear off. Valves get choked, parts crack, pipes leak, lubrication dries etc. Due to pressure for optimum utilisation, capital assets are operated to their fullest limits and are under constant stress. Therefore, regular inspection, lubrication, repair etc. must be undertaken to maintain the reliability and efficiency of equipment.

Proper maintenance helps to maximise production performance by preventing break downs and by minimising the loss caused by break downs. Proper maintenance is essential in all manufacturing concerns because machines break down, parts wear out and tools deteriorate.

8.2 MAINTENANCE AND PRODUCTIVITY

Productivity of a plant depends upon effective and regular utilisation of Production facilities. Proper maintenance of plant and equipment helps to raise productivity by minimising breakdowns and idle resources. Periodic checkup prevent avoidable in operations. Planned overhauls and quick repairs of machinery results in better utilisation of resources. Regular maintenance increases working life of machines and leads to greater utilisation of plant. Improved production economy results in lower unit costs.

By minimising the rate of deterioration, need for fresh capital to replace worn out machinery is reduced. The capital thus saved can be utilised for expansion of plant utilities and employee services.

8.3 TYPES OF MAINTENANCE

Generally, maintenance can be done in following two ways:

1. Breakdown maintenance
2. Preventive maintenance.

In the first case of maintenances, repair can be done after the breakdown occurs while in the second case, maintenance is done on the basis of prediction or on the basis of periodical checking.

1. Breakdown Maintenance: In breakdown maintenance, defects are rectified only when the machine can not perform its function any longer, and the production department is compelled to call on the maintenance engineer for repair.

In this type of maintenance, repair shall have to be done on failure, thus it may disrupt the whole production.

This type of maintenance is expensive due to payment to idol operators, overtime payments to maintenance staff, loss of production and increase of depreciation cost.

2. (*a*) Preventive Maintenance: Preventive maintenance is planned or scheduled maintenance. It is an extremely important function for the reduction of maintenance cost and to keep the good operational condition of equipment and hence increases the reliability.

Preventive maintenance aims to locate the sources of trouble and to remove them before the breakdown occurs.

Best safeguard against costly breakdown is to inspect, lubricate and check up the equipment as frequently as possible.

Thus the repair can be done when one wants to do it, *i.e.*, when it has least effect on the production schedule.

Important function of Preventive maintenance programme are as follows:

(*a*) Inspection or check ups
(*b*) Lubrication
(*c*) Planning and Scheduling
(*d*) Records and analysis
(*e*) Training of maintenance Staff
(*f*) Storage of spare parts

2. (*b*) Preventive Maintenance: This is the maintenance work undertaken to prevent the failure of a machine or plant. It is also known as planned or scheduled maintenance as it is carried out at pre-determined intervals.

Preventive maintenance is carried out before the failure arises or prior to the equipment actually breakdowns.

Preventive maintenance consists of following steps:

(*i*) Systematic and regular periodic inspection of plant and equipment in order to detect chances of possible failure or to diagnose impending failure. This is known as condition monitoring.

(*ii*) Repetitive upkeep, overhauling and servicing of the equipment to prevent breakdown.

(*iii*) Adequate lubrication, cleaning and painting of equipment.

The main advantages of preventive maintenance are:

(*i*) Life of machine and equipment becomes longer.

(*ii*) Production planning becomes easier due to fewer breakdown.

(*iii*) Higher Productivity and better quality.

(*iv*) Safety of Plant and employees is increased.

A new type of preventive maintenance known as predictive maintenance is becoming popular. It involves the use of sensitive instruments to predict trouble. Such maintenance helps in determining the need and time of overhauling. This is discussed later in this chapter.

3. Routine Maintenance: This includes all work undertaken to keep the production equipment in efficient condition. It may cover periodic inspection, cleaning, lubrication, overhaul, repair and replacement etc. All these operations are performed either while the equipment is running or during preplanned shutdowns.

Routine Maintenance is of two types:

(*a*) **Running Maintenance:** It is the work carried out when the equipment is out of service e.g. greasing the running bearings.

(*b*) **Shutdown Maintenance:** It is the work carried out when the equipment is out of service e.g. repairing a boiler tube in power generating plant.

4. Planned Maintenance: This implies that maintenance work is planned in advance and is carried out in a systematic manner. It is also known as Scheduled or Productive Maintenance.

Planned Maintenance involves examination of all plant and buildings in order to service, overhaul, lubricate or repair equipment before breakdown or deterioration in performance.

It aims at reducing machine stoppage and emergency maintenance. The stoppage of equipment due to failure cannot be planned but planning can be done in the sense that when failure takes place everyone concerned knows what to do—how to diagnose the failure quickly, what spare parts and tools are needed and where from these can be obtained.

8.4 MAINTENANCE COST AND ILLUSTRATION

The objective is to minimise total maintenance cost and down time. Economic analysis is helpful in finding a judicious combination of above two types maintenance. In the following diagram *X*-axis measures the time interval between maintenance operations while *Y*-axis measures the cost of maintenance. Curve *Cp* stands for preventive maintenance and curve *Cb* measures breakdown maintenance. The two curves show that with increase in the interval of maintenance, the cost of preventive maintenance goes down but the breakdown maintenance costs rise. The curve *Ct* indicates the total cost of maintenance.

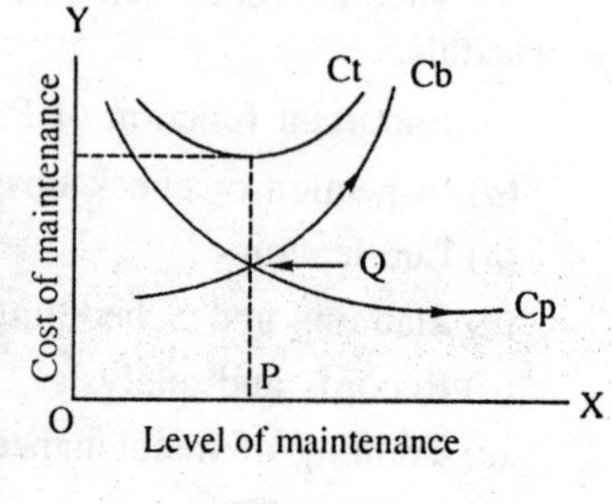

Figure 8.1

The total maintenance cost are minimum at point *Q*. At this point *Cp* and *Cb* curves intersect each other

The relationship between preventive maintenance time and repair time is also significant.

Preventive maintenance policy is justified only when the average downtime and its cost is less than the average time taken to carry out breakdown repairs.

Illustration

A plant is utilising six types of machines. If one machine breaks down the entire assembly line comes to a stop unless the defective machine is repaired or replaced. It takes five hours to replace/repair the machine out of which 1 hour per machine is variable. The machine's wage rate is Rs. 2.50 per hour, repair material cost is Rs. 200 and down time cost is Rs. 100 per hour.

Which of the alternatives maintenance strategies should the company adopt?

1. Replace only the defective machine.
2. Replace the defective machine as also all other machine.

The cost of each strategy will be as follows:

Strategy–I

Downtime Cost	= 5 × 100	= Rs. 500
Machine Cost	= 5 × 2.50	= Rs. 12.50
Materials Cost	=	Rs. 200
	Total	Rs. 712.50

Strategy–II

Total down time	= 4 + 6 × 1	= 10 hours
Down time cost	= 10 × 100	= Rs. 1000
Machine Cost	= 10 × 2.5	= Rs. 25
Materials Cost	= 6 × 200	= Rs. 1200
	Total	Rs. 2225

Thus, strategy 1 is more attractive.

8.5 MAINTENANCE ORGANISATION

A typical maintenance department chart is as follows:

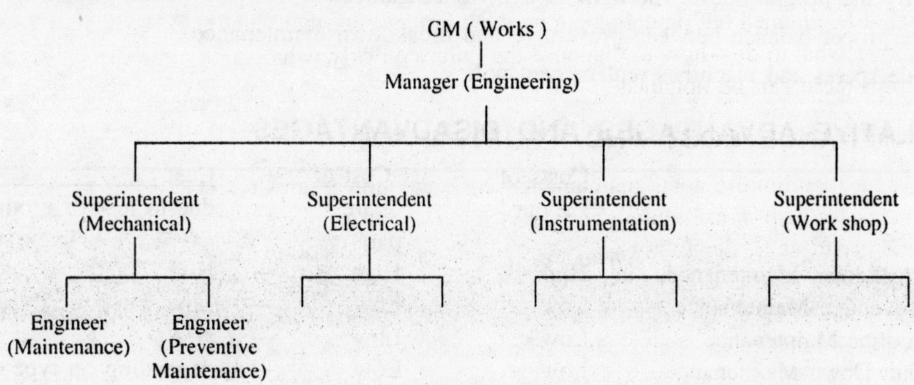

Figure 8.2

Each Superintendent is responsible for the maintenance, over hauls, checking, repairs etc. He should be a qualified and experienced person and should be able to decide the quantum and periodicities and inspection, overhaul etc.

8.6 MAINTENANCE PROGRAMME

The Maintenance Programme should be developed in accordance with the conditions prevailing in the factory. The Programme should be installed for the attainment of desired objectives.

It is preferable to start with a simple programme which can gradually be made a complete one; to provide enough time to train personnel and to permit all concerned to get acquainted with it.

A planned maintenance programme may consist of the following phases:

Phase—I

(*a*) Prepare a list of all machines and equipments to be covered and codify them for the purpose of identification.

(*b*) Collect all pertinent information about each and every machine or equipment on a Machine card or Equipment Record Card. Such information includes maker's name, specification, dates of purchase and installation, physical dimensions, operational specifications and critical spare parts etc.

(*c*) Classify the machines and equipments into critical, subcritical and non-critical.

(*d*) Prepare lubrication schedule and standards.

(*e*) Prepare inspection schedule for all machines and equipments.

(*f*) Design the recording and paper work procedure for proper communication and to maintain record for future use.

Phase—II

(*a*) Develop maintenance organisation specifying various line and staff functions.

(*b*) Determine man power requirements on the basis of estimated workload.

(*c*) Communicate and explain the maintenance plan to all concerned.

(*d*) Train personnel who are to implement the plan.

(*e*) Allocate work to individuals.

Phase—III

(*a*) Modify the programme in the light of experience gained.

(*b*) Strike proper balance between preventive and breakdown maintenance.

(*c*) Decide spares and machines replacement policy.

8.7 RELATIVE ADVANTAGES AND DISADVANTAGES

	Costs of Labour	Cost of Spare parts		Cost due to loss of production
Breakdown Maintenance	High	High	—	High
Preventive Maintenance	Low	Low	—	Low
Routine Maintenance	Low	Low	—	N A
Shut Down Maintenance	Low	Low	—	depending on type of repair
Planned Maintenance	Low	Low	—	

8.8 CONDITION MONITORING

This is part of preventive maintenance and is known as predictive maintenance. Condition of bearing, approximate time of failure is predicted by monitoring the noise coming out of a bearing which is monitored with the help of a stethoscope like gadgets. Similarly, thickness of boiler tubes are monitored by using ultrasonic tests.

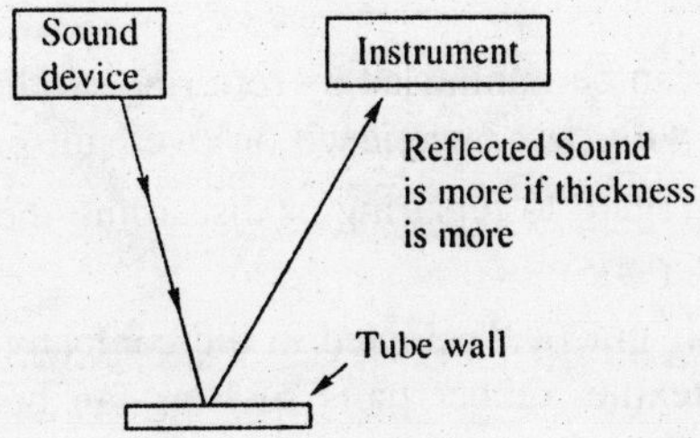

Figure 8.3

Thickness of a rotating shaft is also predicted and replaced before failure.

In case of automobile, the breaks are:

Hydraulic type —
Pneumatic type —
Power type —

condition monitoring is done periodically by checking the sensitivity of the break, monitoring the time and distance for stopping the vehicle.

Many accidents on streets may be prevented by condition monitoring of breaks and types of vehicles. Predictive maintenance is an improved type preventive maintenance.

8.9 OVERHAUL

Overhaul is a planned maintenance for cleaning house-keeping, checking the conditions of vital components and replacing the worn-out parts of a particular equipment/machine or the section of a plant or for the plant as a whole.

Continuous process plants such as Petro-chemicals, Fertilizers and oil Refining etc. which are kept running continuously for 3 shifts a day are subjected to overhaul maintenance for one month every year.

As per statutory regulations, steam boilers of medium and high pressures categories are over-hauled after 11 months' continuous running. The boiler tubes are checked for their remaining thickness with ultrasonic tests followed by hydraulic test and the boiler unit's fitness is duly certified by the Chief Inspectorate of Factories of the concerned state.

Similarly, during the overhaul period the heavy and medium duties material handing equipments such as hoists, cranes and others are maintained and tested for fitness for which suitable fitness certificate is obtained from the Chief Inspector of Factories.

During planned annual overhaul almost all the rotating and moving equipments are attended by thorough cleaning, greasing, oiling, foundation-bolts tightening and transmission belts checking and tightening etc.

The term overhauling signifies giving a new lease of life to an equipment or part of it. Companies undertake periodic overhauling on planned and scheduled basis after pre-determined number of hours of working. In the case of transport industry an engine is overhauled after a pre-determined kilometers of run. In the case of process industry, plant shut down on planned basis, as discussed, takes place.

Thus we notice that the main difference between ordinarily repair and overhaul is about the timing and extent. Repair is usually unscheduled and overhaul is essentially a preventive action to avoid failure.

8.10 SPARES FOR OVERHAUL

In overhauling, some parts require outright replacement whereas the others have to be adjusted. Thus the requirement will be only for those which are to be replaced completely and this requirement cannot be predicted accurately.

However, this uncertainty can be minimised by referring, to the manufactures' catalogue or manual. Also this can be cross checked with past experience on overhaul practices.

The company policy with regard to repairing or discarding the defective part has also an important bearing as procurement of spare parts.

The maintenance and repair practices adopted in the company has a strong influence on the spares requirement. During overhaul, textile, rubber parts such as fan belts, gaskets, houses, etc. are usually replaced 100 per cent. The *ABC* analysis of inventory control is carried out for overhaul so that the Maintenance Engineer can give through to reduce consumption of "*A*" items in the long run by improving the repairing method.

8.11 MEASURING EFFECTIVENESS OF MAINTENANCE PROGRAMME

The effectiveness of maintenance is evaluated in terms of total maintenance cost and downtime costs.

Proper information system is maintained for collecting and storing data about costs and down times.

Following indices are computed on the basis of information relating to:

(*i*) Costs of maintenance

(*ii*) Downtime hours and available machine hours

(*iii*) Number of breakdowns

(*iv*) Labour hours spent on both breakdowns and preventive maintenance

8.12 PROBABLE QUESTIONS

1. What is importance of Maintenance for a Production unit?
2. What are various types of Maintenance?
3. What is Predictive maintenance?
   What do you mean by "overhaul"?
4. What is Optimum Maintenance Cost?
5. Illustrate various Programmes for maintenance.
6. Draw the organisation chart for the maintenance department for a Production Unit.
7. How do you measure the effectiveness of a Maintenance Programme?

9

Manufacturing: Techniques and Processes

• Manufacturing Techniques • Manufacturing Processes • Chemical Process Industries • Motor vehicle Industries • Production Techniques and Processes • Process Industries • Choice of Technology • Technology Forecasting • Future of Technology • Technological Obsolescence • Replacement Decision • Appropriate Technology • Choice of Technology • Information Technology • Creating and Applying Technology • Value Chain Management and Tata Technologies • Uses of Technology in Manufacturing • Probable Questions.

9.1 MANUFACTURING TECHNIQUES

Manufacturing involves physical and chemical changes in raw materials and parts. Under physical change, the material acquires new physical properties such as density, viscosity, solubility, thermal conductivity etc. A physical change is reversible. For example, sugar can be dissolves in water and on heating the sugar can be obtained again.

In a chemical change, the material is transformed with the help of acids and other substances. Such a change is permanent and non reversible. For example, once milk becomes curd, it can not be converted to milk.

In the course of manufacturing, several types of activities are involved e.g. cleaning, washing, repairing, melting, forging etc. Such activities performed on materials and parts are known as manufacturing processes.

In a big factory, separate areas or centres are maintained for different processes of production. For example, metals are melted in the Melting shop, they are cast in the foundry shop by pouring molten metal into moulds, the solid metal is heated and hammered or processed into desired shape in the Forging Shop. The materials formed by casting or forging are machined further to give them desired size and shape.

Manufacturing processes cover the entire spectrum from the completely manual task to automatic systems where labour is of indirect or vigilance nature. Manual tasks and mechanical aids together constitute the major share of production activity. Some manufacturing processes have a considerable technical base such as chemicals and plastics industries.

A good working knowledge of manufacturing process is very useful in efficient management of production.

9.2 MANUFACTURING PROCESSES

Manufacturing processes may be classified into the following categories:

(i) **Fabrication Process:** A fabrication process modifies the physical characteristics of materials with the help of certain labour or machine operations. The fabrication process is generally applied in metal working industries.

Fabrication work involve several operations like forgings, gas welding, flame-cutting etc.

(*ii*) Metal Working Processes:

(*a*) **Forming Process:** Forming Processes involve rough shaping of metals or metal objects. It may be done by hot working such as rolling, forging etc. or by cold working such as binding and drawing. Casting, Gorging, Hot Rolling, Extrusion metal stamping, Powder metallurgy and sizing techniques are all constitute Forming Processes.

(*b*) **Heat Treatment Process:** Heat treatment is the process of heating and cooling solid metals in order to obtain certain desired properties e.g. heating before hot working and annealing after cold working. Heat treatment of steel alloys is nuded to modify physical and electrical properties and to relieve stresses. Mechanical properties of various types of steel such as surface hardness, toughness etc. are changed. For example, steel used in manufacturing cutting tools must be able to successfully machine other metals. Therefore, such steels must be given the right combination of hardness and toughness.

(*c*) **Welding Process:** Welding refers to fusing metals together while they are in the plastic or molten state. Welding process involves the use of heat which is obtained from gas flames, electric arc or electrical resistance. An electrode or filler wire is also used to produce additional metal for filling in and reinforcement.

(*d*) **Surface Treatment Process:** Surface treatment refers to those chemical or mechanical processes which are used to alter the surface characteristic of a metal. The generally used surface treatment processes are Tumbling, shot blusting, painting plastic coating, tile lining, enameling, metal plating, galvanising, Anodizing and lapping etc.

(*iii*) Machining Processes: Machining Processes are concerned with fine shaping of metal objects to precise contours. These processes involve removing a part of the metal. Cutting, grinding and other tools are used to reduce metal blanks to specified shapes and dimensions.

The commonly used machining processes are given below:

- Flamecutting:— generally an oxyacetylene torch is directed by hand for flame cutting of metal plates.
- Sawing:—Hack saw, Circular Saw of Band Saw are used for cutting operation of a metal object.
- Die Casting:— or Screen Cutting is used for cutting Screen threads on the outside surface of a work piece.
- Grinding:—This is used gradually to remove metal from the object and for finishing the surface of a metal object. Grinding is mostly used for finishing machine surfaces to achieve closer dimensional tolerances.
- Drilling—A rotating drill bit is mounted on a spindle for making a uniform holes through the stationary object.
- Boring:—This operation of enlarging a small hole into a bigger hole is done by holding a fixture and a single print rotary cutter is moved through the hole, which cuts the surface to enlarge the dimensions of the hole.
- Reaming:—In this operation an ordinary hole made through drilling or boring is accurately finished or smoothed with the help of a multiple point cutting tool known as "reamer."
- Turning:—This operation is of cutting and removing material from the surface of the work piece. The object is mounted on a lathe rotating at high speed about its axis. A single point cutting tool is placed parallel to the axis and as the object turns the cutter chips the metal.
- Milling:—It is the process of removing extra metal from the object in order to give a fine finish to its surface and to produce a specific shape.

For this purpose, a rotating multipoint cutting tool is used.

- Broaching:—This is the operation of removing metal from inside the hole. It is done with the help of a multiple toothed tool (called broacher) pulled or pushed over the surface of an object.
- Shaping:—This is used for making flat surface with the help of a cutter which reciprocates while the object is stationary.

Polishing:—In this process irregularities from the surface of an object are removed and then a surface layer is put with the help of a brush.

9.3 CHEMICAL PROCESS INDUSTRIES

The physical operations used to manufacture chemicals are called Unit Operations and the chemical operations are called Unit Processes.

Chemical and allied industries may be classified as follows :

(*i*) Inorganic Industries—These include sulphur and sulphuric acid, fertiliser, chloroalkali, cement and explosives etc.

(*ii*) Natural Product Industries—These include oils, soaps and detergents, paints and varnishes, pulp and paper, food processing, and coal chemicals and petroleum etc.

(*iii*) Synthetic Organic Industries—These include petrochemicals, pesticides, pharmaceuticals etc.

(*iv*) Polymerisation Industries—Consist of plastics, rubber, adhesives etc.

(*v*) Metallurgical Industries—This consists of iron and steel, aluminium, copper, lead and zinc etc.

The Unit Processes used in some of the chemical industries are as follows:

Industry	*Unit Processes used*
Chemicals	Oxidation and Reduction
Oils, fats and soaps	Esterification
Cement	Calcination
Plastics and Polymers	Polymerisation
Explosives and Dye Stuffs	Nitration and Sulfonation

9.4 MOTOR VEHICLE INDUSTRY

This is a part of heavy industry for producing Motor Cars, Trucks, Auto Rickshaws, Motor Cycles, Scooters and Mopeds. In other words, all two-wheeler, three wheeler and four wheeler, light, medium and heavy duty vehicles are produced under Motor Vehicle Industry.

The Production Processes involved in this industry are as follows:

Fabrication Process
Metal Working Process
Machining Process
Metal Forming Process
Heat Treatment Process
Welding Process
Surface Treatment Process

Each of the above processes has been narrated in brief or in details earlier in this chapter.

Motor Vehicle Industry uses a large numbers of parts and components for which the main producer of Motor Vehicles depend largely on "The Ancillary Industries".

While major producers of Motor Vehicles are TELCO, Hindustan Motor, Maruti Udyog, Bajaj Auto, Hero Honda, Kinetic Engineering, LML etc. The main ancillary industries are MICO, TVS Sona Steering etc.

9.5 PRODUCTION TECHNIQUES AND PROCESSES

Various Production techniques are used for making finished Products. Production techniques cover the entire spectrum from the completely manual task to automatic systems.

Some Production techniques have a considerable technical base. Chemical Industries, steel making and Hardware and Software Industries are such example.

(*i*) **Fabrication Processes:** Fabrication Processes involves changing the shape of materials with the help of operations such as are welding, gas welding, gas cutting. Large Steel storage tanks which are used for storing liquid petroleum products are made with the help of fabrication processes carried out on steel sheets.

(*ii*) **Steel Making:** Steel making involves remelting the pig iron and processing the molten iron to reduce the carbon content. Several other metals are then added to give physical characteristics to the iron. Blast Furnace and open hearth furnace are used in Steel making.

Liquid steel is cast into Ingots and Ingots are rolled into Sheets by the use of Rolling process.

(*iii*) **Casting:** Casting Process uses Sand and Mould to which liquid metal (Steel, Aluminium etc.) is poured. Then the metal is allowed to solidify.

Various techniques such as Sand casting, Shell—mould Casting, Die-casting and Centrifugal casting etc. are adopted.

(*iv*) **Forging:** Forging is the process of heating the metal into red and then hammering it into shape. Forging operation can be performed in the cold state or hot state. In the latter case, the object is heated to make it pliable and then given the desired shape with the help of a Press machine or forge hammer.

Forging of parts offers benefits like greater strength, lighten weight and better finish.

(*v*) **Hot Rolling:** Hot rolling involves taking the hot ingots from a soaking pit (where it has been kept at an elevated temperature) and rolling it first into blooms (large oblong squares), and then through a series of other rollers into structural shapes. Pipes and tubes are hot rolled products.

Hot rolling also produces structural shapes like angles, *H*–beams, *I*–beams, rails etc.

(*vi*) **Extrusion:** Extrusion is a process in which a billet or slag of metal is forced by high pressure through an Orifice that is shaped to provide the desired form to the finished product.

Automotive and air craft parts, utensils etc. are extruded items.

Extrusion can give various shapes to metal pieces and extrusion machines have been extensively used for wire-drawing, tube-forming and household appliances etc.

(*vii*) **Machining:** Machining is concerned with fine shaping of metal objects to precise contours. Commonly used machining processes are :

- Turning—The operation of cutting and removing materials from the surface of work piece.

  Turning is a lathe operation that forms a cylindrical or conical work surface.

- Grinding—Grinding is used gradually to remove metal from the work piece and for finishing the surface of a metal object.

  Grinding machines with abrasive wheels are used for finishing machined surfaces to achieve closer dimensional tolerances.

- Other machining processes are drilling, boring and milling etc.

Above machining operations are normally carried in a workshop equipped with necessary machines.

9.6 PROCESS INDUSTRIES

In Process Industries, a chemical or ore is transformed into a finished product through a series of chemical and physical changes. Physical operations are called Unit operations and Chemical operations are called Unit Processes.

(*i*) **Inorganic Chemical Industries:** These include Sulfuric Acid, Nitrogen and Phosphorus based Fertilizer, Chloroalkali, Cement, Lime and Mineral Water etc.

(*ii*) **Organic Chemical Industries:** These include Petroleum Refining products, Oils and fats, Soap and detergents. Plastics and Synthetic Fibres and dye stuffs etc.

(*iii*) **Food Processing Industries:** These include Jams, Jelly and Sauce, Biscuits, and Soft Drinks etc. Dehydrated non-seasonal vegetables such as Peas, Cauliflower and Cabbages also form the parts of Food Processing Industries.

(*iv*) **Metallurgical Industries:** This category comprises iron and steel, aluminium, copper, lead and zinc etc. Iron and Steel forms the core sector industries and annual production capacities of iron and steel is normally an indicator of Industrial Progress for a country.

(*v*) **Hardware And Software Industries:** This is the fastest growing industry segment at present in India and India is in a leading position in the world so far as software exports are concerned. Satyam Computers, Zenith Computers, Wipro Ltd. and Infosys Technologies are some of the most reputed Hardware and Software companies in India.

Information Technology and *E*-Commerce are the most lucrative and fastest growing industrial sectors with huge export potential.

9.7 CHOICE OF TECHNOLOGY

In recent decades, mind boggling advances have taken place in the field of science and technology. These developments have led to revolutionary changes in the economic and social life of people, so much so, that the 20th century is known as the 'Age of Technology'.

(*i*) **Concept and Importance:** Technology may be defined as the know how and intellectual input used in doing something. Technology implies the practical application of the principles and techniques of science to day-to-day industrial and commercial use. It is actually called applied science.

It is because of their technological superiority that multinationals launch trend setting product/services. They enjoy technological edge in terms of R & D, product design, process know-how and distribution etc. Sony of Japan, IBM of USA and Hindustan Lever of India are some of the examples. The main benefits of technology are given below:

(*a*) Technological Progress helps to improve productivity thereby conserving scarce resources.

(*b*) Superior technology results in higher quality of products/services thereby increasing customer satisfaction.

(*c*) Improvements in productivity and quality due to technology lead to reduction in cost per unit.

Some example of implications of technology are:

- Developments of new products such as plastics, nylon and battery operated cars.
- Paper less office.
- X-rays, laser, scanning and other developments in medical science.
- Cellular phone, fax, internet, e-mail etc. developments in communication technology.
- Use of Satellites in forecasting and monitoring weather.
- Application of computers in data processing, data storage and data retrieval.
- Use of CAD/CAM in process and equipment design.

- Monitoring and control of huge industrial installations such as Petrochemicals, Power-plants, Petroleum, Refineries and Space stations etc.

At the macrolevel technology is vital factor in economic growth. Advancements in technology help to improve standard of living. Developed countries own much of their living standards to their preeminence in the field of Science and technology.

9.8 TECHNOLOGY FORECASTING

Forecasting is the basis of long term strategic planning. Efficient planning should be done when new technologies become available in future and their implications are considered. Globalisation and liberalisation have made technology forecasting all the more necessary.

To be successful, technology forecasting needs to be integrated with key managerial functions of planning and control. Technology forecasting helps an organisation in achieving and retaining market leadership.

Technology forecasting is the process of predicting the future performance of technology. It is the systematic and scientific anticipation of future trends in technology so as to use them for meeting organisational objectives.

The basic purpose of technology forecasting is to identify technological possibilities and their impact on economy and individual organisations.

The scope of technology forecasting covers:

(*a*) Future technology and products.

(*b*) Technological obsolescence.

(*c*) Technological intelligence.

(*d*) Future Competition and threats.

(*e*) Performance risk.

9.9 FUTURE OF TECHNOLOGY

In a country like India, technological self reliance is a major goal. Therefore, focus should be on the following aspects:

(*a*) Selfreliance and indigenisation.

(*b*) Acquisition and absorption of technology.

(*c*) Cost-Benefit analysis.

(*d*) Need based import of technology.

(*e*) Cost reduction and value engineering.

It is very difficult to say what is going to be the shape of technology in the 21st Century. However, one thing is certain that technology is changing very fast. With this rapid pace, one can expect that technology will be developed to gain mastery over dreaded diseases like cancer and AIDS, and serious problems those may arise from the future shortages of Crude petroleum and electric power etc.

The trend is towards flexible manufacturing, decentralised organisations, specialised products, information technology and communication technology etc.

Future of technology will be such that it will aim at improving productivity and reducing costs. It will help modern factory systems to go in for mass production and standardisation which will bring in the improvement in the living standards of people.

9.10 TECHNOLOGICAL OBSOLESCENCE

Technological progress has created new problems e.g. obsolescence, dehumanisation of jobs, technological unemployment etc. Obsolescence means becoming out of date or comparatively inefficient.

Technological obsolescence implies lowering of the engineering efficiency of machinery and equipment due to introduction of new and better techniques. Obsolescence and deterioration reduce the economic life of plant and machinery.

Ultimately the replacement of plant and machinery becomes necessary.

For example, a handloom becomes obsolete when a powerloom is developed. A value set radio becomes obsolete when solid state ratio set is developed.

Obsolescence is a major issue in the purchase and installation of machinery and equipment.

Technological obsolescence arises due to cotinuous improvements in the techniques and methods of production. It is difficult to predict the rate of obsolescence as it varies widely among different industries.

Management must monitor and anticipate the rate of technological obsolescence in order to design and develop a sound replacement policy.

Following are causes of obsolescence and factors those determine obsolescence:

Causes	*Effect*
Low operating speed	Lower productivity
Low design efficiency	High energy consumption
Inferior design	High repairs and maintenance
Design deficiencies	Frequent breakdowns
Poor design	High Spoilage
In accurate design	Less reliability
Less automation	More labour cost
Less compact design	More floor space

9.11 REPLACEMENT DECISION

In replacement decisions, the basic problem is to decide whether to replace a machine at present or at a future date. It is therefore, necessary to determine whether obsolescence or deterioration has reached the point where the reduction in operating costs expected from replacement justifies the net capital expenditure involved in installing the new machine and disposing of the one.

Need for replacement may arise due to:

• Declining efficiency of existing machine.
• Improvement in machine design ensuring greater efficiency
• Obsolescence caused by technological break through.

A manager will decide to replace an old machine only when he is convinced that he can increase profits by the replacement

For assessing replacement decision, George Terborgh of U.S.A. developed the **MAPI** (Machinery and Allied Products Institute) system. This system requires the use of investment and cost data. **MAPI** system guides a manager as to when to replace economically. It also gives an idea about the minimum cost involved in the postponement of the replacement. The **MAPI** system takes into account the time value of money as well as opportunity cost which are essential for rational decision-making.

9.12 APPROPRIATE TECHNOLOGY

Developed countries no doubt have technological superiority. Developing countries like should use technologies already developed by developed countries, which are appropriate to the needs and resources of rural poor. They require technologies which are neither too capital intensive nor to labour intensive. The developing nations need technologies which can create work places in rural areas and small towns to avoid migration to metropolitan cities. They should adopt technologies which help in creating production methods based largely on local materials and for local use.

Thus, appropriate technology refers to the technology which can satisfy the maximum needs of the country's population.

Appropriate technology covers not only physical technology (machines, processes), biological technology (high yielding crop varieties) but also social technology (education, health, etc.).

People in developing countries should develop living styles suited to their own needs and environment rather than copying western styles and patterns.

9.13 CHOICE OF TECHNOLOGY (with reference to various factors)

Technology is often classified as:

1. Capital intensive technology (High Technology)
2. Labour intensive technology (Low Technology).

Technological choice will determine the type and range of products, capital investment, and profitability.

Choice of technology is a difficult decision and several factors are to be considered.

(*a*) **Nature of Product**—Production of detergents and safety matches for example often involve low technology. Whereas, production of colour tubes, cellular phones, high precision watches requires high technology.

(*b*) **Volume of Production**—Size of market and production volume are major determinants of technology. Firms which later to the global market need automatic technology. Coca Cola Corporation needs superior technology in comparison to a local bottling plant.

(*c*) **Investment Capacity**—Companies which can afford huge capital investment tend to choose high technology, whereas companies which have limited funds prefer manual operations of low technology.

(*d*) **Manufacturing Strategy**—The choice between general purpose machines and special purpose equipments as well as the degree of automation depends on the company's manufacturing strategy.

(*e*) **Technical and Engineering Aspects**—Process specifications, design requirements and engineering feasibility influence technological choice.

(*f*) **Risk and Return**—The desirability of investing in particular technology is judged on the basis of expected return and associated risk.

(*g*) **Social considerations**—Legal and political aspects, employee's attitudes and organisation culture are important considerations in the choice of technology. Labour laws requires employers to use technology that minimises employment of human beings under extremely hot and dusty conditions.

9.14 INFORMATION TECHNOLOGY

Information technology is critical to operations everywhere along the supply chain and to every functional area. computers spawning a huge proportions of current technological changes and innovations.

Computer-based information technology has greatly influenced how operations are managed and how offices work.

Information technology makes cross functional co-ordination easier and links a firm's basic processes. In a manufacturing plant, it can link people with the work centres, databases, and computers. Computer literacy has become essential to success in an organisation

It has basically 4 (four) following components:

(i) **Hardware:** A computer and the devices connected to it. Improved hardware memory, processing capability, and speed have, in large part, driven recent technological change.

(ii) **Software:** The computer programme written to make the hardware work and to carry out different application tasks are called Software. Window 2000 and Tally are the application Software. Software is essential to many manufacturing capabilities, such as computer-aided-design and manufacturing, automated materials handling and flexible manufacturing system etc.

(iii) **Data-bases:** A data base is a collection of interrelated data or information stored on a data storage device such as a computers, hard drive, a floppy disc or tape. A data base can be a firm's inventory records, cost-data, time standard for processes. Thousands of online databases are also available commercially

(iv) **Telecommunications:** The final component of information technology is telecommunications. Fibre optics, telephones, modems, fax machines and their related components make electronic networks possible. Such networks and the compatible software allow computer users at one location to communicate directly with the computer users at another location.

The excellent use of computer networks to conduct business electronically has reduced both time and cost from its supply chain management.

9.15 CREATING AND APPLYING TECHNOLOGY

The innovation process focuses technical and scientific efforts on better ways to meet market needs. One way, for a firm to acquire new technology is to do its own research and development (R & D), which creates new idea or knowledge which is then applied to create and introduce new products, services and production processes.

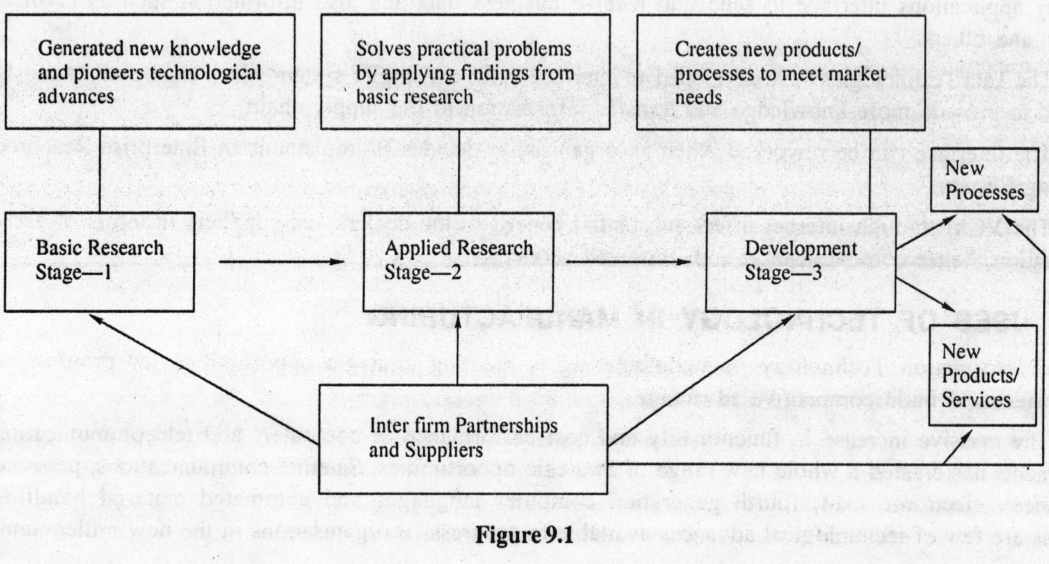

Figure 9.1

R & D passes through the stages to create Products/Services and new processes as shown in Figure 9.1.

R & D Stages: In R & D stages apply equally well to service—providers, although stages 1 and 2 are far less formal and extensive than they are for manufacturers.

Technology Strategy and Technology as a competitive Advantage: Because technology is changing rapidly and many technologies are available, the production managers must take intelligent and well informed decisions about new product and process technologies.

We should examine how technologies should be chosen and how these choices link with strategy to create a competitive advantage.

An appropriate technology is one that fits corporate and operations strategies and gives the firm a sustainable advantage.

Technology strategy deals with technological choice and decides whether a firm should be a leader or follower in technological change and how to evaluate radically new technologies.

A new technology should create some kind of competitive advantage. Competitive advantage is created by increasing the value of a product to a customer or reducing the cost of bringing the products to market.

The potential for increasing value and reducing cost from a new technology is vast.

The most obvious cost reduction strategy is that of reducing the direct costs of labour and materials

9.16 VALUE CHAIN MANAGEMENT AND TATA TECHNOLOGIES

The Tata Technologies, a subsidiary of TELCO has launched Value Chain Management (VCM) system towards a value based interaction between business partners and manufacturers.

Tata Technologies provides the cost effective IT solution to the entire value chain. The VCM system is a WEB based solution to dealers and supplier of TELCO to help them in transacting electronically in an on-line real time mode. As many as over 350 suppliers are transacting with TELCO using VCM E-Commerce.

The system maintains a large value chain database and provides browser based inter active, user friendly applications interface to send and receive business data and also information such as invoice, ohallan and others.

The Tata Technologies have developed an interface to the existing IT system which can be continuously defined to provide more knowledge and transfer information to the supply chain.

The interface can be reworked when an organisation decides to implement an Enterprise Resource Planning System.

The VCM through internet offers substantial benefit to the dealers and suppliers in terms of early information, better communication and improved services.

9.17 USES OF TECHNOLOGY IN MANUFACTURING

Use of Information Technology in manufacturing is creating strategic opportunities for progressive organisations to build competitive advantage.

The massive increase in functionality and cost performance of computers and telecommunication equipments has created a whole new range of Strategic opportunities. Satellite communications, personal computers, electronic mail, fourth generation computer languages and automated material handling systems are few of technological advances available to progressive organisations in the new millennium.

(*a*) **Information Technology and Competitive Advantage:** Information Technology (IT) is now seen as one of the keys to achieving sustainable competitive advantage in modern organisations. Whilst other forms of technology plays important roles, IT in its various forms is all pervasive. Too often, an organisation seizes an opportunity to use technology to improve one aspect of its operation without considering the implementation of technology, the positive and negative effects on various parts of the organisation, aggregated to ensure a net positive outcome.

(*b*) **Electronic Data Interchange (EDI):** Reputed MNC's like Kodak, Coca-Cola, Pepsi-Co. and others have already started using electronic data interchange (EDI) long ago. In India companies such as Bajaj Auto, Maruti Udyog Ltd., Hindustan Lever Ltd. and Godrej etc. have implemented EDI systems in their factories and offices.

EDI involves the transfer of data from files on one computer to another using telephone lines. There are potential benefits for firms who learn not only what EDI can achieve, but also how to use this newly emerging technology effectively.

A major benefit of EDI is service differentiation using information to provide superior service.

The other advantages are:

- Reduction in labour intensive activities.
- Reduction in labour costs.
- Reduction in manual errors.
- Reduction in working capital amount.
- Increase in customer service.
- Elimination of Paper Work.

EDI provides also the following opportunities:

- It can provide an organisation with the ability to maintain control over the inbound movement of raw materials and thereby enabling the organisation to implement JIT manufacturing.
- A company can use EDI effectively to control of flow of finished products to distributor/Retailers and finally to customers.

The decision on adopting EDI can be taken based on internal saving which would offset cost of adopting EDI technology.

(*c*) **Integration using Information Technology:** In developing a cost effective information integration strategy, it is important to realise that, irrespective of organisation structure, all departments and functions are to some extent interdependent and cannot stand alone.

As a minimum requirement, any integration strategy should:

- Identify departments that use common information.
- Determine the logical points at which common data should be entered thereby reducing to a minimum number or times data must be entered.
- Define business and processing policies across applications to be integrated.
- Define common terms and coding schemes.
- Wherever possible, consider using shared data bases.
- Classify data elements as either 'action data' (*i.e.*, purchasing, inventory control etc.) or planning data *i.e.*, Materials Requirement Planning, Sales forecasts etc.

By adopting this approach, companies can ensure that systems are developed that provide real time availability of 'action data' to all who need this information to make good business decisions.

(*d*) **The working of EDI System:** The operational support system of company **A** generates suggested re-order quantities for a number of products which are supplied by company **B**. After recommendations are approved by the Purchase Manager, the system generates a purchase order which is sent electronically to company **B**. Based on this purchased order, the operational support system of company **B** will automatically generate a sales order and perform a credit and a stock availability check. If these checks are passed, company **B** system will electronically send an acknowledgment and will further process the order for order picking and despatch.

An electronic advice will be sent to transport company so that transport will be available on time. At the time of despatch, an advice will be sent electronically to company **A** and after goods have been received, the accounts receivable module will check the invoice against the prices and quantities on the purchase order. If these are passed, an electronic message will be sent to the bank in order to trigger an electronic funds transfer, after which the amounts payable module of company **B** will be updated.

9.18 PROBABLE QUESTIONS

1. Define Manufacturing.
Describe various Processes in fabrication and machining.

2. Write about Metal working processes.

3. Write notes on:
(*a*) Chemical Process Industries.
(*b*) Motor Vehicle Industries.

4. Define Technology.
What is the importance of Technology in Manufacturing?

5. What is Technology for casting?
Write about the future of technology and technological obsolescence.

6. Describe various factors influencing the choice of technology.

7. Describe with examples, how technology helps in gaining competitive advantage in manufacturing.

8. Write notes on:
(*a*) Tata Technologies and value chain management.
(*b*) Information Technology and competitive advantage.
(*c*) Electronic Data Interchange.

10

Material Handling

- *Introduction to the Materials Handling* • *Objectives and Principles of Materials Handling*
- *Materials Handling Equipments* • *Criteria for Selection of Materials Handling Equipment*
- *Efficiency of Materials Handling* • *Probable Questions.*

10.1 INTRODUCTION TO THE MATERIALS HANDLING

A manufacturing company spends sizeable percentage of its total expenditure on materials handling. Its useful planning and application can help in (*i*) reducing unnecessary movement of the workers (*ii*) reducing idle time of the workers and the machines and thereby reducing the overall cost of manufacture.

Material handling is concerned with efficient movement of raw materials, partly finished goods, spare parts and finished goods.

In case of Production layout where the facilities are arranged according to the sequence of operations, the distance between any two consecutive facilities may not be very large and conveyorised transport system or transfer machines may prove to be efficient mode of transfer.

But in case of Process layout the work-pieces have to move from one section to other covering much longer distances.

Therefore, if efficient system is not devised, much time will be lost in transportation.

Proper materials handling system influences the efficiency and cost of manufacturing. Materials handling is an important area for reducing costs, increasing productivity and improving the profitability.

Materials handling adds to the cost of the Product without adding anything to its value. The materials handling system should be so designed as to maximise efficiency and minimise cost. The system should aim at elimination of unnecessary movement of materials and essential movements should be mechanised so as to increase efficiency.

Significance of materials handling is such that improvements in the system can result in faster production, higher plant capacity, lower stock in process and less damage to product in all stages.

10.2 OBJECTIVES AND PRINCIPLES OF MATERIAL HANDLING

The main objectives of materials handling system are as follows:

(*a*) Reduction in manufacturing time.

(*b*) Reduction in labour cost for handling of materials.

(*c*) Increase in employee safety and comfort.

(*d*) Better utilisation of shopfloor and warehouse.

(*e*) Easier control on movement of materials.

Materials handling and Plant layout are complementary to each other. The speed and efficiency of movements of materials determine the Plant and Equipment layout.

The guiding principles for the effective materials handling system should be as under:

(*i*) The best handling is 'no handling'. As this is not possible, the objective should be 'minimum handling'. All types of handling and rehandling should be minimised.

(*ii*) The time and distance for handling should be minimised wherever possible.

(*iii*) Whenever possible flow line and gravity should be used to move materials.

(*iv*) Materials handling equipment should be simple and consistent with the nature of materials and speed of movement. For example, for moving materials over inclined planes, gravity rollers are more appropriate than powered conveyors.

There is tremendous scope for cost-savings in materials handling.

10.3 PRINCIPLES OF MATERIALS HANDLING

(*i*) **Principles of Planning:** Pre-planning of all material handling activities must be done for its overall efficient operation and employment.

(*ii*) **Principle of System Analysis:** All the activities such as receiving of raw materials and finished goods, storage, production, inspection, packaging and transportation should be considered as necessary operation of a system and effort should be made to integrate as many of these activities as practicable.

(*iii*) **Principle of Material Flow:** For minimum flow or movement of material for all the necessary operations, best plant layout should be planned.

(*iv*) **Principle of Simplification:** Handling should be simplified by reducing, combining or eliminating unnecessary movements of work or equipment.

(*v*) **Principle of Gravity:** Force of gravity should be utilised to move materials wherever practicable.

(*vi*) **Principle of Space Utilisation:** The space of the plant should be best utilised for minimum movement of material handling equipment.

(*vii*) **Principle of Unit Size:** The quantity, size or weight of unit load or flow rate should be increased to the possible limit.

(*viii*) **Principle of Mechanisation:** Automation operation should be mechanised.

(*ix*) **Principle of Automation:** Automation should be introduced in production and handling function.

(*x*) **Principles of equipment selection:** While selecting handling equipment due consideration should be given to the type and quantity of material to be handled, movement and method to be used.

(*xi*) **Principle of Standardisation:** Handling methods, type and size should be standardised.

(*xii*) **Principle of dead weight:** The ratio of load carried to the weight of the handling equipment should be increased.

(*xiii*) **Principle of adaptability:** Methods and equipments that can best perform variety of operations should be used if special purpose equipment are not suitable.

(*xiv*) **Principle of Utilisation:** The handling equipment should be best utilised.

(*xv*) **Principle of maintenance:** Preventive maintenance programme and scheduled repairs and replacements should be well planned.

(*xvi*) **Principle of Obsolescence:** Obsolete handling equipments and methods should be replaced by modern, more efficient and versatile equipments.

(*xvii*) **Principle of full capacity:** Handling equipments should be used to its full capacity to achieve target production rate.

(*xviii*) **Principle of performance:** Effectiveness of handling equipments should be determined in terms of expense per unit handled.

(xix) **Principle of Safety:** Safety measures must be incorporated in the handling equipments.

The selected material handling equipment should be very easy and safe to handle.

10.4 MATERIALS HANDLING EQUIPMENTS

Method study is helpful in improving Plant layout and materials handling system. Proper selection and arrangement of physical facilities reduces the number and frequency of movements. A large number of tools and techniques are used for handling materials. The device and method of handling depend upon the type of materials, quantity and frequency of handling and the distance involved.

Materials Handling Equipment are classified under following heads:

(*a*) Gravity Conveyors	—	Ramps, slides, chutes, roller conveyors
(*b*) Power Conveyors	—	Belt and Roller conveyors, Pneumatic conveyors, Screw conveyors, Hydraulic conveyors and Mono Rails etc.
(*c*) Lifts and Hoists	—	Bucket Elevators Escalators
(*d*) Cranes	—	Portable, Travelling, Fixed, Gantry and Derrick etc.
(*e*) Trucks	—	Pallets, Fork Lift Trucks, Tractors and Trailors etc.
(*f*) Other types	—	Acrial Ropeways, Cableways, Revolving floors and Turntables, and Chain Pulley Blocks etc.
(*g*) Earth Moving Equipment	—	Excavators, Dumpers, Trippers, Loaders and Bulldozers.

10.5 CRITERIA FOR SELECTION OF MATERIALS HANDLING EQUIPMENT

Material handling is concerned with efficient movement of raw materials, partly finished goods, finished goods, spare parts and goods that help in production from one place to other in the plant or from outside to the plant.

In case of product layout where the facilities are arranged according to the sequence of operations, the distance between any two consecutive facilities may not be very large and conveyorised transport system or transfer machines may prove to be efficient mode of transfer.

But in case of Process layout the work-pieces have to move from one section to other covering much longer distances. Therefore, if efficient system is not devised much time will be lost in transport.

(*a*) Automated Material Handling: In both manufacturing and service industries, the choice of how, when and by whom materials are handled is an important technological decision. Materials handling covers the process of moving, packaging and storing a product. Moving, handling and storing materials costs both time and money but adds no value to the product. Therefore, Production Managers are always automating the flow of materials to and from an operation.

Whether materials handling automation is justifiable depends on flow strategy, when operations have a flexible flow strategy, job paths vary and there is little repeatability in materials handling. Such variability means that workers must move materials and equipment in open type containers, cars or lift trucks.

However, when operations have a line flow strategy and repeatability is high, handling can be automated.

In addition, other types of flexible automation are also available for firm with floor strategies that fall between these two expenses.

Two automated guiding vehicles used in process industries are Automated guided vehicle (driverless, battery driven truck) (AGV) and Automated Storage and retrieval system (AS/RS), a computer controlled method of storing and retrieving materials. (Same as Parkomat, the automatic Car parking system in Park Street, Kolkata).

1. **Wheel barrow:** A wheel barrow is a shallow box with shafts and wheels and is used for movements of materials within store/works.

Figure 10.1 shows a single wheel hand barrow and Figure 10.2 shows a two wheeled hand barrow.

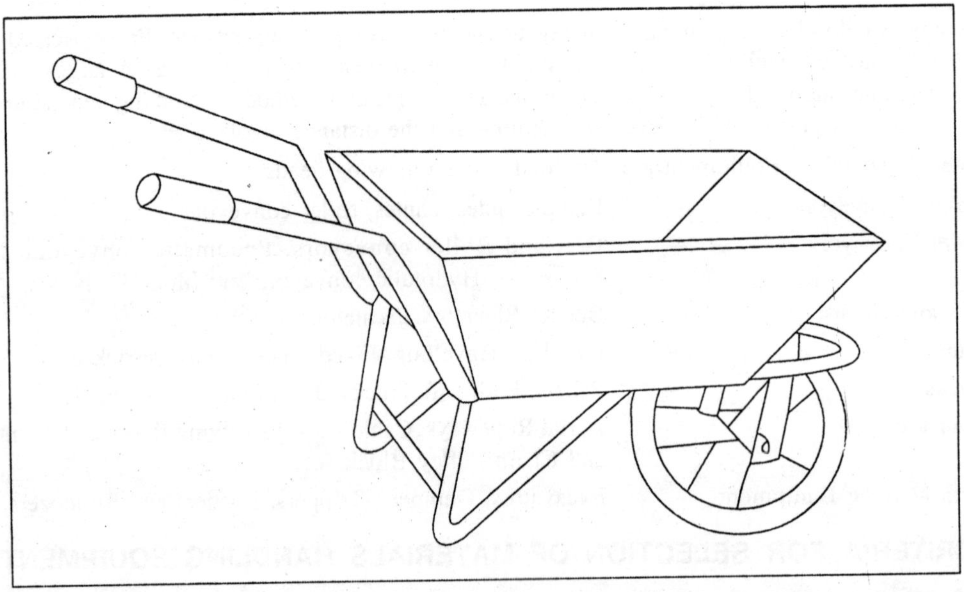

Figure 10.1 Single wheel hand barrow.

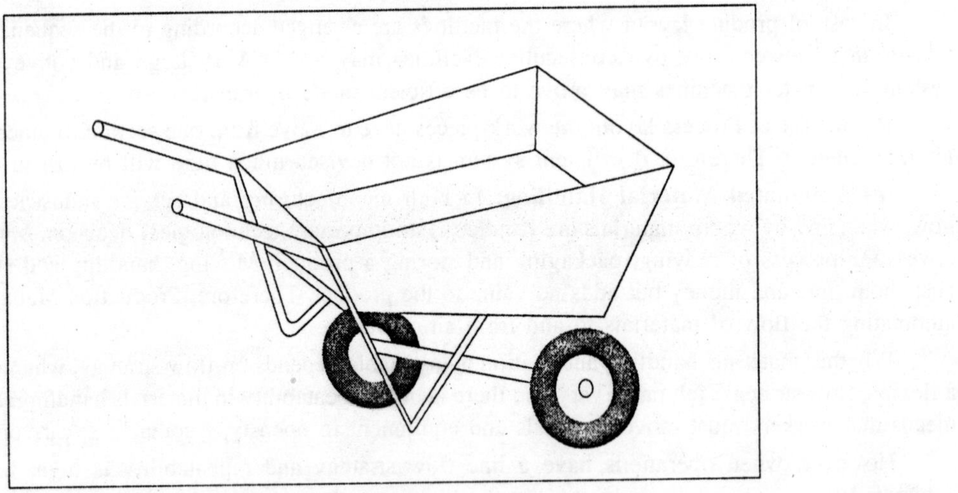

Figure 10.2 Two-wheeled hand barrow.

2. **Hand Trolleys:** Hand trolleys are the metal structures supported on three or four wheels. They may be either open type or closed type. Trolleys are used to transport materials from one location to another. Trolleys can be made in different configurations to satisfy specific needs.

Figure 10.3 shows a four-wheeled platform trolley.

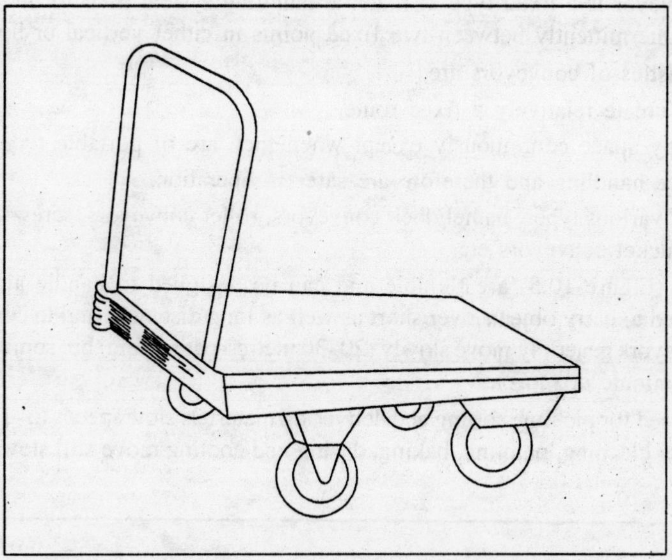

Figure 10.3 Four wheeled platform trolley.

3. **Stillage trucks:** Stillage trucks (Figure 10.4) consist of a wheeled platform manned by a drawbar and fitted with small hydraulic unit actuated by pumping the drawbar to raise or lower the platform. The truck platform is lowered and made to run between the legs of the stillage. Next the platform is raised and truck complete with load is taken away.

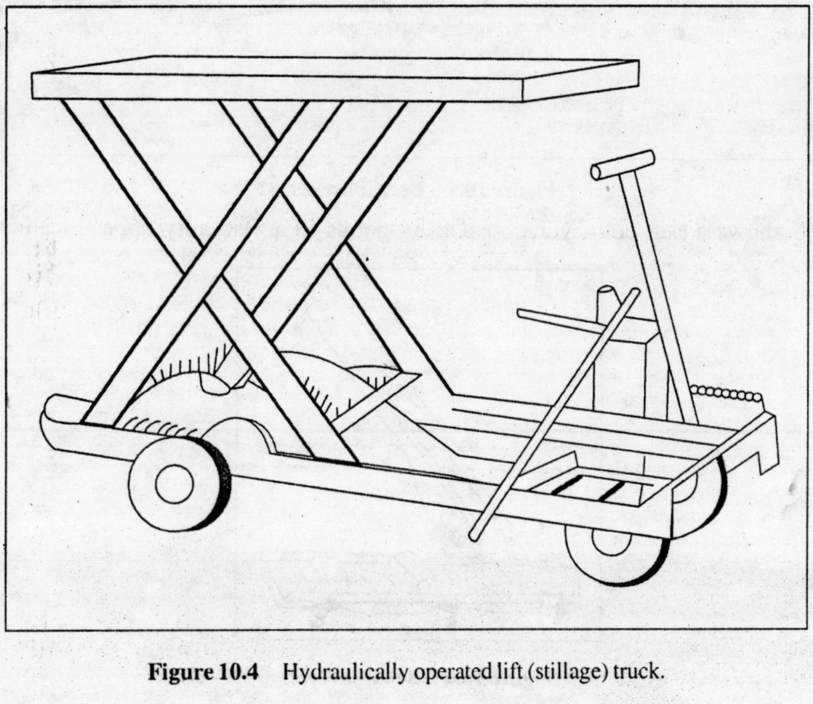

Figure 10.4 Hydraulically operated lift (stillage) truck.

4. Conveyors: Conveyor is a fixed type of material handling system used for moving material either continuously or intermittently between two fixed points in either vertical or horizontal direction.

Salient characteristics of conveyors are:

(*i*) Conveyors create relatively a fixed route.

(*ii*) They occupy space continuously except when they are of portable type.

(*iii*) They reduce handling and therefore are safer in operation.

Conveyors are of various types, namely belt conveyors, roller conveyors, screw conveyors, monorail conveyors and bucket conveyors etc.

(*a*) **Belt Conveyors** (Figure 10.5) are flexible and can be designed to handle almost anything. Belt conveyors are used to carry objects over short as well as long distances and to convey goods to upper floors. Belt-conveyors generally move slowly (20–30 metres-per minute) but some move at high speeds (200 metres per minute or more).

Belt Conveyors used for picking, sorting and delivering materials slow speeds (5–15 metres per minute) and those used for cleaning, painting, baking, drying and cooling move still slowly (0.5–2 metres per minute).

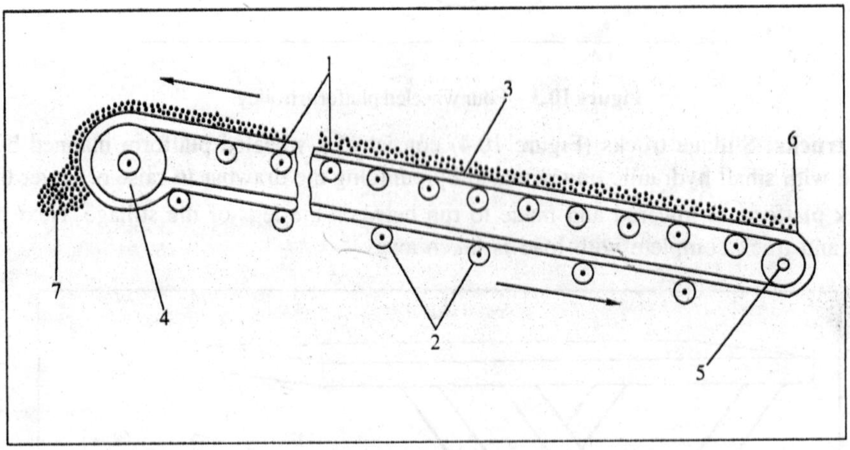

Figure 10.5 Belt Conveyor.

Figure 10.6 shows a belt conveyor transporting goods to a vertically upper location.

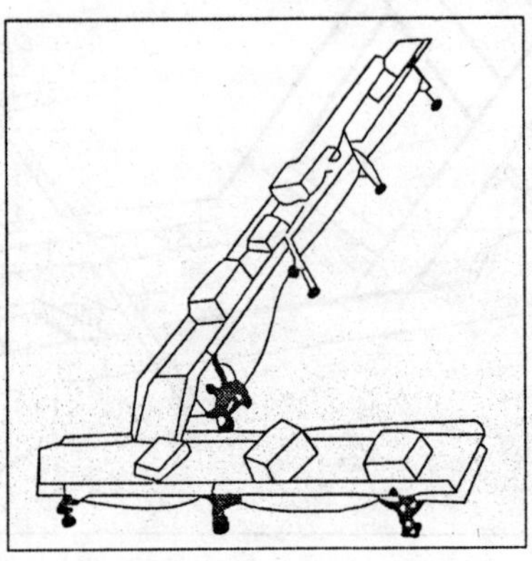

Figure 10.6 Belt Conveyor.

5. Roller Conveyors: Roller conveyors (Figure 10.7) are made of metal frame work bearing horizontal rollers placed at intervals. They use rollers gravity concept and are placed between two destinations so that goods can be pushed along the top of the rollers. The most application is to place a roller conveyor between machines so that a slight push will transfer the work to the next machine to be picked up by the operator on the line.

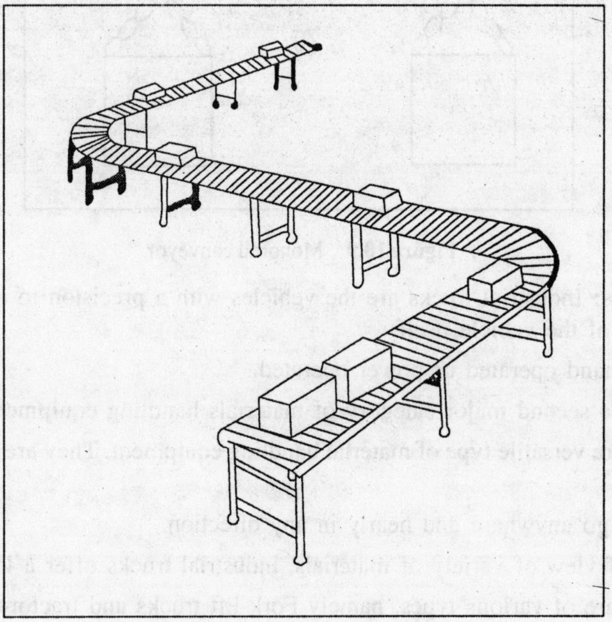

Figure 10.7 Roller conveyor.

6. Screw conveyors: Screw conveyors make use of a propeller like helical screw to push materials in one direction. Screw conveyors are used to handle bulk materials and only those which are not damaged by crushing.

Figure 10.8 shows a Screw conveyor.

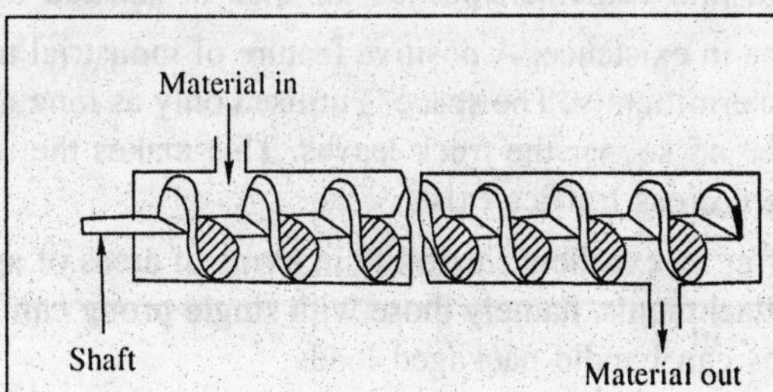

Figure 10.8 Screw conveyors.

7. Monorail Conveyors: Monorail (Figure 10.9) use hooks, racks, baskets etc. to transport variety of items.

The overhead monorail conveyors use a closed-circuit-track to ride parts in space and bring past the point of use at regular intervals.

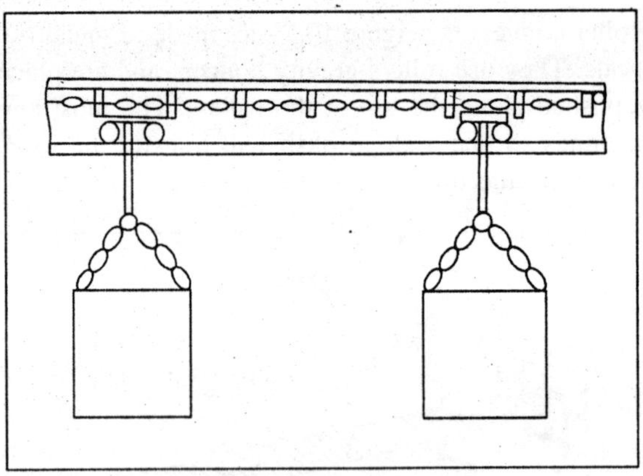

Figure 10.9 Monorail conveyor.

8. **Industrial Trucks:** Industrial trucks are the vehicles with a precision to carry and move materials by transportation of the vehicle itself.

These are either hand operated or power operated.

They represent the second major category of materials handling equipment.

Industrial trucks are versatile type of material handling equipment. They are characterised by freedom of movement.

These trucks can go anywhere and nearly in any direction.

From the point of view of variety of materials, industrial trucks offer a lot of flexibility.

Industrial trucks are of various types, namely Fork-lift trucks and tractor-trailors and others.

Industrial trucks are suitable where:

(*i*) The material require to be picked-up and moved intermittently over different routes. Firms engaged in intermittent manufacturing find that the best use of this material handling facility.

(*ii*) The distances are moderate. Unlike conveyors, there is no restriction on the distance over which materials may be moved.

(*iii*) Material can be put into containers/packed bundled or stacked to form unit loads.

(*iv*) Cross traffic may be in existence. A positive feature of industrial trucks is that they occupy the given space only intermittently. The space is utilised only as long as the truck is in that location and the same is free no sooner the truck leaves. This makes the industrial trucks, useful even in those areas where cross traffics exist.

Industrial trucks offer an excellent flexibility in terms of areas of application. They can be used with a variety of attachments, namely those with single prong can handle paper rolls and those with special clamps can handle packaged loads.

8.(*a*) **Fork lift trucks:** Fork lift trucks (Figure 10.10) have the forks attached to the columns of the truck. Besides being used for loading and unloading and transporting materials and components around the factory, they can be used for stacking materials at heights.

Fork lift trucks are suitable for short-distances (50–70 metres) travel.

Fork lift trucks are usually used for indoor material handling applications. Fork lifts are either diesel operated or battery operated fork lifts (normally used in chemical industries).

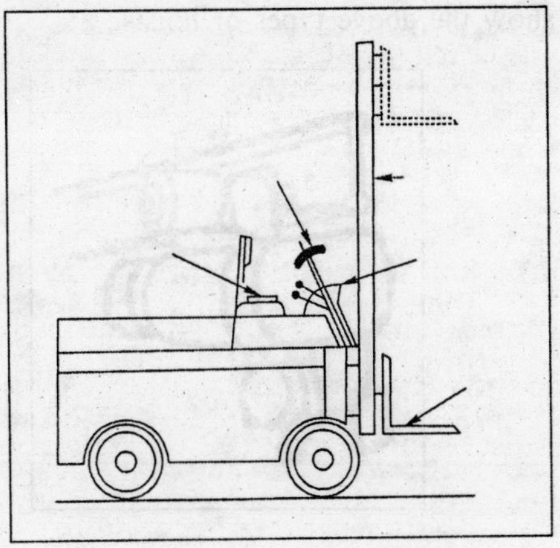

Figure 10.10 Fork Lift Truck.

8.(*b*) Tractor-Trailers: Tractor-Trailers (Figure 10.11) are used to transport materials over long distances.

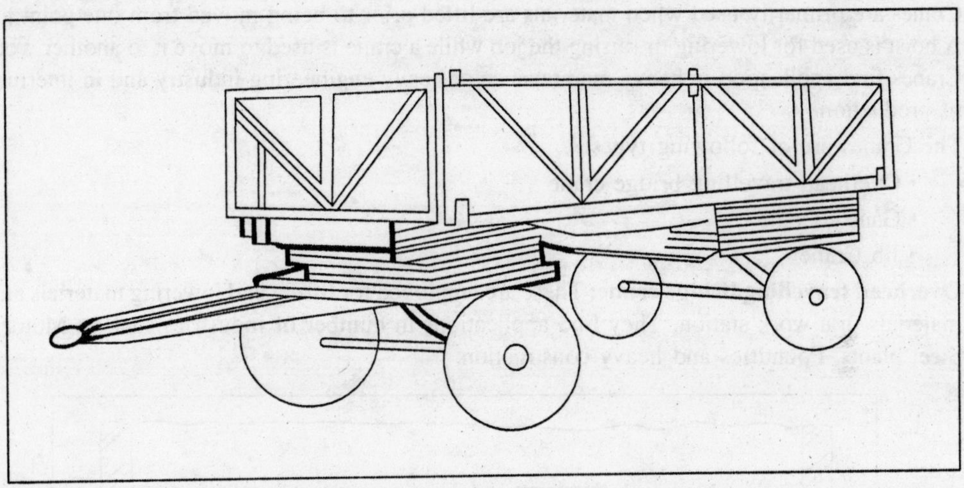

Figure 10.11 A four wheeled heavy duty tractor trailer.

9. Hoist: Hoist are used for loading and unloading of heavy or long objects and they are suitable for:

- Handling goods in assembly/testing department.
- Maintenance of machines and equipment.
- Loading and unloading of heavy jobs from machine.
- Loading and unloading of fixtures for initial machine set up.

Hoist are available in different capacities in terms of lift of the hoist (say 3, 4 and 5 metres etc.), weight/load carrying capacity of hoists (*i.e.*, 250, 500 and 1000 kgs. etc.) and single/double speed.

Hoists are of following types:

1. Chain hoist (manual)
2. Electric hoist
3. Pneumatic hoist.

Following Figure 10.12 show the above types of hoists.

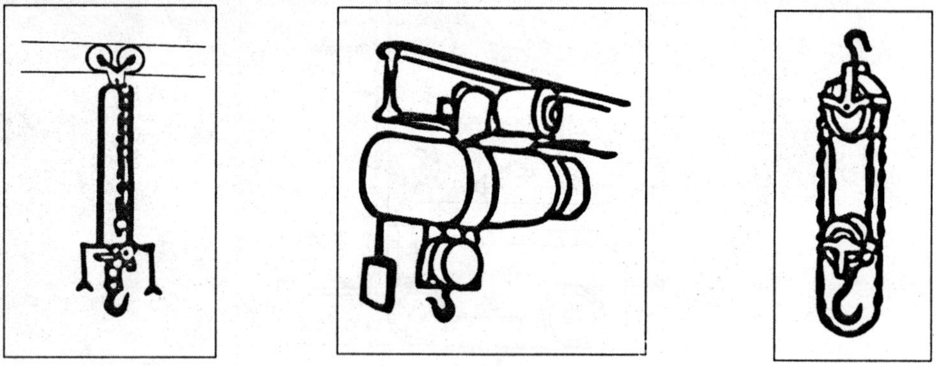

Figure 10.12 Materials handling equipment.

10. **Cranes:** Cranes are overhead devices capable of moving materials vertically and laterally in any area of limited length, width and height.

Cranes are primarily used when materials are lifted prior to being moved from one point to another. A hoist is used for lowering or raising the job while a crane is used to move it to another work station. Cranes find application in heavy maintenance or heavy engineering industry and in intermittent type of production.

The Cranes are of following types:

- Overhead travelling bridge crane
- Gantry Crane
- Jib Crane

(*a*) **Overhead travelling bridge crane:** These are employed for lifting and lowering materials and moving materials in a work station. They find applications in number of industries such as Motor vehicles, Steel plants, Foundries and heavy construction.

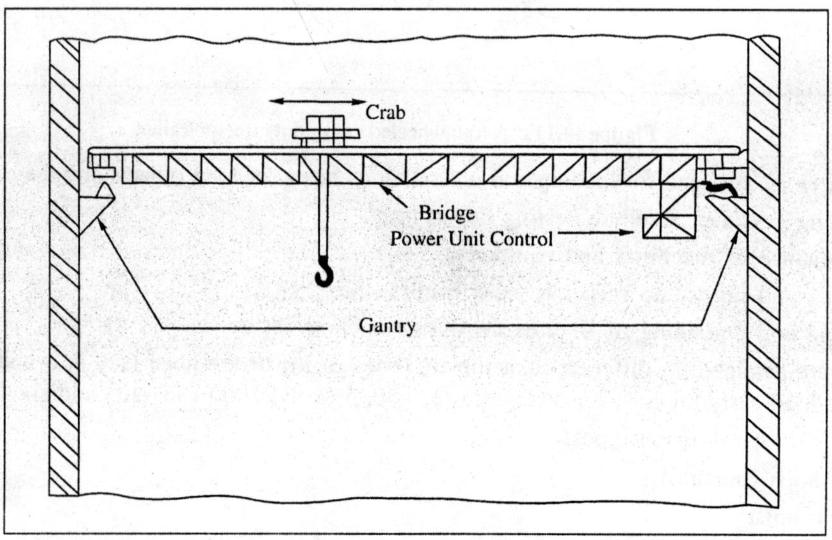

Figure 10.13 Overhead bridge crane.

(*b*) **Gantry Cranes:** Gantry cranes (Figure 10.14) are auxiliary to bridge cranes. They are on wheels and can be transported to the location for use.

Figure 10.14 Gantry Crane.

(*c*) **Jib Cranes:** Jib cranes (Figure 10.15) are preferred where lifting of hobs is required in few locations or where bridge cranes can be erected (say outside near the wall of the building).

A Jib crane is designed for a specific weight *i.e.*, 10 Tons, 30 Tons etc. As per Factories Act, cranes should be overhauled and tested once in a year and fitness certificate is to be obtained from the Chief Inspector of Factories.

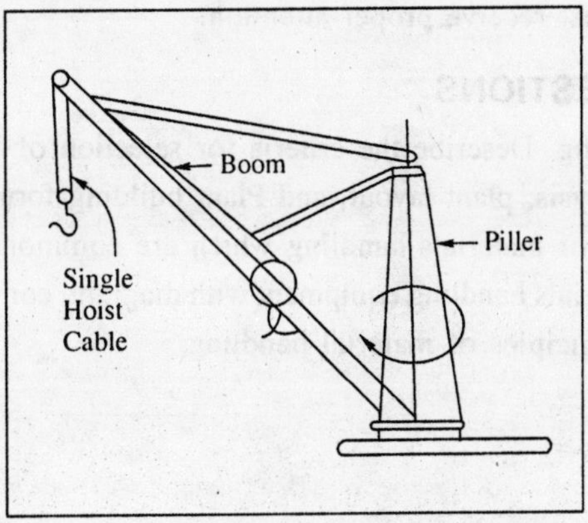

Figure 10.15 A Jib Crane.

10.6 EFFICIENCY OF MATERIAL HANDLING

Material handling efficiency is directly proportional to the size of the load handled. It is generally faster and cheaper to handle small parts by grouping them as one unit and moving them.

The efficiency of the material handling system is judged by the costs of handling materials.

Material handling costs can be classified into the following categories:

(*a*) Labour Cost (*b*) Space cost and (*c*) Cost of handling equipment.

Reduction in these costs (increase in efficiency) of materials handling is the primary objective of management.

Efficiency of material also means minimisation of :

(*i*) Bottlenecks and breakdowns

(*ii*) Misuse of space

(*iii*) Underutilisation of labour

(*iv*) Poor Customer Service

(*v*) Breakage and spoilage of materials

Efficient handling of materials also improves productivity, reduction in fatigue, and better employee safety etc.

The following steps can be taken to improve the efficiency in materials handling:

(*a*) Mechanisation: Use of mechanical devices helps to reduce costs of handling materials. But cost savings should be large enough to cover the cost of owning and maintaining the handling equipment.

(*b*) Better Systems Design: Methods study is useful in improving plant layout and materials handling system.

Proper selection of physical facilities reduces the number and frequency of movements.

(*c*) Effective Organisation Structure: An efficient organisation set up helps in better co-ordination between Production and Maintenance and other departments.

However, many a problems of materials handling can be avoided by improving the existing plant layout.

Material handling activity can be made efficient by using some of the principles of material handling.

Mechanisation of material handling is an important aspect and as such selection of the proper material handling equipment must receive proper attention.

10.7 PROBABLE QUESTIONS

1. Define Material Handling. Describe the criteria for selection of Material handling equipment.

2. "Material handling analysis, plant layout, and Plant building form a composition study."—Justify.

3. Discuss various means of materials handling which are commonly used in manufacturing plants.

4. Describe any three materials handling equipment with diagram, commonly used in a Production plant.

5. Discuss the guiding principles of material handling.

11

Work Study and Productivity

• *Work Study* • *Method Study (Motion Study)* • *Work Measurement, Time and Motion Study* • *Performance Rating: Measuring Achievements* • *Work Sampling* • *Work Study and Productivity* • *Micromotion Studies and Therbligs* • *Ergonomics* • *Probable Questions.*

11.1 WORK STUDY

(i) Introduction: Work-study is based on the assumption that, for every job, in the light of present knowledge there is:

(*a*) one best way of doing it.

(*b*) a scientific method is the best and surest way of finding this 'one best way.'

(*c*) the time taken for doing the job by the best way, can be measured and set as standard.

(ii) Definition: Work-study is the management technique to investigate all the factors affecting the efficiency and economy of an organisation under review in order to improve it.

Work-study is carried out with a view:

(*a*) to standardise the method of doing a task.

(*b*) to determine the standard time for doing a task, for use in wage payment.

(*c*) to minimise the unit cost of production by selecting proper machine tools, optimum cutting parameters and proper process.

(*d*) to minimise the materials movements, operators movement, idle time of the worker's and machines by proper layout of the plant.

(*e*) to eliminate the unnecessary human motion in performing a task.

(*f*) to utilise the facilities such as man, machine and materials most effectively.

(iii) Techniques of work-study: There are 2 techniques:

(*a*) Work measurement

(*b*) Method Study

(iv) Work-study Procedures: The following procedures sequence wise are given below:

(a) Select: Select the job to be studied.

(b) Record: Record all the relevant facts about the job from direct observation.

(c) Examine: Examine each recorded fact clinically.

(d) Develop: Develop the most efficient and economic method of doing that job.

(e) Measure: Measure the quantity of work involved in the job by the developed method and calculate the standard time for doing the job.

(f) Install: Install the new method as standard practice.

(g) Maintain: Maintain the standard practice by regular checks.

111.2 METHOD STUDY (Motion Study)

Method study is defined as a systematic and critical study of the existing method of doing a task, with a view to evolve the most efficient and economic method of doing it.

(*a*) Objective of Method Study

(*i*) To improve the procedure of doing a work or the process of doing the work.

(*ii*) To improve the plant layout.

(*iii*) To minimise the human movements, for minimum fatigue of the operators.

(*iv*) To maximise the utility of man, machines and materials.

(*v*) To improve the overall working environment.

(*b*) Method Study Procedures: Following are the basic steps for Method Study: (Sequence wise)

(*i*) Select

(*ii*) Record

(*iii*) Examine

(*iv*) Develop

(*v*) Define

(*vi*) Install

(*vii*) Maintain.

(*c*) Gilbreth has developed various symbols of Motion Study: Some of them are as follows:

Symbols	Motion
o	Operation
□	Inspection
⇒	Transport
D	Delay
∇	Storage

(*d*) Motion Economy: The best method of performing a job is to observe the principles for increasing the speed to achieve more economy in production and thereby minimising the cost of Production. There are basic 26 Principles of Motion economy which form the basis for improving the efficiency and reducing fatigue in manual work.

1. Principles related to the use of "Human Body". This involves nine Principles such as:

- Both hands should start and complete together at the same time.
- Both hands should not be idle at the same time except during the rest period.
- Use both hands simultaneously and use the best motion sequence.
- Hand motions should be confined to the lowest possible classification in order to reduce fatigue.
- Utilise momentum to assist the worker.
- Smooth continuous motions produce less fatigue.
- Ballistic movements are faster easier and more accurate than controlled movements.
- Sequence of motions should be arranged to build rhythm and automatically into the operation.
- Hands should be relieved of all work that can be done by feet.

2. Principles related to the arrangement of the work place: This also involves nine principles as follows:

- All tools should be placed at a fixed place with easy reach.
- All tools and devices should be placed in front of the operator.
- Provide gravity feed bins and use power or gravity conveyors to transport materials.
- Use chutes or conveyors for drop-deliveries of materials at the required place.
- Storage place of tools and tackles should facilitate the best sequence of motion.
- Illumination must be proper at the work place.
- Provide working tables, stools and chairs for the worker to perform work.
- Chairs provided should make good posture possible.
- Keep the shop in neat and clean condition.

3. Principles related to the design of Tools and Equipment: This involves eight principles as follows:

- Use power operated tools.
- Use foot pedals.
- Reduced noise is good for better performance.
- Tools should be easily available to select operation.
- Wherever possible, two or more tools should be combined.
- Handles on tools and cranks should be designed to permit maximum contact with hands.
- When each finger performs some specific movement, (as in type writing) the load should be distributed in accordance with the inherent capacities of the fingers.
- The location of levers, cross bars and hand wheels etc. should be so decided that the operator can operate with the least change in body position.

All the above principles are covered in the new subject called "Ergonomics". Application of most of the above principles are made in automobiles.

Examples:

1. The shape and size of the handles of motor cycles/scooters have been improved to the present standard through application of above principles to give more comforts to the driver.
2. The racing cycles, motor cycles and cars have different types of handles than ordinary varieties.
3. The length of levers of gears and clutch, the size of the steering wheel, the position of the accelerator and breaks are designed by using above principles with respect to the position of the driver in a manner that they can be operated by the driver within minimum movement of the body.
4. The levers of machine tools such as lathe, drilling machines etc. are coloured, generally in red while the body of these machine tools have grey colour.

11.3 WORK-MEASUREMENT, TIME AND MOTION STUDY

For improving the productivity of an organisation, work-measurement is very important. It is a technique of establishing the proper time required in performing a job or work.

Since it is concerned with measurement of time in relation to motion or movement, it is also called Time and Motion Study.

(*a*) Objectives of Work-Measurement

(*i*) To analyse the activities for doing job with the view to reduce or eliminate some unnecessary or repetitive activities so that human effort is minimised.

(*ii*) To compare the time of performance by alternative methods.

(*iii*) To standardise the efficient method of performing a job.

(*iv*) To stadardise the condition for efficient performance.

(*v*) To determine optimum number of men and machines.

(*vi*) To determine man and machines ratio for effective and efficient utilisation of both.

(*vii*) To provide information and basis for Production, Planning and Scheduling.

(*viii*) To determine the normal time for a job, to be used as a basis for wages incentive schemes for the workers.

(*b*) Techniques of Work-Measurement: Work measurement refers to the study of work content of a job so as to lay down, a fair day's work. A fair day's work is determined by measuring the time for a qualified worker to carry on a specific task at a defined level of performance.

Work measurement is closely related with method study. Time involved in the performance of a job can be standardised only after the work methods, tools and condition are standardised.

The very first step in work measurement is to define the best method.

Major techniques of work-measurement are: (*i*) Time Study (*ii*) Work Sampling (*iii*) Predetermined Motion Time Standards (PMTS) (*iv*) Analytical estimating.

The following are the techniques of work-measurement:

1. Time and Motion Study.

2. Work sampling.

3. Predetermined Motion Time Standard (PMTS)]

4. Analytical estimating

(*a*) Motion Time Analysis (MTA)

(*b*) Basic Motion Time (BMT)

(*c*) Work Factor (WF)

(*d*) Motion time Measurement (MTM)

(*e*) Motion Time Data (MTD)

1. Time Study: Instruments are required: Stop Watch, Motion Picture Camera, Electronic Timer.

Basic Procedure for time study:

(*i*) Select the job.

(*ii*) Break into small elements of activity suitable for measuring the time.

(*iii*) Measure and record the time taken by the operator for each element.

(*iv*) Determine the number of such reading necessary for getting the normal time or representative time for each element.

(*v*) Rate the operator's performance, determine the allowances and then finally calculate the standard time.

$$\underset{\text{(Basic)}}{\text{Normal Time}} = \underset{\text{(Observed time)}}{\text{Actual time}} \times \text{Rating factor}$$

$$\text{Standard Time} = \text{Normal time} + \text{Allowance.}$$

The allowances are Personal allowance, Fatigue allowance, Delay allowance, Continuously allowances, Policy allowances.

(*a*) **Rating Factor:** "Rating" is that process during which the Industrial Engineer compares the performance of the operator under observation with his own concept of normal performance. For every job, there is a normal performance rate. If we assign 100% to normal performance, then other performance rate may be rated lower or higher than this.

(*b*) **Westing House System of Rating:** At Westing-house (USA) a system of rating an operator was developed on the basis of following factors:

(*a*) Skill (*b*) Effort (*c*) Conditions (*d*) Consistency.

Problem 1: The observed time for an element is one minute and ratings are given below:

Skill	—	Excellent,
Effort	—	Excessive,
Condition	—	Good,
Consistency	—	Good

Determine the normal time (basic time) for the element under observation.

Solution. Refer the Performance Rating Table

Skill	=	+ 0.11
Effort	=	+ 0.12
Condition	=	+ 0.02
Consistency	=	+ 0.01
Total	=	0.26 (final and overall rating)

The normal time = Observed time × Rating factor

$$= 1 \times \frac{126}{100} = 1.26 \text{ min.}$$

Note: If the final rating value come (–)ve, then the Normal Time will be less than the observed time.

(*c*) **Synthetic Rating:** Actual time is recorded as before. Performance time for many elements have been standardised and tabulated. These are called PMTS-*i.e.*, Pre-Determine Motion Time Standard.

$$R = \frac{P}{A}$$ R = Performance Rating Factor

P = PMTS in minutes.

A = Average of actual times of an element in minutes.

(*d*) **Time Study:** It is the process of directly observing and recording the time required for performing different elements of a job under specified condition.

The step involved in Time Study are as under:

(*a*) Plan time study performance.

(*b*) Analyse the job into elements.

(*c*) Record the time taken for each element.

(*d*) Determine the rating.

(*e*) Calculate basic time for each element.

(*f*) Assess relaxation allowance for each element.

(*g*) Add contingency allowance.

(*h*) Determine the standard time for the job.

(*e*) **Time and Motion Study:** Time and motion study equipment are following:

(*i*) Stop watch (*ii*) Motion Picture Camera (*iii*) Machine using moving tapes (*iv*) Electronic Timer. Basic Procedure for Timer and Motion Study.

Following steps are essential for carrying out Time and Motion Study for any operation:

1. Select the job for study.
2. Divide the operation for doing the selected job into elements, which could be measured with the time measuring device.
3. Measure and record the time taken by the operator for each element.
4. Determine the number of such readings necessary for getting the normal time or representative time for each element.
5. Rate the operator's performance, determine the allowances and then calculate the standard time.

   Normal Time or Basic Time = Actual time × Rating Factor (observed time)

Rating Factor is known as 'Levelling Factor'. This is expressed as a percentage of the efficiency of representative operator, which indicates how efficient an operator is in comparison to some of his average fellow workers.

11.4 PERFORMANCE RATING: Measuring Achievements

Quantitative measurement of the achievement of objectives is the second step in incentive planning Process. It involves the following activities.

(*a*) **Determining the physical factors** which reflect achievement of the objectives. Quantity of output, time required per unit of output, consumption of materials, power of fuel are examples of such factors.

(*b*) **Analysing the factors** to identify their interdependence, relation to human effort etc.

(*c*) **Developing the standards** of achievement in terms of the selected factors. Work measurement and statistical techniques are used for this purpose. The unit of measurement for relating effort to reward is also decided.

(*d*) **Designing a method** for assessing performance. The achievement is usually measured in the form of an index known as Performance Index or Achievement Index.

This is calculated as follows:

$$\text{Achievement Index} = \frac{\text{Actual Performance}}{\text{Standard Performance}} \times 100$$

A reference index or base index is also decided. Incentive bonus is paid when the performance index exceeds the base index which may vary between reference index and standard index.

Reference index implies the point at which actual performance is equal to the standard performance.

(*e*) **Determining the unit manpower** for the assessment. When an individual is rewarded on his own performance, the incentive becomes most effective. But group incentive schemes may be more appropriate when the performance of a particular worker depends on the performance of other workers in group.

(*f*) **Developing the achievement** must reward relationship. The rate at which the incentive payment increases with increases in performance depends upon reward-performance relationship. As far as possible employees should be rewarded in direct proportion to their performance. Performance-reward relationship should be easy to understand so that employees themselves can calculate the reward.

11.5 WORK SAMPLING

Work Sampling or Activity Sampling is a work measurement technique in which a series of random observation of a worker or machine are taken over a period of time. It is based on the statistical theory of sampling. A sufficiently large numbers of instantaneous observation of an operator of machine are made to obtain a reasonably accurate picture of the time spent on different activities.

Work Sampling is thus a method of finding the percentage occurrence of a certain activity or delay by statistical theory of sampling. It is also known as activity, sampling, random observation method, ratio delay study and activity ratio study.

From the previously determined time study, basic time for each element of the job is calculated. Assess relaxation time and add contingency allowance to determine the standard time for the job.

(*a*) **Work Sampling Method:** Work sampling involves estimating the proportion of time spent by people and machines on activities, based on a large number of observation. These activities might include producing a product or service, doing paper work, waiting for instructions, waiting for maintenance or being idle.

The underlying assumption is that the proportion of time during which the activity is observed in the sample will be the proportion of time spent on the activity in general.

Data from work sampling also can be used to estimate how effective machines or workers are, estimate the allowances needed to set standard for use with other work measurement methods, determine job content and help assess the cost of job or activities.

(*b*) **Work Sampling Procedure:** Conducting a work sampling study involves the following steps:

1. Define the activities.
2. Design the observation form.
3. Determine the length of the study.
4. Determine the initial sample size.
5. Select random observation times using a random number table.
6. Determine the observer schedule.
7. Observe the activities and record the data.
8. Decide whether additional sampling is required.

A work sampling study should be conducted over a period of time that is representative of normal work conditions in which each activity occurs a representative number of times.

A continuous activity throughout the week and month and year, may need study for few weeks only.

The sample size affects the degree of precision that can be expected from work sampling for any desired level of statistical confidence.

Work sampling involves estimating proportions, so the sampling distribution is the binomial distribution.

Confidence Interval for a work sampling study:

p = Sample proportion (number of occurrences divided by the sample size)

e = maximum error in the estimate.

Following interval contains the true proportion with a specified degree of precision:

$p - e \leq p \leq p + e$

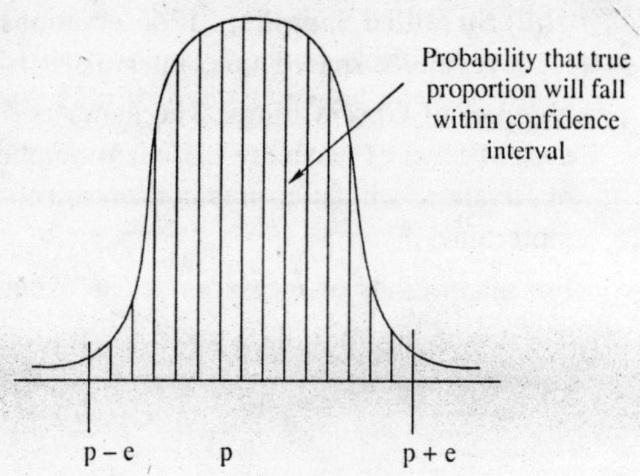

Figure 20.1

(*c*) **Usefulness of Work Sampling:** The work sampling method is used frequently to estimate the proportion of time that people of machines spend on particular activities. Because it offers certain advantages over other approaches. No special training is required for the observers, no stop watches are needed, and several studies can be conducted simultaneously.

In addition, workers themselves often prefer this method of work measurement because it typically is directed at the activities of groups, rather than individuals.

The major disadvantages to work sampling is the large number of brief observations required to provide a reasonable degree of precision for the estimate.

This method is usually not used for setting standards for repetitive jobs.

(*d*) **Work Sampling in Industry:** Consider an industry where there are hundred machines and hundred workers and each worker is preassigned with specific jobs.

The management is interested in finding:

(*i*) the percentage of the day of worker is working and the percentage of the day he is idle.

(*ii*) the working and idle time of a worker to fix up performance rate.

(*iii*) to establish the standard time for an operation.

One method to get these information is to appoint a time study expert who will be present in the factory with stop-watch and continuously note down the working and idle time of the workers. This is a very time consuming method and has its limitations.

Another method known as "work-sampling" was introduced by L.C. Tippett in the British Textile Industry. Work sampling is based on the law of probability. In this method (work-sampling) some random observations are taken of the situation and then conclusions are drawn.

For example, 50 random observations are taken in 10 days in an industry and 35 times the workers are found working and 15 times not working.

It may be interpreted as every day 70% of the time the workers are working and 30% of the time not working in the industry.

(*e*) **Types of Work-Sampling**

(*i*) **Systematic Sampling:** If observation are taken at a fixed interval of time, it is called systematic sampling.

(*ii*) **Random Sampling:** If observations are taken at irregular or random interval of times, it is called random sampling.

(*iii*) **Stratified Sampling:** It observations are taken at random spaced time after a finite number of regularly spaced time intervals it is known as stratified sampling.

(*f*) **Number of Observations:** The numbers of observations, affects the time and cost of study. For any desired level of accuracy sufficient number of observations are must. While inadequate number of observations will fail to predict the result correctly, excess observations will be unnecessary and involve more time.

For many kinds of measurement an accuracy of $\pm$ 5% is considered satisfactory.

The following formula is used for finding this accuracy:

$$S \times P = 2\sqrt{\frac{P(1-P)}{N}}$$

where S = desired relative accuracy

P = Percentage occurrence of an activity or delay being measured expressed as a percentage of the total number of observations as a decimal.

N = Total number of random observations (sample size).

Problem 20.1 Calculate the number of observations necessary for an accuracy of ± 5%, and the confidence level of 95%, if $P = 0.25$.

Solution. In this case $S = \pm 5\% = \pm 0.05$

Using above formula and putting the values

$$0.05 \times 0.25 = 2\sqrt{\frac{0.25\,(1-0.25)}{N}}$$

or

$$N = \frac{4 \times 0.25 \times 0.75}{(0.05)^2 \times (0.25)^2}$$

Problem 20.2 Check whether the number of observations is sufficient for ± 5% accuracy and 95% confidence limit, if:

(*i*) the number of observations of machines working = 3000.

(*ii*) the number of observations of machines idle = 1000.

(*iii*) Total observations = 4000.

Solution. Here,

$$P = \frac{\text{Observations of idle machines}}{\text{Total numbers of observations}}$$

$$= \frac{1000}{4000} = 0.25$$

Using the above formula:

$$S.\,P. = 2\sqrt{\frac{P(1-P)}{N}}$$

$$S \times 0.25 = 2\sqrt{\frac{0.25 \times 0.75}{4000}}$$

$$\therefore \quad S = \pm\, 0.056 = \pm\, 5.6\%$$

Since the valtue of S exceeds ± 5% so the number of observations is insufficient and some more observations are required.

(g) Procedure for making a Work-Sampling study

1. Define the problem:
   (*a*) Objective of the study to be noted.
   (*b*) Describe each element in detail.
2. Obtain permission from the Incharge of the section where study is to be done and convince the operators of the objective of study.
3. The confidence level and accuracy of final result should be determined before hand.
4. Make a pilot study to estimate the value of P.
5. Design the study in the following way:
   (*i*) Calculate the number of observations required for the above level of accuracy and confidence level.
   (*ii*) Calculate the numbers of observes required.

(*iii*) Calculate the numbers of days required for the observations.

(*iv*) Plan the route to be followed by the observers and the timings for each observation.

(*v*) design suitable observation sheet.

(*h*) Take observations as per plan and then analysis and summarise the observations.

(*i*) Recorded all the observations on the sheet.

(*ii*) Summarise all the data at the end of each day.

(*iii*) Determine the control limits.

(*i*) Check the accuracy of data at the end of study and state conclusions.

11.6 WORK STUDY AND PRODUCTIVITY

(*a*) **Productivity and work study:** Productivity improves with the reduction in the wastages of worker's time, machine-time, materials and power etc.

Work-study reduces wastage of time, efforts and increases the efficiency of man and machine. Thus, the work study techniques improves Productivity.

The main objective of a manufacturing organisation is to utilise its resources productivity and profitably.

Productivity holds the key to prosperity of a company, an individual and of the nation.

(*b*) **Factors affecting the Industrial Productivity:** Productivity is a technique of extraction of greater output from the inherent "input creativity" of various resources through the "conversion efficiency". The "conversion efficiency" which changes the level of productivity either individually or jointly.

The important factors are classified as under:

1. **Technological Factors:** Application of automation and more and more mechanisation of manual activities in the plant.
2. **Managerial Factors:** Improved systems of motivation and morale boosting of employees, and application of improved management systems would help.
3. **Financial Factors:** Proper use of funds for research and development activities, use of the latest technology, use of the most productive machine and Process would be beneficial.
4. **Natural Factors:** Favourable climatic conditions can enhance labour productivity.

   The geographical and physical factors such as availability of plenty water for a Pulp and Paper Plant, and sufficient Iron Ore and coking coal for a Steel Plant in the proximity places can enhance productivity.
5. **Sociological Factors:** The genetic characteristics, racial quality, Social attitude towards the work and working conditions can influence on Productivity in plant.
6. **Government Policy:** The Government policy regarding financial incentives, taxation policy, tariff policy, labour laws etc. also affect the productivity.

11.7 MICROMOTION STUDIES AND THERBLIGS

Micromotion studies are expensive to conduct and should be undertaken, if it is economically justified.

Two hundred process charts, simo charts, cycle graphs and chrono cycle graphs are used for the study of operations at the work place.

The above four techniques are the main techniques for micromotion analysis.

The micro motion group of techniques is based on the idea of dividing human activities into divisions of movements or groups of movements according to the purpose for which they are made.

(*a*) **Therbligs:** Therblig is the reverse of the name Gilbreth *i.e.*, Frank B. Gilbreth who had developed 17 nos. of specific division of movement and named each movement as Therblig. ASME (American Society of Mechanical Engineers) later in 1940's had added one additional Therblig "Hold". Thus there are total 18 nos. Therebligs which facilitate the synthesis of activities.

To help people become familiar with Therbligs the charts shown in the table below are required to be coloured as indicated.

Fig. : THERBLIG CHART SYMBOLS

Nos.	Symbol	Name	Description	Colour
1		Search	Locate an article	Black
2.		Find	Mental reaction at end of search	Grey
3.	→	Select	Selection from a number	Light Grey
4.		Grasp	Taking hold	Red
5.		Hold	Prolonged grasp	Gold Ochre
6.		Transport Loaded	Moving an article	Green
7.	9	Position	Placing in a definite location	Blue
8.	#	Assemble	Putting Parts together	Violet
9.	U	Use	Causing a device to perform its function	Purple
10.	#	Dis-Assemble	Separating Parts	Light Violet
11.		Inspect	Examine or test	Burnt Ochre
12.	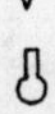	Pre-Position	Placing an article ready for use	Pale Blue
13.		Release Load	Release an article	Carmine Red
14.		Transport Empty	Movement of a body member	Olive Green
15.		Rest	Pause to overcome	Orange
16.		Unavoidable Delay	Idle-outside person's control	Yellow
17.	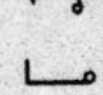	Avoidable Delay	Idle-within person's control	Lemon Yellow
18.	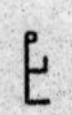	Plan	Mental Process before action	Brown

Each Therblig symbol is used in place of process chart symbol.

A Therblig chart is often used as a first step towards the construction of charts that do possess a time scale.

The most convenient method for collecting such data is by recording the nos. on 16 mm cine film and then analysing the film picture.

(*b*) **The Simo Chart:** Simo stands for simultaneous motion cycle chart. It is one of the recording techniques of micro-motion study and records simultaneously the different Therbligs performed by different parts of the body of one or more operators on a common time scale.

For the work involving the use of hands, it is desired that work should be taken from both the hands. If the participation of both hands are equal, it is the best thing. Type writing is an example of this system.

The SIMO chart for left hand and right hand, inform about the degree of participation of both the hands.

The SIMO chart can be used as a tool for:

(*i*) reducing the work cycle.

(*ii*) reducing the possibility of fatigue due to excessive work done by only one hand or one part of the body.

(*iii*) relaying out the work place.

(*iv*) comparing different work-layouts on the basis of percentage utilisation of the body parts or hands or cycle time.

11.8 ERGONOMICS

(*a*) **Introduction:** Ergonomics is known as Human Engineering and is defined by I.L.O. (International Labour Organisation) as "the application of human biological sciences in conjunction with engineering sciences to the worker and his working environment, so as to obtain maximum satisfaction for the worker, which at the same time, enhances productivity."

Ergonomics consists of words 'Ergo' (mean work) and 'Norms' (means natural laws).

Thus, Ergonomics is a multi-disciplinary Science comprising subjects like Anatomy, Psychology, Physiology, Sociology, Engineering, Anthropology, Physics and Medicine.

The task of ergonomics is to develop such conditions for workers, which are necessary to reduce physical work load to improve working postures, facilitate instrument handling, and thus improves the quality or working life, maximise efficiency of production, operators and to minimise human errors.

(*b*) **Objectives of Ergonomics:** Objectives of the study of ergonomics is to optimise the integration of man and machines in order to increase productivity with accuracy.

It involves in the design of:

(*i*) a work place suitable for the worker.

(*ii*) Machinery and controls, so as to minimise mental and physical strain on the worker to enable the improvement in efficiency.

(*iii*) a favourable environment for performing the task most effectively.

(*iv*) task and work organisation.

(*c*) **Work Place Design:** Pains in the back and neck and other muscular strains due to incorrect seating and working postures are common in industry, where most of the jobs are performed by the operators either in sitting or standing in a fixed posture for a long duration.

This also includes improper table and chair provided to the staff working in an office.

The interaction of the operator with the immediate work place around him is influenced by many factors such as seat design, the working desk and adjacent machine.

These factors are responsible for the position and postures of the users, and hence their efficiency.

(*d*) **Location of Tools and Materials:** All tools and materials required must be located within the normal grasp area and as far as possible in front of the worker. This will enable him to travel lesser distances to pick up and put these tools and materials frequently at desired place so as to save time and energy. For the assembly job, it is desirable to provide such arrangement so that the components can slide along the smooth surface and the worker picks them up. It will greatly reduce time and effort.

(*e*) **Proper Chairs:** Chairs permitting proper posture for the workers and staff should be provided. This is possible when the working on the work bench. Performing a job on floor in sitting position or on table in standing position requires more energy.

The height of chair and the work bench must be arranged in such a way so that the worker may not feel any difficulty while working. Their height must be such that the top of bench remains at the height of the elbow of the worker.

If possible, the height of the bench must be such that worker can work both in sitting and standing position.

(*f*) **Working Desk:** As explained earlier, all the tools and materials must be located within the normal grasp area and as close in front of the operator as possible.

Working desk must be so designed so that use of both hands can be taken simultaneously.

(*g*) **Proper Work-Place layout:** Proper Work-Place layout also helps in maintaining proper body and eye motions of operators, which minimises fatigue for the worker.

11.9 PRODUCTIVITY

(*i*) **Productivity and Production:** Productivity is the ratio between inputs (resources) and output (goods and services). There is a reciprocal relationship between cost and productivity. An increase in Productivity leads to a fall in the cost per unit and subsequently to a rise in profits.

Symbolically, $\text{Productivity} = \dfrac{\text{Output}}{\text{Input}}$

Thus, productivity is the ratio between the output of wealth produced and input of resource used up in the process of production.

Productivity concept guides the management in production systems and in measurement of success In other words, Productivity is the quality that indicates how the labour, capital, materials and energy are effectively utilised.

Higher productivity generally results in lower per unit costs and thereby in higher profits.

Productivity is different from production. Production may be increased but productivity may fall due to inefficient use of input resources.

Lastly, Higher Productivity help to increase the prosperity and standard of living of people in a country. It is through higher productivity that workers can expect higher wages, shareholders can expect better dividends and customers can expect lower prices.

(*ii*) **Measurement of Productivity:** Productivity has become a crucial economic and social issue. For a manager, productivity is a measure of work performance. Without continuous productivity improvement, an enterprise can not successfully face competition.

Higher productivity is beneficial for all industry, Government and Public. Higher Productivity requires elimination of waste in all forms. It is necessary to identify and eliminate the wastage of materials, machinery, time, manapower, space and the other resources. Several techniques e.g. work study, value analysis, operation research, *SOC*, inventory control, ergonomics etc. are used for this purpose.

Productivity may measured on aggregate basis or separately for different individual inputs.

Overall Productivity: From an overall view point, Productivity is the ratio of total outputs to total inputs.

Total Productivity Index (*TPI*)

$$= \frac{\text{Total value of output}}{\text{Total cost of inputs (Land + Labour + Material + Energy and Fuel + Capital)}}$$

Total productivity may be calculated for a department or for the whole organisation or for an industry or for the nation as whole. Total productivity by itself does not indicate anything. It has to be related to earlier years to find the trend.

The simplest and straight forward method for measurement of productivity is to convert all inputs into money value. The amount of money spent on wages, on materials and on capital equipment when added together would indicate input.

However, many adjustments are needed for work in progress, stock in hand, depreciation on capital equipment and the interest payable on capital. Further adjustment must be made for inflation.

To avoid the problem of inflation, method called "Man Year Approach" may be used. Under this approach all the inputs are converted into man years as follows:

(*a*) Labour – Average number of persons employed during the year.

(*b*) Materials – Money spent on materials during the year divided by average industrial income in the country at that time.

(*c*) Capital – (Cost of Capital divided by average industrial income) divided by years of amortisation.

Cost of capital refers to interest payments, depreciation etc.

The sum of *a*, *b* and *c* will yield resources man years.

$$\text{Total Productivity Measure } (TPM) = \frac{\text{Total Output}}{\text{Resource man years}}$$

This measure can be calculated for the total enterprise as well as for individual departments.

In order to judge the trends in Productivity, Productivity index number for various years can be calculated by taking productivity in base year as 100.

Ratio of Profit to value added is a better measure provided adjustment is made for inflation.

Productivity of an individual inputs is known as factor (partial) productivity. It is helpful in identifying in depth the causes for low productivity and initiate appropriate corrective action. It is only an approximation because productivity is the outcome of all factors (Materials, Labour and Machinery etc.) taken together.

Measurement of inputs possess similar problems. Input factors are many and varied. Some of them may not be measurable at all e.g. managerial skill. When it is difficult to compare the output and input in physical terms, they have to be converted into money terms for the purpose of comparison. Then productivity is defined as the ratio of net value of output to the net value of input all expressed at constant prices. But price fluctuations create errors in measurement. Monetary measurements do not measure correctly the changes in quantity. Measurement of productivity is even more difficult in service enterprises.

Productivity may be measured either on an aggregate basis or an individual basis. In the first case output is compared with all the input factors taken together. This is known as total productivity. In the second case output is compared with any one of the input factors and this is called partial productivity or factor productivity.

$$\text{Total Productivity Index} = \frac{\text{Total Output}}{\text{Total Inputs}}$$

$$\therefore \text{Total productivity} = \frac{\text{Value of Total Production of goods \& Services}}{\text{Labour + Material + Capital + Energy as Total Cost of Inputs}}$$

This index measure the efficiency of the entire organisation in the use of all the resources. It is a strategic yardstick for evaluating the operating efficiency of the entire plant or firm.

Factor of Indices

In order to measure the efficiency of individual operations or specific factors of productivity, productivity indices for individual inputs are computed. Labour Productivity Index is the most common measure of productivity. The labour input is measured in terms of man hours. One man working for one hour is called a man hour.

$$\therefore \text{ Labour Productivity index} = \frac{\text{Output in units}}{\text{Man hour worked}}$$

The index does not indicate the idleness of labour due to machine breakdown, power, failure etc.

$$\text{Similarly, Machine Productivity Index} = \frac{\text{Total Output}}{\text{Machine hours worked}}$$

$$\text{Material Productivity Index} = \frac{\text{Total Output}}{\text{Quantity of Material used}} \times 100$$

$$\text{1. Material Productivity} = \frac{\text{Total Output (Volume)}}{\text{Quantity of Materials used}} \times 100$$

$$\text{2. Labour Productivity} = \frac{\text{Standard man hour earned}}{\text{Man hours taken}} \times 100$$

$$= \frac{\text{Standard cost of output}}{\text{Actual wages paid}} \times 100$$

Standard cost means the costs which should have been incurred in production.

3. Machinery/capital Productivity: Productivity of Plant and machinery is generally measured with the helps of Capital output ratio.

$$\text{Capital Productivity} = \frac{\text{Total Output}}{\text{Capital employed}}$$

Changes in this ratio can be used to judge trend in productivity over time and across industries.

***(iii)* Factors Influencing Productivity:** Productivity is the outcome of several factors. These factors are so interrelated that it is difficult to identify the effect of any one factor on productivity.

These factors may broadly be divided into two categories—1. human factor and 2. technological factors.

1. Human Factor: Human nature and human behaviour are the most significant determinants of Productivity of Productivity. Human factors may further be classified into following categories as given below:

(*a*) Ability to work: Productivity of an organisation depends on the competence and calibre of its people—both workers and managers. Ability to work is governed by education, training, experience, aptitude etc. of the employees.

(*b*) Willingness to work: Motivation and morale of people is the second important group of human factors that determine productivity.

(*c*) Morale and Productivity: Most behavioural scientists regard morale as a group phenomenon. Morale is a concept that describes the level of favourable attitudes of the employees collectively to all aspects of their work—the job, the company, the working conditions, fellow workers, supervisors etc. Attitudes express what the individuals think and feel about their jobs.

The attitudes towards the organisation constitutes morale for an employee. Employee's feelings of cohesiveness, group interest and identification with the company mission together with the optimism about success of the group are important factor which contribute to morale.

Morale and Productivity go hand and higher the morale, higher the productivity and vice-versa. But their co-relation does not bear any arithmetic proportion. That is, an increase of fine percent in morale does not guarantee a proportional increase in productivity.

A more accurate statement about high morale is that it indicates a pre-disposition to be more productive if leadership is effective along with proper production facilities and individual's ability.

Productivity is a function of four factors—(*i*) Organisational factors (*ii*) Individual factors (*iii*) attitudes and (*iv*) morale

Attitudes and morale are determined by the satisfaction of individuals which is again affected by organisational and individual factors.

Thus Productivity is a functions of several variables, of course, morale may be one of the important factors.

Successful managers believe that behavioural management requires a positive integration of goals so that people working together will achieve the desirable high morale with high productivity.

Sometimes, it may be possible *t* achieve high productivity with low morale but it is a short time phenomenon. Because, in a course of time, employees will show resistance and dissatisfaction resulting in low productivity.

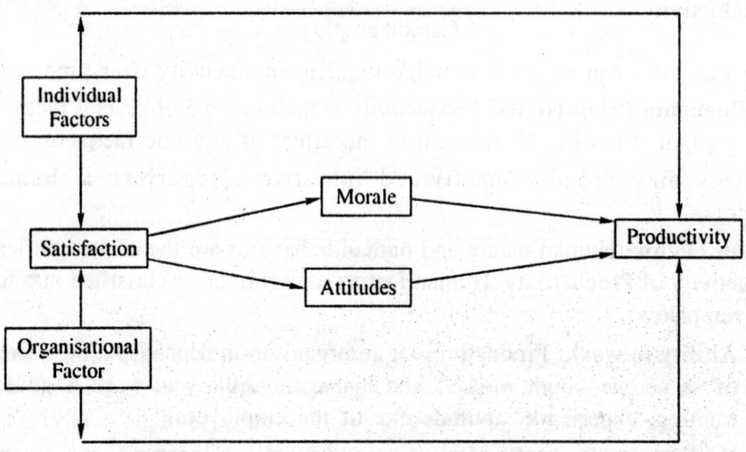

Figure 11.2 Satisfaction-Morale-Productivity Model.

Above model diagram gives the relationship between satisfaction and productivity via morale and attitudes.

Behavioural scientists F. Herzberg and V.H. Vroom have held optimistic views of evidence and suggested that there are enough data to justify the morale as a factor in improving the productivity (worker's output).

Thus, on the basis of above, it can be concluded that for higher productivity, high morale is necessary.

(*d*) **Incentive Schemes:** Wage incentive scheme seeks to motivate employees in paying extra remuneration. Profit sharing or bonus, labour welfare measures and good working conditions also help in this objective.

(*e*) **Workers participation in Management:** Labour participation in management is considered an effective tool for improving productivity. It helps in developing mutual understanding and co-operation between management and labour.

(*f*) **Production Planning and Control:** Scientific task planning ensure timely supply of inputs, proper maintenance of plants, effective work scheduling and regulation of day to day activities in the plant. It facilitates full utilisation of plant capacity and achievement of production targets.

(*g*) **Automation:** Mechanisation, automation and rationalisation are major break through for increase in productivity.

(*h*) **Management By Objective (MBO):** MBO is the process whereby superior and subordinates jointly identify the specific measurable goals, define results expected of an individual and jointly assess the contribution of every individual. It is an approach for integrating the individuals with the organisation. The focus of MBO is on participative goal setting, joint evaluation of performance and results to be achieved. It is also known as Management By Results.

(*i*) **Job Enrichment:** Job enrichment is the process of redesigning a job in order to enlarge its scope and to give the worker more to do. Its purpose is to improve job satisfaction, motivation and morale workers. When the job is engineered to workers the dehumanisation element is reduced so as to improve productivity and to reduce costs. It provides an opportunity for the satisfaction of higher level needs.

The following methods can be adopted for job enrichment:

(*i*) Give workers new and more varied task to perform.

(*ii*) Provide greater freedom and self control in performing jobs.

(*iii*) Give opportunity to do whole task rather than an element of it.

(*iv*) Give employee greater responsibilities of their own work.

(*v*) Provide an opportunity to the workers to become an expert on a particular task.

(*vi*) Supply production report directly to the workers.

(*j*) **Flexitime:** Flexitime is a relatively new work pattern which is a major departure from tradition. It allows the workers to set their own work hours subject to a minimum number of hours per week. During a particular period all workers are required to be present. Such a period is called 'core hours'. Subject to these limitations workers are given freedom to decide when they will work. Flexitime helps to reduce worker alination and to raise productivity.

(*k*) **Quality of Work Life (QWL):** QWL is a new techniques for improvement of productivity and quality of work. A QWL programme consists of the following elements:

- **Labour Management Co-operation:** a major change is required in the philosophy and attitude of the management and labour. The attitude of antagonism and opposition must be replaced by feeling of togetherness. Supervisors and workers must learn to work together and to mutually solve problems. The philosophy of win loose relationship must give way to the feeling that management and labour both gain or loose together. Management must take the initiative unilaterally to develop mutual operation and constructive relationship on the production floor.

- **Collective Bargaining:** The collective bargaining agreements must be based on the mutuality of interest on the shop floor. A more constructive bargaining relationship should be developed.
- **Participative Management:** Management must adopt a more open and democratic style in place of classical style of use of authority. Employees must be permitted to participate in the decision making process. The jointly made decisions should be whole heartedly implemented by both management and workers.

(*l*) **Quality Circles (QC):** A quality circle is a small group of workers which regularly meet to discuss problems, investigate causes, recommend solutions and if authorised take corrective action.

A leader is appointed to direct and guide the circle. A facilitator makes integration of programmes easier at all levels. The co-ordinator supervises the facilitators and directs administration of the programme. There is a steering committee which overseas and directs the efforts of all quality circles in the organisation.

The purpose of a quality circle program is to improve motivation, product quality. It is designed to optimise the man power by capturing the creative and innovative power of the work force. It provides workers and opportunity to participate in decisions making about their work. As a result they take greater interest in their jobs.

The procedure adopted by a quality circle consists typically of the following steps:

(*a*) Identify the problem.

(*b*) Discuss the problem.

(*c*) Analyse its causes.

(*d*) Develop a solution.

(*e*) Present the solution to management for necessary action.

The main objective of quality circles are as follows:

- To promote job involvement and work motivation to employees.
- To promote team work.
- To improve quality of products and services.
- To provide training in problem solving and decision making.
- To improve organisational communications.
- To improve labour relations.

A quality circle program is based on the philosophy that quality and output can be improved through the participation of employees in solving work problems.

2. Technological Factors: Technological factors exercise significant influence on the level of Productivity. The main technological factors are as follows.

- Size and capacity of plant.
- Production design and standardisation.
- Timely supply of materials and fuel.
- Rationalisation and automation measures.

- Repairs and maintenance.
- Production planning and control.
- Plant layout and location.
- Materials handling system.
- Inspection and quality control.
- Machinery and equipment used.
- Research and development.
- Inventory control.
- Reduction and utilisation of waste and scraps etc.

3. **Managerial Factors:** The competence and attitudes of managers have an important bearing on productivity. In many organisation, productivity is low despite latest technology and trained manpower. This is due to inefficient and in different management.
4. **Natural Factors:** Natural factors such as physical, geological and climatic condition exert considerable influence on Productivity.
5. **Sociological Factors:** Social customs, traditions and institutions influence attitudes towards work and job.
6. **Political Factors:** Law and order, stability of Government, etc. are essential for high productivity in industries.
7. **Economic Factors:** Size of market, banking and credit facilities, transport and communication systems, are important factors influencing productivity.

11.10 WORK STUDY AND METHOD STUDY

(*a*) **Work Study:** Work study means the application of systematic analysis to the work of men and machines so as to improve methods and establish time value for that work. It is the systematic and analytical study of work processes and work methods to improve productivity. Work study helps to increase productivity through standardisation and simplification of work.

Work study seeks to achieve the following objectives:

(*i*) Optimum utilisation of plant and equipment.

(*ii*) Most effective use of human effort.

(*iii*) Reasonable workload for employees.

Work study is shown thus:

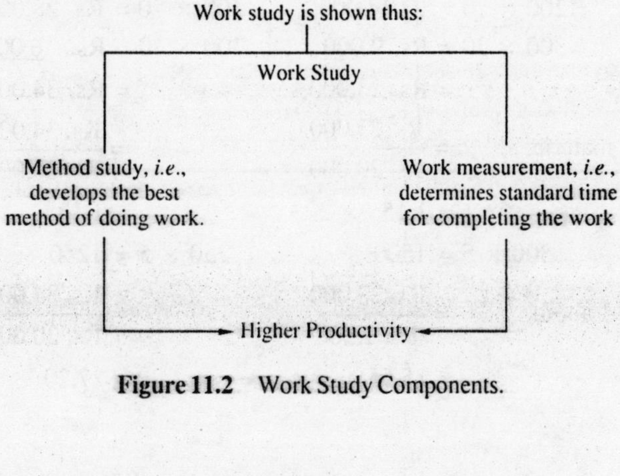

Figure 11.2 Work Study Components.

Method study involves the following steps:

- Select ... Work to be studied
- Record ... all relevant facts
- Examine ... the facts critically
- Develop ... a new method
- Install ... the new method
- Maintain ... the standard method by routine checks.

Method study helps to improve productivity by (*a*) eliminating unnecessary tasks (*b*) reducing the number of operations (*c*) combining the interrelated tasks (*d*) re-arranging the tasks (*e*) simplifying the process.

Case Study on: Productivity and selection of proper material for manufacturing operation.

Example: A factory can manufacture two products *A* and *B* using two material *P* and *Q*. Product *A* is expected to sell at Rs. 70 Unit and *B* at Rs. 30 per unit. The operating data are as follows:

	With material P	*With material Q*
Output	*A* 200 Units & *B* 300 Units	*A* 400 Units. *B* 200 Units.
Quantity of raw material usage	1000 kgs.	1000 kgs.
Labour usage	300 man hours	250 man hours
Electricity consumption	1000 kw. hrs.	1500 kw. hrs.
Cost of raw material per kgs.	Rs. 20	Rs. 30
Labour per man hour	Rs. 5	Rs. 5
Electric energy per kw. hr.	Rs. 1.50	Rs. 1.50

Compare the Productivity of Material
Labour
Electric Energy
in using materials *P* and *Q*

Comment on the relative advantages of using either of the materials.

Solution.	***P***	***Q***
Quantity of material used	1000 kgs.	1000 kgs.
Cost of raw materials per kg.	Rs. 20	Rs. 30
(*i*) Total cost of materials used	Rs. 20,000	Rs. 30,000
(*ii*) Value of output	200 × 70 = Rs.14,000 300 × 30 = Rs. 9,000 = Rs. 23,000	400 × 70 = Rs. 28,000 200 × 30 = Rs. 6,000 = Rs. 34,000
Productivity of raw material	$= \frac{\text{Rs. } 23{,}000}{\text{Rs. } 20{,}000}$ = 1.15	$= \frac{\text{Rs. } 34{,}000}{\text{Rs. } 30{,}000}$ = 1.13
(*iii*) Cost of labour	300 × 5 = 1500	250 × 5 = 1250
Productivity of Labour	$= \frac{\text{Rs. } 23{,}000}{\text{Rs. } 1{,}500}$ = 15.55	$= \frac{\text{Rs. } 34{,}000}{\text{Rs. } 30{,}000}$ = 27.20

(*iv*) Cost of Electrical energy	= 100 × 1.50	= 1500 × 1.50
	= Rs. 1500	= Rs. 2250
Productivity of energy	$= \frac{\text{Rs. } 23{,}000}{\text{Rs. } 1{,}500}$	$= \frac{\text{Rs. } 34{,}000}{\text{Rs. } 2{,}250}$
	= 15.55	= 15.01
(*v*) Total cost (*i*) + (*ii*) + (*iv*)	= Rs. 23,000	= Rs. 33,000
Net Gain (*ii*) – (*v*)	= Nil	= Rs. 1,000

Therefore, it is more economical to use material *Q*.

Summary for Productivity-Enhancement

FACTORS INFLUENCING PRODUCTIVITY

1. **Human Factor** — Ability to work.
   Willingness to work.
   Wage incentive schemes,
   Labour participation in management,
   Communication system,
   Promotion policy,
   Union-management Relation,
   Quality of Leadership.
2. **Technological Factors** — Size and capacity of plant,
   Production design and standardisation,
   Timely supply of inputs,
   Automation Measures,
   Repairs and Maintenance,
   Plant layout and location,
   Materials handling
   Inspection and Quality control,
   Research and Development
   Inventory control
   Recycle and reduction of waste
3. **Managerial Factors:** Competence and attitude of Managers have important bearing on productivity.
4. **Natural Factors:** Physical, geological, climatic.
5. **Sociological Factors:** Social customs, Tradition and institutions influence attitude towards work.
6. **Political Factors:** Law and order, Stability of Government.
7. **Economic Factors:** Size of market, banking and credit facilities, transport and communication.

11.11 COST EFFECTIVENESS INDEX

$$\text{Cost Effectiveness Index} = \frac{\Sigma Q_2\ P_2 / \Sigma Q_1\ P_1}{\Sigma I_2\ C_2 / \Sigma I_1\ C_1}$$

Q = Quantity, *I* = Input, *P* → Price, *C* → Costs

1, 2 stand for base year and current year respectively

Σ = Summation.

Definition ⟶ Cost effectiveness index is a measure of relationship between current period costs and base period costs which may be standard or ideal costs.

CEA ⟶ Cost effectiveness Analysis.

CEA is defined as a quantitative analysis of the costs involved and the likely benefits associated with alternative productive systems for the purpose of selecting the preferred alternatives and the equipment or tools associated with it.

Application of CEA ⟶

(*i*) To assist executive judgement in making better choice among alternative systems, particularly in situation where economic resources are a major constraint.

(*ii*) To keep identify the specific areas where there is scope for cost reduction.

(*iii*) To provide necessary data for cost estimation and for analysis of uncertainty.

Cost analysis is concerned primarily with the development of relationship between the costs of a system and its performance.

Effectiveness and Efficiency: Management should focus on doing effective (result oriented) activities in an efficient (cost saving) manner.

11.12 COST CONTROL

(*i*) **Meaning of cost control:** Cost Control involves all managerial efforts designed to control cost of operations. Cost control is applicable to all phases of operations management e.g. production, distribution, R & D, personnel and finance etc. Cost control is a technique of monitoring the costs and keeping them under check.

Cost control has two aspects (*a*) reduction in specific expense (*b*) more efficient use of every rupee spent.

(*ii*) **Benefits of cost control:** Profits depend upon the difference between selling price and the cost of operation. Generally, a firm has little or no control over selling price. Therefore, it must keep its costs under control. In fact, cost control is an essential element for the prosperity of an enterprise.

The main advantages of cost control are as follows:

1. Obtaining higher productivity from given resources.
2. Economic stability and prosperity of the industry.
3. Improvement in the competitive position of the enterprise.
4. Enhancement of the profitability of the enterprise.

(*iii*) **Techniques of cost control:** The main techniques used in cost control are as follows:

(*a*) Standard Costing

(*b*) Budgetary Control.

(*a*) **Standard Costing:** It implies the establishment of pre-determined costs for some future period for each cost unit, the comparison of costs actually incurred with those pre-determined costs and analysis of variances to their causes and incidence.

Standard costing is preparation of standard costs and their use to measure financial results with the purpose of maximising efficiency by executive action.

Standard costs are set up as unit costs and are broken down into the following categories:

1. Standard direct material costs
2. Standard direct labour costs
3. Standard direct expenses
4. Standard fixed overhead costs
5. Standard variable overhead costs
6. Standard selling and distribution costs.

After establishing standard costs, actual product cost figures are collected and compared with the corresponding standard costs. Adverse variances are analysed to determine their causes.

(*b*) **Budgetary Control:** A budget may be defined as a financial and/or quantitative statement, prepared and approved in advance for a definite period of time to reflect the expected results for attaining given objective.

Budgetary control is a system whereby, actual results are compared with budget figures and appropriate corrective actions are taken.

Budgetary control is not only a tool of cost control but of managerial planning and co-ordination too.

Budget plans and budgetary control figures offer opportunities for reduction of costs.

Budget control can be used for setting targets of cost savings. Suitable rewards for achievement of budgetary performance and correcting action for failure must be taken in time. Individuals must be held responsible for costs they can control.

(*iv*) **Variance Analysis:** Variance refer to the difference between standard cost and actual cost. When the standard cost exceeds actual cost, variance is said to be positive and favourable. On the other hand, unfavourable or negative variance implies excess of actual cost on standard cost. Calculation and analysis of variance is an important element of standard costing.

(*v*) **Importance of cost accounting:** Cost accounting is that part of the accounting system which is concerned with the determination and analysis of the costs of particular departments, jobs or products within the enterprise.

Cost accounting is the basis of cost and budgetary control system which are essential in the successful operation of a modern industrial concern.

Cost accounting provides useful cost data relating to inventory control, economic lot size, records points etc.

The profit making capacity depends to a great extent on the efficiency with which cost are controlled.

Benefit of cost accounting are:

(*a*) It provides the necessary information for setting up cost standards.

(*b*) It provides information for price determination.

(*c*) Variable costs e.g. costs for materials, labour, fuels spares and maintenance etc. are necessarily controlled after comparing against standard data.

(*d*) Many successful organisations work out actual variable cost figures and provide information about contribution of the product on daily basis (contribution = selling price – total variable costs) to cost.

11.13 COST REDUCTION

(*i*) **Objectives of cost reduction:** Cost is the basis of any rational action. The entire process of decision making is based on cost-benefit analysis. Cost determination is the fundamental step as prices and other decisions require cost data. Profit is the excess of price over cost.

Price is an external factor and is not always in the control of management. On the other hand, cost is an internal and controllable factor. Thus an enterprise can increase its competitiveness and profitability by reducing costs.

Cost reduction involves critical examination of the purposes for which costs are incurred with a view to reduce or eliminate the reasons for expenditure.

It involves appraisal of resource utilisation so as to minimise wastage and inefficiency and to maximise productivity. It also requires critical examination of work standards and work methods so as to develop higher standards and better work methods. Cost reduction is an approach rather than a technique.

Cost reduction implies deliberate savings in the cost of production and distribution through the elimination of wastes and inefficiency. It involves reduction in Unit costs by improvements in product design and related techniques of practises.

(*ii*) **Cost versus Expenditures:** Cost reduction is a planned programme. Reduction in cost due to windfalls, fortuitous receipts, changes in fiscal policies, etc. do not form part of cost reduction analysis. Cost reduction means reduction in Unit costs and does not necessarily imply reduction in total expenditure. It may involve increase in expenditure.

For example, a firm may spend more on research and development to improve product design so as to reduce unit cost of production. Cost reduction is based on the basic philosophy that there is always a better ways of doing things and an improvement is possible in everything. And for achieving this objective, expenditures are to be effectively incurred on research and design, product development, product design and specialised training of personnel.

(*iii*) **Cost Reduction and Cost Control:** Both cost reduction and cost control are tools of increasing profitability. But the two differences in terms of their procedures and approach.

The differences between Cost Reduction and Cost Control are as follows:

(*a*) **Nature:** Cost reduction is a corrective function where as Cost Control is a preventive function.

(*b*) **Emphasis:** The emphasis on cost reduction is on present and future costs. Cost control lays emphasis on present and past behaviour of costs.

Cost Control is a routine function where as cost reduction seeks improvement in the way work is done.

(*c*) **Standards:** Cost control involves setting cost standards, analysis variances from the standards and taking corrective actions. Cost reduction is not concerned with standards. It involves obtaining potential savings.

Cost control attempts to keep actual costs in like with established cost standards. Cost reduction challenges these standards forthwith. It tries to reduce costs on a continuous basis.

(*d*) **Application:** Cost reduction can be applied to each and every area of business. But cost control is limited to areas where standard costs can be set.

(*e*) **Aim:** Cost Control seeks to achieve lowest possible cost under given conditions. On the other hand, cost reduction recognises that no condition is permanent. It calls for change in conditions if they result in lower cost.

(*f*) **Content:** Cost Control represents efforts involved in attaining targets or standards. Cost reduction symbolises achievement in reducing costs.

(*g*) **Continuity:** Cost reduction programme can be finished. Cost control on the other hand, is an ongoing or never ending process.

Example: Under cost control, the tendency is to accept standards once they are fixed and leave them unchallenged over a period. In cost reduction, on the other hand, standards must be constantly challenged for improvement.

There is no phase of business which is exempt from cost reduction.

Products, processes, procedures and personnel are subject to continuous scrutiny to see where and how they can be reduced in cost.

Cost reduction involves cutting down costs whereas cost control involves maintaining costs in accordance with established standards.

(*iv*) **Cost Reduction Programme:** Cost reduction has immense significance in business as it exercises marked influence on the future of a business enterprise.

A business firm may increase profits by:

(*a*) Increasing the selling price of its products, by

(*b*) Increasing the volume of sales, or by

(*c*) Reducing the cost of operation.

In the highly competitive world, no individual firm can raise prices or sales volume to significant extent. Therefore, the only practical way to raise profits is to minimise costs. Cost reduction improves the competitiveness of a business firm. Lower costs make for lower prices and higher demand and sales. For instance, television enjoyed limited demand/sale in the late seventies and early eighties because of high price, but with reduction in cost and price, the demand of T.V. sets had started increasing from the mid eighties till the current period.

Need to reduce selling price and expand market is an important reason for a cost reduction programme.

Every cost reduction programme is designed to reduce costs of operations below their present level.

Cost reduction programme aims for maximising profits due to following reasons:

(*a*) It works both successful and less profitable companies against indulging in extravagance.

(*b*) It tries to avoid extra costs creeping in during inflationary periods.

(*c*) It serves to educate everyone in the company for attempting to keep costs down.

A cost reduction programme has following steps:

(*a*) Locating cost centres and grouping them according to departmental responsibility.

(*b*) Conducting a value analysis exercise for each cost centre to identify scope for cost reduction and to optimise efficiency.

(*c*) Using appropriate corrective measures to minimise costs. For any cost reduction programme to be successful.

- Workers and Unions may be taken in confidence for the exact purpose of the programme.
- Persons responsible for cost reduction programme should be given proper training.
- Funds required for several heads may be arranged in advance before commencement of programme.

(*v*) **Techniques of cost Reduction:** The main techniques used for cost reduction is as follows:

(*a*) Cost Accounting and Analysis

(*b*) Ratio Analysis

(*c*) Break Even Analysis

(*d*) Work Study

(*e*) Management Audit

(*f*) Value Analysis

(*g*) Organisation

(*h*) Methods

(*i*) Standardisation and Simplification

(*j*) Production Control

(*k*) Inventory Control

(*l*) Quality Control

(*m*) Automation

Cost-Benefit Analysis involves comparison between cost incurred in using the resources and the benefits accruing from these resources. The objective of cost benefit analysis is to minimise waste through the best possible use of resources.

Value Analysis is significant as an useful techniques of cost reduction.

(*vi*) **Break Even Analysis:** Break-even-analysis is a simple and inexpensive technique which focuses a microscopic picture of the profit structure of a business firm. It highlights the areas of economic strengths and weaknesses and reveals the profit vulnerability of the firm to changes in business condition. However, break even an analysis is based on several assumptions which are not true in practice. The selling price, rate of decrease in variable cost are assumed to be constant. It is assumed that there will be no changes in input prices, product-mix, labour efficiency and technology and there is no change in inventory level.

Break-even analysis is a static picture as it assumes constant relationship of output to costs and revenue. Break-even analysis is based on accounting data which may suffer from several limitations like neglect of imputed costs, arbitrary depreciation estimates, in appropriate allocation of overheads etc.

The break-even chart has been exhibited earlier. Break-even analysis is useful in several types of managerial decisions.

The following example helps the management for an important decision which is beneficial for the organisation:

Example: *ABC* company is examining a proposal to expand its plant capacity which is expected to increase its annual sales from Rs. 40 lacs to Rs. 60 lacs. The expansion will involve an increase in fixed cost from Rs. 15 lacs to Rs. 20 lacs. The variable cost is likely to remain unchanged at 50% of the Sales revenue.

Should the company go in for expansion?

Solution. Break Even Point (*BEP*) at Present Capacity

$$= \frac{15,00,000}{50\%}$$

BEP at proposed capacity $= \frac{20,00,000}{50\%} = \text{Rs. } 40 \text{ lacs.}$

Increase in break-even point = Rs. 10 lacs.

As the increase in Sales (Rs. 20 lacs) is greater than the increase in *BEP*, the company should go in for expansion.

11.14 PROBABLE QUESTIONS

1. What do you mean by "Work Study", "Method Study" and "Work Measurement"?

2. What are the objectives of Method Study?
Describe the techniques of Method Study.

3. What are the objectives of Time Study?
State the methods adopted for Time Study.

4. Write notes on:
(*a*) Performance Rating Factor
(*b*) Standard Time
(*c*) Ergonomics.

5. Define Ergonomics.
Describe the objectives of the study of ergonomics.

6. Describe "Micro-Motion Study".
Illustrate suitable example of its application.

7. What are Therbligs?
State their significance. Provide the name, abbreviation and symbol of each of 17 Therbligs.

8. Write notes on:
(*a*) Work-Sampling
(*b*) Simo Chart
(*c*) Pre determined Motion Time Standards (PMTS).

9. What are the advantages of "PMTS" over ordinary Time Study?

10. Discuss in brief, "Work Sampling" and state some of its applications.

12

Inspection and Quality Control

• Quality Control • Quality • Inspection and Quality Control • Quality, Inspection and Quality Control • TQM and the Deming • The Kaizen Systems for Improvement • The Japanese 5 S Systems • Ishikawa Diagram • Quality Function Development (QFD) • ISO 9000 and ISO 14000 Certification • Statistical Process Control (SPC) • Case Example—Six-Sigma Quality • Six-Sigma Quality • International Organisation for Standardisation (ISO) • TQM and Strategic Management • Probable Questions.

12.1 QUALITY CONTROL

(*i*) Quality Control Organisation:

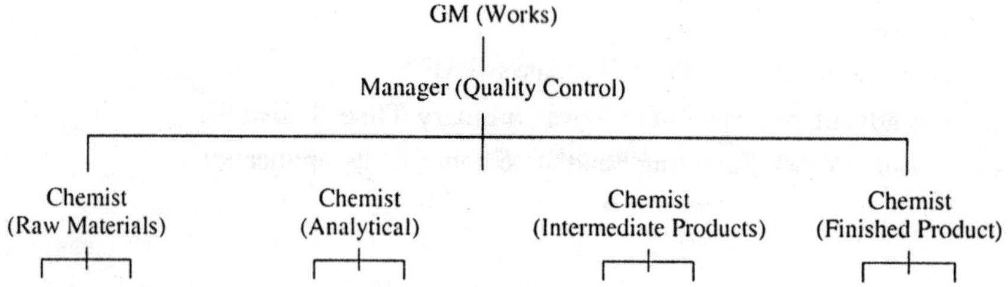

Figure 12.1

A typical organisation chart for Quality Control Department.

(*ii*) Objectives of Quality Control

(*a*) To set up standards of quality acceptable to the customer and economical to achieve and maintain.

(*b*) To locate and identify the process faults so as to control defective, scrap and west.

(*c*) To take necessary corrective measure so as to maintain the quality of products.

(*d*) To ensure that sub-standard products do not reach the customers.

(*iii*) Advantage of Quality Control: There are many advantages by controlling the product quality. Some of them are listed below:

1. Quality of Product is improved which in turn increases sales.
2. Scrap rejection and rework are minimised thus reducing wastage, so the cost of manufacturing reduces.
3. Good quality product improves reputation.

4. Uniformity in quality can be achieved.
5. Improvement in technical knowledge and engineering data for process development and manufacturing design.

12.2 QUALITY

Quality is fitness for use. Quality consists of parameters those meet customer's satisfaction when he or she uses the product or service.

Quality is the important survival criteria in the competitive situation. For supply of products or services in the domestic market a businessman tries to maintain the quality norms specified by the Bureau of Indian Standards as per International Standard Organisation (ISO) are to be followed.

Thus corporate leaders consider quality of Products and services they deal with as very important and vital for survival and growth of their business.

(*i*) **Controlling Quality Level:** Quality is defined as that feature of a product which influences its capacity to satisfy a given need. Quality characteristics are directly measurable. Quality is also classified as specificational, functional, aesthetic and usage.

Perfection in any type of quality is rarely possible and it may mean infinite cost. Quality control is an important function designed to ensure that manufactured product meets meaningful specifications. Quality control is defined as an effective system for integrating the quality development, quality maintenance and quality improvement efforts of the various groups in an organisation so as to unable production and service at the most economical levels which allow for full customer satisfaction." It includes all the activities performed to fulfil the quality objectives of the organisation.

Quality control enters into all phases of the manufacturing process. It begins with designing of product so that it has high customer appeal in terms of appearance, function, life etc.

(*ii*) **Reliability and Inspection:** Reliability refers to the extent to which the product may perform in function. A product's useful life span or the expected duration of its performance constitutes its reliability. There is a close interrelationship between reliability and quality control. For Diesel Generators, Thermal Power Plants and Steel Plants etc., reliability is most essential.

A well planned and organised quality control system starts controlling quality from design stage and continues to work until trouble free product is supplied to the customer. Customer satisfaction can be achieved only when the customer is happy with the performance, reliability and serviceability of the Product.

Reliability can be measured as the probability of performing without failure a specified function under given conditions for specified period of time.

Inspection implies comparing quality characteristics of a product with predetermined standards or accepted specifications of quality. Inspection is a post mortem operation carried out after the product is manufactured. It includes all types of testing carried out to determine whether the prescribed standards are adhered to or not.

The ultimate aim of Inspection is to separate products into "accepted" and "rejected" categories. The rejected units may be rectified or sold at a discount or sold as scrap.

Such rejection results in wastage of materials, labour and money. Quality control takes place while the production process is continuing while inspection is done after completion.

Purchased materials, manufacturing process, finished products all need inspection. Therefore, proper policies, procedures and practices should be laid down for inspection. Quality control is designed to minimise the high costs of inspection and rejection.

(*iii*) **Objectives and Benefits of Quality Control:** The ultimate aim of quality control is to provide products which are dependable, satisfactory and economical.

The main objective of quality control is to ensure economical production of products of uniform quality which is acceptable to the customer. An effective quality control programme provides the following benefits to the organisation.

(*a*) Scrap, rework and other losses are minimised.

(*b*) Costs of materials, fuels and labour are reduced as a result.

(*c*) Uniformity and reliability of Products improve sales turnover.

(*d*) Customer complaints are minimised.

(*e*) Quality consciousness is increased.

(*iv*) **Statistical Quality Control:** Statistical quality control (*SQC*) is a scientific technique of controlling quality by means of statistical techniques. It has been defined "the" technique of applying statistical methods based upon the mathematical theory of probability to quality control problems with the purpose of establishing quality standards and maintaining adherence to these standards in the most economical manner."

Statistical quality control is designed to regulate in process manufacturing and to take corrective action in such a way that products do conform to the quality standards as they are produced. For this purpose *SQC* involves not only setting quality specifications but evaluating processes and equipments to make necessary improvements thereon. *SQC* is concerned with quality of conformance while inspection is concerned with quality design.

(*a*) **Variations in Quality:** A certain amount of variability is inevitable in any manufacturing process. This variability arises due to two types of causes—Chance variation and assignable variations.

Chance Variations (or internal variations) are inherent and inevitable in the process. A normal distribution curve is given below. It is specified by the central value (arithmetic mean X) and the measure of spread (standard deviations) as shown.

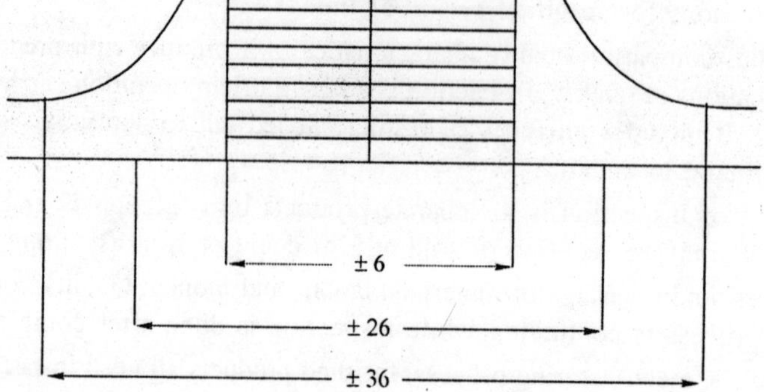

Figure 12.2

Normal Curve has the following important properties:

1. $X \pm 6 = 68.27\%$ of all observations
2. $X \pm 26 = 95.45\%$ of all observations
3. $X \pm 36 = 99.73\%$ of all observations

Thus, only 0.27% (3 out of 1000) observation lie outside $X \pm 36$ limits. Techniques of *SQC*. Statistical Techniques used in *SQC* are:

(*a*) **Control Charts:** These are used to control quality of products and parts during the course of their actual manufacture. A control chart is a graph which indicates the tolerance, *i.e.,* limits within which variation from the average quality are to be permitted.

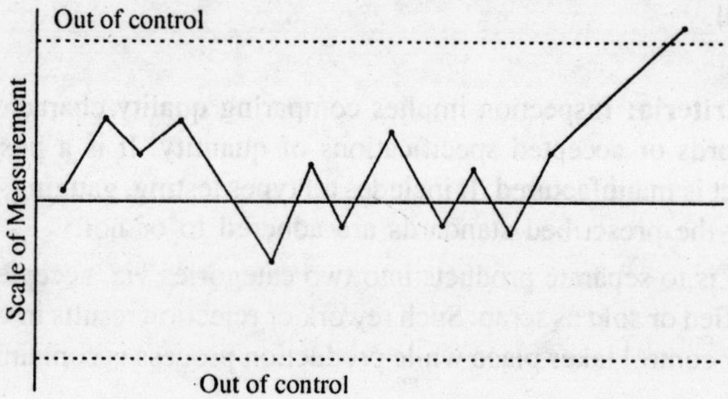

Figure 12.3 Quality Control Chart.

Control Charts are further discussed later in this chapter.

(*b*) **Acceptance Sampling:** 100% inspection involves lot of time and money. Therefore, sample inspection is used in most of the cases. A random sample of every lot is taken. The results of the sample are used to see whether the quality specification is met.

The whole lot is accepted if the random samples show conformance to standard quality and it is rejected if the sample results shows non-conformance. In order to avoid Producer's risk and customer's risk in Acceptance sampling, Lot Tolerance Percentage Defective (LTPD) is determined. This is the highest level of defects beyond which a lot will not be accepted. The probability of acceptance of an LTPD lot should be one e.g. 0.1. It is a measure of quality which is unacceptable.

(*v*) **Operating Characteristics Curve (*OCC*):** While judging various acceptance sampling plans, their performance is compared over a range of possible quality levels. *OCC* gives a picture of such performance. *OC* of an acceptance sampling plan indicates the ability of the plan to differentiate between good and bad lots. It is seen from the Curve that as quality of lot deteriorates (Percent defective *P* increases), the probability of acceptance of the lot gets reduced (*Pa* decreases).

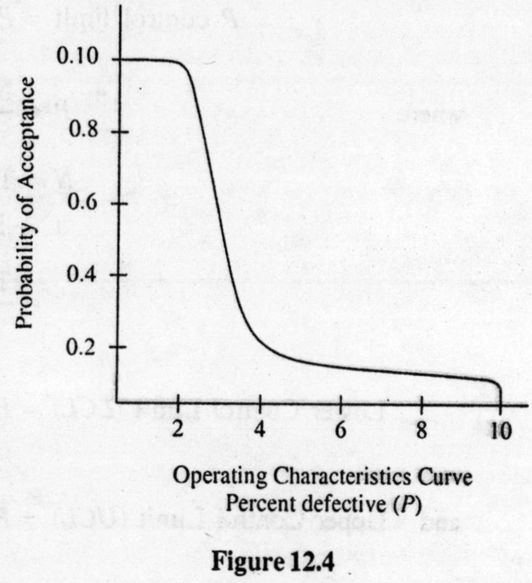

Operating Characteristics Curve
Percent defective (*P*)

Figure 12.4

(*vi*) **Bureau of Indian Standard:** To protect the interest of the consumers, Indian Standard Institution is serving in

India. I.S.I. serves consumers through certification Marks Scheme. Under this Scheme, I.S.I has been vested with the authority to grant licenses to manufacturers to apply the I.S.I. mark on their products in token of their conformity to the desired Indian standards.

To control the quality, I.S.I. inspectors carry out surprise inspection of the factories of the licensee. Thus I.S.I. mark gives guarantee to the purchaser that the goods with this mark have been manufactured under a well defined system of quality control.

12.3 INSPECTION AND QUALITY CONTROL

1. Types and Criteria and Inspection.
2. Significance of Quality Control.
3. Statistical Quality Control.
4. Control Charts.

1. **Inspection, Types and Criteria:** Inspection implies comparing quality characteristics of a product with predetermined standards or accepted specifications of quantity. It is a post mortem operation carried out after the product is manufactured. It includes all types testing, gauging, etc., that are carried out to determine whether the prescribed standards are adhered to or not.

The purpose of inspection is to separate products into two categories viz. accepted and rejected. The rejected units may be rectified or sold as scrap. Such rework or rejection results in wastage of materials, labour and money. Quality control takes place while production process is containing while inspection is done after completion.

Purchased materials, manufacturing process and finished products need inspection. Proper policies, procedures and practices should be laid down for inspection. Inspection does not add to the value or quality of the product. But it ensures that substandard products are not supplied to the customer. Quality control is designed to minimise the high costs of inspection and rejection. Under quality control, a small sample of the product being produced is tested for quality and steps are taken during the process stage to ensure that the products meet desired standards. The purpose is to prevent the production of defective products.

2. **Control Chart:** Formula for determining control limits for

$$P \text{ control limit } = P \pm 3\sqrt{\frac{P(1-P)}{n}}$$

where

$$P = \frac{\text{Number of Operator idle Observation}}{\text{Total Number of Observations}}$$

$$N = \text{Total Number of Observations}$$

$$n = \text{Number of daily Observations}$$

$$= \frac{\text{Total Number of Observations}}{\text{Number of days observed}}$$

$$\text{Lower Control Limit } (LCL) = P - 3\sqrt{\frac{P(1-P)}{n}}$$

and

$$\text{Upper Control Limit } (UCL) = P + 3\sqrt{\frac{P(1-P)}{n}}$$

Problem 12.1 The following observations were recorded by a work sampling study group:

Data of Study	*Total Number of observation*	*Number of observation "of operator idle"*	*Percent of day operator idle*
1 – 3	100	9	9
2 – 3	100	9	9
3 – 3	100	12	12
4 – 3	100	7	7
5 – 3	100	7	7
6 – 3	100	8	8
7 – 3	100	10	10
8 – 3	100	8	8
9 – 3	100	7	7
10 – 3	100	3	3
Total	1000	80	

Solution. The control limits for $P = P \pm 3\sqrt{\dfrac{P(1-P)}{n}}$

$$N = \text{Total Number of observations} = 1000$$

$$n = \text{Number of daily observations}$$

$$= \frac{\text{Total Number of observations}}{\text{Number of days studied}} = \frac{1000}{10} = 100$$

$$P = \frac{\text{Number of 'Operator idle' observations}}{\text{Total Number of observations}} = \frac{80}{1000} = 0.08$$

Control limits $= 0.08 \pm 3\sqrt{\dfrac{0.08 \times (1 - 0.08)}{n}}$

$$\therefore \quad UCL = 0.08 + 3\sqrt{0.0009}$$

$$= 0.08 + 3 \times 0.03$$

$$= 0.08 + 0.09$$

$$= 0.17 = +17\%$$

$$LCL = 0.08 - 3\sqrt{0.0009}$$

$$= 0.08 - 3 \times 0.03$$

$$= 0.10 - 0.09$$

$$= 0.01 = +1\%$$

Problem 12.2 Determination of standard time. The work-sampling can be used to estimate the standard time of an operation with the help of the following formula:

Standard time in (min)

$$= \frac{[\text{Total working time or study time (min)}] \times \left(\dfrac{\text{Percent working}}{100}\right) \times \left(\dfrac{\text{Average performance rating}}{100}\right)}{\text{Quantity Produced during observation period}} + \text{Allowance}$$

Problem 12.3 An operator was kept under observation for 10 days. He was found working on 400 occasions and abstaining including idle 100 times. He produced 200 jobs during these days. The observation per day was for 5 hours only and the total number of observations were 500. Take 120 as performance rating for operator and 20% as allowance. Calculate the standard time.

Solution. Standard time

$$= \frac{[\text{Total working time or study time (min)}] \times \left(\frac{\text{Percent working}}{100}\right) \times \left(\frac{\text{Average performance rating}}{100}\right)}{\text{Quantity Produced during observation period}} + \text{Allowance}$$

Total working time, or study time = $10 \times 5 \times 60 = 3000$ min.

Percentage working $= \frac{\text{Number of observation for working}}{\text{Total observation}} \times 100$

$= \frac{400}{500} \times 100 = 80\%$

Performance rating $= 120$

$\therefore$ Standard time $= \frac{3000 \times \frac{80}{100} \times \frac{120}{100}}{200} + \text{Allowance}$

$= 14.4 + \text{Allowance of } 20\%$

$= 14.4 \times 1.2$

$= 17.28$ min.

2. (*a*) **Control Charts:** A fundamental aim of *SQC* is to ensure system of differentiating between the variation due to chance causes and those due to assignable causes so that the latter can be identified and removed thereby improving the quality. The basic tool used for this purpose is called control chart.

A control chart is a visual display of the inspection results of the samples of a product. It incorporates carefully derived statistical limits which help to discriminate between random variability and assignable variability.

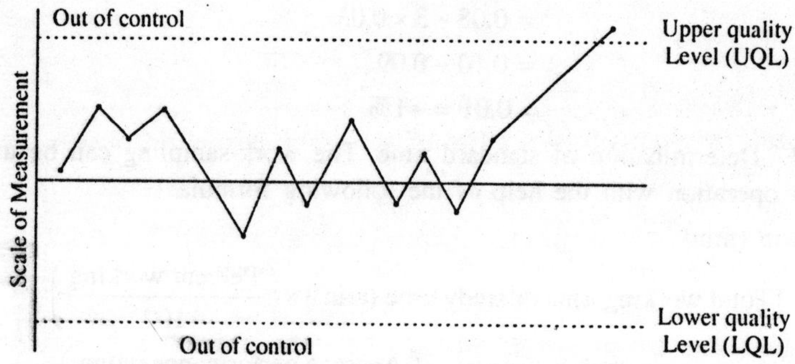

Figure 18.5 Quality Control Chart.

3. Types of Control Charts: These are as follows:

(*a*) $\overline{X}$—chart—known as the average chart—measures the central tendency of the process.

(*b*) *R*—chart—known as the range chart—measures the spread of the process. $\overline{X}$—chart and *R*—chart are used together and known as $\overline{X}$–*R* charts.

(*c*) *P*—chart—known as the fraction defective chart—records the proportion of defective items in a sample.

(*d*) *np*—chart—known as the number defective chart—records the number of defective items in a sample.

(*e*) *c*—chart—known as the defects chart, records the number of defects in a component.

Some times $\overline{X}$ chart does not give satisfactory results, this may occur due to old machine or worn out parts. Here the *R*–chart (Range chart) is used as additional tool of control. *R*–chart does not replace $\overline{X}$—chart but simply supplements with additional information.

12.4 QUALITY, INSPECTION AND QUALITY CONTROL

(*i*) Quality has 4 stages

Stage—I. Inspection: 'Inspection phase' has the following features:

- Inspection stage employs simple inspection based systems.
- Inspection is conducted at various stages of manufacture, raw materials or Input stage, Intermediate stage and Finished Product Stage.
- Non-conforming products are segregated from good ones.

Stage—II. Quality Control: Quality Control (inspection based) has the following features:

- Acceptance function.
- Data on defects is generated from the inspection results.
- Sampling inspection plans are adopted for Product Control thereby replacing 100% inspection by sampling inspection.
- Statistical Quality Control (Control charts) are employed for Precess Control.

Stage—III. Quality Assurance: Quality Assurance has the following features:

- Quality Control (inspection based) is substituted by Quality Assurance (prevention based).
- Quality planning and quality manuals are prepared with an object to build quality into the manufacturing process.

Stage—IV. Total Quality Management: TQM is the current stage in quality and has the following features:

- TQM covers all kinds of industries manufacturing and service.
- TQM implementation requires initiative of top management and removal of inter-departmental barriers.
- TQM places great emphasis on customers (internal and external) focus.
- TQM believes that systematic training is essential to attach greater quality.
- TQM lays greater thrust on business processes and advocates continuous improvement in every business activity. TQM is long term process initiated by Management to bring about a cultural change in the organisation and to integrate every employee, every function and process in order to provide total customer satisfaction. TQM builds in quality with product/service and improves the profitability.

(ii) **Quality Control:** Quality control is the mechanism by which products are made to measure upto specifications determined from customer's demand and transformed into engineering and manufacturing requirements.

Quality control refers to the systematic control of those variables encountered in manufacturing process which affects excellence of the end product.

There are **three basic aspects** of Quality Control:

1. **Acceptance function:** This refers to the inspection of goods to ensure that they are up to the specifications thereby segregate those which are defectives. Acceptance function of quality is called 'Inspection' and it includes elements like receiving inspection, process inspection, finished goods inspection etc.
2. **Preventive function:** This refers to the identification of defects in materials, components and machining processes etc., and thereby avoiding or minimising occurrence of defectives. Prevention function of quality is called 'Quality Control'.
3. **Assurance function:** This refers to verification that every quality characteristic is assumed to meet a pre-determined performance standard at each in manufacturing process.

   The assurance function includes elements line customers' complaints quality audit etc. Most of the Indian industries are found to perform the acceptance function while little attention is paid to preventive and assurance functions.

(iii) **Inspection versus Quality Control:** Even though they are closely related, they differ in the following:

1. Quality control aims to produce better quality products at the least cost and inspection is one of the tools used by it.
2. Quality control determines the causes of variations in the characteristics of the products and suggests methods to minimise these variations while, Inspection is the application of tests and measuring devices to compare the products their performance with specified standards.
3. Quality Control determines what, when and how much to inspect while Inspection actually conducts examination.

(iv) **Benefits of Inspection and Quality Control:** Inspection and Quality Control:

1. Ensures adequate maintenance of quality necessary to satisfy customers and to meet competition of competitors.
2. Ensures that parts are within the specified limits of accuracy and they fit properly during assembly.
3. Gives economy in production through reduction of defective work.
4. Prevents labour and machine time from being spent on work already identified as defective.
5. Provides required control on work produced by the incentive workers since they need to be paid only for the acceptable quantities.

(v) **Cost of Quality Analysis:** This is used to highlight the cost savings that can be achieved by doing the work right the first time. The analysis involves qualifying all costs associated with maintaining acceptance quality levels, such as the costs of preventing errors, and then comparing these with the costs increased by failures, to achieve acceptance quality, such as the cost of rework.

Cost of quality analysis helps to identify those opportunities for improving that offer the largest cost savings.

Deming Cycle: For Total Quality Management, Deming has listed the following parameters:

(*i*) Create constancy of purpose towards improvement.

(*ii*) Adopt and institute proper leadership.

(*iii*) Create an environment after every member to work without fear.

(*iv*) Install proper co-ordination.

(*v*) Encourage every body to accomplish the objectives.

12.5 STATISTICAL PROCESS CONTROL (SPC)

Application of statistical methods at the process control stage is known as Statistical Process Control. Customer quality assurance schemes now pushing the manufacturers towards the use of process control. The greater degree of process control allows an overall reduction in inspection and test effort. This helps in area other than covering total quality related costs such as vendor rating, efficient management of non-production areas like purchasing, design and even marketing.

(*a*) **Implementation of SPC Programme:** Essential steps in the process are:

1. Formalize the Procedure
2. Check the specification
3. Emphasize the need for process quality control
4. Plan for quality training
5. Follow up
6. Take one problem at a time
7. Record all observed data in detail
8. Measure the capability of the process
9. Make use of the data on the Process.

(*b*) **Economical Aspects In Control Charts:** The production of defective output results in the costs of sorting, scrap, rework dealing with customer complaints, replacement under warranty etc.

A more serious but very difficult cost to ascertain is that associated with the loss of goodwill, following the sales of defective or non-conforming products.

Designers of economic models use following costs:

- Fixed costs of sampling, inspecting, testing and measuring.
- Variable cost of sampling, measuring, calculating and plotting each sample value on control charts.
- Cost of correcting and assignable cause.
- Total loss in profit when the process is running out of control.

It has been experimented that the savings due to control of poor quality products, better control over the quality of purchased product, use of more economical materials or methods due to their greater reliability, are sometimes spectacular. Quality is a dynamic phenomena and is being improved continuously with the new developments in technology and management technique.

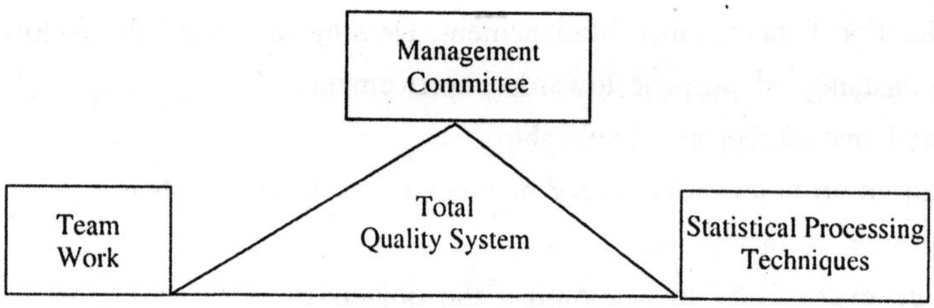

Figure 12.8 TQM Model.

(c) Some Statistical Terms:

(i) Universe of Population: It is a common source from which one or more units are collected. Suppose one cylinder block is picked up from a collection of 100, manufactured by a particular industry. It could be said that a unit of cylinder block has been picked up from its universe or population. Cylinder blocks of same size and capacity, but manufactured by different operators, or by different machine tools or at different plants, will form different populations. Units from different population may be alike but not same in every respect.

(ii) Attributes: When a record shows only the number of articles conforming and number of articles or items or units failing to conform to any specified requirement or specification, it is said to be a record of attributes.

The Products or articles are inspected and if a defect is observed the product is not accepted, the dimension of defect is not important.

Say a tube having a crack will be rejected, the size and shape of the crack are unimportant. So, in measurement by attributes the products are inspected on the principles of 'go' and 'no go' gauges. If a product conform to a specification, it is accepted otherwise rejected. The difference between the actual quality or dimension of the products under inspection with the specified values are not measured.

(iii) Frequency Distribution: Frequency means how many times a particular dimension or data occurs during an observation.

12.6 QUALITY AS A COMPETITIVE WEAPON

Attaining quality in all areas of manufacturing is a difficult task. To make things even more difficult, consumers change their perceptions of quality. For instance, change in life-styles and economic conditions have drastically altered consumer perceptions of automobile quality. Since the oil crisis took place in the early 1970's, consumer preferences shifted from power and styling to fuel economy.

Subsequently, the 1980's onwards the safety factor has taken additional importance. And 1990's onwards the reliability aspect has gained prominence for almost all consumer durable commodities including automobiles.

In general, a business's success depends on the accuracy of its perception of consumer expectations and its ability to bridge the gap between those expectations and operating capabilities. Consumers are much more quality-minded now than in the past.

A product or service that is perceived by customers to be of higher quality stands a much better chance of gaining market share than does one perceived to be of low quality, even if the actual levels of quality are the same.

Good quality can also pay off in higher profits. High quality products and services can be priced higher than comparable inferior quality ones and yield a greater return for the same sales volume.

Management is better able to compete on both price and quality.

(1) Quality and cultural change

The challenge of quality management is to instill an awareness of the importance of quality in all employees and to motivate them to improve quality.

Through Quality Management, everyone is expected to contribute to the overall improvement of quality.

One of the main challenge in developing the proper culture of Quality Management is to define Customer and Customer Satisfaction for each employee.

Employees even who have little contact with external customers should be given to underabout how their jobs contribute to the customer's satisfaction.

In Quality Management, everyone in the organisation must share the view that quality control is an end in itself. Errors or defects should be detected and corrected at the source, not passed along to an internal department.

This philosophy is called quality at the source.

In addition, firms should avoid trying to "inspect quality into the product" by using the services of Inspectors to weed out defective products after operating have been performed.

(2) Employee development

On the job training programmes can help improve quality. Training is imparted for new process and method to few selected skilled workers to adopt correct practices for increasing productivity and reduce the numbers of product defects.

Managers also need to develop skills and subsequently can train their subordinates. The prospect of merit pay and bonus can give employees some incentives for improving quality and a firm may link monetary incentives directly to quality improvements.

However, continuous improvement based on, Japanese "Kaizen" concept is the philosophy of continually seeking ways to improve quality and productivity.

Continuous improvements involve identifying bench marks of excellent practice and installing a sense of employee ownership in the operation.

The basis of continuous improvement philosophy are the beliefs that virtually any aspect of an operation can be improved and that the employees most closely associated are in the best position to identify the appropriate changes should be made.

The idea is not to wait until a greater problem occurs before acting.

Firms those are involved in the continuous improvement train their employees to use the **"Plan-do-check-act"** cycle, more commonly known as **"The Deming Wheel"**, for problem solving in the operation.

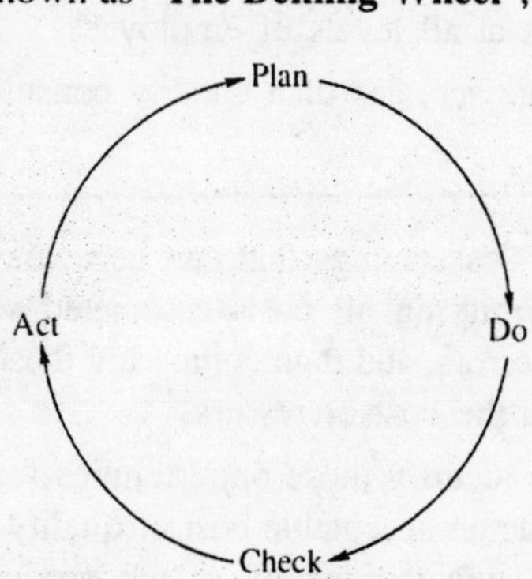

Figure 12.1 The Deming Wheel.

12.7 TOOLS FOR IMPROVING QUALITY AND PERFORMANCE (7QC TOOLS)

The first step in improving the quality of an operation is data collection. Data can help uncover operation requiring improvement and the extent of remedial action needed.

There are **Seven Tools** for organising and presenting data to identify areas for quality and performance improvement. These are as follows:

(*i*) **Check List:** It is a form used to record the frequency of occurrence of certain product or service characteristics related to quality; *i.e.,* weight in kilogram, Diameter in metre, etc.

(*ii*) **Histogram and Bar Chart:** Histogram summarises data measured a continuous scale showing the frequency of distribution of some quality parameter. A bar chart shows series of bars representing the frequency of occurrence of data with periods.

(*iii*) **Pareto Charts:** Pareto (Italian Scientist) concept of 80–20 rule states that 80 percent of the activity is caused by 20 percent of factors. An employee can attack 80 percent of quality problem by concentrating on 20 percent factors. The vital factor is Pareto Chart.

(*iv*) **Scatter Diagram:** A scatter diagram is a plot of two variables showing whether they are related and can be used to verify. Each point on the diagram represents one data observation which may cause quality problem.

(*v*) **Cause-and-effect diagrams:** One way to identify a design problem that needs to be corrected is to develop a "cause-and-effect-diagram." This relates a key quality problem to its potential causes. The diagram (developed by K. Ishikawa) help management to trace customer complaints directly to the operation involved.

(*vi*) **Graphs:** Graphs represent data in a variety of pictorial formats, such as line graphs and pie charts. Line graphs represent data sequentially with data points connected by line segments to highlight trends in the data. Line graphs are used in the control charts. Pie charts represent quality factors as slices of a pie and these charts are useful showing a factor as a percentage of total.

(*vii*) **Control Charts:** These charts are described under Statistical Process Control.

(1) Quality management characteristics and a firm with quality problems

The definition of quality is conformance of requirements. The system of getting quality is prevention, and not appraisal. The quality performance standard must be free of any defect. The management of quality is the cost to get it.

A firm facing quality problem must systematically document the deviation in quality parameters. The company should check clearly the quality performance standards and compares with the best.

The management must have clear idea about the cost of quality and be sincere about the quality and performance training programmes at all levels of employees.

If necessary, they should hire the services of a Quality consultant.

12.8 COST OF QUALITY

This analysis is used to highlight the cost savings that can be achieved by doing the work right at the first time. The analysis involves quantifying all costs associated with maintaining acceptable quality levels, such as the costs of preventing errors, and then comparing these with the costs incurred by failures, to achieve acceptable quality, such as the cost of rework.

Cost-of-quality analysis helps to identify those opportunities for which the improvements achieved offer the largest cost savings. To decide an acceptable cost of quality, we may consider the value offered by the finished product. While increasing the quality of the product, we tend to increase its cost of Production as shown in figure. The value added the finished Product tends to grow much lesser rate.

A firm would rather accept level of quality at which the value Product exceeds its cost of production. While, ascertaining the cost of quality of the Product, one should achieve a trade-off between the losses on account of defects and the cost of inspection and quality control.

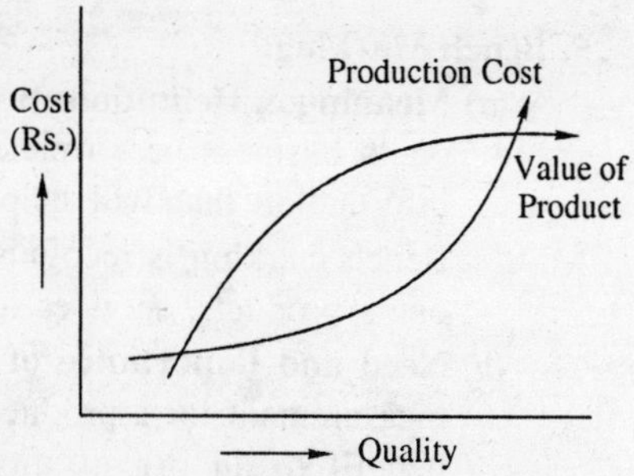

Figure 12.2

Cost of Quality Constitute the following:

(*i*) Cost of prevention of defects, that is, costs of training and applying acceptance sampling of raw materials, SQC, Six Sigma and other techniques.

(*ii*) Cost of detecting defects in the final product, that is costs incurred in the outgoing inspection of products before they are delivered to customers.

(*iii*) Cost of scrap and rework of defective products, which includes the costs of extra paper work, delays, and rescheduling required etc.

(*iv*) Cost of warranty claims, which includes loss of good will of the customers.

12.9 HOW TO MAKE A SUCCESSFUL BENCH MARKING PROCESS

The bench marking performance parameters are as follows:

(*i*) Profit Margins.

(*ii*) Return on Investment.

(*iii*) Cycle Times.

(*iv*) Percentage defects.

(*v*) Sales volumes per employee.

(*vi*) Unit cost of a Product/Service.

Depending on above the following four types of Bench markings are adopted.

1. **Internal Bench Marking:** Identifies the internal performance standards of an organisation.
2. **Competitive Bench Marking:** Compare companies performances which deal with similar product/ service.
3. **Functional Bench Marking:** Functional Bench marking (also known as Industry Bench Marking) tends to involve comparisons between firms that share some common technological and market characteristics and to concentrate on specific functions.

   Example: CESC, Kolkata compares its billing process with that of BEST, Mumbai.
4. **Generic or Process Bench Marking:** This focuses on excellent work process rather than on the business practices of an organisation. It has the potential of revealing the best of best practices.

   The vital factors to be considered for a successful Bench Marking are:

   1. Choose the right things to bench mark.
   2. Involve the right people.
   3. Have a common understanding of what is involved.
   4. Gain a thorough understanding of one's situation.
   5. Choose suitable partners.
   6. Turn good ideas into practical projects.
   7. Manage the improvements.
   8. Bench marking is a continuous process.

5. Bench Marking:

(*a*) **Meaning & Definition:** Bench marking is the process of continuously measuring and comparing one's business performance against comparable processes in leading organisation to obtain information that will help the organisation identify and implement improvements.

Bench marking is recognised by the industry leaders as the continuous process of measuring one's products, services and business practices against the toughest competitors.

(*b*) **Need and importance of Bench Marking:** Bench marking lies at the heart of performance measurement for a product, service or business practice. A bench marking exercise can be of benefit to an organisation since it forces the participants to look closely at their own organisations processes and question them.

Bench marking by definition forces an organisation to change its focus from the internal to the external environment by attempting to compare its performance with that the best-in-class companies.

A business firm becomes engaged in bench marking in order to remain competitive. The process of bench marking leads to the organisation having a better understanding of its competitive environment and its customers needs.

The Xerox corporation, USA was the pioneer in conducting the bench marking exercise.

(c) The Bench marking Exercise:

	Objectives	*Without Bench Marking*	*With Bench Marking*
1.	Becoming Competitive	Internally focussed Evolutionary	Understanding of competitions, ideas change from proven practices
2.	Industry best practices	Few solutions frantic catch-up activity	Many options, Superior performance
3.	Defining customer	Based on history or gut feeling requirements	Market reality objective evaluation perception
4.	Establishing effective	Lacking external focus goals and objectives	Credible, unarguable, Reactive Proactive
5.	Developing true measures of Productivity	Pursuing pet Projects strengths and weaknesses not understood Route of least resistance	Understanding outputs based on industry best practices

The guide to conduct a bench marking exercise involves following:

- Senior management commitment
- Set clear cut objectives
- Choose bench marking partners
- Getting acquainted with one's partner
- Conduct Analysis
- Continuing the process.

(*d*) The following are some of the formal bench marking systems that have been developed over the years:

(*i*) Quality function deployment (QFD) This bench marking approach has been developed by Japanese managers. It takes the customer's requirements as the starting point and aims to improve performance by converting customers perceptions of suppliers performance into an improvement agenda.

(*ii*) ISO 9004. As part of the ISO 9000 series of quality management frame works, ISO 9004 provides a frame work of constant comparison for any type of business.

(*iii*) The Malcom Baldridge National Quality Award bench marking frame work: This is an award for quality awareness started in 1987 in the US.

The frame work is based on four basic elements.

- The role of senior managers in promoting quality excellence.
- The processes used to achieve the objectives of the organisation.
- Quality achievements.
- Customer satisfaction.

19.10 CONTROL OF QUALITY AND TOTAL PRODUCTIVE MAINTENANCE (TPM)

Maintenance is the key to zero defect programme. Japanese Management expert S. Nakajima introduced the concept of TPM in 1984, the ultimate aim was to maximise the output-to-input ratios. It aims to improve capital productivity.

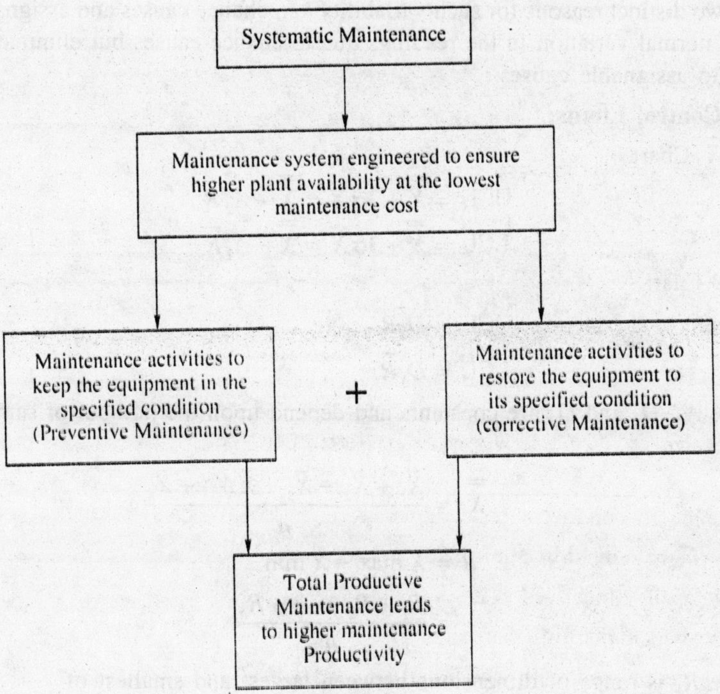

Figure 19.3

A TPM company first quantifies overall equipment effectiveness, which is a function of the availability of the machines after accounting for the failures, break-downs and set up times.

Thus
$$\text{Availability} = \frac{\text{Loading Time} - \text{Down Time}}{\text{Loading Time}} \times 100$$

$$\text{Performance Efficiency} = \frac{\text{Theoritical Cycle} \times \text{Processed Amount}}{\text{Operating Time}} \times 100$$

TPM uses autonomous and planned maintenance, total employee involvement and team-work and continuous improvement.

The important steps in a TPM Programme are as follows:

(*i*) Plant audit and assessment

(*ii*) Formation of functional committees for Maintenance, Training, Safety and Quality.

(*iii*) Selection of Production line/lines.

(*iv*) Focus on eight aspects such as Autonomous maintenance, improvement activities, Zero defect and Zero loss, Efficiency of support services, Process-Flow System and Zero accidents.

TPM and TQM complement each other.

12.10 CONTROL CHARTS

A control chart is an important statistical tool used for the study and control of repetitive processes. This has been devised by W.A. Shewart and it is based on the fact that variability exists in all repetitive processes.

There are two distinct reasons for such variability *i.e.,* chance causes and assignable causes. A control chart accepts the normal variation in the readings due to chance causes but eliminates entirely the errors in readings due to assignable causes.

(*v*) The Control Limits:

For $\overline{X}$ Chart

$$\text{UCL} = \overline{\overline{X}} + 3\sigma\overline{X} = \overline{\overline{X}} + A_2\overline{R}$$

$$\text{LCL} = \overline{\overline{X}} - 3\sigma\overline{X} = \overline{\overline{X}} - A_2\overline{R}$$

For R Chart

$$\text{UCL} = D_4 R$$

and

$$\text{LCL} = D_3\overline{R}$$

where A_2, D_3 and D_4 are constants and depend upon the number of samples per unit or sub-group size.

and

$$\overline{\overline{X}} = \frac{\overline{X}_1 + \overline{X}_2 + \overline{X}_3 + \overline{X}_4 --- + \overline{X}_n}{n}$$

$$R = X\max - X\min$$

$$\overline{R} = \frac{R_1 + R_2 + --- + R_n}{n}$$

where R_1 is range of dimensions between largest and smallest of

X_1', X_1'', X_1''' and $X_1^{nnn} - n$ readings of sample I

(*vi*) Lack of Control: Lack of Control is indicated if the points fall outside the control limits on either x or R – Charts.

(*vii*) Purpose of Control Charts

1. To establish whether the process or operation is in statistical control or not.
2. To determine whether the process capability is compatible with the specifications or not.
3. To detect the trend of readings for further planning, adjustment and resulting of the tools.
4. To get prior information about when the process is likely to be out of control.

(viii) Advantages of Control Charts:

1. The control charts separate out the assignable causes and chance cause for variations in observation, thus bring substantial improvement in product quality.
2. There is reduction in spoilage of work and re-work.
3. The inspection work also reduces.
4. The use of control chart is not limited to manufacturing only but can be applied to many business variables to discover their average values, their range of variation that can be taken as a matter of change and the presence or absence of assignable causes.

(d) Factors for Determining the 3 Sigma Control: Following table shown factors for determining the 3 sigma control limits for $\bar{\chi}$ and R charts.

Number of observations in Sub group n	*Factor for $\bar{\chi}$ chart, A_2*	*Factor of R Chart*	
		Lower Control Limit, D_3	*Upper Control Limit, D_4*
2	1.88	0	3.27
3	1.02	0	2.57
4	0.73	0	2.28
5	0.58	0	2.11
6	0.48	0	2.00
7	0.42	0.08	1.92
8	0.37	0.14	1.86
9	0.34	0.18	1.82
10	0.31	0.22	1.78
11	0.29	0.26	1.74
12	0.27	0.28	1.72
13	0.25	0.31	1.69
14	0.24	0.33	1.67
15	0.22	0.35	1.65
16	0.21	0.36	1.64
17	0.20	0.38	1.62
18	0.19	0.39	1.61
19	0.19	0.40	1.61
20	0.18	0.41	1.59

(e) Numerical Problems on Control Charts:

Problem 18.4 A machine manufacturers plugs to a nominal diameter of 0.500 ± 0.30 cm. Five samples were taken randomly from the manufactured lot and 3 measurements were taken on each sample at different lengths. The readings are shown in tabular form as shown on next page.

Calculate the Control Units on $\bar{\chi}$ and R charts:

Sample	*Three Measurements per Sample (cm) (x)*

	1	2	3
1	0.488	0.489	0.505
2	0.494	0.495	0.499
3	0.498	0.515	0.487
4	0.492	0.509	0.514
5	0.490	0.508	0.499

Solution. For sample 1,

$$\bar{X}_1 = \frac{0.488 + 0.489 + 0.505}{3} = \frac{1.482}{3} = 0.494$$

$$\bar{X}_2 = \frac{0.494 + 0.495 + 0.499}{3} = \frac{1.488}{3} = 0.496$$

$$\bar{X}_3 = 0.50$$

$$\bar{X}_4 = 0.505$$

and $$\bar{X}_5 = 0.499$$

$$\Sigma\bar{X} = \bar{X}_1 + \bar{X}_2 + \bar{X}_3 + \bar{X}_4 + \bar{X}_5 = 2.494$$

$$\therefore \quad \bar{\bar{X}} = \frac{\Sigma\bar{X}}{\text{Number of Samples}} = \frac{2.494}{5} = 0.499$$

Calculation of Range

For Sample 1,

$$R_1 = (X\,\text{max} - X\,\text{min}) \text{ for sample 1}$$

$$= 0.505 - 0.488 = 0.017$$

and $$R_2 = 0.499 - 0.494 = 0.005$$

$$R_3 = 0.515 - 0.487 = 0.028$$

$$R_4 = 0.514 - 0.492 = 0.022$$

$$R_5 = 0.508 - 0.490 = 0.018$$

$$\bar{R} = \frac{R_1 + R_2 + R_3 + R_4 + R_5}{\text{Number of Samples}}$$

$$= \frac{0.017 + 0.005 + 0.028 + 0.022 + 0.018}{5} = 0.018$$

(*f*) Trial Control Limits

1. **Control Limits for *R* Chart:** Now, $UCL = D_4\ \bar{R}$ and $LCL = D_3\ \bar{R}$. The sub group size 3 (since the Number of observations per sample is 3). From the table for 3 sigma control limits given before,

   For Number of observation $= 3 \rightarrow D_4 = 2.57$ and $D_3 = 0$.

   $\therefore \quad UCL = D_4\bar{R} = 2.57 \times 0.018 = 0.0463$ & $LCL = 0$.

2. **Control Limits for $\bar{X}$ chart:**

   $$UCL = \bar{X} + A_2\bar{R} \ \&\ LCL = \bar{X}\,A_2\,\bar{R}$$

From the above (3 sigma control limits) table for $n = 3$ $A_2 = 1.02$ for sub group size 3, $X = 0.499$ and $\overline{R} = 0.018$

Therefore, $UCL = 0.499 + 1.02 \times 0.018$
$= 0.5174$

and $LCL = 0.499 - 1.02 \times 0.018$
$= 0.4807$

Observation: No values of $\overline{\chi}$ and R are out of the control limits. Therefore, the trial control limits are actual control limits.

Problem 12.5 The surface hardness of crank pins were measured along their lengths. On each 3 measurements were taken. In all six pins were randomly selected from a lot of 10 and measurements were taken. The readings are given below. Complete the control limits for $\overline{\chi}$ and R charts.

Sample	*Three Measurements per Sample (x)*		
	1	*2*	*3*
1	100	102	101
2	102	101	101.5
3	104	101	101.5
4	99	102	101
5	94	100	104
6	97	99	100

Solution. $\overline{\chi}_1 = \dfrac{100 + 102 + 101}{3} = 101$

$\overline{\chi}_2 = 101.5, \quad \overline{\chi}_3 = 102.2$

$\overline{\chi}_4 = 100.7 \quad \overline{\chi}_5 = 99.3$

$\overline{\chi}_6 = 98.7$

$$\therefore \quad \overline{\overline{\chi}} = \frac{\Sigma\overline{X}}{6} = \frac{603.4}{6} = 100.46$$

$R_1 = 102 - 100 = 2, \ R_2 = 102 - 101 = 1$

$R_3 = 104 - 101 = 3, \ R_4 = 102 - 99 = 3$

$R_5 = 104 - 94 = 10, \ R_6 = 100 - 97 = 3$

$$\overline{R} = \frac{R_1 + R_2 + R_3 + R_4 + R_5 + R_6}{6} = \frac{22}{6} = 3.7$$

Trial Control Limits

1. For $\overline{X}$ – chart

$$UCL = \overline{\overline{X}} + A_2\overline{R}$$

for 3 readings – $A_2 = 1.02$ (from above table)

$= 100.46 + 1.02 \times 3.7$

$= 104.37$

$$LCL = \overline{\overline{X}} - A_2\overline{R} = 100.46 - 1.02 \times 3.7$$
$$= 97.54$$

Observation: No value of $\overline{X}$ is out of control limit.

2. For R – Chart

$$D_3 = 0 \quad \text{and} \quad D_4 = 2.57 \text{ (from above table)}$$
$$UCL = D_4\overline{R} = 2.57 \times 3.7$$
$$= 9.50$$

and $LCL = 0$

12.11 PROBABLE QUESTIONS

1. Define Quality Management and illustrate importance of Quality for a business.
2. Describe Seven QC tools for improving performance.
3. What do you understand "Cost of Quality"? Illustrate with diagram.
4. Describe Philip Crosby's methods for improving Quality.
5. What is Bench Marking? How do you make a successful Bench Marking Process?
6. What is Zero-Defect? How do you install a Zero-Defect Programme?
7. Describe the importance of Total Productive Maintenance System with diagram.
8. Describe the significance of Total Quality System in Service Sector.
9. What are multiple dimensions qualities in the service sector?
10. Write about the contribution of TQM for customer satisfaction in Services Sector

13

Total Quality Management (TQM)

> *• The Japanese 5 S Systems • Ishikawa Diagram • Quality Function Development (QFD) • ISO 9000 and ISO 14000 Certification • Statistical Process Control (SPC) • Case Example—Six-Sigma Quality • Six-Sigma Quality • International Organisation for Standardisation (ISO) • TQM and Strategic Management • Probable Questions.*

13.1 TQM AND THE DEMING

Dr. Edward Deming was a pioneering personality to have influenced the Japanese manufacturing industries in the last century. The Union of Japanese Engineers and Scientists (JUSE) in 1950 took his expert advice to improve the poor state of Japanese industries in terms of poor quality and poor-price.

Dr. Deming was an authority on the statistical control of Quality and his expert guidance had helped the Japanese industries to a great extent. The JUSE set up the Deming Prize in 1951 for the Japanese companies and later it was thrown open to the rest of the world.

The Deming Prize has 3 categories.

1st category is the Deming Application Prize that is given to companies or divisions of companies that have enhanced performances through TQM in a given year.

Mahindra and Mahindra Ltd. a reputed automobile manufacturer in India had won this prize in 2003-04 for its tractor division.

The second category of the Deming Prize, for individuals that goes to TQM scholars and Practitioners.

The third kind of Prize is the Quality Control Award for Operations Business Units given out for exceptional implementation of TQM. The Deming Prize tests applications on their ability to adopt Deming's principles across the company. The companies are not asked to conform to any given model but are examined on whether the methods chosen were the best of their market and the impact of their choice on the future.

The Deming Prize is conducted and managed by JUSE and the examinations are carried out by five sub-committees and based on their examination reports the Deming Prize committee awards the prize.

The Deming Prize as an endorsement of quality practices of the highest order.

(*a*) The Deming's 14 Points Quality Practices:

1. Create constancy of purpose.
2. Adopt the new philosophy.
3. Cease dependence on inspection to achieve quality.
4. Minimise total costs.

5. Improve continuously quality and productivity.
6. Practise job training for employees.
7. The objectives of Supervision should be to help employees and machines to do better job.
8. Remove fear to enable everyone to work effectively.
9. Maintain inter-departmental co-ordination and cohesion.
10. Improve systems to eliminate the causes of low quality and low productivity. It is needless to associate workers for the improvement of system.
11. Improve all-round supervision as means of guidance and checks.
12. Quality Supervision with meaningful leadership should be instituted in the shop floor.
13. Institute vigorous programme of education and self improvement.
14. Send message that the transformation is everybody's job.

(*b*) The Deming Prize and Indian Companies: The Deming Prize was thrown open to companies outside Japan in 1985 and some Indian companies as stated below have won the awards.

The Deming Application Prize goes to companies or divisions that have achieved distinctive performance improvement through the application of TQM in a specific year.

Some other Indian companies have also won the Quality Control Award for operations Business Units.

1. Sundaram-Clayton, Breaks Division of TVS Group won the Deming Application Prize in 1998. The company is a major exporter of auto components throughout the world.
2. Sundaram Breaks Linings also is a TVS group company won Deming Prize in 2001. It makes breaks linings and asbestos free friction material. It is a small scale unit with turnover less than 100 crore a year.
3. TVS Motor company, the first two-wheeler company had won the prize in 2002.
4. Mahindra and Mahindra, Farm Equipment Sector won the prize in 2003.
5. Rane Breaks Linings, a Rane group company based in Chennai won the Prize in 2003 for its continued focus on quality for a long time and obtained certificates in ISO 9001 and ISO 14001. It makes steering, suspension systems, seat belts and valves etc.
6. Sona Koyo Steering Systems: The flagship company of the Sona Group. It makes out components for major customers like Maruti Suzuki, Hyundai Motors, Hindustan Motor, Telco and M & M etc.
7. Birla Cellulosic, Kharach—A group company of Grasim Industries had won the prize in 2003.

13.2 THE KAIZEN SYSTEMS FOR IMPROVEMENT

Kaizen is Japanese concept of seeking to continually improve the operation. Like Quality it also is applied to process improvements. Continuous improvement involves identifying benchmarks of excellent practice and instilling the sense of employee ownership in the process.

The based of continuous improvement philosophy are the beliefs that virtually any aspect of an operation can be improved and that the people must closely be associated with an operation are in the best position to identify the changes that should be made.

Continuous improvements can also focus with problems of customers or suppliers. The expression KAIZEN captures the underlying philosophy of almost all techniques of Japanese Management.

KAI = Change and ZEN = Good (for better)

KAIZEN means continual improvement

Kaizen means improvement through self discipline and self efforts.

Improvement should be continuing in nature and improvement should cover all aspects of life: personal, social, environmental and work place.

When applied to workplace KAIZEN means continuing improvement involving everyone—managers and workers.

(*a*) Nature and Types of Improvement through Kaizen: There are two ways of achieving improvement:

- People–Oriented.
- Investment–Oriented.

Kaizen believes in People-Oriented improvement.

(*b*) Management has two broad approaches:

- Process–Oriented.
- Result–Oriented.

Kaizen believes in Process–Oriented approach.

Kaizen believes in improvement in small doses with existing resources and without making much financial investment.

6. (*a*) Getting Started with continuous improvement instilling a philosophy of continuous improvement in an organisation may be a lengthy process, and several steps are essential to its eventual success. These steps are:

1. Train employees in the methods of statistical process control (SPC) and other tools for improving quality and performance.
2. Make SPC methods a normal aspect of daily operations.
3. Build work teams and employee involvement.
4. Utilise problem-solving tools within the work-teams.
5. Develop a sense of operator ownership in the process.

It is to be noted that employee involvement is central to the philosophy of continuous improvement. However, the last two steps are crucial if the philosophy is to become part of every day operations.

Problem solving addresses the aspects of operations that need improvement and evaluates alternatives for achieving improvements.

A sense of operator ownership emerges when employees feel as though they own the processes and methods they use and take pride in the quality of the product or service they produce.

It comes from participation on work team and in problem solving activities which instill in employees a feeling that they have some control over their work place and tasks.

(*b*) **Problem-Solving Process:** Continuous most firms actively engaged in improvement train their work teams to use the plan – do – check – act cycle for problem solving. Another name for this approach is the Deming wheel.

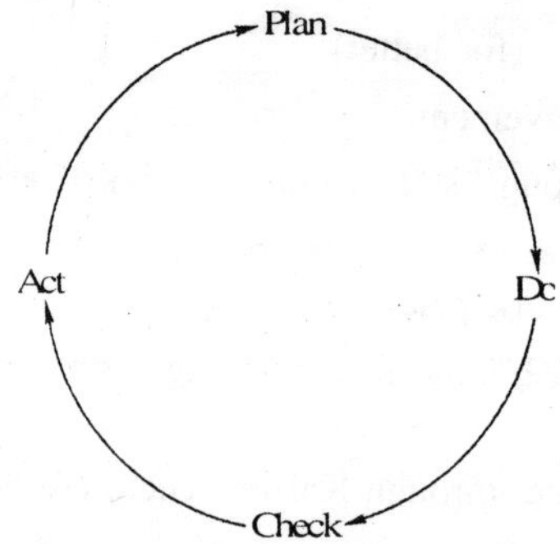

Figure 13.1 Plan – Do – Check – Act or PDCA Cycle.

- **Plan:** The team selects a process that needs improvement. The team then documents the selected process, analyse data, set qualitative goals for improvement and discuss various ways to achieve goals.
- **Do:** The team implements the plan and monitors progress. Data are collected continuously to measure the improvements in the process.
- **Check:** The team analyses the data collected during the "do" step to find out how closely the results correspond to the goals set in the "plan" step. If major short coming exists the team may have to reevaluate the plan or stop the project.
- **Act:** If the results are successful the team documents the revised process so that it becomes the standard procedure for all who may use it.

The idea of continuous improvement is to reduce or eliminate activities that do not add value and thus are wasteful (*i.e.,* such as inspection).

Continuous improvement projects might focus on reducing materials handling time by rearranging machine locations to minimise the distances travelled by materials or improving the methods for producing the parts to reduce the need for inspection and rework.

13.3 THE JAPANESE 5 S SYSTEMS

Focus: Work Place. The Five 'S' Movement (Highly useful and popular in Japan). These are very good practices at work place.

Start the day with:

Step 1	–	Seiri	–	Straighten up following: Work-in-Progress Unnecessary tools Unused machinery Defective Products Papers and Documents
Step 2	–	Seiton	–	Put things in order Tools, Parts, Papers
Step 3	–	Seiso	–	Clean up Gemba (work place)

Step 4 – Seiketsu – Personal cleanliness
Step 5 – Shitsuke – Discipline and Punctuality.

13.4 ISHIKAWA DIAGRAM

Dr. Kaoru Ishikawa founded Ishikawa diagram which is also known as cause and effect diagram. It depicts the relation between an "effect" and various possible "causes" for the effect. The purpose is to generate the maximum number of ideas regarding possible causes for a problem in a structural manner by using brain storming technique.

The generation of Ishikawa diagram consists of (*i*) Identify the problem for which causes are to be searched (*ii*) Determine the main categories of causes (*iii*) Brainstorm to collect as many causes in each category (*iv*) Discuss the relative importance of the causes (*v*) shortlist few causes through a consensus or vote (*vi*) Test to verify the findings.

Quality Function Deployment (QFD)

QFD is a key to improving quality through TQM for linking design of products or services to the processes which produce them. It is a means of translating customer requirements into the appropriate technical requirements for each stage of product or service development and production.

QFD approach seeks to answers to following six questions:

(*i*) Voice of customer	–	What do the customers need and want.
(*ii*) Competitive Analysis	–	How are we doing compared to our competitors in relation to customer's satisfaction.
(*iii*) Voice of the engineer	–	What technical measures relate to our customers's need?
(*iv*) Correlations	–	Relationships between voice of customers and voice of the engineer.
(*v*) Technical comparison	–	Performance of our Products services compared to competitors.
(*vi*) Trade – offs	–	What are potential technical trade offs? QFD encourages inter functional communication for the purpose of improving the quality of Products and services.

13.5 ISO 9000 AND ISO 14000 CERTIFICATION

ISO's guide lines for ISO 9001 and ISO 14001 certification are available on ISO's web site www.iso.org.

Buy using ISO's guide lines, an organisation will avoid the pitfalls of false, misleading or confusing statements in their or confusing statements in their communications about ISO 9001 or ISO 14001 certification and thus avoid harming the credibility of the organisation.

By following guide lines, an organisation will be demonstrating the same rigor in their communications about certification as it has done implementing its ISO 9001 quality management system or ISO 14001 environmental management system.

The ISO guidelines are intended to help organisations apply good practice when publicizing, communicating and promoting their certification to stake holders including staff, customers and business partners and to the general public.

ISO 9001:2000, the single standard has replaced the 1994 versions of ISO 9001, ISO 9002 and ISO 9003. Both the ISO 9000 (quality) and ISO 14000 (environment) families of standard now confirm only one certification standard respectively. ISO 9001:2000 and ISO 14001:1996. ISO itself does not audit organisation and does not issue 9001 or ISO 14001 certificates. This is carried out independently of ISO by more than 750 certification bodies around the world.

(*a*) **ISO 9000–Quality Management:** ISO 9000 series standards are for the Quality Management Systems for an organisation and do not directly relate to the outgoing product quality. This set of standard has a very strong emphasis on improvement of the product quality and reduction in cost through strengthening the systems and product realisation process. Over the last decade, these standards have been modified to build in a strong focus towards process orientation, top management commitments to quality and the basic framework of the Quality Management Principles in the activities of the organisations.

If any organisation implements these standards true to its spirit, then it is bound to gain by the improved efficiency and consistent output of product quality.

The Quality Management Systems and their implementation can be done effectively only if the eight principles of Quality Management as listed in the Standard form from the basic fabric of the management system of the organisation.

(*b*) **Total Quality Management:** TQM is a long term system initiated by the top management to bring about a cultural change in the organisation and to integrate every employees, every function and every process in order to provide total customer satisfaction.

Quality consists of utility/service function, customer satisfaction and aesthetic function. In TQM, market data on customer's satisfaction is fed back to design for continuous improvement in satisfaction level. This cycle may be formed as Quality Circle, Deming cycle or PDCA cycle.

Following activities are practised at every stage in TQM Process.

Sales and Marketing
Product Planning
Product Design
Product Preparation
Manufacturing
Inspection and Testing

Quality Assurance (QA) is part of TQM, which comprises of following six standards:

ISO 8402	–	Concepts and definition (for QA)
ISO 9000	–	Quality Management and Quality Assurance Standards – selection and use.
ISO 9001	–	Model for quality assurance in design/development.
ISO 9002	–	Model for QA in Production and Installation.
ISO 9003	–	Model for QA in final inspection and testing.
ISO 9004	–	Guidelines on development of quality measurement systems to minimise costs and maximise benefits.

The Quality Circle team decides the most appropriate factors under which the probable causes and other information could be listed.

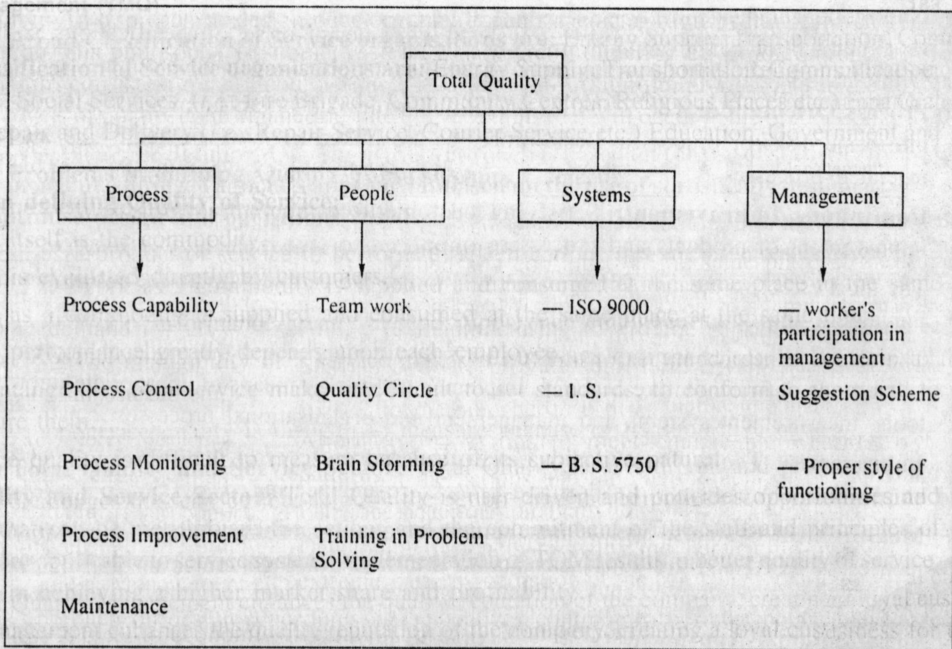

Figure 13.2 The four elements of total quality.

It depends upon the defects or effects in the product or the system which is to be eliminated or improved upon.

These factors can be: Manpower, Machine Tools or equipment; Method or process, Material, Fixture, Environment, Supplier, Office, Market and Vendor etc.

(*i*) **TQM:** There are four fundamental elements of Total Quality Management:

These are (*i*) Process (*ii*) People (*iii*) Systems (*iv*) Management.

13.6 QUALITY AND TQM

Quality: Quality is defined as being the value which conforms to standards, specifications and fitness for use. Quality is that value which meets customer's expectations. Quality is judged by the user rather than the producer.

TQM: TQM provides a valuable test-bed for many key areas of management theory such as leadership, strategy and employee involvement. TQM is a set of techniques and procedures used to reduce or eliminate variation from a production process, or service delivery system in order to improve efficiency, reliability and quality.

TQM is seen as consistent with open management styles, delegated responsibility and increased autonomy to staff. TQM is an integrative management concept for continuously improving the quality of goods and services delivered through the participation of all levels and functions.

(*i*) **Important Principles of TQM are as follows:**

(*a*) **Customer Orientation:** Customer orientation provides a common goal for all organisational activities and members, and incorporates both quality of design and conformance to quality specification.

A customer's requirements must be translated into a design or set of specifications, so that the activities needed to produce the required product or service can be brought together.

(*b*) **Process Orientation:** The activities performed within an organisation can be broken down into basic tasks or processes. Basic processes are linked in series or quality chains to form extended processes.

(*c*) **Continuous Improvement:** Satisfying customer requirements involves the continuous improvement of products and processes.

The most effective means of improvement is to use the people who do the job to identify and implement appropriate changes.

The above principles are implemented in a specific manner and the mode of implementation is itself one defining feature of TQM. Implementation is by means of appropriate improvement tools, measurement systems and management and organisational processes.

Improvement Tools: These embrace statistical process control methods, to be used by all employees, process simplification and process–re–engineering.

Measurement Systems: Monitoring the cost of quality and customer satisfaction are novel metrics of TQM and are supplementary to the more traditional measurement of defects or variation.

Organisational Approaches: These include quality improvement or action teams, quality committees, cross-functional planning, self-inspection, exposure of employees to customers and collaborative quality improvement with suppliers.

(*d*) **Quality Circle (QC):** The concept of Quality Circle is based on respect for the human individual, as against the traditional assumption based on suspicion and mistrust between management and employees. Quality Circles build mutual trust and create greater understanding between the management and the workers. Co-operation and no confrontations is the key elements of its operation.

Quality Circles aim at building people; developing them, arousing genuine interest and dedication to their work to improve quality, productivity, cost reduction etc.

(*i*) **Objectives of Quality Circles:** Some of the broad objectives of Quality Circle are as follows:

1. To improve quality, productivity, safety and cost reduction.
2. To give chance to the employees to use their wisdom and creativity.
3. To encourage team spirit, cohesive culture among different levels and sections of the employees.
4. To promote self and mutual development including leadership quality.
5. To fulfill the self-esteem and motivational needs of employees.
6. To improve the quality of work-life of employees.

(*ii*) **Implementation of Quality Circles in an Organisation:** For the success of Quality Circle Programme, following actions are necessary in an organisation.

1. Few managers representing production, quality control, design process planning form the Quality Circle and steering committee. This acts as a Policy making body and would monitor the Q.C. in the organisation.
2. Top management should attend the orientation courses designed for them.
3. A committed top and middle management is necessary.

(*e*) **Taguchi Philosophy:** An approach to design developed by Japan's Genichi Taguchi has received considerable attention. His philosophy is simple. Instead of constantly directing effort to control a process so as to assure consistent quality conformance, it is better to design the product or service to achieve desired levels of quality conformance despite the variations that will occur in the production process or service delivery system.

Based on his work in manufacturing, **Taguchi's approach is based on the use of statistically designed experiments to optimise design and operations costs.**

This approach requires a product or service to perform to specifications in extreme conditions.

For Example:

(*i*) Above-average demand	—	Ability of manufacturing to provide capacity uplifts.
(*ii*) Absenteeism	—	Staffing plans to provide short-term cover.
(*iii*) Dietary needs	—	Range of options to provide alternative menus.
(*iv*) Weather shifts	—	Alternative activities to meet changeable weather patterns
(*v*) Unexpected demand	—	Plans to meet early arrivals.
(*vi*) Working conditions	—	Developing products to withstand harsh climates or extreme patterns of use.

The effects of this approach on design procedures and objectives continue to be most noticeable. In part it forces the process/delivery system and product/service design to come together and agree the parameter to meet a range of conditions and to build these into specifications.

13.7 CASE EXAMPLE—SIX-SIGMA QUALITY

Jack Welch, General Electric's Chairman and *CEO*, has set a corporate goal of becoming, by the year 2000, a six sigma quality company, which means a company that produces virtually defect free products, services and transactions.

As he outlined in his addressed to GE's 1996–97 AGM "3 to 4" Sigma Quality is typically 10–15 percent of revenues. In GE's case, with over $70 billion in revenues, that amounts to some $7–10 billion annually, mostly in scrap, reworking of parts and rectifying mistakes in transactions. So the financial rationale for embarking on this quality journey is clear.

But beyond the pure financials, there are even more important rewards that will come with dramatically improved quality. Among them, the unlimited growth from selling products and services universally recognised by customers as being on a completely different plane of quality than those of your competitors.

Six-sigma will be an exciting journey and the most difficult and invigorating stretch goal we have ever undertaken.

The magnitude of the challenge of going from 35,000 defects per million to fewer than 4 defects is huge. It will require us to reduce defects rates 10,000 fold – about 84 percent to five consecutive years– we want to make our quality so special, so valuable to our customers, so that our products and services become their only real value choice."

Six-sigma Quality

The drive to improve existing levels of quality conformance has been elaborated in the mandate of Six-Sigma quality. In the 1980's Motorola's Semi Conductor Products division laid down for itself the six-sigma challenge; that is 3.4 defects per million transactions or virtually error free output. And it set the goal of achieving ± 6 sigma capability in all phases of the business including product design, manufacturing, sales and services.

Most companies currently fall well short of that.

Typical Processes generate about 35,000 defects per million which sound a lot, but is consistent with the defect levels of most successful companies – in statistical terms this constitutes three and a half sigma.

Other companies are also recognising the competitive advantages of setting quality conformance goals that will change the rules of the game.

Six Sigma Quality Standard

Specification Limit	*# defects per million*	*Percent good quality*
± 1 Sigma	697700	30.22
± 2 Sigma	308700	69.13
± 3 Sigma	66810	93.32
± 4 Sigma	6210	99.37
± 5 Sigma	233	99.98
± 6 Sigma	3.4	99.99

13.8 MUMBAI DABBAWALLAHS A CASE STUDY OF SIX SIGMA

The British public was not too happy with Prince Charles' marriage, but Raghunath D. Megde, leader of the 5000-strong Mumbai *dabbawallahs*, was kicked: '*Yeh hamare yaar ki shaadi hai*'. Camilla Parker Bowles had a wedding present from India no member of the British royalty has ever had. So what if she has to be content with only being called Her Royal Highness the Duchess of Cornwall, and at best Princess Consort, if her husband ascends the throne. In her gifts, she found a traditional *chhavvari* (six yards long) Maharashtrian silk sari and a matching blouse—probably green in colour. Her husband was not overlooked either—he got a traditional *pheta* (turban). These were gifts to the couple from the *dabbawallahs* of Mumbai. Raghunath D. Medge and Sopan Laxman Mare, leaders of the 5000-strong Mumbai *dabbawallahs* (Nutan Mumbai Tiffin Box Suppliers Charity Trust, the organization that runs this service), were two special invitees of Prince Charles. The Prince remembered the gifts they sent on hearing of his wedding and was touched by their sentiment. The Queen told Medge she knew about the tiffin-carriers of Mumbai from TV and newspapers while Prince Charles said it was nice of them to come and then added to convey his greetings and good wishes to other members.

Prince Charles talking to Mumbai *dabbawallahs* in 2003

No wonder Medge said at the end of the wedding, 'We will never forget the attention we got from Prince Charles. Now we are being given attention by our own VIPs back home too.' He added, 'We felt like being in a fairyland at Windsor. It was like a dream, spending time at a 900-year old castle and treated equal to Dukes, Duchess, and other dignitaries. We are grateful to him as we said in our wedding greetings card 'thank you for enlightening the life *dabbawallahs*'. The *dabbawallahs*' trust with Prince Charles started in 2003, when he was on a visit to India. Medge was elated by Prince Charles' visit. 'We are glad that this 'raja of England' (King of England is interested in our work. Tragically, no leader of India has ever inquired about our work and our trouble he said. Medge and the organization's secretary Gangaram Talekar, garlanded the Prince, placed a shawl on him, and offered him a white Gandhi cap which he politely declined to wear. This brief ceremony took place in the premises of the Western Railway Headquarters, opposite Churchgate Station in South Mumbai. Medge and Talekar then explained the intricacies of their business to the Prince, showing him a long rectangle tray that carries up to 40 boxes. They explained how the boxes that are collected from various houses in the suburbs are sorted and sent specific stations, where they are sorted to be sent various offices. Explaining the rationale for the Prince's visit to the *dabbawallahs*, a British High Commission official said the idea was to show him something that was unique to Mumbai. 'I don't think any other city anywhere in the world or even India has such a system,' she said, adding, 'also, the Prince of Wales is always keen to meet people, so we felt this would be ideal.' Back home, after the wedding of Prince Charles, these leaders of the *dabbawallahs* are getting similar attention. Medge, who was invited at Chennai to receive the 'Lucas TVS NIQR' Award, received a standing ovation in Le Royal Meridien. After receiving this award from the National Institution for Quality and Reliability, he said 'it is surprising to note that after doing business for more than 100 years now, our model of enterprise had become a global case study for MBAs and PhD students.' Their business model had caught the attention of even the hallowed 'Forbes.' The American business magazine conferred the 'Six Sigma' plus rating on *dabbawallahs*, meaning only one error in six million deliveries, alongside the likes of GE and Motorola in terms of efficiency and quality of service. Their modus operandi too has been well documented by the likes of BBC and Dutch and German film makers. There are close to 5,000 *dabbawallahs* operating in Mumbai city supplying 1,70,000 *dabbas* (tiffin boxes) every day. Their operations are so complex that if even one thing goes out of place, it would lead to chaos, so much so that even when Prince Charles came to visit them, they did not delay their operations. A lot of people believe that the food *dabbawallahs* deliver is also cooked by them. In reality, they only deliver food to the people of Mumbai which is cooked in the homes of the people by their wives, sisters, or mothers. The tiffin box that the food is delivered in also belongs to the customer. *Dabbawallahs* have a unique colour coding system that they put on the boxes. Their ancestors started by first using coloured threads. Then they switched to using pieces of cloth and now *dabbawallahs* use oil paint and symbols. The first colour symbolizes a 'group.' A group comprises 10 to 20 people who service one station. Just like a cricket team there are a few substitutes in case someone falls ill. Each group picks up about 40 tiffins from their area and delivers them to the local railway station. There they are sorted according to their destination. The alphabet written on the tiffin box stands for the person who collects the tiffins from the house, and the number is for its destination. From the Six Sigma point of view, the *dabbawallahs* have to take care of two critical to quality (CTQ) characteristics—the tiffins must be delivered to the customer in office at the scheduled time without any delay and secondly, the empty tiffin box must be returned back at the customer's home without any mix up. Rarely do *dabbawallahs* get complaints of someone's tiffin getting mixed up or lost. It happens only once in a month or two when they get a complaint. On following up on the complaint they generally find that it was stolen by a hungry beggar. They then keep a lookout for it in the market and on spotting it buy it back and return it to the rightful owner. *Dabbawallahs* claim that they never misplace anything due to any confusion on their part. It obviously is a puzzle for many who wonder how they have managed to reach such levels of efficiency with such an untrained work force. Medge says, 'It just depends on hard work and sincerity, only when you fly high can you reach the stars. The uneducated have an ability to memorize and retain more as opposed to the educated who are used to writing down everything.'

Dabbawallahs charge Rs. 250–300 per month from a customer. That includes picking up the tiffin from home, delivering it to the office, and then returning the empty tiffin back home. Every station on Mumbai's western, central, and harbour railway lines has two groups ranging between 15 to 40 people. 'All of us are entrepreneurs who come together to deliver as a whole. We work exactly like the post office with hub and spoke operations,' says the 63-year old Jairaj Surve, a *dabbawallah*. The meals picked up from clients by 9–9.30 a.m. are brought to the closest railway station. Numbers and symbols painted on the aluminium cases help to sort out the *dabbas* according to the destination. Over the next hour, they are loaded in trains and taken to their destinations, where they are once again sorted out on the basis of office, street, and floor. Even as the *dabba* is picked up from a client's home and delivered by one person, it is delivered and picked up from the workplace by another person. It goes through 3 to 4 hands before reaching its destination. Till 1980, it was a worker-employer relationship, whereby there used to be a contractor who would employ 20–25 workers under him. However, the railway strike of 1975 under Datta Samant which lasted for 20–22 days, caused huge losses for the *dabbawallahs*. Their losses were further compounded by the mill strike. This made them wonder what would happen if their workers were to go on strike. This was the reason that every worker was made a shareholder. This way they put in more effort and since everyone is a shareholder, there is no question of a union. There are elections for the post of the president of the trust and the person getting majority votes becomes the president. There is a show of hands and the person getting the most hands win. There are disputes between *dabbawallahs* at time, but they are settled on the 15th of every month in the Panch Committee. *Dabbawallahs* have their own mini-government which levies a fine on the workers for making mistakes like not turning up for duty or drinking alcohol while on duty. No dispute has even reached the police or the courts.

13.12 TOTAL QUALITY IN SERVICE SECTOR

Service Sector in India is very prominent and its contribution towards country's GDP is over 50%. The development of the service industry has facilitated service trading at a rate faster than in manufacturing.

The development of the service industry has become an important national economic indicator. In terms of organisational operation, service means a functional component that is deeply involved with design, planning, procurement, engineering, repair, maintenance, warehousing, distribution and marketing.

Service is an activity that has some element of intangibility associated with it, which involves interaction with customers or with property in their possession and does not result in a transfer of ownership.

Service has four characteristics.

- Intangibility — Abstract and intangible.
- Heterogeneity — Non-standard and highly variable.
- Inseparability — Services are typically produced and consumed at the same time with customer participation in the process.
- Perishability — Service cannot be stored.

The Service System is an integration of all these components, involving a large number of white-collar staff working with a purpose to satisfy the varying needs of customers.

The distribution between a Product and a Service is done on the basis of their tangible and intangible elements. If the source of a product's core benefit is more tangible than intangible, it should be considered a Product; and if it is more intangible than tangible, it should be considered a service.

The proportion of intangibility attached to any service brand further complicates its marketing for the Service providers.

(*a*) **Broad Classification of Service organisations are:** Energy Supply, Transportation, Communication, Health Care, Social Services, (*i.e.,* Fire Brigade, Community Centres, Religious Places etc.) Financial Services, Repair and Delivery (*i.e.,* Repair Service, Courier Service etc.) Education, Government and Law etc.

(*b*) **Problems in defining Quality of Service:**

- Work itself is the commodity.
- Work is evaluated directly by customers.
- Work as a commodity is supplied and consumed at the same place at the same time.
- Work performance greatly depends upon each employee.
- The intangibility of a service makes it difficult to set standards, to conform to them and to measure them.
- Service quality is difficult to measure because of its subjective nature.

(*c*) **Total Quality and Service Sector:** Total Quality is user-driven and provides opportunities and challenges that can be met through the actions and the commitment of the staff and principles of TQM are more applicable to service system. Implementation of TQM results in better quality of service, which help in achieving a higher market share and profitability.

Quality Management enhances the quality reputation of the company, creating a loyal customer base, less subject to economic fluctuation. Quality Management helps a service business for establishing the link between quality and productivity.

The quality improvement will lead to increase in sales, production of low cost products, better salaries and promotional avenues and high morale for employees.

Lastly, the cultural change at which TQM aims will help a service business to attend to its customers need in a better way, thus promoting a satisfied customer base.

(*d*) **Quality of Service:** Quality is defined as constantly meeting or exceeding customer expectations. This approach relies on the ability of a firm to determine customer requirements and then meet them.

Bery has identified the principal dimensions customers use to judge service quality. These are:

1. **Reliability:** Customers expect companies to deliver the promised level of service each time and every time dependably and accurately.
2. **Responsiveness:** The Service should be delivered promptly and the company should respond to the customer's demands.
3. **Assurance:** The service employees should be knowledgeable, courteous and able to convey trust and confidence.
4. **Empathy:** The customer should be provided caring and individualised attention.
5. **Tangibility:** The physical evidence associated with the service facilities should be clean and the employees should be well trained.

Further, Garvin (1988) and Stamatis (1997) prescribed following dimensions of Service quality such as:

Function, Features, Conformance, Reliability, Serviceability and Perception.

13.13 MULTIPLE DIMENSIONS OF SERVICE QUALITY

- Accessibility
- Aesthetics
- Appropriateness
- Effectiveness
- Efficacy
- Efficiency
- Personal Perspectively
- Reliability
- Reputation

- Assurance
- Availability
- Conformance
- Continuity
- Courtesy
- Durability
- Empathy
- Features
- Flexibility
- Freshness
- Maintainability
- Performance
- Responsiveness
- Robustness
- Safety
- Security
- Serviceability
- Timeliness

13.14(*a*) TQM AND CUSTOMER SATISFACTION IN THE SERVICE SECTOR

Philip Kotler (1996) defined customer delivered value as the difference between total customer value and total customer cost.

Total customer value is the bundle of benefits customers expect from a given service. Customer added value is set of service value, product value, personal value and image value and total customer cost is composed of monetory price, time cost, energy cost.

Kotler adds that to-day, companies do compete on the basis of a value delivery system. A value delivery system depends on the combinative capabilities of product and service delivery processes.

Thus, Total Quality Management creates a network of people and organisations those are involved with each other through upstream and downstream linkages in the different processes and activities that produce value in the form of products and services in the hands of ultimate customers. Implementing a strategy based on customer's satisfaction means, above all, setting up a programme of self-evaluation.

The success of awards for quality (Deming Prize, Malcolm Baldrige National Quality Award etc.) is linked essentially to self-evaluation.

In other words, firms use the principles and criteria of quality-excellence when setting up a process of self-evaluation for the quality system itself.

In relation to awards, customer satisfaction is seen as one component of the quality system, and sometimes, as in the Baldrige Award, it is the most important one.

13.14(*b*) IDENTIFICATION OF QUALITY PARAMETERS FOR A SERVICE

The quality of a service is defined by a set of four parameters:

(*a*) **Timeliness:** Service time is defined as the total time that elapses from the entry of a customer in the service system to his exit from the system.

(*b*) **Access Time:** This is the length of time that elapses from the clients first, effort to gain the service provider's attention until the effort succeeds.

(*c*) **Queuing Time:** Waiting time or Queuing time is the result of the variable load. In such cases, the customer can be provided with reading material or a television set or he can have games offered to his children.

In the case of an eventuality

Designing for Service continuity

Many service designs include provisions for maintaining continuity of service in the event of failures. For example, Telephone companies and Airlines make use of alternative routings in the event of standard routings becoming unavailable.

(*d*) **Action Time:** Action Time is commonly defined as the interval between taking the customer's order and providing the service requested. For an Airline, the emphasis on travel time may be from terminal to terminal. The customer will make decisions on this point-to-point basis.

Customer satisfaction is assessed on the basis of the characteristics of the service provided.

To gauge customer satisfaction, the questions an organisation asks itself are:

- How large is the potential market for the service?
- What percentage of the market must be satisfied for the company to realise a project?
- How important is continued use of the service?
- Is the organisation essentially interested in problem solving?

Useful information on customer satisfaction can be obtained through market surveys, questionnaires, observations and customer complaints and claims.

13.14(*c*) *TQM IMPLEMENTATION FOR A SERVICE SYSTEM*

TQM implementation requires a thorough and systematic analysis of customer operations systems, processes and functions, defining and establishing quality parameters; developing and putting in place systems of measurement and control and integrating all these with the business.

Steps are as follows:

Step 1: It requires a well defined purpose patience and discipline to initiate, develop and propagate to implement a TQM Performance.

Step 2: The process through which service functions operate must be well identified and its quality, dimensions defined for proper implementation and review.

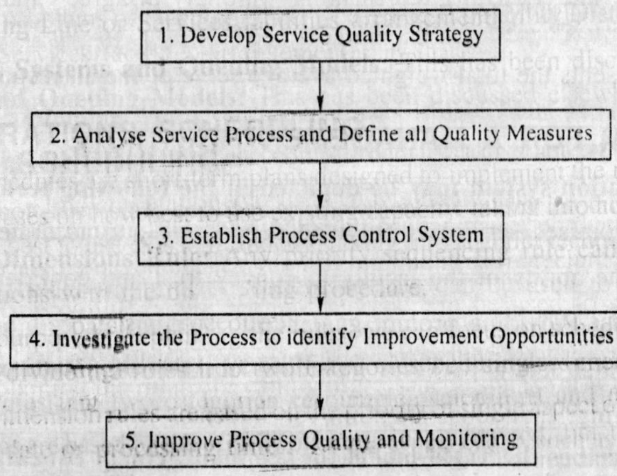

Figure 13.5 Framework for Improving Service Quality.

Step 3: For continuous monitoring of the service process, it is essential to establish process control. The focus should be on an understanding what needs to be measured and controlled to meet customer requirements.

Step 4: It is required to identify internal process problems affecting customer satisfaction and costs exploring process improvement opportunities.

Step 5: The goal for the improvement stage is to achieve and sustain a new level of process performance.

This requires, regular review of quality improvement opportunities and quality management performance with all employees.

An understanding of quality needs of customers, designing and developing process systems, measures and controls and continuous feed back and evaluation for improvement with participation and involvement of one and all are the necessary integration of TQM implementation plan.

13.15 MEASURING SERVICE QUALITY USING SERVQUAL

SERVQUAL is a questionnaire designed to measure the gap between the expectations and perceptions of a customer from a particular service.

The questionnaire consists of five categories such as:

- Tangibles
- Reliability
- Responsiveness
- Assurance
- Empathy.

These five categories are the result of a factor analysis applied to ten dimensions namely: Tangibles, Reliability, Responsiveness, Communication, Credibility, Security, Competence, Courtesy, Understanding the customer and access.

There are 22 questions in all for this questionnaire and the responses of customers are recorded on a scale ranging between 1 and 7, with I representing "Strongly disagree" and 7 representing "Strongly agree."

'SERVQUAL' represents the total weighted average score of the all responses for the 22 questions.

13.16 TQM SYSTEM FOR A MANAGEMENT INSTITUTE

1. Quality of an education system may be depicted in the following terms:

(*a*) **Reliability:** Promised service is provided dependably and accurately.

(*b*) **Assurance:** The ability of the faculty to convey trust and confidence.

(*c*) **Responsiveness:** Providing prompt guidance to students.

(*d*) **Tangible:** Infra-structural facilities including laboratories, computers with internet etc.

(*e*) **Empathy:** Caring, Individual attention for students.

2. Diagram below describes the TQM model for the management education system (Figure 13.6)

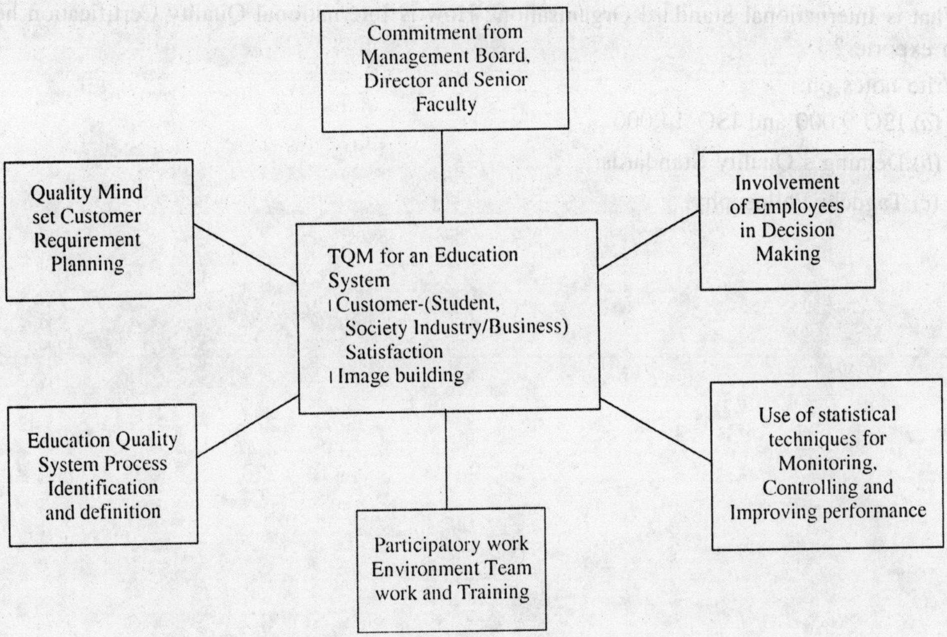

Figure 13.6 A proposed TQM Model for a Management Institute.

The main emphasis of TQM on:

- Internal and external customer satisfaction.
- Responsibility and commitment of top management.
- Implementation of rules and regulations.
- Quality System and Process.
- Training and Interactive sessions.

For a TQM interface between Institute and Industries/Business, the top management including the faculty should keep in mind the following:

- Education is human resource development and not an assembly line for the Supermarket.
- The principles of TQM remain unchanged, but the specifics of the application involve new elements.

13.17 PROBABLE QUESTIONS

1. Define Quality and Quality Control. State the principles and purposes of quality control.

2. Distinguish among Quality Control, Inspection and Quality Assurance. What is Reliability?

3. Describe Quality Control function. What are the benefits of Quality Control?

4. What is Statistical Quality Control? State its importance in a manufacturing organisation.

5. Write notes on:

(*a*) Total Quality Management

(*b*) Quality Circle

(*c*) Six Sigma.

6. What is International Standard Organisation? How is International Quality Certification helpful for an exporter?

7. Write notes on:

(*a*) ISO 9,000 and ISO 14,000

(*b*) Deming's Quality Standards

(*c*) Taguchi Philosophy.

14

Operations Management

• *Operations Scheduling* • *Job Shop & Batch Shop* • *Service System* • *Operations Scheduling* • *Gantt Charts* • *PERT/CPM: Network Scheduling* • *Manufacturing* • *Probable Questions.*

14.1 OPERATIONS SCHEDULING

One of the important steps in the planning and control of manufacturing operations is the scheduling of output and production for different items and operations. It establishes the time sequence of operation and indicates the time required for each job or operation. Scheduling develops a time-table for manufacturing. A schedule is a programme showing list of items to be produced in a given period of time. It determines when an operation is to be performed or when work is to be completed.

(*a*) **Objectives of Scheduling:** The basic purpose of scheduling is to ensure that the right things are done at the right time with the right items or people to create the product or service output through the most efficient utilisation of resources.

Proper Scheduling helps:

1. To obtain balanced use of time among different work centres.
2. To utilise labour in such a way that the desired output is produced within established lead time.
3. To deliver products in time.
4. To produce goods at minimum cost.

Scheduling is intimately connected with routing, loading, inventory control etc. For example, a schedule can not be prepared without a knowledge of required routing because route serves as a resource for scheduling. Similarly, scheduling indicates lead times which are useful in determining inventory policies.

(*b*) **Elements of Scheduling:** The various steps in scheduling of operation are as follows:

1. **Demand Forecast:** Long term (5–10 years) and short-term sales forecasts are made.
2. **Master Scheduling:** Scheduling begins with the preparation of a master scheduling on an overall basis. The master schedule, represents the broad operations plan to be accomplished in a given period of time. It is prepared on the basis of sales forecast, routesheet, plant capacity and availability of different inputs.

   Master Schedule is an aggregate schedule which helps in making best possible utilisation of production facilities and capacity in meeting estimated demand.

(*c*) **Operation Schedules:** Operation or shop schedules are prepared from the Master Schedule. These schedule deal with different products or jobs of total operational plan. The particular set of operations contained in an operation schedule should dove tail into the main master schedule. The different shop schedules should be properly co-ordinated. The operation schedule breaks down the monthly production target into weekly or daily targets. The master schedule is segregated into different jobs on the basis of delivery schedules and productive capacity.

Detailed schedule for a shop or department should contain controls to ensure that individual jobs do not get out of phase with the master schedule.

14.2 JOB SHOP AND BATCH SHOP

A Job Shop is a firm that specialises in low-to-medium-volume production utilising job or batch processes.

Jobs in this type of flexible flow environment are difficult to schedule because of the variability in job routings and the continuous introduction of new jobs to be processed.

Dispatching procedures are schedules used in **Job Shop** that allows the schedule for a work station to evolve over a period of time. The decision about which job to process next (or whether to let the work station remain idle) is made with simple priority rules whenever the workstation becomes available for further processing information on operating conditions can be incorporated into the schedule as it evolves.

Dispatching procedures determine the job to process next with the help or priority sequencing rules. When several jobs are waiting in line at a workstation, priority rules specify the job processing sequence. These rules can be applied by a worker or incorporated into a computerised scheduling system that generates a dispatch list of jobs and priorities for each workstation.

Critical Ratio: The critical ratio (*CR*) is calculated by dividing the time remaining to a job's due date by the total shop time remaining for the job, including the set up, processing, move and expected waiting times of all remaining operations, including the operation being scheduled.

The Formula
$$CR = \frac{\text{Due date} - \text{Today's date}}{\text{Total shop time remaining}}$$

A ratio less than 1.0 implies that the job is behind schedule, and a ratio greater than 1.0 implies that the job is ahead of schedule. The job with the lowest CR is scheduled next.

The job with the earliest due date is scheduled next.

Batch Shop: A batch shop differs from the Job Shop with respect to volume, variety and quantity. The primary difference is that volumes are higher because similar products or services are provided repeatedly.

Variety is achieved more through an assemble-to-order strategy than the job process's make-to-order strategy. Some of the components going into the final product or service may be produced in advanced. Another difference is that production lots or customer groups are handled in larger quantities (or batches) than they are with Job processes.

14.3 THE SERVICE SYSTEM

The Service system may be described by the number of lines and the arrangement of facilities.

(*a*) **Number of Lines:** Waiting lines may be designed to be a simple line or multiple lines. Generally, single lines are utilised at airline/railway booking counters or inside a bank. Multiple lines are utilised at grocery shop, cinema counters, drive-in-bank counters or petrol pumps.

(*b*) **Arrangement of Service Facilities:** Service facilities consist of the personal and/or equipment necessary to perform the service for the customer. Manager should choose an arrangement based on customer volume and the nature of services performed.

Some services require a single step, also called a phase, whereas others require a sequence of steps. In a single channel, single phase system all services demanded by a customer can be performed by a single line and go through the service facility one at a time.

The Single Channel, multiple phase arrangement is used when services are best performed in sequence by more than one facility, yet customer volume or other constraints limit the design to one channel. Customers form a single line and proceed sequentially from one service facility to the next. An example of this system is checking and completion of various custom formalities before boarding an aircraft for foreign travel.

The Multiple–Channel, single phase arrangement is used when demand is large enough to warrant providing the same service at more than one facility or when the services offered by the facilities are different customers form one or more lines, depending on the design.

The Multiple channel, multiple phase arrangement occurs when customers can be served by one of the first phase facilities but then require service from a second phase facility and so on.

An example of this arrangement is Laudromat. Washing machines are the first-phase facilities and dryers are the second phase facilities. Some of the washing machines and dryers may be designed for extra-large loads thereby providing the customer a choice of channels.

(*c*) **Priority Rule:** The priority rule determines which customer to serve next. Most service systems use first come, first served (FCFS) rule. The customer at the head of the waiting line has the highest priority.

A preemptive discipline is a rule that allows a customer of higher priority to interrupt the service of another customer. For example, in a hospital emergency patients with the most life-threatening injuries receive treatment first.

Operations Research problems of Queuing Theory based on Probability Distribution are best examples of Waiting Line or Services facilities arrangement.

(*d*) **Services Systems and Queuing Models:** This has been discussed elsewhere in the book.

14.4 OPERATIONS SCHEDULING

Operations Schedules are short-term plans designed to implement the master production schedule. Operations scheduling focuses on how best to use existing capacity, taking into account technical production constraints.

(*a*) **Single Dimensions Rule:** Any priority sequencing rule can be used to schedule any number of workstations with the dispatching procedure.

For the purpose of explaining the rules, we can focus on scheduling several jobs on a single machine. We can divide the rules into two categories *i.e.,* single-dimensions and multiple dimension rules.

Single-dimension rules are based on the priority of single aspect of job, such as arrival time at workstation, the due date or processing time.

(*b*) **Multiple-dimension Rules:** These rules apply to more than one aspect of the job compared to single dimension rules.

(*c*) **Johnson's Rule:** Johnson's rule is a procedure that minimises makespan in scheduling a group of jobs on two workstations. S.M. Johnson showed that the sequence of jobs at the two stations should be identical and that therefore the priority assigned to a job should be the same at both.

The procedure is based on the assumption of a known set of jobs, each with a known processing time and available to begin processing on the first workstation.

The procedure is as follows:

Step 1: Scan the processing times at each workstation and find the shortest processing time among the jobs not yet scheduled. If there is a tie, choose one job arbitrarily.

Step 2: If the shortest processing time is on workstation 1, schedule the corresponding job as early as possible. If the shortest processing time is on work station 2, schedule the corresponding job as late as possible.

Step 3: Eliminate the last job scheduled from further consideration. Repeat step 1 and 2 until all jobs have been scheduled.

Johnson rule determines the production sequence for a group of jobs so as to minimise the makespan has two advantages:

1. The group of jobs is completed in minimum time.
2. Utilisation of two-stations floor shop is maximised. Utilising the first workstation continuously until it processes the last job so as to minimise the idle time on the second workstation.

Note: Makespan–The total amount of time required to complete a group of job.

A company has received an order to refurbish 5 motors for a plant which were damaged in a fire. The motors will be repaired at 2 workstations in the following manner:

Workstation 1: Dismantle the motor and clean parts.

Workstation 2: Replace parts as necessary, test the motor, and make adjustments.

The customer's shop will be inoperable until all the motors have been repaired, so the plant manager is interested in developing a schedule that minimises the makespan and has authorised round-the-clock operations until the motors have been repaired.

14.5 GANTT CHARTS

A pictorial chart known as "Bar Chart" or "Gantt Chart" was for the first time developed by Henry Gantt in 1900 A.D. and is used to deal with planning of activities.

The Gantt chart consists of two co-ordinates, the horizontal represents the time elapsed and the vertical represents the activities performed.

The activities are shown in the form of bars as shown below:

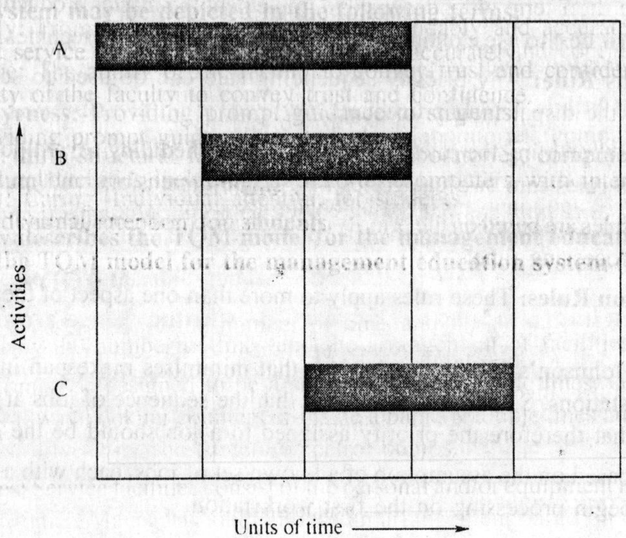

Figure 14.1

The length of the bar shows the time that the job or activity takes for completion.

Problem 14.1 Draw the bar chart (Gantt Chart) for the following examination work:

A	Design Questionnaire	10 days
B	Print Question paper	3 days
C	Distribute to various centres	6 days
D	Answer Questionnaire	1 day
E	Collect answer books at main office	6 days
		26 day

Solution. All the above activities are interdependent and in the order of sequence. The total duration is 26 days. The Gantt chart can be drawn as shown below:

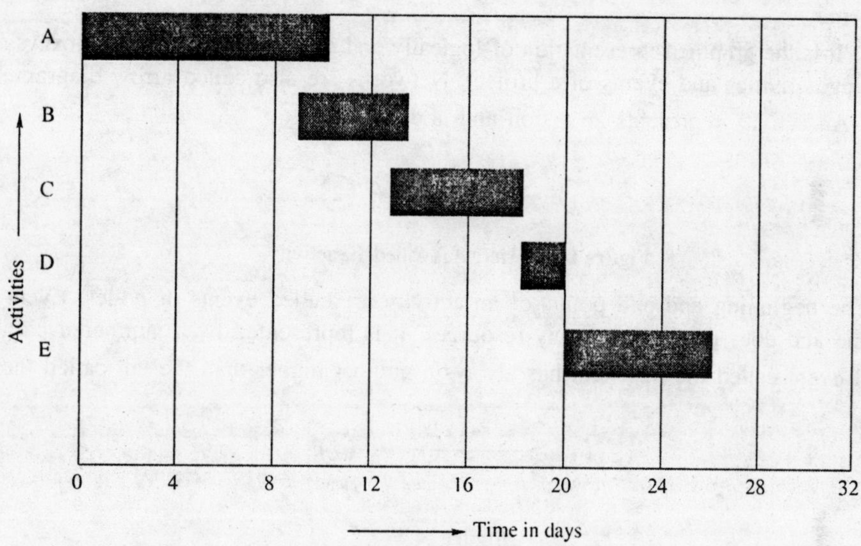

Figure 14.2

(*a*) **Limitations of a Gantt Chart:** The bar chart can not indicate clearly the interdependency among various activities. The fact that two or more activities are scheduled for simultaneous or overlapping time does not always make them related or interdependent.

- The bar chart does not indicate the progress of work, hence it cannot be used as control device.
- The third most important limitation of the bar chart is that it can not reflect the uncertainty or tolerances in the duration times estimated for various activities.

14.6 PERT/CPM: NETWORK SCHEDULING

Network scheduling is a technique used for planning and scheduling large projects in the field of construction, maintenance, fabrication etc. There are two basic planning and control technique that utilise a network to complete a predetermined project or schedule.

These are Programme Evaluation Review Technique (PERT) and Critical Path Method (CPM). The work involved in a project can be divided into three phases corresponding to the management functions of Planning, Scheduling and Control.

Planning: This phase involves setting the objectives of the project and the assumptions to be made. It also involves the lighting of jobs to be performed to complete the project under consideration.

Scheduling: This consists of laying the activities according to the precedence order and determining:

(*i*) The start and finish times for each activity.

(*ii*) The critical path on which the activities require special attention.

(*iii*) The slack and float for the non-critical paths.

Controlling: This phase is exercised after the Planning and Scheduling, which involves the following:

(*i*) Making periodical progress reports.

(*ii*) Reviewing the progress.

(*iii*) Analysing the status of the project.

(*iv*) Management decision regarding updating, crashing and resource allocation etc.

1. Basic Terms

Network: It is the graphic representation of logically and sequentially connected arrows and modes representing activities and events of a project. Networks are also called arrow diagram.

Activity: An activity represents an action and is denoted by:

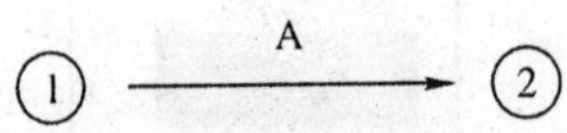

Figure 14.3 Here *A* is called the activity.

Event: The beginning and end points of an activity are called events or nodes. Event is a point in the time and does not consume any resources. It is represented by a numbered circle.

The head event called the *j*th event has always a number higher than the tail called the *i*th event.

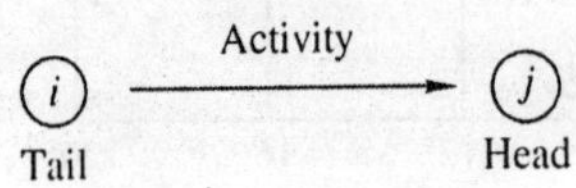

Figure 14.4

Preceding, Succeeding and Concurrent activities: Activities which must be accomplished before a given event can occur are termed as preceding activities. Activities which can not be accomplished until an event has occurred are termed as succeeding activities.

Activities, which can be accomplished concurrently are known as concurrent activities.

Dummy Activity: Certain activities which neither consumes time nor resources but are used simply to represent a connection or a link between the events are known as dummy activities.

It is shown in the network by a dotted line. The purpose of introducing dummy activity is:

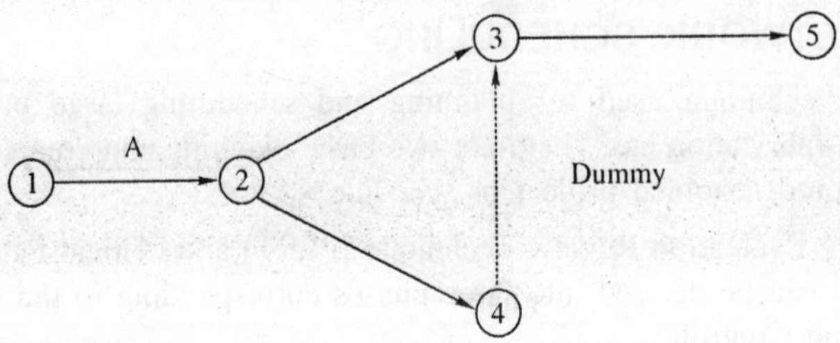

Figure 14.5 This means, '*D*' can only start after '*C*' is completed.

1. To maintain uniqueness in the numbering system as every activity may have distinct set of events by which the activity can be identified.
2. To maintain a proper logic in the network.

14.6.1 Rules of Network Construction

There are a number of rules in connection with the handling of events and activities of a Project network that should be followed.

1. Try to avoid arrows which cross each other.
2. Use straight arrows.
3. No event can occur until every activity preceding it has been completed.
4. An event can not occur twice *i.e.,* there must be no loops.
5. An activity succeeding an event can not be started until that event has occurred.
6. Use arrows from left to right. Avoid mixing two directions, vertical and standing arrows may be used if necessary.
7. Dummies to be introduced if it is extremely necessary.
8. The network has only one entry point called the start event and one point of emergence called the end or terminal event.
9. Event numbers should be unique and numbering should be carried out on sequential basis left to right.

14.6.2 Construction of Network

Problem 14.2 Construct a network for the project whose activities and their precedence relationships are as given below:

Activities	*A*	*B*	*C*	*D*	*E*	*F*	*G*	*H*	*I*
Immediate Predecessor	—	*A*	*A*	—	*D*	*B, C, E*	*F*	*E*	*G, H*

Solution. *A* & *D* are start activities and *I* is the terminal activity. *B*, *C* start with same event. *F* have predecessors *B*, *C*, *E*. *E* is the predecessor of both *F* and *H*, hence we have to introduce a dummy activity.

D1 dummy activity.

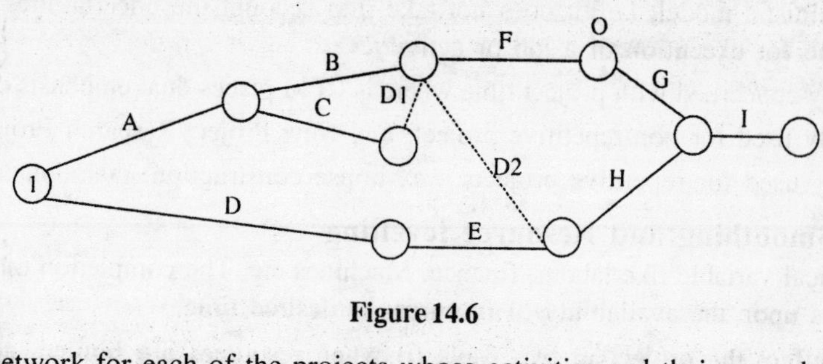

Figure 14.6

Construct a network for each of the projects whose activities and their precedence relationship are given below:

Activities	*A*	*B*	*C*	*D*	*E*	*F*	*G*	*H*	*I*	*J*	*K*
Predecessor	—	—	—	*A*	*B*	*C*	*D*	*E*	*E*	*H, I*	*F, G*

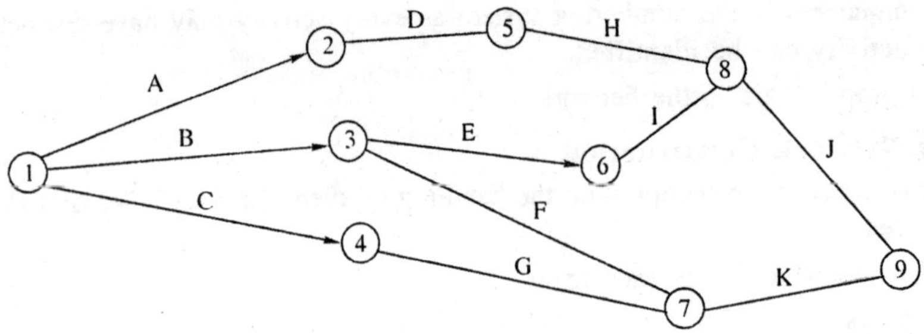

Figure 14.7

A B C are start activities concurrently,
J, *K* have 2 preceding activities.

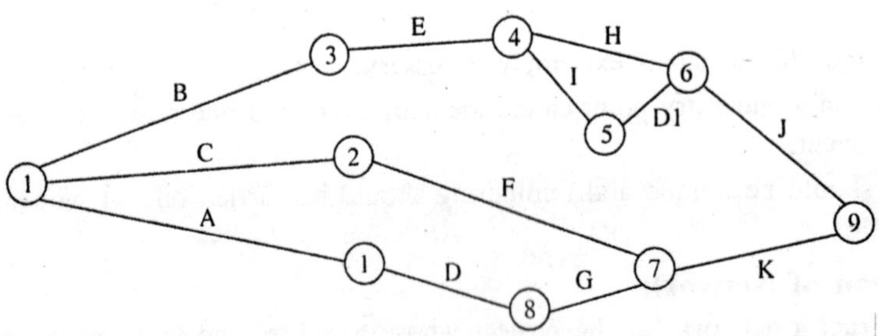

Figure 14.8

14.6.3 PERT/CPM

1. PERT is event oriented where as CPM is activity oriented.
2. PERT is a Probabilistic model, *i.e.*, it takes into account uncertainties involved in the estimation of time of job or an activity, *i.e.*, optimistic, probabilistic and pessimistic.

$$\text{Time of an activity} = \frac{\text{Optimistic Time} + 4\ \text{Probabilistic time} + \text{Pessimistic time}}{6}$$

   CMP is a deterministic model, *i.e.*, it does not take into account the uncertainties involved in the estimation of time for execution of a job or activity.
3. PERT in primarily concerned with project time whereas CPM places dual emphasis on time and cost.
4. PERT is generally used for non-repetitive project, *i.e.*, New Project/Research Project.
   CPM is generally used for repetitive projects, *i.e.*, house construction, maintenance etc.

14.6.4 Resource Smoothing and Resource levelling

A resource is the physical variable like labour, finance, Machines etc. The completion of a project on the scheduled date depends upon the availability of resources at desired time.

Resources may affect the project in two ways (*i*) when resources are limited, activities may be delayed due to non-availability of the resources. Therefore, in such circumstances, main constraint is resource and maximum demand of any resource is not exceed a certain limit. In such cases, activities are to be rescheduled so that total demand of resource at any time remain within the limit, which may increase the project duration. This is known as **Resource Levelling.** (*ii*) When main constraint is the project duration, it is kept unchanged. This means activities on critical path remain unchanged, so that total Project duration is maintained. For this purpose, activities having slack are shifted, so that a uniform demand of resource is maintained. This process is known as **"Resource Smoothing"** or **"Load Smoothing."** The Process of distributing the resources is called **"Resource Allocation."**

Problem 14.3 Draw the network for the following activities and find the critical path and total duration of Project:

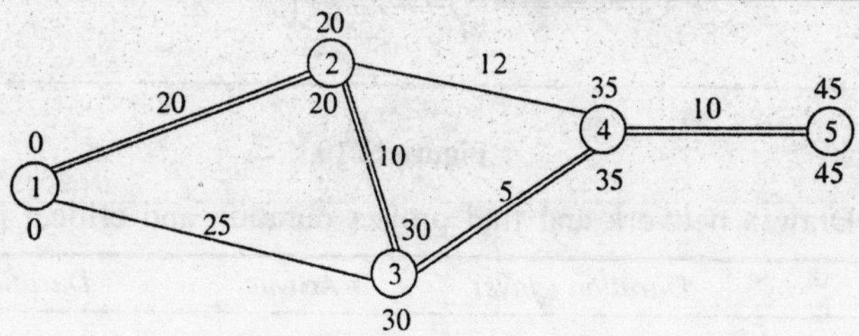

Figure 14.9

Longest duration path 1 – 2 – 3 – 4 – 5 = 20 + 10 + 5 + 10

= 45 days

Early Start Time (EST) – Write at top of Event

Late Start Time – Written at bottom of Event

LST – EST = Float

For critical path event → Float is zero.

Ans.: → Critical path and Project duration 45 days.

Problem 14.4 Draw a network and find critical path and duration of project.

Activity	*Duration (days)*	*Activity*	*Duration (days)*
1 – 2	13	5 – 6	10
2 – 3	8	5 – 7	6
3 – 4	10	6 – 8	8
3 – 5	11	7 – 8	7
3 – 5	11	8 – 9	14
4 – 6	9	9 – 10	18

Path (1) 1 – 2 – 3 – 4 – 6 – 8 – 9 – 10 = 13 + 8 + 10 + 9 + 8 + 14 + 18

= 80 days

(2) 1 – 2 – 3 – 5 – 6 – 8 – 9 – 10 = 13 + 8 + 11 + 10 + 8 + 14 + 18

= 82 days

(3) 1 – 2 – 3 – 5 – 7 – 8 – 9 – 10 = 13 + 8 + 11 + 6 + 17 + 14 + 18

= 77 days

Longest duration path is (2) → 82 days.

For Event 4 Float 33 – 31 = 2 days.

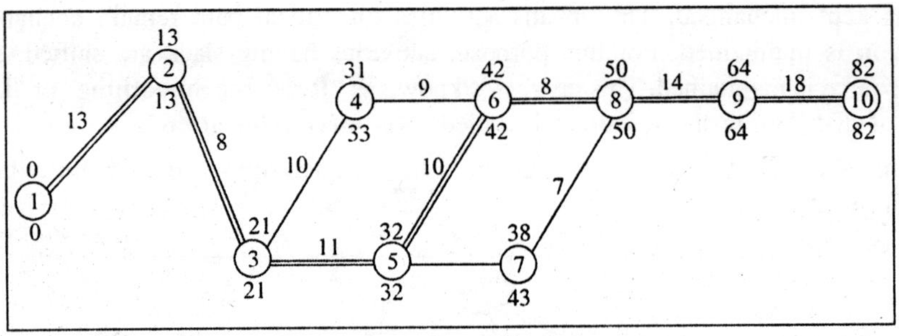

Figure 14.10

Problem 14.5 Draw a network and find project duration and critical path.

Activity	*Duration (days)*	*Activity*	*Duration (days)*
1 – 2	3	4 – 7	4
1 – 4	2	5 – 6	4
1 – 5	2	6 – 9	6
2 – 3	4	7 – 8	5
3 – 8	2	8 – 9	3
4 – 6	7		

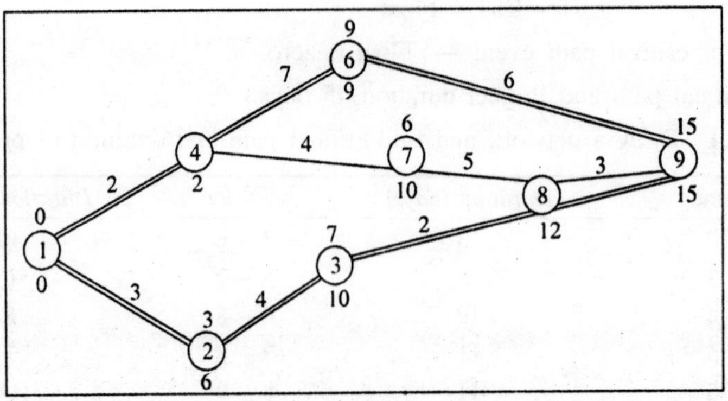

Figure 14.11

Path (1) 1 – 4 – 6 – 9 = 2 + 7 + 6 = 15 weeks.

(2) 1 – 4 – 7 – 8 – 9 = 2 + 4 + 5 + 3 = 14 weeks.

(3) 1 – 2 – 3 – 8 – 9 = 3 + 4 + 2 + 3 = 12 weeks.

Longest path → Critical path → Project Duration = 15 weeks.

i.e., (1) 1 – 4 – 6 – 9 = 2 + 7 + 6 = 15 weeks.

Critical path in bold.

Event having floats ②^{3} ③^{7} ⑧^{11}

6 10 12

Problem 14.6 Draw the network of a Project whose duration of activities are given below. Find the critical path, estimate early start times, late start times of each event and Project completion time in months.

Activity	Duration (days)
1 – 2	3
2 – 3	4
2 – 4	4
3 – 7	4
4 – 5	2
4 – 7	2
5 – 6	3
6 – 7	2

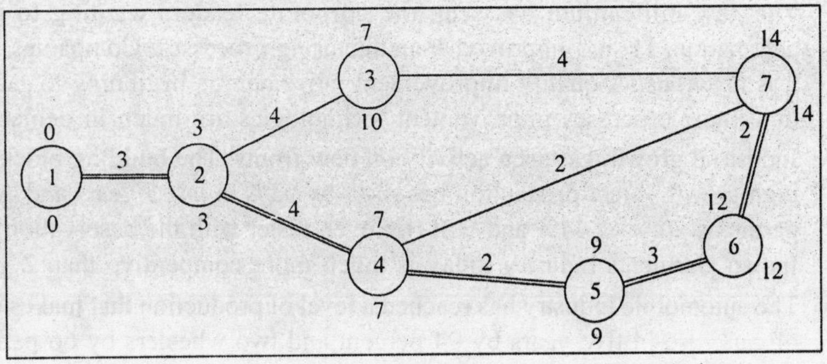

Figure 14.12

Path (1) 1 – 2 – 3 – 7 = 11 months.

(2) 1 – 2 – 4 – 5 – 6 – 7 = 14 months → Longest path = Critical path

(3) 1 – 2 – 4 – 7 = 9 months

(*i*) (2) is critical path — shown in double line.

(*ii*) Project completion time = 14 months.

(*iii*) ESTs and LSTs of events on critical path shown above. These events have no floats.

(*iv*) Event 3 is not on critical path and this has EST = 7 months and LST = 10 months with a float of 10 – 7 = 3 months.

14.7 MANUFACTURING

World class manufacturing is a way of achieving the competitive advantage from manufacturing. It is the pursuit of superior performance in quality, lead time, cost and customer service through continuous improvement by using principles such as Just-in-Time manufacturing, TQM and employee-involvement.

World class companies such as General Electric, Mitsubishi and Samsung etc. optimize the problems-solving abilities of their employees in applying both modern techniques and traditional industrial Engineering technique.

As time advances and new business theories and strategies are developed and tested, companies generally, become better at what they do. Levels of excellence improve and standards previously seen as the ultimate are achieved easily.

(*a*) **Manufacturing in India:** Industry growth includes manufacturing in registered and unregistered enterprises as well as in infrastructure and other sectors.

Manufacturing declined to 1.5 and 2.5 percent in 1998 and 1999, revived to 4.4 and 7.1 percent in 2000 and 2001, fell to 3.7 in 2002. While the last 2 years were 6.2 and 7.1 percent respectively.

The liberalisation of the Nineties, lowering of import duties, opening of the market to domestic and foreign competition, removal of controls, led to companies increasing capacity, modernising technology, investing to improve productivity, building new plants.

From 1998, the private sector corporates were restructuring capital and borrowing, improving business focus, reducing numbers of employees, improving productivity and working capital management, not investing in more fixed investment.

These were also the years in which the equity markets had lost confidence in equity market due to insider trading and price rising. Those companies that had the resources to invest were doing the things for improving their margins.

The new millennium has seen the corporate leaders wanting to improve quality, productivity, automation, IT and improved manufacturing processes. Companies have learnt to make more with less materials. A quality improvement movement is beginning to affect and oracle, Six Sigma and other new processes improvement technologies are much in demand.

Industrial growth has seen activity on new fronts. The building blocks of manufacturing have shown high growth. Steel production has risen by 53% in last 5 years and Aluminium by 51%. Readymade garments grew @ 44% and will rise even faster with the deservation to small scale 2 years ago. The Indian Garments industry today is much more competitive than 2 years ago.

The automobile industry has reached a level of production that makes it a driver of growth. Production of cars rose in five years by 94 percent and two wheelers by 66 percent. The petroleum industry is in an expansion mode with new LNG terminals being built, pipelines and refineries, petrochemical plants and the like.

The explosion in telecommunication has meant not merely growth in instruments, but also in the manufacture and laying of cables and other infrastructure. The power sector is gearing up for very significant expansion after the passage of the Electricity Act 2003. With all these, the growth in manufacturing has been about 7 percent.

As India becomes more integrated into the global economy and the rural markets begin to show improving demand, this growth is expected to further accelerate. In manufacturing, India needs growth in labour and skill intensive, improvement and expansion intensive. The strengthening of rupee will lead to greater import of equipment.

Expansion of capacities, productivity and cost improvements, better design and quality of products will be some of the consequences of industry reaction to competition and opening up. Demand also shows significant improvement. This time it is not merely driven by more purchasing power, but helped by easily available bank credit.

Banks in India are now getting ready to enter the rural markets with offer of loans for purchase of house hold goods by rural consumers. It is essential that industrial development should reach masses and not be confined to the upper and urban classes.

Manufacturing is at long last set to grow rapidly, making the structure of the economy more consistent with our low standards of living.

SME-Sector: The Indian banks including all India FIs are now adopting good risk management system for lending funds to the small and medium enterprises since this segment is emerging as a major growth centre along side retail finance as commercial banks with liquidity fund that large companies are not keen on loans.

Competitive Advantage: Competitive advantage can be derived only by paying attention to technology, cost and quality, apart from improved management strategies and better financial controls in other areas of production. Lower cost of production and high quality of products play a significant role in the international trade.

Continuous technological upgradation and modernisation play a crucial role in improving quality and reducing cost of production. Besides, not only production techniques in manufacturing have to be improved but considerable use of information and communication technologies has also to be increasingly made use by all types industries, small and large, to face global competition in the emerging scenario.

The fact is to be kept in mind that all types of industries in India during the last five decades had operated in the sheltered market situation, almost free from competition and the management had paid scant attention to modernisation and up gradation of technologies during this period.

(*b*) **Service Systems:** Production system produces goods and commodities which are tangible items, can be stored and used as and when necessary. Service system produces services which are intangible in nature, can not be stored, but to be used as and when produced.

Telecom, transportation, ITes, hospitality, tourism, education and healthcare services are some of the growing service sectors in India in the 21st century.

The contribution of services sector to India's GDP at present in over 50 percent.

14.8 PROBABLE QUESTIONS

1. What is scheduling? Describe various uses of scheduling.
2. What are the objectives of scheduling? State how will you prepare a master schedule for a production facility?
3. What is Gantt chart? Describe the utility of Gantt chart in planning a project.
4. Write notes on:
   (*a*) Johnson's rule of Scheduling jobs in machines.
   (*b*) PERT/CPM.
   (*c*) Flexible manufacturing system.
   (*d*) Critical Ratio.
   (*e*) Job shop and Batch shop.
5. Distinguish between PERT/CPM techniques. What do you mean by "Dummy Activity", "Critical path" and "Float"?
6. What is the difference between "Resource Smoothing" and "Resource levelling"?
7. Describe the advantages of Network techniques. What are the limitations of Gantt Charts?

15

Process Management

• *Process Management/Process Decisions* • *Symbols Used for Flow Process Charts* • *Operation Process Chart* • *Flow Process Chart* • *Work Station Design* • *Assembly Line Balancing* • *Process Flow Diagram* • *Equipment Replacement Analysis* • *Probable Questions.*

15.1 PROCESS MANAGEMENT/PROCESS DECISIONS

15.1.1 Process Management

Process management is the selection of the inputs, operations, work flows, and methods that transform inputs into outputs.

Process decisions deal with the proper mix of human skills and equipment and which parts of the processes are to be performed by each.

Process decisions become important when quality is to be improved, competitive priorities are changed, demand for a product/service is changed, competitors gain advantage and the cost of main input materials are different.

1. **Process Decisions:** Corporate managers must consider following five common Process decisions while dealing with processes for offices, service providers or manufacturers.
   - **Process Choice:** This determines whether resources are organised around products or processes in order to implement the process flow strategy. The Process choice decisions depends on the volume and degree of customisation to be provided.
   - **Vertical Integration:** This is the degree to which a firm's own production system or service facility handles the entire supply-chain. The more a firm's production system handles the raw materials, other inputs and outputs, the greater is the degree of vertical integration.
   - **Resource Flexibility:** Resource flexibility is the case with which employees and equipment can handle a wide variety of products, output levels, duties and functions.
   - **Customer Involvement:** This reflects the ways in which customers become part of the production process and the extent of their participation.
   - **Capital Intensity:** This is the mix of equipment and human skills in a production process, the greater the relative cost of equipment, the greater is the capital intensity.
2. **Process Choice:** Process choice involves Project, Job, Batch Line and Continuous types of the Process operation that best supports the flow strategy.
   - Examples of Project Process are building a Project team, running a political campaign, constructing a new project etc.
   - Examples of Job Process are machining a casting as per customer order, handling special delivery mails etc. which create flexibility needed to produce a variety of Products or services. Customisation is relatively high and volume for any one product or service is low.

- Examples of Batch Process are scheduling air travel for a group, making components that supply an assembly line and manufacturing capital equipment which create an assemble-to-order, strategy compare to the job process make-to-order strategy.

  A batch process differs from the jobs process with respect to volume, variety and quantity. The primary difference is that volumes are higher because the same or similar products or services are provided repeatedly.

- Examples of Line Process are products line automobiles, appliances, fast-food restaurants the process of which lies between the batch and continuous process. Volumes are high and products or services are standardised which allow resources be organised.
- Examples of Continuous Process are petroleum refineries, chemical plants, distilleries etc. which results in high volume output.

3. **Vertical Integration:** Vertical integration decides which services and products should be made in-house and which of them should be outsourced. In other words this is the economics of make-or-buy decision. This theory is explained in details elsewhere in this book.
4. **Resource Flexibility:** The choices that management makes concerning competitive priorities determine the degree of flexibility required of a company's resources—its employees, facilities and equipment. When new products and services call for short life cycles or high customization, employees need to perform a broad range of duties and equipment must be general purpose.

   Flexible Work Force: Members of a flexible work force are capable of doing many tasks, either at their own work stations or as they move from one work station to another. Such flexibility in work force calls for higher skills and requisite education and training.
5. **Customer Involvement:** This decides how much should customer be involved in the process. The amount of customer involvement may range from self-service to customization of product. A good degree of customer involvement is in custom-designed and build homes.
6. **Capital Intensity:** Capital intensity decides how much should a firm depend on machinery and automated process. Capital intensity is the mix of equipment and human skills in the process; the greater the relative cost of equipment, the greater is the capital intensity.

   Automation in a process has both advantages and disadvantages; hence the automation decision requires careful examination.
7. **Process Re-engineering:** Re-engineering is the fundamental rethinking and radical redesign of processes, to improve performance dramatically in terms of cost, quality, service and speed. Process Re-engineering is about reinvention, rather than incremental improvement.

   Bell Telephone Inc., U.S.A. had used Re-engineering process to Re-engineer its telephone business and became a very profitable company. Re-engineering requires focusing on a core process in the company and often uses cross-functional teams, information technology, leadership and Process analysis. Process Re-engineering is also discussed elsewhere in details in this book.
8. **Process Improvement:** Process improvement is the systematic study of the activities and flows of each process to improve it. Its purpose is to learn the numbers, understand the process and dig on the details. Once a process is thoroughly understood, it can be improved. In order to provide better quality at a lower price, the companies must continually review all aspects of their operations. There are multiple approaches for Process improvement and two basic techniques are analysing Process flow diagrams and Process Flow Charts.

   Total quality Management is another technique which focuses on quality improvements. Improvements can be made in quality, throughout time, cost, errors, safety or on-time delivery.

   Maruti Udyog Ltd. in India is a remarkable company which has achieved large improvements in Operations and Marketing since the beginning of the new millennium.

9. Process Planning: Process planning is the key decision in production as it affects the efficiency of production. It is essential to design the process for production after determining the transformation system for all necessary inputs into desired outputs.

While planning a process, the designers have to consider various factors like capacity, lead time, efficiency, effectiveness, flexibility and safety. The suitable technology and necessary equipment for the production process are also to be considered while planning the process.

In process planning, other important parameters like productivity, minimum or nil wastes, least cost of production, desired quality and environment friendly operations are also to be considered. Process study goes hand in hand with work-study, R & D, product design and plant engineering.

Decision regarding process selection for production depends upon both economic and non-economic considerations. The incremental cost of each alternative and the volume of manufacture are important economic considerations.

Non-economic considerations may differ from situation to situation depending on factors like machine/ equipment availability, safety and environmental pollution hazards and Governmental regulation etc.

10. Process Design-Procedures: Following steps are adopted for designing a production process:

(*i*) **Product Design:** Complete specifications for the product with necessary quality parameters and the most economical method of production are necessary considerations in the Product design stage.

(*ii*) **Bill of Materials:** A comprehensive list of all materials and auxiliary items including vital spare parts is prepared and considered in this stage.

(*iii*) **Layout:** The layout of production and service facilities including maintenance is suitably worked out for the plant and the most economical layout which results in the least unit cost of production is considered.

(*iv*) **Tool Design:** The machines, equipment and tools most appropriate for the product, volume of output etc. are worked out before the plant layout is finalised.

(*v*) **Control System:** Necessary control of materials, machines and manpower is established to ensure effective utilisation of all production facilities.

Process design carried out in above manner is also known as Process Engineering.

Process Planning and Plant Layout

Work Flow	*Product Layout*	*Process Layout*
System Design	Continuous	Intermittent
Work Routing	Built into Equipment	Individual Instructions
Material Handling	Fixed Path-equipment	Variable Path equipment
Production Run	Long	Short
Type of work flow	Batch shop like	Job shop like
Work Centre		
Work Volume	Large	Small
Product Requirement	Standard Product Line	Non-standard Product
Capacity	Capacity	Individual equipment capacity
Type of loading	Assembly line balancing	Worker-machine balance
R & D efforts	on product	on process

Critical analysis of on going activities together with improvements planned is the main consideration in Process planning and designing analysis.

15.2 SYMBOLS USED FOR FLOW PROCESS CHARTS

Frank Gilbreth used a number of symbols to represent the activities essential for accomplishing a job. In 1947 ASME had established following five standards symbols.

O	—	Operation	—	It indicates activity concerned with manufacturing, working or accomplishing.
□	—	Inspection	—	It indicates verification of quality and/or quantity.
→	—	Transportation	—	It indicates the movement of workers, materials or equipment, from one work-station to other or stores etc.
D	—	Delay	—	It indicates interference or temporary storage between two work-stations.
∇	—	Storage	—	It indicates permanent storage.

15.3 OPERATION PROCESS CHART

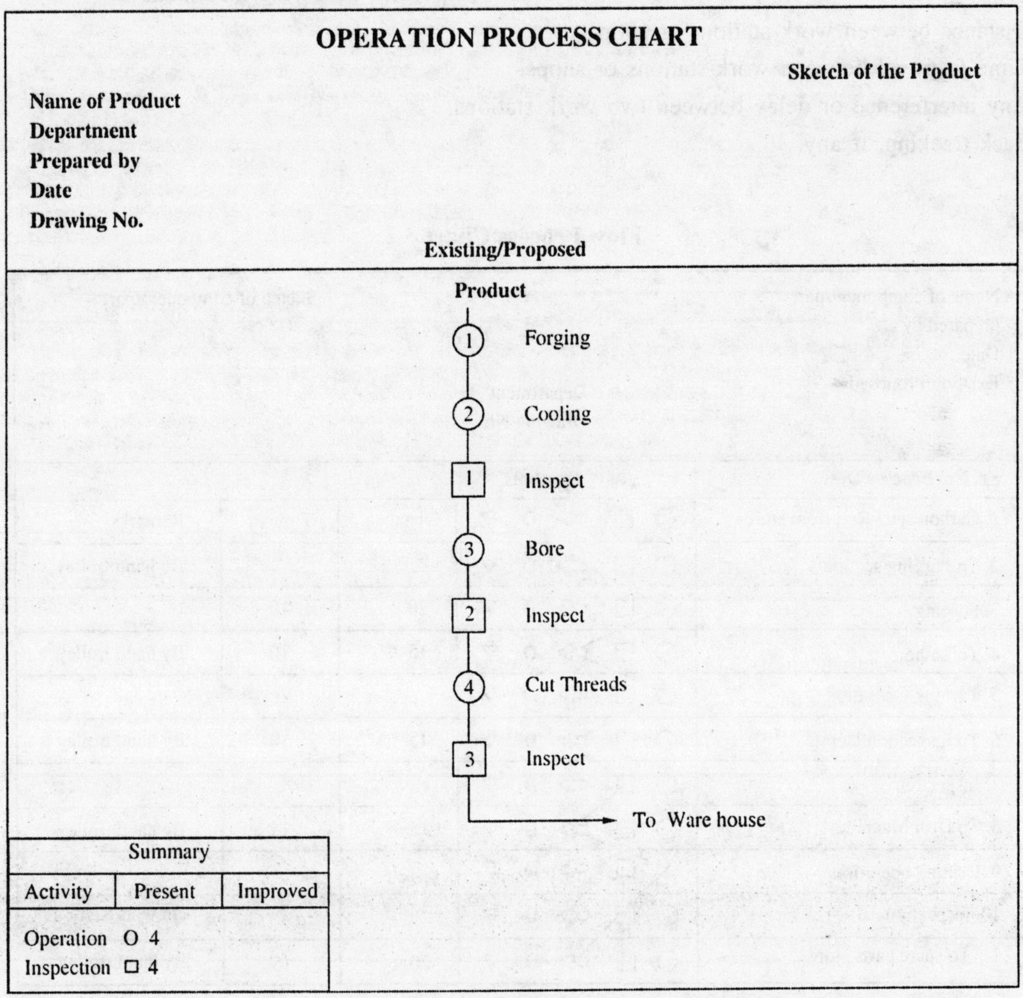

Figure 15.1

The Operation Process Chart is a graphic representation of a process, which contains the following information. It makes use of only two symbols for operating and inspection.

(*i*) Name of the product or assembly or sub-assembly.

(*ii*) Name of the person making the chart.

(*iii*) Date of making the chart.

(*iv*) Sketch of the product.

(*v*) Operations as per their sequence.

(*vi*) Inspections.

(*vii*) Name of the department.

(*viii*) Drawing Number.

15.4 FLOW PROCESS CHART

It is also a graphical representation of the process. It incorporates following information:

(*i*) Distance between work-stations or shop

(*ii*) Time to travel between work-stations or shops.

(*iii*) Any interference or delay between two work stations.

(*iv*) Back tracking, if any.

Flow Process Chart

Name of component/part prepared by Date Existing/Proposed	Department Drawing No.			Sketch of component/part
Sr. No. Process Des.	**Symbols**			
1. Carbon steel Rod from stores	○ □ ⇨ D ▽	Distance	Time in	Remarks
2. To Forging section	○ □ ⇨ D ▽			By hand trolley
3. Forging	○ □ ⇨ D ▽	20	10	
4. To Lathe	○ □ ⇨ D ▽	15	10	By hand trolley
5. Turning Operation	○ □ ⇨ D ▽			
6. To Inspection Deptt.	○ □ ⇨ D ▽	15	10	By hand trolley
7. Inspection	○ □ ⇨ D ▽			
8. To Drill Machine	○ □ ⇨ D ▽	15	15	By hand trolley
9. Drilling operation	○ □ ⇨ D ▽			
10. Inspection	○ □ ⇨ D ▽			On work station
11. To spare parts store	○ □ ⇨ D ▽	20	15	By hand trolley

Summary

Activity		Nos.
Operation	O	3
Inspection	□	2
Transportation	⇒	5
Delay	**D**	nil
Stores	∇	2

Figure 15.2 Flow Process Chart for a Carbon Steel Rod in the existing operation and layout.

15.5 WORK STATION DESIGN

Work Station or Work place may be defined as the floor space occupied by the worker and the machine or a group of machines. In the design of work station layout generally following space requirements are taken into consideration.

(*i*) The rectangular space occupied by the length and width of the machine or group of machines.

(*ii*) Floor space required by the workers to perform work.

(*iii*) Clearance space for feeding the work, on and off the machine.

(*iv*) Space for racks and bins etc. which may be required for the process.

In plant layout while allotting space for work stations, provision for materials storage inside the plant should be made on the basis of following:

(*i*) The quantity of raw materials required for production per hour.

(*ii*) Volume and weight of partially processed parts awaiting moving from one machine to the next machine.

(*iii*) Volume and weight of parts on the move from one department to the next department.

(*iv*) Volume and weight of scrap.

15.6 ASSEMBLY LINE BALANCING

Assembly line balancing refers to the process of balancing work stations on a product line in term of equal lines required to meet the desired rate of output.

A balanced line has a series of progressive related operations with approximately equal standard times for each so that the work flows at a steady rate from one operation to the next.

Assembly line involves the arrival of individual component parts at the work place and departure of these parts assembled together in the form of assembly or sub-assembly.

It contains a series of assembly station through which a product must pass in an orderly established sequence.

The assembly process can be broken down into work stations according to the requirements. An ideal situation would have equal work content measured in terms of time. In this situation, perfect balance would exist.

Assembly line balancing problems are approached in two ways.

1. Fixed cycle time to optimise the number of stations.
2. Fixed number of work stations to minimise the cycle time.

The main objective and line balancing are:

(*i*) to minimise the balancing loss

(*ii*) to minimise the number of work stations

(*iii*) to spread the loss between work stations.

15.7 PROCESS FLOW DIAGRAM

In the earlier chapter a detailed layout had shown the various departments producing necessary components for the sub-assembly and final assembly lines of a light-commercial vehicle (Passengers Cars).

It is important for the Production Manager to understand the Process, Flow Sequence, sub-assembly and assembly lines to enhance productivity thoroughly and apply improved techniques such as re-engineering, MRP, JIT, Kanban and T & M etc. for improving the overall efficiency and productivity.

Suitable mechanisation and automation should be adopted in the sub-assembly and assembly lines to enhance productivity, reduce the cost of production and to gain competitive advantage.

Bajaj Auto, Hero Honda and Maruti Udyog etc. have adopted these successful strategies for their operations.

Given below is a Process Flow Scheme of Effluent Treatment for a Process Industry. Students would benefit themselves by studying the process, flow sequence and the scheme in details and then join a group discussion to offer their recommendations for improving the process and reducing the overall cost of operation (*see* Figure 15.3).

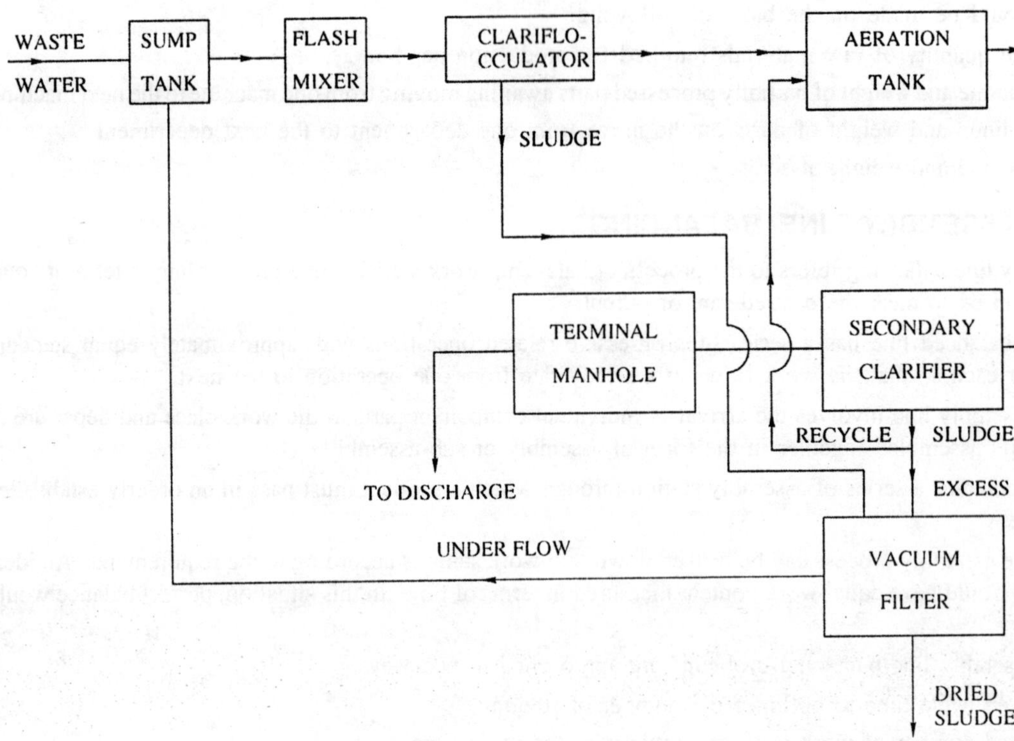

Figure 15.3 Process Flow Scheme of Effluent Treatment for a Process Industry.

15.8 EQUIPMENT REPLACEMENT ANALYSIS

Equipment Replacement Decision

(*a*) Replacement of Capital equipment that deteriorates with time:

(*i*) Without considering time value of money.

(*ii*) With time value of money.

1. Equipment Replacement Decision: Equipment replacement decision plays an important role in the economic running of any concern for years. A firm has to face three types of replacement decision.

(*a*) The replacement of capital equipment, as it weaves out or becomes obsolete.

(*b*) The capital equipment required for expansion.

(*c*) The displacement of old technology by the new *i.e.,* the introduction of an improved equipment in the market which may produce cheaper products.

Replacement decision requires several considerations. As it involves large capital investment, hence a wrong decision may adversely effect the profitability of whole concern. Therefore, a scientific approach to solve such problems is essential.

2. Reasons for Replacement of Equipment

(*a*) Deterioration

(*b*) Obsolescence

(*c*) Inadequacy

(*d*) Working conditions *i.e.,* machinery unsafe in operation or more noise or cause more pollution may have to be changed.

3. Guidelines for Replacement Analysis and Replacement Policy: Large number of factors are responsible to replace the equipment before the expiry of the estimated life and some of them are:

(*a*) To reduce production cost

(*b*) To reduce fatigue

(*c*) To improve quality

(*d*) To increase output.

(*e*) To secure greater safety and reliability.

There are certain rules which may be used as guidelines for replacement analysis.

(*a*) For Equipment in use: Consider the following:

(*i*) Operating cost

(*ii*) Repair and maintenance

(*iii*) Down time cost

(*iv*) Salvage value

(*v*) Rebuilding cost

(*b*) For New Equipment: Consider the following:

(*i*) Initial cost

(*ii*) Interest on capital investment

(*iii*) Salvage value at the end of useful life.

(*iv*) Cost advantage of improved product.

(*v*) Labour savings.

4. Methods for Replacement Studies: Following methods are used without considering time value of money.

(*i*) Pay back period method

(*ii*) Total life average method

(*iii*) Annual cost method

(*iv*) Rate of return method.

(*i*) Payback period method: This method determines as to how long it will take (in years) to pay back invested capital.

Let P = Pay back period in years

C = Cost of original equipment

R = Annual return expected

Then $P = \frac{C}{R}$

This method has drawbacks since it does not take into account insurance, interest and maintenance cost.

(*ii*) Total Life Average Method: In this method, all the costs involved in buying, operating and maintaining an equipment or asset are added together into one total figure and this sum is divided by the total estimated life to get an average annual cost.

Problem 15.1 An existing piece of equipment has its market value of Rs. 10,000, maintenance cost Rs. 1,000 per year and has a life of 10 years without any salvage value. The interest rate is 10%. The proposed equipment has an installed cost of Rs. 1,00,000, maintenance cost of Rs. 800 per year, a life of 50 years and salvage value of Rs. 15,000. Suggest whether proposed equipment should be purchased or not.

Solution.

Factor	*Exhg. Eqpt.*	*Proposed Eqpt.*
1. Depreciation	Rs. 10,000	Rs. (1,00,000 – 15,000) = Rs. 85,000
2. Maintenance	Rs. 1000 × 10 = Rs. 10,000	Rs. 800 × 50 = Rs. 40,000
3. Interest 10% (see the calculation below)	Rs. 5,500	Rs. 2,16,750
4. Total life cost	Rs. 25,500	Rs. 3,41,750
5. Average cost/year	= Rs. 25,500 ÷ 10 = Rs. 2,550	Rs. 3,41,750 ÷ 50 = Rs. 6,835

Since the average cost per year of extg. equipment is much lower the new equipment should not be purchased.

Interest is calculated by the following method:

Interest for extg. equipment:

Total life 10 years

Hence, yearly reduction in cost $= \frac{10,000}{10}$ = Rs. 1,000

Interest for the first year @ 10% $= \dfrac{10,000}{10} \times 10 = \text{Rs. } 1,000$

Now cost of equipment in second year $= 10,000 - 1,000 = 9,000$

$\therefore$ Interest for 2nd year @ 10% $= \dfrac{9000 \times 10}{100} = \text{Rs. } 900$

Difference of interest in two consecutive years = Rs. 1,000 – Rs. 900 = Rs. 100

Total interest of 10 years life is calculated by the formula

Total interest $= \dfrac{n}{2}[2a - (n-1)d]$

n = Total life of equipment = 10 years

a = First year's interest = Rs. 1,000

d = Difference between two consecutive years interest

= Rs. 1,000 – Rs. 900 = Rs. 100

Hence Total Interest $= \dfrac{10}{2}[2 \times 1000 - (10-1)\,100]$

= 5 [2000 – 900]

= Rs. 5,500

For New Equipment n = 50 years

yearly cost reduction $= \dfrac{85,000}{50} = \text{Rs. } 1,700$

1st years interest @10% $= \dfrac{85,000}{100} \times 10 = \text{Rs. } 8,500$

Now cost of equipment in 2nd year

= Rs. (85,000 – 1,700) = Rs. 83,300

$\therefore$ Interest for Second year @ 10% $= \dfrac{83,300}{100} \times 10 = \text{Rs. } 8,330$

$\therefore$ Difference between two consecutive years interest

= Rs. (8,500 – 8,330) = Rs. 170

$\therefore$ Total interest for 50 years $= \dfrac{n}{2}[2a - (n-1)\,d]$

$= \dfrac{50}{2}[2 \times 8500 - (50-1)\,170]$

$= 25\,[17000 - 49 \times 170]$

$= 25 \times 8670 = \text{Rs. } 2,16,750$

***(iii)* Annual Cost Method:** This method is to compare the annual costs of obtaining service from different equipments

Annual Cost = Capital Recovery + Operating Costs

Capital Recovery (CR) is given by

$$CR = (P - L) \times \text{Capital recovery factor} + L \times i$$

$$= (P-L)\left[\frac{i(1+i)^n}{(1+i)^n-1}\right] + L \times i$$

P = Cost of equipment

L = Salvage value

i = Interest rate in %

n = Life of equipment in years

Here $\left[\frac{i(1+i)^n}{(1+i)^n-1}\right]$ is called capital recovery factor (CRF).

Problem 15.2 The cost details of two equipments are given below. Find the most economical one.

S. No.	*Factor*	*Equipment I*	*Equipment II*
1.	Initial cost (P)	Rs. 15,000	Rs. 25,000
2.	Annual operating cost	Rs. 800	Rs. 500
3.	Life n	6 years	6 years
4.	Interest rate (i)	5%	5%
5.	Salvage value (L)	1000	4000

Given CRF for i = 5% n = 6 years = 0.1970

Solution.

Equipment I	*Equipment II*
CR $= (15000 - 1000) \times 0.1970 + 1000 \times \frac{5}{100}$	CR $= (25000 - 4000) \times 0.1970 + 4000 \times \frac{5}{100}$
$= 14000 \times 0.1970 + 50 = 2808$	$= 21000 \times 0.1970 + 200 = 4337$
∴ Total annual cost	Total annual cost
= CR + Operating cost annually	= CR + annual operating cost
= Rs. 2808 + Rs. 800 = Rs. 3608	= Rs. 4337 + Rs. 500 = Rs. 4837

∴ Total annual cost of equipment I is less therefore, equipment I is to be chosen.

Problem 15.3 The following are the data for two equipments, suggest whether to purchase the equipment or not:

Sr. No.	*Existing equipment Market value*	*Proposed Equipment*
1.	Rs. 40,000	Installed cost Rs. 90,000
2.	Overhauling charges to make it work for next 5 years = Rs. 20,000	Expected life 15 years
3. Resale value	Rs. 30,000	Rs. 10,000
4. Maintenance cost per year	Rs. 200 more than Proposed equipment	Rs. 100/year
5. Interest rate	10%	10%
6. For n = 5 and i = 10% CRF = 0.2638 For n = 15, i = 10% CRF = 0.1315		

Problem 15.4 The cost of a M/C is Rs. 6,100 and its scrap value is Rs. 100. The maintenance costs are as follows:

Year	1	2	3	4	5	6	7	8
Costs	100	250	400	600	900	1250	1600	2000

When should the *m/c* be replaced?

Solution. The scrap value is Rs. 100. Generally the scrap value is at the end of useful life. But in this problem we should use data for each year of life.

Years of life	*Cumulative maintenance cost Rs.*	*Capital Cost Rs.*	*Total Cost Rs.*	*Average cost per year*
1	100	6100	6100	6100/1 = 6100
2	350	6000	6350	6350/2 = 3175
3	750	6000	6750	6750/3 = 2250
4	1350	6000	7350	7350/4 = 1837
5	2250	6000	8250	8250/5 = 1650
6	3500	6000	9500	9500/6 = 1583
7	5100	6000	11100	11100/7 = 1585
8	7100	6000	13100	13100/8 = 1637

The lowest average cost is in the 6th year. Hence, replacement should be at the end of every six years. **Ans.**

(*a*) **Replacement Analysis with time value of money:** This method is accurate and reasonable and used to evaluate the present value of new equipment. For the purpose of comparison, future costs are translated into today's value of money.

A "present worth of rupee" is today's value of money invested (at certain interest rate) after given number of years from today. If we have Rs. 5,000 to invest and want to know what will be its worth in 10 years @10% interest.

The formula used is:

$$F = P(1 + i)^n$$

F = Future worth of money

P = Present amount of money

i = Interest rate

n = Number of years

$$\therefore \quad F = 5000\,(1 + 0.10)^{10} = 5000\,(2.594) = \text{Rs. } 12.970$$

Thus Rs. 5,000 to-day is worth Rs. 12,970 after 10 years from now, or in other words Rs. 12,970 after 10 years from now has a present worth of Rs. 5,000.

∴ To determine the present worth of a sum to be paid in n years hence that is

$$P = \frac{F}{(1+i)^n}$$

$(1 + i)^n$ is called compound amount factor. Value of $(1 + i)^n$ is seen from tables for equal payment series. Present worth factor (PWF) can be calculated by putting the values of ***n*** and "***i***" in above equation.

Problem 15.5 Initial cost on equipment is Rs. 10,000 annual operating cost is Rs. 10,000 and life of equipment is 8 years. If the salvage value is Rs. 1,000 and interest rate is 5%, find the present worth of the equipment.

Given PWF2 for $n = 8$, and $i = 5\%$ is 6.4632

PWF1 for $n = 8$, and $i = 5\%$ is 0.6768

Solution. Initial cost $= \text{Rs. } 10{,}000$

Present worth of annual operating costs $= 1000 \times (\text{PWF2})$ for 8 years and 5%

$= 1000 \times 6.4632 = \text{Rs. } 6463.20$

Present worth of salvage value $= 1000 \times (\text{PNF1})$ for 8 years and $i = 5\%$

$= 10,000 \times 0.6768 = \text{Rs. } 676.8$

∴ Present worth of equipment $= 10,000 + 6463.20 - 676.80$

$= 15,789.40$ **Ans.**

Problem 15.6 If one has to receive a payment of Rs. 10,000 in 10 years, what should be the present worth @10% interest.

$$P = \frac{10,000}{(1+0.1)^{10}} = \text{Since}$$

$$\frac{1}{(1+0.1)^{10}} = 0.3855 \text{ is known present worth factor}$$

$$\therefore \quad P = 10,000 \times 0.3855 = \text{Rs. } 3,855 \textbf{ Ans.}$$

Problem 15.7 A machine costing Rs. 10,000 has yearly operating charges of Rs. 200. If it has a 10 year life and money is worth 6%, what is the present worth of the cost for service provided by the machine?

Given: PWF = @6% – 10 years = 7.2965.

Solution. (*i*) Initial cost of machine = Rs. 10,000

(*ii*) Present worth of operating charges

= Rs. 200 × (PWF) 2 for 10 years and $i = 6\%$

∴ = 200 × 7.2965 = Rs. 1459.30

Total Present worth of Machine

= Rs. 10,000 + Rs. 1459.30

= Rs. 11.459.30 **Ans.**

(*b*) **Replacement of Items that completely fail—Individual versus Group Replacement:** There are certain items that deteriorate with time necessitating increase in maintenance cost and operation costs. Such as bearings, springs, piston rings etc.

However, there are many situation in which items do not deteriorate with time but fail suddenly such as *electric bulb, resistor in radio, T.V., computer, rectifier etc.*

Therefore, it is quite important to know in advance as to when the failure is likely to take place. Although individual failure is unpredictable, the statistical characteristics of group may be considered as stable. Rigorous inspection and condition monitoring may be required to detect imminent failure, and once, they are detected, preventive replacement could be taken up.

15.8.1 Replacement Policies

1. **Individual Replacement Policy:** Under this policy an item is replaced immediately after an item fails or reaches some predetermined service life, say *T*, but not failed (*i.e.*, replacement after failure or after reaching a service life).

2. **Group Replacement Policy:** Under this policy, all items are replaced after a fixed interval of time, irrespective of whether they have failed or not. There is a provision that if any item fails before the optimal time, it may be individually replaced.

The cost involved in the above two replacement policies will not be the same. The optimal value of replacement time T, which will minimise the total cost involved have to be found out which will vary from system to system. For example, the policy may be for replacement of *bulbs in a factory*, or replacement of bearings in a machine shop, or replacement of *piston rings from a fleet of automobiles*, or replacement of valves of hydraulic pumps etc.

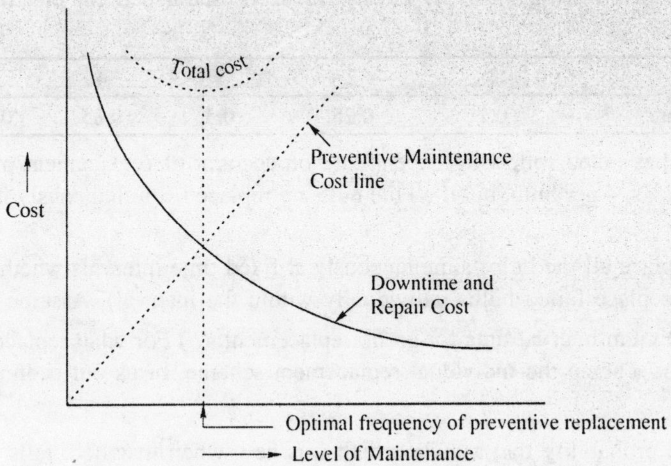

Figure 15.4. Cost versus Level of maintenance.

With the increase in frequency of preventive replacements, fewer actual breakdowns are expected. The total cost curve presents a minimum value for a particular frequency of replacement, that is optimal frequency of replacement.

Consider a case where the breakdown and repair cost did not decline sharply but declined very slowly and the preventive replacement cost increased steeply. In such cases, the preventive replacement may not be justified as there may be no minimal of the total cost.

- **Mortality Table:** It is virtually impossible to predict the time at which a system will fail. However, with the help of mortality table or life table, probability distribution of failure time can be obtained, *i.e.*, the probability distribution of life span of items (or system) can be obtained.

For each item the probability distribution is different which is made on the basis of large samples so that the prediction may have good reliability. The real problem is to determine the rate of failure that occur during a certain span of time.

Certain system consist of large number of low cost identical items which are prone to failure with time, such as *Street Light Bulbs*. It may be economical to replace all such items at a fixed interval of time T, whether they have failed or not and at the same time go on replacing failed items as and when they fail.

The *problem arises to find the optimum group replacement time interval T*.

Let N = Total number of items in the system.

$N(t)$ = Number of items surviving at time t.

$N(t-1)$ = Number of items surviving at time $(t-1)$

The number of items failed during period 't' and $(t - 1) = N(t) - N(t - 1)$

The probability of failure of items during period (t) and (t – 1)

$$= \frac{N(t-1) - N(t)}{N}$$

The conditional probability that an item survived upto time (t – 1) and will fail in the next period.

$$= \frac{N(t-1) - N(t)}{N(t-1)}$$

Problem 15.8 The following mortality rates have been established for electric bulbs used in an industrial complex.

End of Week	1	2	3	4	5	6
Probability of failure	0.1	0.25	0.5	0.85	0.77	1.00

The management has noted following expenditure on account of replacement of bulbs. To replace a bulb in service, it costs Rs. 4 per bulb, but if all the bulb are replaced simultaneously it is done for Rs. 0.5 a bulb only.

It is decided to replace all the bulbs simultaneously at fixed time intervals whether or not they have failed (and continue to replace failed bulbs individually within the interval). Assume 1000 bulbs in use:

Determine: (*i*) Optimum interval time for group replacement. (*ii*) For what replacement cost per bulb under group replacement scheme the individual replacement scheme, turns out economical?

Solution.

Let PC = The probability that a bulb, which was new when installed, fails during *i*th week of its life

= Probability of failure at the end of *i*th week – probability of failure at the beginning of *i*th week.

Therefore, $P_1 = 0.1$ $\quad P_2 = 0.25 - 0.1 = 0.15$

$P_3 = 0.50 - 0.25 = 0.25$

$P_4 = 0.85 - 0.50 = 0.35$

$P_5 = 0.97 - 0.85 = 0.12$

$P_6 = 1.00 - 0.97 = 0.03$

As given in the problem, all bulbs are sure to fail by the sixth week.

i.e., $P_7 = P_8 = P_9 = P_{10} = 0$

Let No = Number of original bulbs (*i.e.,* in the beginning)

Ni = Number of bulbs replaced at the end of *i*th week, when all the 1000 bulbs are new initially.

Then, N_1 = Number of bulbs being replaced by the end of 1st week.

= Number of bulbs in the beginning × Probability that a bulb fails during 1st week of its installation.

$= No \times P_1 = 1000 \times 0.1 = 100$

and N_2 = Number of bulbs replaced by the end of second week.

= Number of bulbs in the beginning × Probability of failure in second week + Number of bulbs replaced in 1st week × Probability that these fail during 1st week.

$= No \times P_2 + N_1 \times P_1$

$= 1000 \times 0.15 + 100 \times 0.1$

$= 150 + 10 = 160$

and $N_3 = No \times P_3 + N_1 \times P_2 + N_2 \times P_1$

$= 1000 \times 0.25 + 100 \times 0.15 + 160 \times 0.1$

$= 250 + 15 + 16 = 281.$

and $N_4 = No \times P_4 + N_1 \times P_3 + N_2\, P_2 + N_3 \times P_1$

$= 1000 \times 0.35 + 100 \times 0.25 + 160 \times 0.15 + 281$

$= 350 + 25 + 24 + 28.1$

$= 427.1.$

and $N_5 = No \times P_5 + N_1 \times P_4 + N_2\, P_3 + N_3 \times P_2 + N_4\, P_1$

$= 1000 \times 0.12 + 100 \times 0.35 + 160 \times 0.25 + 281 \times 0.15 + 427.1 \times 0.1$

$= 120 + 35 + 40 + 42.15 + 42.7$

$= 279.85 = 280.$

and $N_6 = No \times P_6 + N_1 \times P_5 + N_2\, P_4 + N_3 \times P_3 + N_4\, P_2 + N_5\, P_1$

$= 1000 \times 0.03 + 100 \times 0.12 + 160 \times 0.35 + 281 \times 0.25 + 427.1 \times 0.15 + 280 \times 0.1$

$= 30 + 12 + 56 + 70.25 + 64.065 + 28$

$= 260.315 = 260.$

So,	$No.$	N_1,	N_2,	N_3,	N_4,	N_5,	N_6,	N_7
	1000	100	160	281	427.1	280	260	295

$N_7 = No \times P_7 + N_1\, P_6 + N_2\, P_5 + N_3\, P_4 + N_4\, P_3 + N_5\, P_2 + N_6\, P_1$

$= 1000 \times 0 + 100 \times 0.03 + 160 \times 0.12 + 281 \times 0.35 + 427.1 \times 0.25 + 280 \times 0.15 + 260 \times 0.1$

$= 0 + 3 + 19.2 + 98.35 + 106.8 + 42 + 26$

$= 295.35$

$= 295.$

It is seen that, the number of bulbs failing each week increases till the 4th week, then decreases and again increases from 7th week.

In this way, *Ni* will continue to oscillate till the system attain a steady state in which condition the proportion of bulbs failing each week is reciprocal of their average life (expected life).

The average expected life of each bulb

$$E(n) = \sum_{i=1}^{6} \chi i\ pi \qquad \chi i = \text{Nos. of weeks}, \quad pi = \text{corresponding probability of failure}$$

Substituting the valves and χi and pi we get:

$$E(x) = \chi_1 p_1 + \chi_2 p_2 + \chi_3 p_3 + \chi_4 p_4 + \chi_5 p_5 + \chi_6 p_6$$

$$= 1 \times 0.1 + 2 \times 0.15 + 3 \times 0.25 + 4 \times 0.35 + 5 \times 0.12 + 6 \times 0.03$$

$$= 3.33 \text{ weeks.}$$

and under steady state condition, the average number of failure or replacement per week

$$= \frac{N}{\text{mean life}} = \frac{1000}{3.33} = 301 \text{ bulbs/week}$$

∴ Cost of individual replacement, weekly

(Rs. 4/bulb) $= 301 \times 4 =$ Rs. 1204 **Ans.**

- Now, to find out the cost of replacement under group replacement policy.

  Given group replacement cost = Rs. 0.5,

  and Individual replacement cost = Rs. 4.00

Table 15.1 Group Replacement Policy

End of week	*Total cost of replacement Rs. = Group replacement cost + Individual replacement*		*Average cost weekly, Rs.*
1	$1000 \times 0.5 + 100 \times 4$	= 900	900
2	$1000 \times 0.5 + 4(100 + 160)$	= 1560	$\frac{1560}{2} = 770$
3	$1000 \times 0.5 + 4(100 + 160 + 281)$	= 2664	$\frac{2664}{3} = 888$
4	$1000 \times 0.5 + 4(100 + 160 + 281 + 247)$	= 4372	$\frac{4372}{4} = 1093$
5	$1000 \times 0.5 + 4(100 + 160 + 281 + 427 + 280)$		$= 5492 \ \frac{5492}{5}$
= 1098			

It is seen that the average minimum cost is in second week, so it is optimal policy to have group replacement after every two weeks.

If P = Price per bulb under group replacement scheme

Then $\frac{1000 \times P + 4\ (100 + 160)}{2} > 1204$ (*i.e.*, cost of individual replacement weekly)

or $500\ P \times 520 > 1204$

or $500P > 1204 - 520$ or 684

or $P < \frac{6.84}{5} = 1.368$ or Rs. 1.368 = Rs. 1.37

Since group replacement cost per bulb is Rs. 0.5 which is less than Rs. 1.368, the group replacement policy is to be preferred.

Problem 15.9 For a certain type of electric bulbs the following mortality rates have been recorded:

Week	1	2	3	4	5
Percent failing by the end of the week	10	25	50	80	100

There are 2000 bulbs in use and its costs Rs. 6 to replace an individual bulb which has fused. If all bulbs are replaced simultaneously it would cost Rs. 2 per bulb. Which policy of replacement should be adopted for incurring minimum total cost. What should be the interval of replacement?

Hint: Probability during 1st week 10%

$$P_1 = \frac{10}{100} = \frac{1}{10} = 0.1$$

$$P_2 = \frac{25 - 10}{100} = \frac{15}{100} = 0.15$$

and $$P_3 = \frac{50 - 25}{100} = 0.25$$

$$P_4 = \frac{80 - 50}{100} = 0.30$$

$$P_5 = \frac{100 - 80}{100} = 0.20$$

15.9 PROBABLE QUESTIONS

1. What is Process Management? What are the common decisions for any process?
2. Describe how a process choice is made?
3. What is Process Re-engineering? How is a process improved?
4. What is Replacement Analysis? Describe different factors responsible for replacing an old equipment.
5. Describe the merits and demerits of individual replacement vs. group replacement for the equipment which may fail suddenly.
6. Describe the procedures involved for Process Planning and Process design.

16

Quality Management

- *FOrecasting: Methods and Procedural steps in Forecasting.*

16.1 MEANING OF DEMAND FORECAST

Forecasting is one of the important aspects of administration. The corner-stone of successful marketing planning is the measurement and forecasting to market demand. According to American Marketing Association "Sales forecast is an estimate of sales, in monetary or physical units, for a specified future period under a proposed business plan or programme and under an assumed set of economic and other forces outside the unit for which the forecast is made".

A sales forecast is an estimation of sales volume that a company can expect to attain within the plan period. A sales forecast is not just a sales predicting. It is the act of matching opportunities with the marketing efforts.

Sales forecasting is the determination of a firm's share in the market under a specified future. Thus sales forecasting shows the probable volume of sales.

16.2 FACTORS INFLUENCING A FORECASTING

Following factors help in making an accurate sales forecast

(*i*) **General Economic Condition:** The general economic trend such as inflation, recession and deflation etc. affect the business and these influence the sales forecasting.

A thorough knowledge of the economic, political and the general trend of the business facilities to build a forecast more accurately.

(*ii*) **Consumers:** Products like, wearing apparel, luxurious goods furniture, vehicles are sold and sales depend on size of population, age, education, gender etc.

(*iii*) **Industrial Behaviours:** Markets are full of similar products manufactured by different firms, which compete among themselves to increase the sales. As such, the pricing policy, design, advanced technological improvements, promotional activities etc. of similar industries must be carefully observed. Unstable conditions—Industrial unrest, government control through rules and regulations, improper availability of raw materials etc. directly affect the production, sales and profits.

(*iv*) **Changes Within Firm:** Future sales are greatly affected by the changes in pricing, advertising policy, quantity of products etc. A careful study in relation to the changes on the sales volume may be studied carefully. Sales can be increased by price cut, enhancing advertising policies, increased sales promotions, concessions to customers etc.

(*v*) **Period:** The required information must be collected on the basis of period-short run, medium run and long run forecasts.

16.3 IMPORTANCE OF FORECASTING

(*i*) Supply and demand for the products can easily be adjusted by overcoming temporary demand, in the light of the anticipated estimate and regular supply is facilitated.

(*ii*) A good inventory control is advantageously benefited by avoiding the weakness of understocking and overstocking.

(*iii*) Allocation and reallocation of sales territories are facilitated.

(*iv*) It is a forward planner as all other requirements of raw materials, labour plant layout, financial needs, warehousing, transport facility etc. depend in accordance with the sales volume expected in advance.

(*v*) Sales opportunities are searched out on the basis of forecast, and thus discovery of selling success is made.

(*vi*) It is a gear, by which all other activities are controlled as a basis of forecasting.

(*vii*) Advertisement programmes are beneficially adjusted with fully advantage to the firm.

(*viii*) It is an indicator to the development of finance as to how much and when finance is needed and it helps to overcome difficult situations.

(*ix*) It is a measuring rod by which the efficiency of the sales personnel or of sales department can be measured.

(*x*) It facilitates scheduled production and avoids idle time and helps to improve efficiency.

16.4 METHODS OF FORECASTING

Approaches to forecasting techniques and procedures vary form firm to firm. There are many methods. A firm may manufacture the products or distribute the products or both. Forecasting can not be done on mere guessing, but on the basis of reliable statistical data collected for this purpose.

A dealer or a manufacturer must anticipate the future need and provide necessities to fulfil the needs. The following are the various methods of sales forecasting.

(*i*) **Jury of Executive Opinion:** This method of sales forecasting is the oldest. One or more of the executives, who are experienced and have good knowledge of the market factors make out the expected sales. The executives are responsible while forecasting sales figures through estimates and experiences.

All the factors—internal and external—are taken into account. This is a type of committee approach. This methods utilises the experiences and judgements of senior executives.

This is not based on factual data but an economical, simple and quick method.

(*ii*) **Sales Force Opinion:** Under this method, salesman or intermediaries are required to make out an estimate sales in their respective territories for a given period. Salesman are in close touch with the consumers and possess good knowledge about the future demand trend. All the sales force estimates are processed, integrated, modified and a sales volume estimate formed for the whole market, for the given period.

In this, specialised knowledge is utilised but success depends on the competency of salesman.

(*iii*) **Test Marketing Result:** Under the market test method, products are introduced in a limited geographical area and the result is studied. Taking this result as a base, sales forecast is made. This test is conducted as a sample on pre-test basis in order to understand the market response.

This system is reliable as forecast is based on actual result but it is a time consuming process and study is made on the basis of a part of a market.

(*iv*) **Consumers' Buying Plan:** Consumers, as source of information, are approached to know their likely purchases during the period under a given set of condition. This method is suitable when there are few customers. This type of forecasting is generally adopted for industrial goods. It is suitable for industries, which produce costly goods to a limited number of buyers, wholesalers, retailers etc. In this method, user's intentions are known and first hand information is possible.

But in this system, buyers may change their buying habits, and it is difficult to identify actual buyers. Long run forecast is not possible.

(*v*) **Market Factor Analysis:** A company's sales depend on the behaviour of certain market factors. The principal factors which affect the sales may be determined. By studying the behaviour of the factors, forecasting should be made. Correlation is the statistical analysis which analyses the degree of extent to which two variables fluctuate with reference to each other.

Regression Analysis is a statistical device which help us to estimate or predict the unknown values of one variable from the known values of another variable.

For example: You publish a text book on "Banking", affiliated to different universities. The permitted intake capacity of each and the medium through which the students are taught are known. Is it a compulsory or optional subject?

By getting all these details and also by considering the sales activities of promotional work, you may be able to declare the probable copies to be printed.

The key to the successful use of this method lies in the selection of the appropriate market factors. Thus the demand decision makers have to consider price, competitions, advertising, disposable income, buying habits, consumption habits, consumer price index, change in population etc.

This habits, consumption habits, consumer price index, change in population etc.

This is a sound method which analyses market factors in detail. The disadvantages are that it is costly, time-consuming and done for a short-run process.

(*vi*) **Expert Opinion:** Various consultancy agencies have entered into the field of sales. The consultancy agencies have specialises experts in the respective field. This includes dealers, trade associations etc. They may conduct market researches and possess readymade statistical data. Firms may make use of the opinions of such experts. These opnions may be carefully analysed by the company and a sound forecasting is made.

In this method specialised knowledge is used and more accurate forecasts are made.

However, the success of forecast depends on competency of experts and reliability of data used.

(*vii*) **Economic Model Building:** This is a mathematical approach of study and is an ideal way to forecast sales. This method is more useful for marketing durable goods.

It is in the form of equations, which represent a set of relationships among different demand determining market factors.

This analysing the market factors (independent variable) and sales (dependent variable), sales are forecast.

This system does not entirely depend upon correlation analysis. It has great scope, but adoption of this method depends upon availability of domplete information.

The market factors which are more accurate, quick and less costly may be selected for a sound forecasting.

(*viii*) **Past Sales (Historical Method):** Personal judgement of sales forecasting can be beneficially supplemented by the sue of statistical and quantitative methods. Part sales are a good basis and on this basis future seales can be formulated and forecast.

Today's sales flow into tomorrow's sales activities. This approach is adding or deducting a set of percentage to the sales of previous year.

(*ix*) **Other Factors (Subjective Techniques):** Apart from the above, the following factors may also be consideredc.

(*i*) Availability of raw materials.

(*ii*) Plant capacity.

(*iii*) Government policies.

(*iv*) Buying habits of consumers.

(*v*) Fashion changes.

(*vi*) Distribution system.

(*vii*) Financial, capacity.

(*viii*) Market Competition.

(*ix*) National Income Movement.

(*x*) Sales promotion.

16.5 FORECASTING—TREND METHODS.

Mostly trend is used for forecasting in practice. Popular trends are:

(*a*) Least Square Method and

(*b*) Moving Average Method.

(*a*) **Least Square Method:** This is one of the best method to determine trend. In most cases, we try to fit a straight line to the given data. The line is known as "line of best fit" as we try to minimise the sum of squares of deviation between the observed and the fitted values of the data.

The basic assumption here is that the relationship between the various factors remains unchanged in future period also. If Y is the demand and X the period for a certain items, then,

$y = a + bx$ – linear relationship a and b can be estimated with the help of past information about X and Y.

If x and y are the deviations of x and y (variances) from respective means, the least square estimates of a and b are given by

$$\hat{a}\frac{\Sigma y}{n} \text{ and } \hat{b}\frac{\Sigma xy}{\Sigma x^2}\ n = \text{nos. of observation.}$$

The calculation of Σy, Σxy and Σx_2 can be done with the help of given data and y an x.

(*b*) **The Moving Average Method:** This method can be used to determine the trend values for given data without going into complex mathematical calculations. The calculations are based on some predetermined period in weeks, months, years etc. The period depends on the nature of characteristics in the time series and can be determined by plotting the observations on graph paper.

The moving average is an average of some fixed or predetermined number of observations (given by period) which moves through the series by dropping the top item of the previous averaged groups and adding the next item in each successive average.

16.6 DELPHI METHOD OF DEMAND FORECAST

Developed by Rand Corporation, USA. Panel 7 experts not known to each other are requested by a co-ordinator to give their opinions for a questionnaire handed over to each & them. The co-ordinator collects the opinions and compile them to compose the demand forecast. This method has been found to be expensive.

16.7 TREND PROJECTIONS

Every company has accumulated data on the sales of its products for the past many years. This firm arranges such sales data chronologically and then prepare time series relating to sales to represent the pattern of effective demand for a particular product.

The time series is used to prepare a trend line which is projected into the future.

Following two methods are used for trend projections:

(*i*) The method of moving averages

(*ii*) The method of least squares

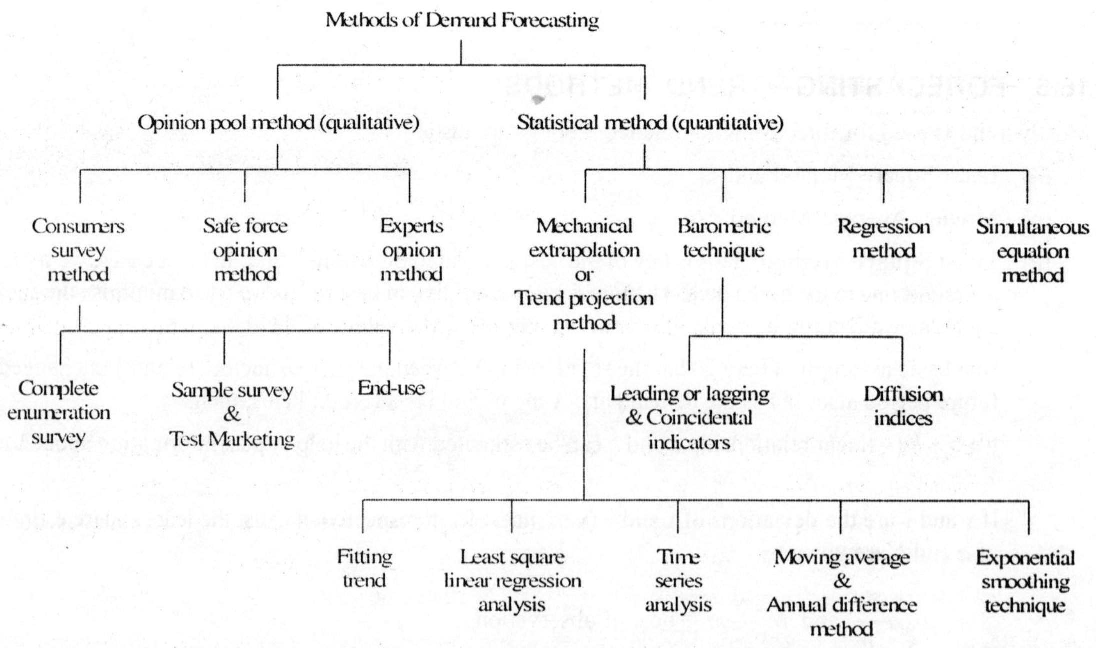

(*a*) *The method of moving averages:* It is a simple method involving calculations of moving averages for 3-4 years period to find out the trend.

In this way, the firm calculates the moving averages or the trend of demand which is plotted on a graph with horizontal axis representing the years. From the graphical presentation, demand forecasting is projected through the extension of curve for the years ahead.

(b) *The method of least squares:* It is more scientific than moving average method and is most commonly used.

It uses the straight line equation $Y = a + bx$

where, Y = Demand for the product a & b are constant.

X = Determinant or the variable on which Y depends.

Say, Agricultural product/demand (Y) depends on quantity of rainfall (×) A straight line known as "the line of best fit is used and we try to minimise the sum of squares of deviations between the observed and fitted value of data.

(c) *Regression Analysis:* This method is based on demand forecasting on certain economic indicators such as

Personal disposable income

Demands for agricultural equipment

Demands for building materials

After collecting above information, one is concerned in establishing the relationship between the demand for a product and the particular economic indicator through the method of least squazres and derives the regression equation.

The linear relationship is exopressed by the equation.

$$Y = a + bx$$

where Y = Demand for the product

X = Economic indicator.

One, the equation is derived, the value of Y is esxtimated for any value of x.

There are however two major limitations to regression analysis.

(*i*) It is not easy to locate an appropriate economic indicator for demand forecasting of a particular product.

(*ii*) The regression analysis is not applicable for a new product as no past sales data are available.

16.8 DETERMINANTS OF DEMAND FORECAST

Good can be broadly classified into three categories.

(*a*) Capital Goods—Equipment, Machinery

(*b*) Durable Consumer Goods—Automobiles, TV Sets, Refrigerator.

(*c*) Consumer Goods (non-durable)—Soft drinks, Cigarettes, Viscuits.

A. Damand Forecasting for Capital Goods: Demand for capital goods are of two kinds:

(*a*) Replacement Demand

(*b*) New Demand

Demand Forecasting for capital goods has to consider the following factors.

(*i*) Extent of excess capacity in the industry using the capital goods.

(*ii*) Forecast of demand for the commodity which the capital good is capable of producing.

(*iii*) Existing inventory of capital goods.

(*iv*) Age distribution of existing stock.

(*v*) The rate of obsolescence.

(*vi*) The availability of funds and cost of funds to a firm planning for capital goods.

(*vii*) The natural of tax/duties applicable on re-equipment.

(*viii*) The prices of substitutes and complementary goods.

(*ix*) The market structure within which the capital goods operate.

After collecing the above information, a firm can take the help of regression analysis to forecast the demand for capital goods in question.

B. Demand Forecasting for Consumer-durable Goods: Demands for consumer durable goods are of 2 kinds.

(*a*) Replacement demand

(*b*) New demand

Demand forecasting for consumer-durable goods has to consider the following factors.

(*i*) Changes in size and characteristics of population

(*ii*) Saturation limit of the market

(*iii*) Existing stock and age distribution

(*iv*) Replacement demand Vs New demand

(*v*) Income levels of Consumers

(*vi*) Consumer Credit outstanding

(*vii*) Tastes and preferences of Consumers

(*viii*) Advertising efforts.

After collecting above information, a firm can resort to the Survey of Consumer plan and then the data can be fed into a regression model to forecast the demand for the Consumer durable goods, Econometric model consisting of a mathematical equations of independent and dependent variables is used for demand forecast for consumer durable goods.

C. Demand Forecasting of Consumer Goods: Population and its characteristics (i.e. culture, habits) Income level, purchasing power or disposable income, price of goods, Advertising efforts are important criteria for consumer goods.

Size and characteristics of population for consumer goods demand are very important and it si commonly known as demography, and refers to the total population, income groups, social status, age and sex imposition, urban rural ration, geographical characteristics, level of education etc.

Demand for consumer goods is influenced by all the above factors.

With the help of demographic variables, demand for each market segment can be estimated as distinct from the total market demand.

D. Demand Forecast—Industry Examples: The estimated demand for a product determines the maximum amount of its output. Every business firm needs to make a forecast of sales before deciding the quantity to be produced.

A proper demand or sales forecast helps in preparing appropriate production schedules so as to avoid overstocking and delays in meeting demand.

In the long-run, demand forecast facilitate capacity planning.

Before introducing a new product in the market, it is always desirable to first forecast its demand.

For example, Hindustan Unilever Ltd. made extensive demand forecast, before introducing any of their consumer product such as Close Up Toothpaste and Lux or Life Byoy toilet soaps.

Forecasting demand for new products is important for two reasons. First, when a businessman wants to introduce new products for diversification and growth, he needs an estimate of likely demand. Secondly, every product has a life span and a firm has to go in for new products when old products decay and die out.

Methods of Demand Forecasting—Survey Method

Initially when some business managers attempted to forecast the demand for their products, they depended on their personal judgement and past-experience and made intelligent guesses bout future demand and sale prospects for their products.

In course of time, however, specialist took over and used increasingly sophisticated statistical techniques and mathematical formulae to clarify demand relationships and arrive at accurate demand forecasting.

The following are some of the methods employed for demand forecasting.

(*a*) **Survey of Buyers Intentions:** A direct method of demand fore-casting for a short period is to find out what consumers prefer and intend to buy.

For this, a company may undertake surveys of what buyer's plan to buy during a forthcoming period say a year.

The opinion survey can take the form of interview of the buyers.

The survey method is useful when the bulk of the sale is to a few industrial buyers.

(*b*) **Collective Opinion Survey:** In this method, opinions of many top executives of companies connected with purchase or sale of the product are collected and compiled.

This method is based on first hand information of the consumers.

(*c*) **Survey of Experts' Opinion:** A company may engage experts in the field of market research and demand forecasting to analyse the past and present economic conditions, undertake sample surveys of the market, carry out opinion polls and then forecast demand. Delphi Method used by Rand Corporation, USA uses opnions of a panel of experts not known to each other. A co-ordinator of the company collects individual opinions and combine them to arrive at a conclusion. The Delphi method is primarily used to forecast the demand for new products. Though it provides valuable insights, it is rather expensive as the experts may charge high fees for their opinions.

16.10 PROBABLE QUESTIONS

1. Define forecasting. What is the importance of forecasting?
2. (*a*) Write about factors influencing forcasting

   (*b*) What are various types of forecasts?
3. What are various methods of forecasting?

UNIT-II

Materials Management

1

Materials and Inventory Management & Control

• *Materials Management—Need, Scope, Advantages, Objective* • *Materials Planning* • *Definition and Types of Inventory* • *Economic Order Quantity* • *Inventory Control* • *V-E-D Analysis* • *FSN Analysis* • *Perpetual Inventory* • *MRP* • *Inventory Analysis for pares Consumable and Components* • *JIT* • *KANBAN* • *Non-Production of Scrap* • *EOQ Models* • *Probable Questions.*

1.1 MATERIALS MANAGEMENT—DEFINITION, IMPORTANCE, NEED, SCOPE, ADVANTAGES, OBJECTIVES

(*a*) **Definition:** Materials Management is a management function responsible for the coordination of planning, sourcing, purchasing, moving, storing and controlling materials in an optimum manner so as to provide a pre-decided service to the customer at a minimum cost.

(*b*) **Importance & Need:** In some industries line steel, cement, Pharmaceuticals & Fertilizer, total cost of materials consists about 50–55% of total cost of production and in sugarcane, cotton & Engineering industries this is 60–65%.

Roughly,

Cost of Production = Cost of Materials + Conversion Cost
+ Cost of Wages & Salaries + Cost of Over heads.

The importance of materials management lies in the fact that any significant contribution made by the materials deptt. in reducing materials cost will go a long way in improving the profitability and the rate of return on investment.

In the present global economy, there is increased competition from domestic and foreign supplies and, hence reducing cost of materials will help in competitive advantage.

Materials are important item of current assets in a company.

The Return on Investment (ROI) depends on a great deal on the manner of utilisation of materials.

$$ROI = \frac{\text{Profit}}{\text{Investment}} = \frac{\text{Profit}}{\text{Fixed Assets} + \text{Current Assets}}$$

Since fixed assets constitute Capital already sunk and the only scope for improving the return on investment lies therefore in the efficient management of materials, which constitute the bulk of the current assets.

Therefore, in this context, the control of materials assumes great importance.

(*c*) **Scope and Advantages:** Materials management covers all aspects of materials and their supply necessary for convecting raw materials into finished products. It is thus concerned with planning and programming of materials (material planning), materials purchase for research, procurement of materials and Capital goods (purchasing), receiving, storing, keeping, warehousing, inventory control, packaging materials movement, disposal of scrap, surplus and obsolete materials.

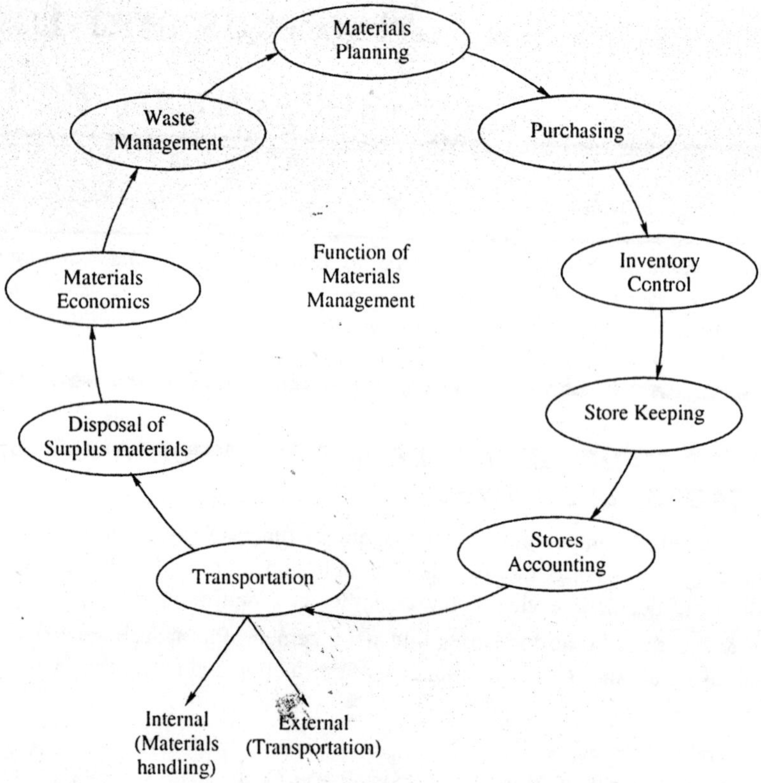

Figure 1.1

Reduction in Unit Cost of Production: Reduction in cost is something which is within the control of the company. The total cost of a Profit centre consists of four main constituents *i.e.*, material cost, labour cost, conversion cost & overhead cost, and in these materials cost is the major portion of the total cost.

Materials in Indian scenario constitute more than 50% of the cost of production and in some cases it is 60–70%. This makes the materials management. The bigger single area having tremendous scope for cost reduction. A well coordinated materials management programme may lead to 15 to 20% of cost reduction.

A rupee saving on material cost in almost equivalent to ten rupees of sale. Moreover, a sale is one time sale, while saving in material cost is a recurring benefit.

Effective materials management, therefore has a tremendous effect on the profitability of the firm. Though materials department is the biggest spending department, it has the potential to save money to a large extent.

In a company, the fixed Capital is deployed in fixed assets like land, bldg. plant and machinery, jigs and fixtures etc. and very little can be done to save anything in it. This leaves us with the working

Capital which is locked up in inventory in the form of raw materials, work-in-progress and finished goods, etc. which can be released if profit materials management techniques such as scientific inventory control, JIT, MRP etc. are employed.

(*d*) **Objectives of Materials Management:** There are ten objectives of materials management:

- To maintain steady flow of materials to ensure uninterrupted production.
- To achieve economy in cost of materials by adopting cost reduction techniques like value analysis, JIT & MRP etc.
- To ensure consistency of quality by providing right materials of right quality and quantity.
- To reduce inventory investment through inventory control techniques
- To improve corporate image by improving good buys-sells relation.
- To maintain good records of purchase, stores, traffic, etc to eliminate possibility of corruption.
- To preserve/conserve materials in stock so that losses due to pilferage, deterioration, obsolescence etc are kept at minimum.
- To reduce operating cost by minimising/eliminating wastage and improving productivity of materials.
- To improve competitive advantage of the firm by producing the best quality products using quality materials at the lowers possible cost.
- To help the firm at the firm of shortage of raw materials.

(*e*) **Materials Management:** Profit centre concept: The objective of Materials Management should be to ensure continuity of supply of uniform quality with lowest cost of the right item or service. Purchasing function storing function and inventory control function involve major volume of cash outflow and cash out lay in any organisation.

In view of this substantial outlay, financial losses arising from have been high.

By the same token, cost reduction can be achieved by better planning and setting realistic objectives and through materials management improvements on better management procedures.

In many progressive large Companies Material Management works as a Profit Centre Concept in relation to materials management for running units and for new project ventures. These are under taken in multiple locations in the country or abroad.

1.2 MATERIALS PLANNING

(*a*) Materials Planning is the scientific way of determining the requirements of raw materials, bought out parts and others and ensuring, their availability in the right quantities, at the right time with minimum capital lock up.

Materials planning is an important function of materials management.

(*b*) **Bill of Materials (BOM):** Bill of Materials is also called the parts list and is a document generated at the design stage. It details the structure of the product by dividing the final assembly into major assemblies, major assemblies into sub-assemblies and sub-assemblies into parts.

The individual parts, as far as possible, are listed in the manner in which each part is assembled.

Bill of Materials provide details such as part number, description, quantities required, materials specification etc.

For determining the materials requirements, each product is split into its basic requirements (i.e., bought out parts etc.) with the help of its bill of materials.

The quantity required for item is multiplied by the quantity of the product to be produced to arrive at the total requirement of each item.

The requirements are adjusted for the rejection during manufacturing.

Bill of materials technique is best suited for engineering industries since in these, a large number of components are required for assembling an end-product.

Micro factors for Materials planning are price trends, business-cycles, Govt policies & credit policies where as Micro factors are corporate objectives, Plant Capacity utilisation, lead time inventory level, working capital etc.

(*c*) **Materials Requirement Planning (MRP):** On the basis of Production Schedule of the finished product requirements of materials can be calculated. The system of calculating the requirements of input materials at different points of time on the basis of production plan is called Materials Requirement Planning (MRP).

The basic objective of MRP is to ensure the supply of right quantities of parts at the right time. MRP is used for dependent demand items.

For independent demand items other Computer Programmes such as IMPACT (Inventory Management Programme and Control Technique) are used.

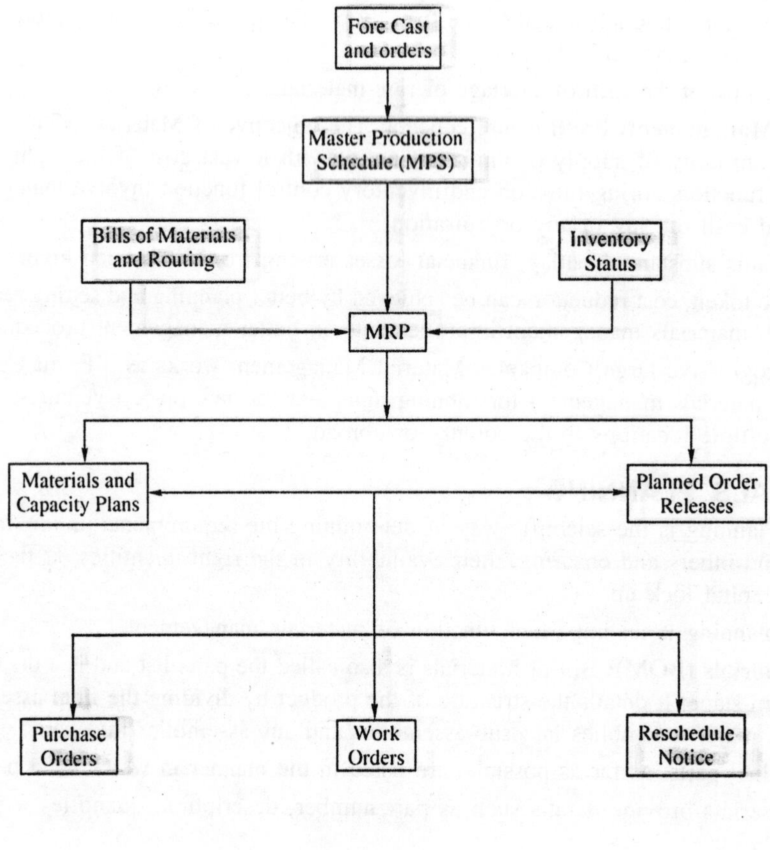

MRP in perspective

Figure 1.2

MRP System is Compatible to Computer station.

It is applicable in Production Situation.

The Master Production Schedule (MPS) of end product dictates the demands for parts and subassemblies.

MRP inputs are:

(*a*) Master Production Schedule

(*b*) Bill of Materials

(*c*) Inventory Status.

MRP Software computes component requirement and procurement schedules.

MRP is a system of order scheduling for dependent demand situation.

This system anticipates the requirements of finished products, and based on this information and other inputs, generator statements.

MRP is a push system, unlike JIT, which is a Pull system.

It is push in the sense that statements of requirements are in line with the delivery schedules and thus assemblies, components and raw materials get pushed into the process.

Thus, MRP is a time-bound materials-ordering system. The basic element of MRP is the independent/ dependent demand.

Independent pattern of demand is shown by finished products, component and sub-assemblies to be sold as spares. This demand is calculated by using known orders/fore casts. This constitutes MPS. MRP taken advantage of the fact that demand for all sub-assemblies, components and raw-materials are dependent upon the demand for finished products. Thus they show dependent demand. For these item a fore cast is necessary.

The following diagram illustrates MRP in perspective.

(*d*) Benefits of Material Requirement Planning

(*i*) MRP estimates the dependent demand of components from the production schedules of their parents, these provide a better forecast of component requirements

(*ii*) MRP system provide useful information for planning capacities and estimating financial requirements.

(*iii*) MRP systems automatically update the dependent demand and inventory replenishment schedules of components when the production schedules of parent items change.

(*e*) MRP Explosion: The key input of an MRP system are a BOM, MPS and Inventory status. Using this information, the MRP system identifies action that a Production operation must take to stay on schedule, such as releasing new production orders, adjusting order quantities and expediting late orders.

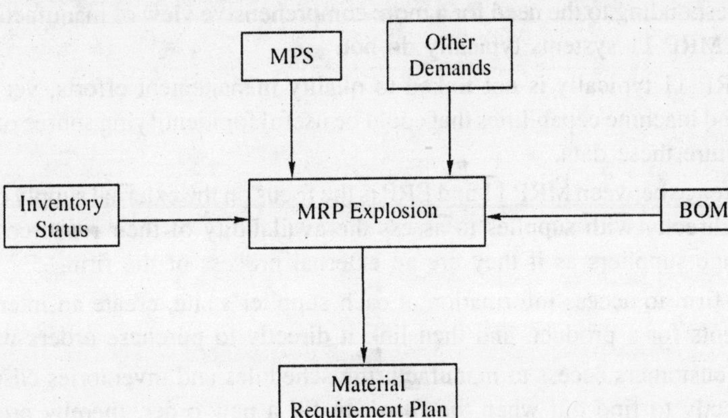

Figure 1.3 Shows MRP Inputs.

An MRP System translates MPS and other sources of demand, such as independent demand for replacement parts and maintenance item, into the requirements for all subassemblies, components and raw materials needed to produce the required parent item. This process is called on MRP explosion because it converts the requirements of various final products into material requirements plan that specifies the replenishment schedules of all the subassemblies, components and raw materials needed by final products.

(*f*) MRP 11 is known as Manufacturing Resource Planning. The basis MRP system has its roots in the batch manufacturing of discrete parts involving assemblies that must be stocked to support future manufacturing needs.

The focus is on producing schedules that meet the materials needs identified in the master production schedules.

Mfg. resource planning (MRP 11) is a system that ties the basic MRP system to the company's financial system.

The focus of MRP 11 is to aid the materials managers by providing information based on the production plant to all functional areas.

MRP 11 enables managers to test "what if" scenarios by using simulation.

For example, managers can see the effect of changing the MPS on the purchasing requirements for certain critical supplies.

Information from MRP 11 is used in mfg, purchasing, marketing, finance, accounting and engineering. MRP 11 reports help in developing and monitoring the overall business plan and recognise sales objectives, manufacturing capabilities and cash flow constraints.

MRP 11 is used extensively and it provides benefits beyond that of MRP alone.

The real benefit of **MRP 11 is that it also enables a high degree of integration with other automated processes in the organisation.** MRP 11 is a push system.

(*g*) **Enterprise Resource Planning:** ERP on the onset of supply, chain management, *E*-commerce and global operation has created a need to provide and exchange information directly with other companies and customers. In some companies, MRP 11 is evolving into a new form, *i.e.,* Enterprise Resource Planning (ERP).

ERP is a system that has additional capabilities for quality management field service, maintenance, distribution, marketing and supplies management. In addition, these system have databases structured for ease of external access and the ability to access the information system of other companies.

ERP system are responding to the need for a more comprehensive view of manufacturing. They supply information that MRP 11 systems typically do not.

For example, MRP 11 typically is not linked to quality management efforts, yet a lot of data may exist on defects and machine capabilities that could be useful for identifying source of quality problems. ERP System capture these data.

The biggest difference between MRP 11 and ERP is the focus on the external supply chain. ERP enables the firm to deal directly with supplies to assess the availability of their resources. ERP can enable the firm to manage suppliers as if they are an external process of the firm.

ERP enables the firm to access information at each supplier's site, create an internal work order to satisfy requirements for a product, and then link it directly to purchase orders with the suppliers.

ERP also allows customers access to manufacturing schedules and inventories customers can quarry the schedule directly to find out when the firm can fill a new order, thereby providing the firm a competitive edge over other manufacturers.

(h) Benefits of ERP: ERP bring together people who work on shared tasks within the same enterprise or in their dealings with supplies and customers.

Enterprise have to ensure a smooth flow of information at all levels and between all parts of their organisation to access up-to-data information.

Benefits of ERP in industries are as follows:

- Reduction on lead time
- On time delivery to customers
- Customer's repurchase orders
- Reduction in Production Cycle time
- Work-in-Process inventory is reduced.

There are also some intangible benefits like better customer satisfaction, reduced quality costs, increased information accuracy etc.

With the liberalisation of Indian economy and the consequent competition, enterprises in India have realised the need to adopt ERP solutions.

ERP enables a firm to use information as a means to gain increased competitive advantage by achieving the most effective practices results in the company adjusting faster to changes in the environment like competition, government policies, consumer preferences etc.

Manufacturing companies in India in the fields of Steel, FMCG, Automobiles and Pharmaceuticals have implemented ERP solutions successfully.

A Corporate House having multiple location mfg. units is benefited by implementing ERP to improve the demand/supply imbalance between different plants.

ERP becomes more effective when management also links a human resource module to the ERP system.

Top management should involve itself in all the stages of ERP implementation, review the results and take appropriate follow up actions. Then only ERP will be effective in any organisation.

(i) ERP Approach: The approach to ERP is to first develop a business model comprising the business processes or activities that are the essence of the business. The business activities are shown as one large system with interconnections and sequences. Based on business strategy and objectives, a business model consisting of business processes is developed.

These processes are managed and controlled by various individuals in various organisation.

The ERP is developed to provide the required information to the organisation to manage the processes that are part of to manage the processes and that are part of the business model. The data base is the source of information and drives an ERP.

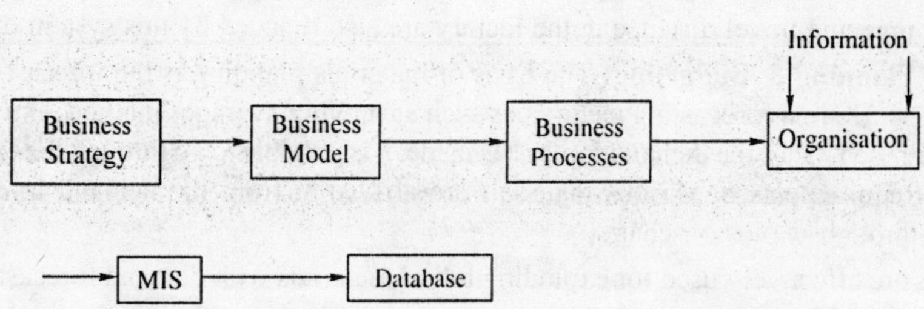

Figure 1.4 Building an MIS for ERP–The data base drives ERP.

(*j*) **BPR and ERP:** Now, throughout the world, the latest business busy world, Business Process Reengineering BPR or simply Business Engineering (BE), is fully underway.

Various Companies have created special groups, often led by senior executive, that focus solely on BE.

BPR or BE revolves around Information Technology (IT) and continuous change. It is the constant refinement of an organisation's changing needs.

BE is the re-thinking of business processes to improve the speed, quality and output of materials service.

The reason why so many companies are engaged in extensive re-engineering efforts is that society is shifting from an age where labour and machinery drove productivity to an age where productivity depends on knowledge and information. We now live in the age of information. This shift has created major social, technological and market change, all of which have led to the increasing importance of BPR or BE.

Recent developments in IT have not only made BPR possible on a radical and extensive scale, but also more effective. Today, IT and BPR go hand in hand.

The heart and soul of BE lies in radical, process oriented business solutions, which have been greatly enhanced by IT of Client/Server computing. Most of the ERP Systems are based on the Client/Server Solution model and business engineering blueprint that represent an advanced integration of business process reengineering and IT.

ERP rum in close association with BPR of the company. BPR will initially question the value-added potential of the particular process and then go on to put some systems and procedures in place.

ERP, hence, function as the key enables in any BPR. The key factor is that every company that implements ERP has to reengineer its processes in one form or the other.

ERP is essentially an activity that encompasses the entire organisation, number of Plants and Locations. MRP and MRP 11 Packages address primarily the requirements of a manufacturing set up, and ERP address the information requirements of the entire enterprise.

The focus of ERP has not only been on addressing the current requirements of an organisation but also on providing the opportunity for continually improving and refining business processes.

Thus ERP is the Manning of four Ms of an enterprise's resources—Man, Money, Materials and Machines to their best synergistic values.

(*k*) **Cellullar Manufacturing:** The use of work cells is frequently used in lean manufacturing environments. A work cell is more than a single machine location but smaller than a manufacturing department. A small group of workers are brought together in one part of the factory to produce a certain product. In their cell they will have all the machines, resources and materials available to produce the product. This cellular manufacturing system speeds up processing time and the communication and team work between workers are improved by this technique.

The travel time and travel distance in the factory are also reduced by this system of cellular working.

(*l*) **Materials Planning & Budgeting:** The basis of materials planning is the forecast of demand for the end-products. Demon forecasting techniques such as moving averages method, exponential and Trend Analysis are used. Once the demand forecast is made, it is possible to go through the exercise of materials planning. Requirements of various materials are arrived at from the demand forecast, using bill of materials, through explosion charts.

Computers are effectively used for exploding bill of materials with demand forecasts. Bill of materials is a document which shows for a given component the list of materials required, unit consumption and location code.

An explosion chart is just a series of bills of materials grouped together in a matrix form so that combining the requirements for different components can be made.

Materials budget can be prepared once the materials requirements are worked out on the basis of demand forecasting techniques, sales forecasts for products required, product-mix and product feature etc. and the bills of materials together with delivery schedule.

Thus the purchase budget takes into account the inventory on hand and orders on hand.

It is the usual practice to formulate budgets both in terms of quantity and money.

The process of preparation of materials budget is exhibited below:

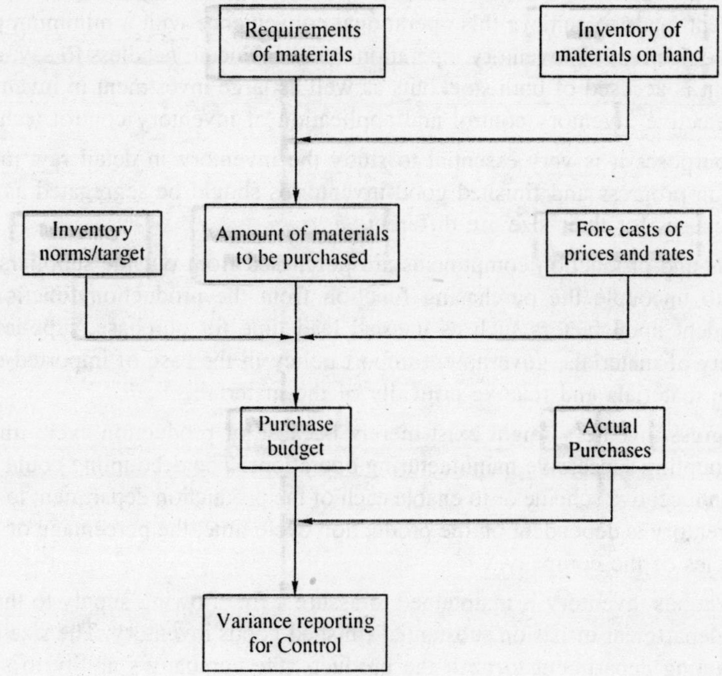

Figure 1.5

The main purposes served by the budget are as follows:

(*i*) The materials management department knows exactly its resources availability so that it can plan its purchases and long term contracts in the must much optimum manner taking into account price trends, markets position etc.

(*ii*) To record the prices on which the budget was formed and to compare it finally with the actual prices so that controllable and uncontrollable elements are clearly brought out.

(*iii*) To help the financial management of materials by clearly stating the fund requirements for the budget period (usually a year) as well as the shorter horizons (quarterly or monthly)

The much important element of budgeting is the review and control aspect. The control aspect should include corrective action with regard to expenditure where the budget target has been exceeded appreciably.

Periodic statements should be prepared and the budget should be compared with actuals so that major variances can be high-lighted for action.

1.3 DEFINITION AND TYPES OF INVENTORY

In financial parlance inventory is defined as the sum of the value of raw materials, fuels and lubricants, spare parts, maintenance consumables, semi processed materials and finished goods stock at a given point of time. The operational definition of inventory would be, the amount of raw materials, fuel and lubricants, spare parts and semi processed materials to be stocked for the smooth running of the plant. Since these resources are idle when kept in the stores, inventory is defined as an idle resources of any kind having an economic value.

Inventories are maintained basically for operational smoothness which they can effect by uncoupling successive stages of production, whereas the monetary value of inventory series as a guide to indicate the size of the investment made to achieve this operational convenience with a minimum possible investment in inventories. The objectives of inventory, operational and financial, needless to say, are conflicting. The materials department is accused of both stockouts as well as large investment in inventories. The solution lies increasing a selective inventory control and application of inventory control techniques.

For control purposes it is very essential to study the inventory in detail raw materials, production components, work in progress and finished good inventories should be segregated as the reasons for the existence and the causes for their size are different.

Raw materials and production components are purchased from outside suppliers and the reason for their existence is to uncouple the purchasing function from the production function. The size of this inventory is dependent upon factors such as internal lead time for purchase, supplier lead time, vendor relations, availability of materials, government import policy in the case of imported material, the annual consumption of the materials and relative critically of the material.

Work in progress inventory might exist merely because of production cycle time or could also be maintained for decoupling successive manufacturing operations. The decoupling could be employed either for implementing an incentive scheme or to enable each of the production department to plan independently. The size of this inventory is dependent on the production cycle time, the percentage of machine utilisation, the make/buy policies of the company.

The finished goods inventory is maintained to assure a free flowing supply to the customers and for this the marketing department insists on substantial finished goods inventory. The size also depends on the ability of the marketing department to push the products, the company's ability to stick to the delivery schedule of the client—the shelf life and the warehousing capacity.

Two factors which influence the inventories of all types are the accuracy and details of the final forecast—all the inventories are geared for future requirements and are therefore, sensitive to this factor-and available storage space-the logical sequence to this factor is the shelf life of the items stored, a factor for consideration in the case of perishable goods.

(*a*) **ABC analysis: (Always better control):** ABC analysis is a basic analytical management tool which enables top management to place the effort where results will be greatest. This technique popularly known as Always Better Control or the alphabetical approach, has universal application in many areas of human behaviour. The technique tries to distribution of any characteristic by money value of importance in order to determine its priority. In materials management, this technique has been applied in areas needing selective control, such as inventory, criticality of items, obsolete stocks, purchasing order, receipt of materials, inspection, store-keeping and verification of bills.

The annual consumption analysis of any organisation would indicate that a handful of top high value item - less than 10 percent of the total number will account for a substantial portion of about 75 percent of a total consumption value, and these few vital items are called '*A*' items which need careful attention of the materials manager. Similarly, a large part bottom items-over 70 percent of total number can account for only 10 percent of the consumption value and are known as '*C*' class. The items that lie between the top and the bottom are called '*B*' category items.

The object of carrying out *ABC* analysis is to develop policy guidelines for selective control. Normally once *ABC* analysis has been done, the following broad policy guidelines can be established in respect of each category.

Table 1.1

'A' Items High Consumption Value	*'B' Items Moderate Value*	*'C' Items Low Consumption Value*
1. Very strict control	Moderate Control	Loose control
2. No safety stocks (or very low)	Low safety stocks	High safety stocks
3. Frequent ordering or weekly deliveries	Once in three months	Bulk ordering once in six months
4. Maximum follow up and expediting	Periodic follow up	Follow up and expediting in exceptional cases
5. Rigorous value Analysis	Moderate Value Analysis	Minimum Value Analysis
6. As many sources as possible for each item	Two or more reliable sources	Two reliable sources for each item.
7. Minimisation of waste obsolete and surplus	Quarterly control over surplus and obsolete items	Annual review over surplus and obsolete material
8. Maximum efforts to reduce lead time.	Moderate	Minimum

The following Figure 1.6 also explains the *ABC* analysis.

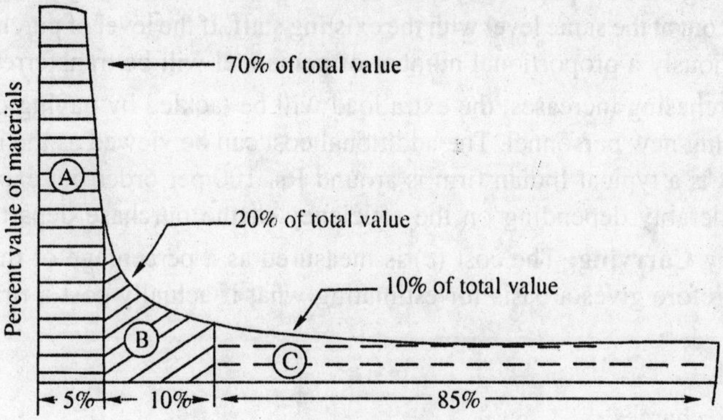

Figure 1.6

Advantages of *ABC* Analysis: This approach helps the materials manager to exercise selective control and focus his attention only on a few items when he is confronted on a lakh of stores items. By concentration on '*A*' class items the materials manager is able to control inventories and show visible results in a short span of time. By controlling the '*A*' items and doing a proper inventory analysis, obsolete stocks are automatically pin pointed. Many organisations have claimed that *ABC* analysis has helped in reducing the clerical costs and resulted in better planning and improved inventory turnover. *ABC* analysis has to be resorted to because equal attention to '*A*', '*B*' and '*C*' items will not be worthwhile and would be very expensive. Concentrating on all the items is likely to have a diffused effect on all the items, irrespective of the priorities.

(*b*) **Norms for Inventory:** The norms for inventory could be set by either the top management or the materials management department. The top management usually sets monetary limits for investment in inventories. The materials department then has to allocate this investment to the various items and ensure the smooth operation of the company. It would be worthwhile if the inventory norms (limits) are made in consultation with the materials department. The norms thus evolved should be specific and quantified. The achievement of the targets set is the responsibility of the materials department.

In the setting up of the norms, the involvement of the persons who are directly responsible for maintaining the inventories is very desirable. Other departments involved in setting the norms are finance, production, marketing and materials control. The norms of inventory should be converted to specifically spelt out parameters like the number of stock outs permitted, the sales to inventory ratio and inventory to consumption ratio.

(*c*) **Cost of Ordering:** Every time an order is placed for stock replenishment, certain costs are involved, and, for most practical purposes it can be assumed that the cost per order is constant. The ordering cost (*c*) may vary, depending upon the type of items, raw materials like steel against production components like casting. However, it is assumed that an estimate (*c*) can be obtained for a given range of items. The cost of ordering (*c*) includes:

- Paper work cost, typing and despatching an order.
- Follow-up cost and the follow up required to ensure timely supplies-includes the travel cost for purchase follow up, telephone, telex and postal bills.
- Costs involved in receiving the order, inspection, checking and handling of the stores.
- Any set up cost of machines if charged by the supplier, either directly indicated in quotations or assessed through quotations for various quantities.
- The salaries and wages of the purchase department. This is relevant for consideration if the purchasing function is carried out at the same level with the existing staff. If the level of purchasing activity decreases significantly, obviously a proportional number of personnel will be transferred to other departments.

  If the level of purchasing increases, the extra load will be tackled by paying overtime to the existing staff or by recruiting new personnel. The additional cost can be viewed as the marginal cost of orders. The ordering cost is a typical Indian firm is around Rs. 100 per order but experience shows that this cost varies considerably depending on the efficiency of the purchase department.

(*d*) **Cost of Inventory Carrying:** The cost (*c*) is measured as a percentage of the unit cost of the item. This measure therefore gives a basis for estimating what if actually cost a firm to carry stocks. This cost includes:

- Interest in capital,
- insurance and tax charges,
- storage cost-any labour, excluding handling of receipts of new orders-the cost of provision of storage area and facilities like bins, racks etc.,
- allowance for deterioration or spoilage,
- salaries to stores staff and
- obsolescence.

The inventory carrying cost varies and in a typical Indian industry is about 30 percent. A major portion of this is accounted for by interest on capital which depends on the fiscal policies of the government. A few firms differentiate the cost as fixed and variable cost. In the analysis of and use of mathematical formula, only the variable costs of ordering should be considered as fixed cost will be constant irrespective of the number of order placed or inventory carried.

(*e*) **Understocking cost or overstocking cost:** Understoking cost, (Ku) is the cost incurred when an item is out of stock. It includes the cost of lost production during the period of stock out and the extra cost per unit which might have to be paid for an emergency purchase.

Overstocking cost is the cost (Ko) for a specific period of time. This time varies in different contents-it could be the lead time of procurement or the entire life time of a machine. In the case of one time purchase overstocking cost would be—Purchase Price-Scrap price.

1.4 ECONOMIC ORDER QUANTITY (EOQ)

Inventories are built to act as a cushion between supply and demand. The supply could be a one time supply (static) or a continuous repetitive one (dynamic). The demand on its part could be totally known (certain), be known over a range of probable values (risks) or be totally unknown (uncertain). Thus six different inventory models can be perceived.

	Supply	*Demand*
1.	Static	Certain
2.	Static	Risk
3.	Static	Uncertain
4.	Dynamic	Certain
5.	Dynamic	Risk
6.	Dynamic	Uncertain

Out of these six possible inventory models the static certain model is very obvious. The supply is one time and the quantity is known. Hence allowing for the lead time, the quantity can be ordered so that it is received when situation which is dynamic and repetitive ceases to be uncertain after a certain lapse of time. The static uncertain model is based on regret matrix which is discussed in detail in the chapter on purchasing under uncertainty. The three remaining models, then are static risk, dynamic certain and dynamic risk.

The cost relevant of consideration in these three models are:

Table 1.2

Inventory	*Understocking Cost*	*Overstocking Cost*	*Inventory carrying cost*	*Ordering cost*
Static-Risk	✓	✓	—	—
Dynamic-Certain	—	—	✓	✓
Dynamic-Risk	✓	✓	✓	✓

(*a*) **Static Risk Model:** This model is useful for project purchases and purchase of capital and insurance spares. Examples of this category are publication of calendars, diaries, year books, buying capital spares etc. which are one time decisions but the quantities can be estimated in the probability values. The cost relevant for consideration are the understocking and overstocking. It is pointless to consider the supply side cost as the purchase is not repetitive. The optimal stocking policy in this situation is to stock upto level "*S*"—*S* denotes service level—where *F* (*S*) is the cumulative probability of demand upto "*S*" i⌐ equal to $\frac{\text{Ku}}{\text{Ku} + \text{Ko}}$. The *EOQ* for this model thus is $\frac{\text{Ku}}{\text{Ku} + \text{Ko}}$. ...(*i*)

(*b*) **Dynamic certain (EOQ) Model:** The costs relevant for consideration in this model are cost of ordering and inventory carrying. Since the demand is certain the understocking and overstocking costs becomes irrelevant for consideration. The EOQ is equal to $\sqrt{\frac{2MCo}{SCc}}$ where

M = Annual Demand of The Item.

S = Unit Cost of the item.

Co = Ordering Cost

Cc = Carrying Cost

(*c*) **Cost Sensitivity Analysis:** The economic order quantity is given by $\sqrt{\frac{2MCo}{SCc}}$ where values of C and Ce are estimated as averages for all the items in the stores. The average are used for convenience in designing an inventory model. It can be proved that these estimates are useful for practical consideration. This is done by carrying out a cost sensitivity analysis.

(*d*) **Derivation of EOQ:** Let the annual demand be "*M*" (deterministic). Let *C* be the cost of ordering and Ce the inventory carrying cost and *S* unit price of an item.

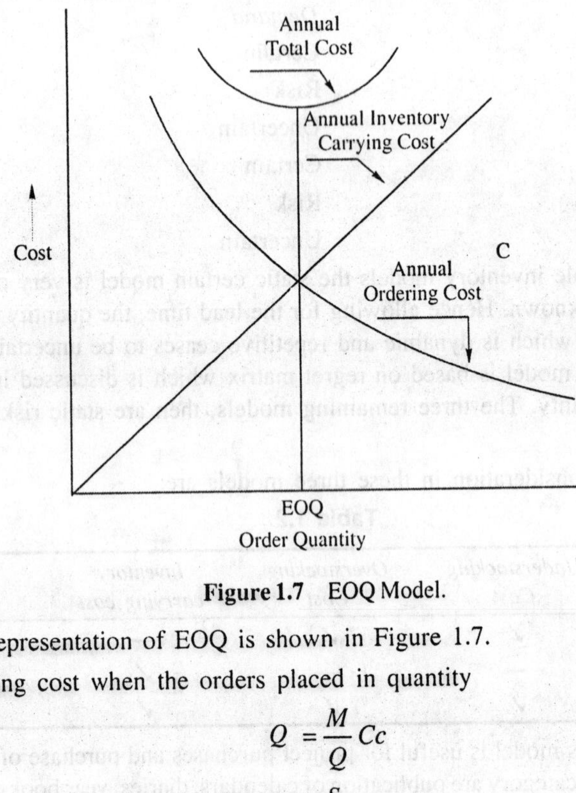

Figure 1.7 EOQ Model.

The graphical representation of EOQ is shown in Figure 1.7.

The total ordering cost when the orders placed in quantity

$$Q = \frac{M}{Q} Cc$$

$$\text{Carrying Cost is} = \frac{S}{2} S.Cc$$

$$\text{The total annual cost is} = \frac{M}{Q} Co + \frac{Q}{2} SCc$$

For cost be minimum

$$\frac{dc}{do} = 0 = \frac{-M}{Q^2} Co + \frac{1}{2} SCc$$

or

$$\frac{M}{Q^2} Co = \frac{1}{2} SCc$$

$$Q^2 = \frac{2\,MC}{SCc}$$

This treatment is given again later.

or $$Q\text{ (Optimum)} = EOQ = \frac{2\,MC}{SCc}$$

1.5 INVENTORY CONTROL

(i) Meaning of Inventory: The term inventory refers to the stock of raw materials, parts and finished products held by a business firm. It is the aggregate quantity of materials, resources and goods that are idle at a given point of time. Inventory consists of usable but idle resources.

In practical sense, Inventory consists of the following:

- raw materials
- work in-progress
- bought-out components
- finished goods
- maintenance spare parts
- consumable supplies.

(ii) Need for Inventory

(i) To carry on day today operation

(ii) To ensure regular production

(iii) To maintain a safety margin

(iv) To take advantage of price

(iii) Objectives of Inventory Control: The main objectives of controlling inventory are as follows:

(i) To maintain capital investment in inventory by eliminating exclusive stocks.

(ii) To ensure availability of needed inventory for uninterrupted production and for meeting consumer demand.

(iii) To provide a scientific basis for planning of inventory needs.

(iv) To tide over demand fluctuations by maintaining reasonably safety stock.

(iv) Advantages of Inventory Control

(i) It improves the liquidity position of firm by reducing unnecessary tying up of capital in excess inventories.

(ii) It ensures smooth production operation by maintaining reasonable stock of materials.

(iii) It protects the firm against variations in raw materials delivery time.

(iv) It facilitates production scheduling, avoids shortage of materials.

(v) It helps to minimise loss by obsolescence, deterioration and damage etc.

1.5.1 Nomenclatures

Lead Time: It refers to the interval between placing an order for a particular item and its actual receipt.

Safety Stock: It implies the stock of inventory held as a safety measure against fluctuation in demand and lead time. Safety stock is function of lead time. The longer the lead time, the greater the safety stock.

1.6 EOQ MODELS

ICC — Inventory Carrying Cost

OC — Ordering Cost

IC = Inventory Cost includes Cost of inventory + insurance + obsolescence.

OC — includes salaries of staff of Purchase Dept. + Cost of stationeries + Cost of Mail etc.

These two are opposing cost.

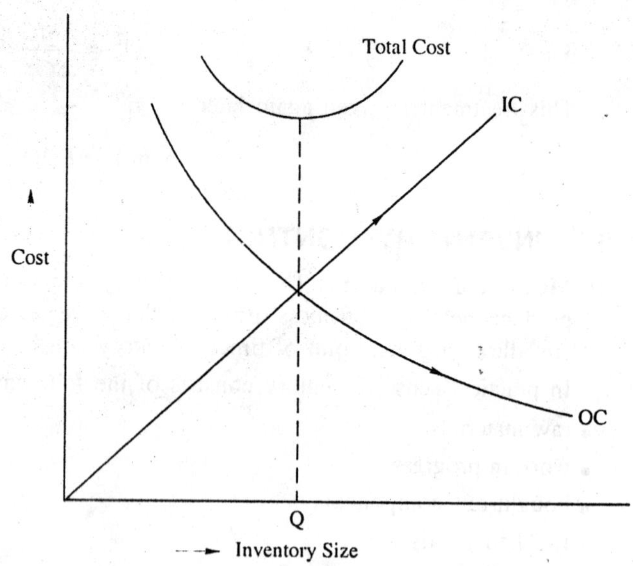

Figure 1.8

1.6.1 Derivation of EOQ

Suppose N = Annual requirement in Units

C = Unit cost of item

I = Inventory carrying rate expressed as percentage of unit cost

A = Cost of ordering (Procurement) of economic lot Q

YC = Total annual cost

$Q = EOQ$

$YC = NC$ + Inventory Carrying Cost + Ordering Cost of N Units.

$$= NC + \left(\frac{Q}{2}\right) C.1 + \left(\frac{A}{Q}\right) N.$$

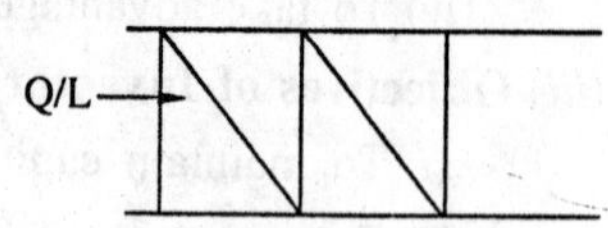

Figure 1.9

for economic lot size, total cost is minimum

$$\therefore \quad \frac{\alpha\, yc}{\alpha\, Q} = 0 = 0 + \frac{C.I}{2} - \frac{A\,N}{Q^2}$$

or $$\frac{C.I}{2} = \frac{A\,N}{Q^2} \quad \text{or} \quad Q^2 = \frac{2AN}{C.I}$$

$$\therefore \quad Q = \sqrt{\frac{2AN}{C1}}$$

In this derivation, reserve stock has not been taken into account.

1.6.2 EOQ Model—Without Shortage

When, supply is instantaneous, consumption is continuous and there is reserve stock.

Figure shows this pattern.

R = Reserve Stock

Yc = Material Cost + Procurement Cost + Inventory Carrying Cost

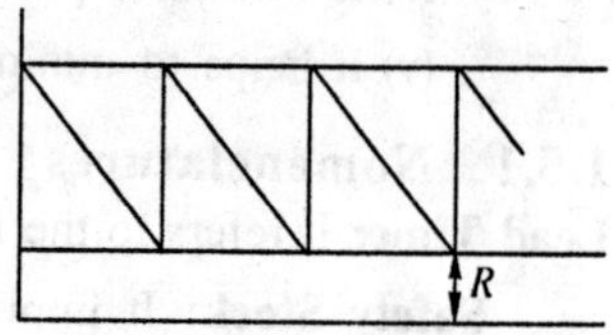

Figure 1.10

$$= N.C. + \frac{A}{Q}\cdot N + I\cdot\left(R+\frac{Q}{2}\right)C \quad \left[Q \text{ gradually decreases to zero so } \frac{Q}{2} \text{ is taken as average}\right]$$

$$= N.C. + \frac{A}{Q}\cdot N + IRC + \frac{I\cdot Q\cdot C}{2}$$

For economic lot size, $\dfrac{dYC}{dQ} = 0 = \dfrac{d}{dQ}\left[N.C. + \dfrac{AN}{Q} + IRC + \dfrac{I\cdot Q\cdot C}{2}\right]$

Let R = Reserve stock be expressed as a fraction of Q *i.e.*, $R = Qf$

$$\therefore \quad \frac{dYC}{de} = 0 = \frac{d}{dQ}\left[N.C. + \frac{AN}{Q} + I\cdot Qf\cdot C + \frac{I\cdot Q\cdot C}{2}\right]$$

$$= 0 - \frac{AN}{Q^2} + I\cdot f\cdot C + \frac{IC}{2}$$

or $$\frac{AN}{Q^2} = IC\left(f+\frac{1}{2}\right) = IC\left(\frac{2f+1}{2}\right)$$

or $$\frac{AN}{Q^2} = IC\left(\frac{1+2f}{2}\right)$$

or $$Q^2 = \frac{2\,AN}{IC\,(1+2f)}$$

$$\therefore \quad Q = \sqrt{\frac{2AN}{IC(1+2f)}}$$

$Q = EOQ$ with reserve stock

Reserve Stock = Qf.

i.e., fraction of Q

A = Cost of ordering of Q lot

N = Yearly requirement

C = Unit cost

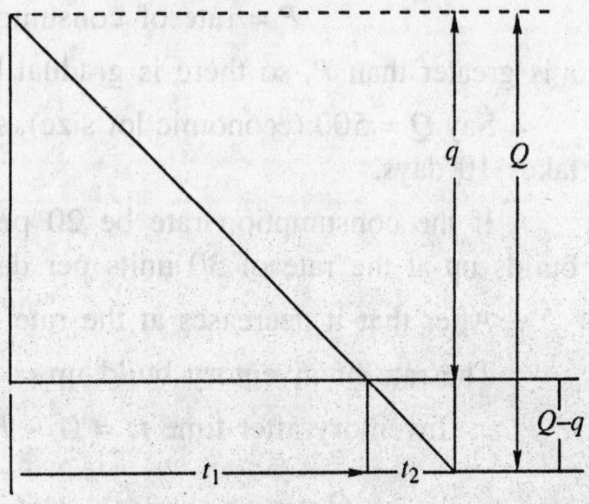

Figure 1.11

1.6.3 EOQ model with shortage

q = maximum inventory

$Q = EOQ$

n = nos. of orders placed annually $= \dfrac{N}{Q}$

$Q - q$ = shortage for which supplies is charged

penalty $C1$ = cost per unit time

N = Yearly requirement

Cycle time $= t = t_1 + t_2$

Above figure is the model for economic lot size with shortages, instantaneously supply and continuous consumption.

Total yearly cost = Yc = Material cost + cost of Procurement + Inventory Carrying cost + shortage cost

$$= NC + \frac{A}{Q}N + C \cdot I \cdot \frac{q}{2}t_1 \cdot n + \frac{Q-q}{2}t_2 \cdot n.\, C_1$$

Geometrically $\frac{t_1}{t} = \frac{q}{Q}$, from $t_1 + t_2 = t$

$$t_1 = \frac{q}{Q} \cdot t \text{ and } t_2 = \frac{Q-q}{Q} \cdot t$$

$$q = Q\frac{CI}{CI + C_1}$$

and $$Q = \sqrt{\frac{2AN}{CI}} \times \sqrt{\frac{C_1 + CI}{C_1}}$$

Since $$\frac{C_1 + CI}{C_1} > IQ > \sqrt{\frac{2AN}{CI}}$$

1.6.4 EOQ model with price breaks (Model with quantity discount)

Model for economic lot sizes with supply and consumption rates varying, no shortage and no reserve stock.

r = rate of supply

P = rate of consumption

r is greater than P, so there is gradual build up of inventory at the rate $(r - p)$.

Say $Q = 500$ (economic lot size), suppose it is to be supplied at the rate 50 per day, so total supply takes 10 days.

If the consumption rate be 20 per day. So the inventory builds up at the rate of 30 units per day till the 10th day.

After that it decreases at the rate of consumption P.

The rate of inventory build up = $r - P$

∴ Inventory after time $t_1 = (r - P)\, t_1$,

$$Q = rt_1 \quad \therefore \quad t_1 = \frac{Q}{r}$$

∴ Inventory after time $$t_1 = (r-p)\frac{Q}{r}$$

$$= Q\left(1 - \frac{P}{r}\right)$$

∴ Average inventory $$= \frac{Q}{2}\left(1 - \frac{P}{r}\right)$$

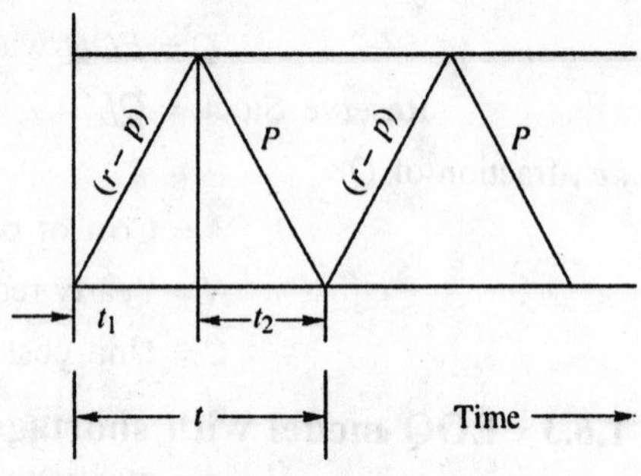

Figure 1.12

Yearly Cost

Yc = Material cost + cost of Procurement + Inventory Carrying cost

$$= NC + \frac{A}{Q} \cdot N + \frac{Q}{2}\left(1 - \frac{P}{r}\right)C \cdot I$$

For minimum Yc $$\frac{\alpha YC}{\alpha Q} = 0 = \frac{\alpha}{\alpha Q}\left[NC + \frac{AN}{Q} + \frac{Q}{2}\left(1 - \frac{P}{r}\right)C \cdot I\right]$$

$$= 0 - \frac{AN}{Q^2} + \frac{1}{2}\left(1 - \frac{P}{r}\right) C \cdot I$$

or $$\frac{AN}{Q^2} = \frac{1}{2}\left(1 - \frac{P}{r}\right) C \cdot I$$

or $$Q^2 = \frac{2AN}{C \cdot I\left(1 - \frac{P}{r}\right)}$$

$$\therefore \quad Q = \sqrt{\frac{2AN}{C \cdot I\left(1 - \frac{P}{r}\right)}}$$

Case 1: If $r = P$ *i.e.,* rate of supply is equal to rate of consumption then there is no inventory build up, so no inventory carrying cost.

Then Q becomes infinite $Q \to \alpha$ *i.e.,* the economic batch size is infinite.

Problem 1.1 A manufacturer gets order of 24,000 units for a year. The supply should be instantaneous. The customer does not maintain any buffer stock, so he will not tolerate any shortage in supply. The inventory holding cost is 10% of unit cost and the setup cost of machine, fixture etc. is Rs. 350.00 per run.

Find the optimum size of production lot for minimum total cost. How many runs will be requirec for this and the duration of each run?

What is the cycle time? Assume the capacity of the equipment as 3000 units per month. Each uni cost Rs. 5.

Solution. Q = Economic lot size

N = Yearly requirement = 24,000

A = Set up cost per unit of Q = Rs. 350.

C = Rs.5 and I = 10% of C = 0.1 × 5 = 0.5

$$Q = \sqrt{\frac{2\,AN}{C \cdot I}} = \sqrt{\frac{2 \times 350 \times 24{,}000}{0.5}} = 5800 \text{ Units.}$$

∴ Optimum size of Production lot = 5800 units.

$$\therefore \text{ Nos. of runs for a year} = \frac{24{,}000}{5{,}800} = 4.1$$

∴ Nos. of runs = 5

and he will have 4 runs of 5800 each and 5th run will produce

24000 – 5800 × 4 = 800 units.

$$\text{Duration of each run} = \frac{Q}{\text{Production rate}} = \frac{5{,}800}{3{,}000} = 1.93 \text{ months}$$

and the length of a cycle or time between two successive supply

$$= \frac{5{,}800}{24{,}000} \times 12 = 2.9 \text{ months}$$

Problem 1.2 (Example with shortage): A company estimates that the demand of a certain item to be used by its production department will be 1000 units in the next 12 months. If the company can not procure the item in time, due to shortages there will be a loss of Production, the cost of which is estimated to be Rs. 100 per unit per year.

The inventory carrying cost is 30 percent per unit per year, the cost of procurement Rs. 75, cost of each item Rs. 50. Determine the optimum, procurement size so as to minimise the total cost.

Solution. Use formula for EOQ model with shortage

$$Q = \sqrt{\frac{2AN}{C \cdot I}} \times \sqrt{\frac{C_1 + CI}{C_1}}$$

Here A = Cost of Procurement Rs. 75

$N = 1000$ $\qquad I = 30\% = 0.3$

$C =$ Rs. 50

$C_1 =$ Rs. 1000

Substituting $Q = \sqrt{\frac{2 \times 75 \times 1000}{50 \times 0.3}} \sqrt{\frac{100 + 50 \times 0.3}{100}}$

$= 100 \times 1.04$

$= 104$ **Ans.**

Problem 1.3 (Example with price breaks): The rolling mill of a steel industry has the capacity of 60,000 a year. The demand in the domestic market is 30,000 only. It depends for the raw material on other department of a sister concern. The supply of raw material is restricted to 300 per day. The average rate of rolling is 2000 per day.

Calculate the economic lot size, if cost of unit material is Rs. 50, inventory carrying cost is 0.20 of unit cost and the set up cost is Rs. 5000.

Solution. In this case, rate of supply and rate of consumption are different, so use the formula for EOQ model as:

$$Q = \sqrt{\frac{2AN}{C \cdot I\left(1 - \frac{P}{r}\right)}}$$

Here, $A =$ Rs. 5000

$N =$ Rs. 30,000

$C =$ Rs. 50

$I = 0.20$

$r = 300$ (Supply rate)

$p = \frac{60,000}{300}$

$= 200$ consumption rate

$$= \sqrt{\frac{2 \times 5000 \times 30,00}{50 \times 0.2\left(1 - \frac{200}{300}\right)}}$$

$$= \sqrt{\frac{30 \times 104}{10 \times 1/3}}$$

$= 9486$ units **Ans.**

Problem 1.4 Consider an item with following parameters

$N = 200$ units per year.

$C =$ Rs. 25 $\quad I = 20\%$ $\quad C_1 = 1.05$ (shortage per unit) = Rs. 5

Calculate the economic lot size and time between each procurement.

Solution. Since it is case of shortage, we use the formula

$$Q = \sqrt{\frac{2AN}{CI}} \times \sqrt{\frac{C_1 + CI}{C_1}}$$

Here A = Rs. 5, $C_1 = 1.05$ C = Rs. 25 $I = 0.2$ $N = 200$

$$Q = \sqrt{\frac{2 \times 5 \times 200}{25 \times 0.2}} \times \sqrt{\frac{1.05 + 25 \times 0.2}{1.05}}$$

$$= \sqrt{400} \times \sqrt{4.3}$$

$$= 20 \times 2.1 = 42$$

and the time between procurement

$$\frac{N}{Q} = \frac{42}{200} \times 12 = 0.21 \times 12 = 2.52$$

Say 2 ½ months

and if no shortage were permitted then $Q = 20$.

2.7 (*a*) V-E-D ANALYSIS—SELECTIVE INVENTORY CONTROL

V stands for 'vital' items—non-availability of such items would stop production.

E stands for "Essential" items, non availability of such item renders temporary dislocation or loss of production. In case of stock out of such items expensive procurement may have to be made, if no number stand by facility is available.

D stands for 'Desirable' items—these items are necessary but do not cause any immediate loss of production. The stock-out of desirable items may entail very nominal expenditure in procurement and may cause minor disruption for a short duration.

The ***V-E-D*** analysis or classification is done mainly for maintenance spares according to their criticality.

ABC analysis categories items to their consumption value, where as ***V-E-D*** analysis determines the effects of items on production and their services.

2.7 (*b*) F-S-N ANALYSIS—SELECTIVE INVENTORY CONTROL

F—refers to 'Fast moving' items

S—refers to 'Slow moving' items

N—refers to 'Non-moving' items.

In this exercise, quality and consumption rates of all items are analysed and accordingly classified Such classifications help in arranging (storing) items in the stores.

For example, the fast moving items should be kept near the exit of the store. Like wise, slow-moving items and non-moving items would take back seats in the stores. The non-moving (*i.e.*, rare-moving) items should take positions at the top rack of stores.

To carry out this analysis, the date of receipt and date of issue of all items are noted down and their movement rates (*i.e.*, consumption rates) are ascertained.

Problem 1.5 The demand of an item is uniform at a rate of 25 units per month. The fixed cost is Rs. 150 each time a production run is made. The production cost is Rs. 1 per unit and inventory carrying cost Rs. 0.25 per unit per month. If the shortage cost is Rs. 15 per unit per month, determine how often to make a production seen and of what size it should be?

Solution. This is a case of *EOQ* model with shortage

Use formula $$Q = \sqrt{\frac{2AN}{C \cdot I}} \times \sqrt{\frac{C_1 + CI}{C_1}}$$

Here, A = Rs. 150 $N = 25$, C = Rs.1 1 = 0.25 Cl = 15

$$Q = \sqrt{\frac{2 \times 150 \times 25}{1 \times 0.25}} \times \sqrt{\frac{15 + 1 \times 0.25}{15}}$$

$$= 173.2 \times 1.0082$$

$$= 174.62$$

$$= 175 \text{ units}$$

$\therefore$ Optimum Production lot size = 175

and Production run $= \frac{175}{25} = 7$ months

Problem 1.6 The demand for a particular automobile part in a shop is 800 a year. The cost of placing an order for this part is Rs. 15. The unit cost of the part is Rs. 20. There is some possibility of shortage. However, to discourage this, a heavy penalty of Rs. 10 per unit is imposed. Assume inventory carrying charge at Rs. 0.20 of unit cost.

Determine 1. EOQ. 2. Time between placing orders and 3. Nos. of orders to be placed.

Problem 1.7 For above problem, if shortage is not permitted but the supply is continuous at the rate of 150 units a month.

Find 1. EOQ 2. Time between placing orders and 3. Nos. of orders to be placed.

1.7.1 EOQ model with Quantity discount

When quantity discounts are available, the economic lot size could be evaluated after several calculations. Some manipulations in formula

$$Q = \sqrt{\frac{2AN}{CI(1+2f)}}$$ is required without shortage.

Let us take an example

If $Q \leq 500$ The unit cost is Rs. 6.00 (C_1)

If $501 \leq Q \leq 1000$, the unit cost is Rs. 5.50 (C_2)

If $1000 \leq Q \leq 5{,}000$, the unit cost is 5.00 (C_3) and so on.

The above formula becomes:

$$Q = \sqrt{\frac{2AN}{CI(1+2f)}}$$ [R = Reserve = Qf fraction]

Value of C—is taken C_1, C_2 and C_3 as above.

Schedule of *Price breaks* is covered under *Quantity discount.*

1.7.2 Two-Bin Perpetual Inventory System

When Bin-2 is depleted, an order is placed when a replishment order is received, Bin-1 is filled to the re-order point level.

The remainder of the order is placed in Bin-2.

Obviously, if Bin-1 is at the re-order point level, all of the incoming items are placed in Bin-2. When Bin-2 is emptied, a new order is placed.

The two-bin system is not feasible for many kinds of items, but when, it is, a great deal of clerical work is eliminated.

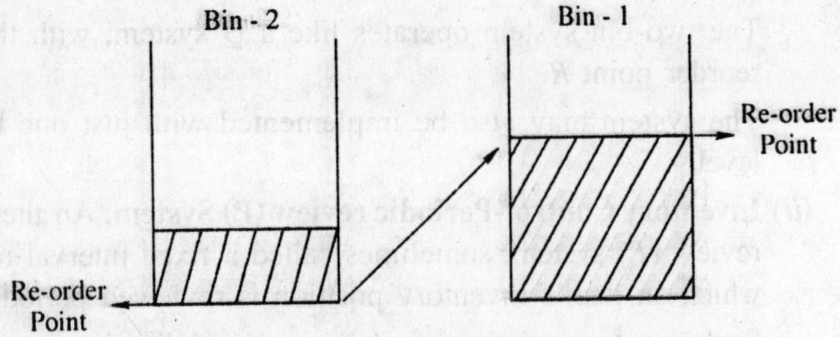

Figure 1.13

1.8 PERPETUAL INVENTORY

Record shows the quantity received, quantity issued and the balance left in the inventory on any date. By knowing the balance, the re-order point and the order-quantity could be calculated.

Perpetual inventory system is used as a check on the accuracy of Stores Keeping.

(a) Diagram for Periodic inventory system and

(b) Perpetual Inventory System

(a) Periodic Inventory System

—the order quantity is variable

—it depends on stock on hand at review point.

(b) A perpetual inventory system where always same quantity is ordered.

These are illustrated in details here.

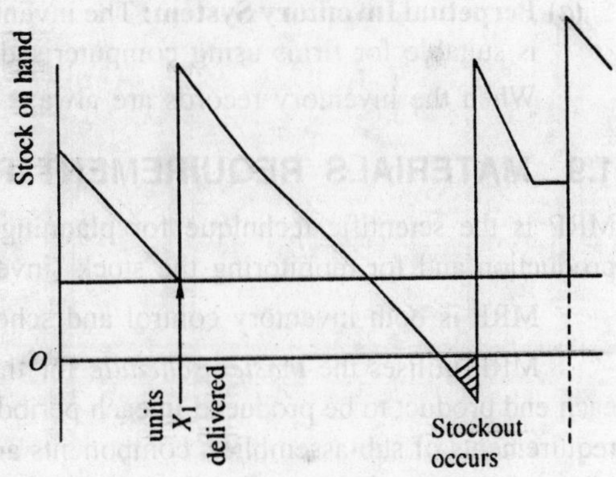

Figure 1.14 (*a*)

(i) Inventory Control-Two-Bin System: The concept of a *Q* system can be incorporated in a visual system, that is a system that allows employees to place orders when the inventory visibly reaches a certain level. Visual systems are easy to employ since records are not to be kept on the current inventory position. Visual systems are intended for use with low-value items that have a steady demand, such as nuts and bolts or office stationeries.

A visual system version of the *Q* system is the **two-bin** system in which an item's inventory is stored at two different locations. Inventory is first withdrawn from one bin. If the first bin is empty, the second bin provides back-up to cover demand until a replenishment order arrives. An empty first bin signals the need to place a new order. Premade order forms placed near the bins let employees send one to purchasing department. When the new order arrives, the second bin is restored to its normal level and the rest is put in the first bin.

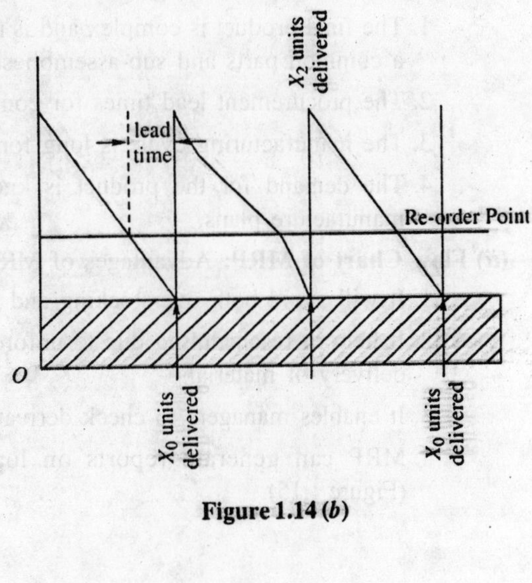

Figure 1.14 (*b*)

The two-bin system operates like a Q system, with the normal level in the second bin being the reorder point R.

The system may also be implemented with just one bin by marking the bin at the reorder point level.

(*ii*) **Inventory Control-Periodic review (P) System:** An alternative inventory control system is the periodic review (P) system, sometimes called a fixed interval reorder system or periodic reorder system, in which an item's inventory position is reviewed periodically rather than continuously.

Such a system can simplify delivery scheduling because it establishes a routine. A new order is always placed at the end of each review, and the time between orders **(TBO)** is fixed at P. Demand is a random variable, so total demand between reviews varies. In a **P** system, the lot size, **Q**, may change from one order to the next, the time between orders is fixed. An example of a periodic review system is that of a soft drink supplies making weekly rounds of retail stores. Each week, the supplies reviews the store's inventory of soft drinks and restocks the store with enough items to meet demand and safety stock requirements until the next week.

(*a*) **Perpetual Inventory System:** The inventory position is known when a review is made and this system is suitable for firms using computerised record keeping arrangement.

When the inventory records are always current, the system is called a *Perpetual inventory system.*

1.9 MATERIALS REQUIREMENT PLANNING (MRP)

MRP is the scientific technique for planning the ordering and usage of materials at various levels of production and for monitoring the stock (inventories) during these transactions.

MRP is both inventory control and scheduling technique.

MRP utilises the *master schedule* for the end products (a master schedule shows the quantities of each end product to be produced in each period of the planning horizon), *product structure* for determining requirements of sub-assemblies, components and raw materials procurement/manufacturing lead times and inventory status of products, sub-assemblies, parts and materials and utilising these data bases in a series of steps it draws up the timings of procurement/manufacture of all sub-assemblies, parts and raw materials required over the production horizon to meet the given end production schedules.

(*i*) **MRP is useful in following cases:**

1. The final product is complex and is made up of several levels of assemblies which have many a common parts and sub-assemblies.
2. The procurement lead times for components and raw materials are relatively long.
3. The manufacturing cycle is long for the finished product.
4. The demand for the product is known and it is desirable to make specific procurement/ manufacture plans.

(*ii*) **Flow Chart of MRP:** Advantages of MRP

1. It will avoid both overstocking and stock outs.
2. It help in rescheduling due to unforeseen events such as changes in order quantity, delay in delivery of materials.
3. It enables managers to check derivation on capacity.
4. MRP can generate reports on load, capacity, net requirements and inventory status (Figure 1.15).

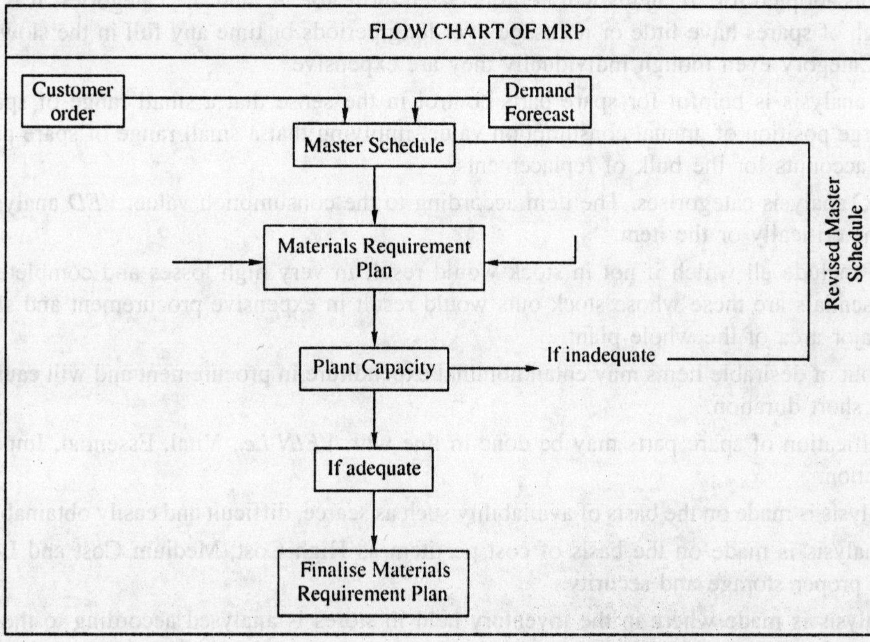

Figure 1.15

1.10 INVENTORY ANALYSIS FOR SPARES, CONSUMABLE AND COMPONENTS

A typical illustration of *ABC* inventory control analysis for spares, consumables and components is given below:

Category	*Items*		*Annual*	*Consumption*
	Nos.	*%*	*Rs-lacs*	*% of total*
A	828	9.2	88.8	74.0
B	1890	21.0	21.6	18.0
C	6282	69.8	9.6	8.0
Overall	9000	100.0	120.0	100.0

The '*A*' items representing 'the vital few' account for bulk of the consumption value of spares, components and consumables and hence the major amount of capital is teed up. These must be closely controlled with regard to reorder points. Safety stocks, order quantities, following up the purchase order etc.

Records relating to consumption, issue, budgets and fore casts must be accurately built up for *A* items.

On the contrary, the '*C*' items constitute the friend many, *i.e.,* a large number of items but a small percentage of total investment in rupees. The order for these may be placed once or twice a year with liberal safety stock.

Combinedly, all these benefits enable a small producer to supply an item to a large company at a lower market price than it would cost the company to produce it.

The controls adopted for '*B*' items will be in between those for '*A*' and '*C*' categories. It is possible that a large rough of spares have little or no usage over long periods or time any full in the slow moving Category or *C* Category even though individually they are expensive.

The *ABC* analysis is helpful for spare parts control in the sense that a small range of spare parts account for a large position of annual consumption value, implying that a small range of spare parts, due to their failure, accounts for the bulk of replacements.

While *ABC* analysis categorises. The item according to the consumption value, *VED* analysis helps in identifying the critically or the item.

Vital item include all which if not in stock would result in very high losses and complete closure of the plant. Essentials are these whose stock outs would result in expensive procurement and stop page of work in a major area of the whole plant.

The stockout of desirable items may entail nominal expenditure in procurement and will cause minor disruption for a short duration.

VED Clarification of spare parts may be done in line with *VEIN i.e.,* Vital, Essential, Important & Normal clarification.

(*a*) **SDE:** Analysis is made on the basis of availability such as scarce, difficult and easily obtainable items.

(*b*) **HML:** Analysis is made on the basis of cost per item as High Cost, Medium Cost and Low Cost to help in proper storage and security.

(*c*) ***XYZ*:** Analysis is made where in the inventory held in stores is analysed according to the number and value.

These analysis helps to identify the service level which forms the basis of inventory policy.

(*d*) **Safety stock:** The need for safety stock in any inventory situation arises due to uncertainty in lead times particularity the supplier lead time as well as fluctuation in demand profile, of any item.

The quantity of safety stock to be maintained is dependent on the degree of service level desired.

The service level can be measured in terms of the percentage of demand which can be met immediately from the stock.

1.11 JIT (JUST–IN–TIME) SYSTEM OF INVENTORY

(*a*) **Just-In-Time Philosophy:** The basis concept is not to make anything till it is needed. It further extends however to manufacturing, but can be extended to distribution, sales, marketing and finance.

It is applicable to both manufacturing and service industries. In JIT, we have to meet customers requirements of quality, cost and delivery time. The factors which affect these requirement are wasteful and so must be eliminated. For instance, factors like interest, unnecessary equipment and holding large inventories tend to increase costs and so must be eliminated. JIT teaches us an effective method of manufacturing.

(*b*) **JIT System of Inventory:** It is also called zero-inventory operation. It is actually a philosophy which can be installed after eliminating all unwanted operation and waste. It is a continuous process. It seeks to eliminate raw materials stock and finished stock. It has to adhere to other norms of manufacturing excellence like right time delivery every time, perfect quality and right implementation of plan. It pre-supposes complete co-operation between management and works.

The internal and external suppliers are the key to success in JIT system. Quality and timely supply schedule are necessary for it. JIT has been successfully employed in Japan, Taiwan ans S.Korea.

JIT reduce inventory carrying costs. The scope of misspelling JIT in an Integrated Company is more where there is very less reliance or no reliance on external supplies.

JIT in Indian situation, can only be installed. If the supplies carry stocks for the company, which make the participation in the JIT programme. Even a slight trend towards JIT will be a big step forward.

Practice of JIT is followed for selectively for large valued (*i.e.,* say *A* & *B* types inventories) and not for all items.

JIT production system avoids idle time and accelerates flow of product due to reduction in lead times.

JIT production system encourages preventive maintenance and development of suitable venders.

In India, where there is shortage of proper materials, power and other infrastructural input, transportation bottleneck, the installation JIT Production system may be difficult.

JIT system of a large company that makes an assembled product will require its suppliers to deliver the components needed for the final product within a very short time (say 3-4 hrs before required) before the assembly process.

Thus, for the JIT production process, the company has to practise the following. Everything is ordered. Production is "Just-in-Time." There is a neccessary linkage between stock less production and quality-every item, must be made correctly just in time and every time.

There is key element of productivity gain and there is no waste.

JIT system encourges usage of all manpower. Materials and Machines. Just-In-Time (JIT) approach was first developed in Japan by Toyota Motor Corporation in 1970s and was initially known as the "Totoya manufacturing system" or 'Toyoterism.' The label 'Just-in-time' was applied later.

The Central idea of JIT is to reduce the seven wastes as follows.

- Over production
- Waiting
- Transporting
- In appropriate processing
- Unnecessary inventory
- Defects.

1.12 KANBAN

Kanban means 'visible record'. Generally, Kanban is thought as a card. In manufacturing, it is a card that is attached to a barked or container containing an order for production. The container with card is just filled up with the items, no more, no less- and is always excellent quality.

Kanban will work well only the context of a Just-in-Time system in general, and in the contest of the set-up time/lot size reduction feature of JIT in particular.

Kanban is the Japanese word for a small card or tag, which is attached to a bin.

The use of Kanban is essentially a production management system for the production employees in the plant.

1. The production Kanban authorises the preceding stage to produce the required quantity of components or subassemblies that are listed.
2. The conveyance Kanban is attached to the container, when it is transported from one stage to the mat operation stage. Use of two Kanban will expose production bottlenecks and encourage finding out solution.
3. The product on control presses begin with the invention of the job card or Kanban in each container of materials. The finished goods inventory of one production department becomes the raw material inventory of the next downstream department.

4. The final assembly rate determines, the production quantum for both vendor-supplied parts and for immediate predecessor or production department, which in turn, determines the production rate for all other production sections.

1.13 NON-PRODUCTION OF SCRAP

Quality problems in the form of scrap or reworked products are waste of the first order.

The Japanese developed several strategies to counter this problem. In one case, they built their factory with no area to store scrap on the principle that having an area for scrap encouraged its production.

Quality circles were created, where workers were allocated time specifically given over to discussing quality issues and their elimination, the latest being "Zero Defect."

The philosophy of Kaizen, or continuous improvement was adopted as working culture in these organisations with support at the very top.

Systems of quality management such as TQM and ISO 9000 seek to achieve the same ends.

The causes of "Scrap" production may not originate in the factory itself and may be caused by sub-standard raw materials being supplied to the process.

Increasingly, suppliers performance is appraised and measured in defective parts per million. Working in a positive environment with supplies to eliminate problems quickly is the preferred approach.

Involving suppliers in new product development helps eliminate potential problems before they are translated into the production process.

Many companies have now adopted six sigma as a formal process improvement technique. Literally, this aims to control a process to the point of ± six sigma (*i.e.*, standard deviations), which equals to 3.4 defects per million. The processes technique normally consist of DMAIC (define, measure, analyse, improve and control).

1.14 PROBABLE QUESTIONS

1. (*a*) Describe Materials Management as a Profit Centre Concept.
   (*b*) What is Inventory?
   Describe with examples various types of inventories.
2. What is meant by "Inventory Control"?
   Describe *A-B-C* inventory control policy with diagram.
3. Explain the importance of Inventory Control in an industrial organisation.
4. What is Economics lot size? Explain how the standard order quantity is determined and point out how it help in inventory control?
5. Describe briefly the different elements of inventory carrying costs.
6. Find the "EOQ" from the following data:
   Average annual demand = 30,000
   Inventory Carrying Cost = 12% of the unit value per year.
   Cost of placing an order = Rs. 70
   Cost/Unit = Rs. 2
7. Write notes on:
   (*a*) Material Requirement Planning
   (*b*) JIT inventory system.
   (*c*) Perpetual inventory system.
   (*d*) Periodic inventory system.

2

Purchase Management

• *Importance of Purchasing* • *Negotiation* • *Purchase Budget* • *Purchase Systems* • *Vendor Development* • *Purchase of Capital Equipment* • *International Purchasing* • *Make or Buy Decision* • *Legal Aspects of Purchasing* • *Reference to Contract Act* • *Probable Questions.*

2.1 IMPORTANCE OF PURCHASING

Purchasing has come to stay as the most important function of materials management. The moment a buyer places an order he commits a substantial portion of the finance of the corporation which affects the working capital and cash flow position. He is a highly responsible person who meets various salesmen and thus can be considered to have been contributing to the public relations efforts of the company. Thus the buyer can make or mar the company's image by his excellent or poor relations with the vendors.

2.1.1 Goals of Purchasing/Purchase Policy

The basic objective of purchasing function is to ensure continuity of supply of raw materials, sub contracted items and spare parts and at the same time reduce the ultimate cost of the finished goods. In other words, the objective is not so much to procure the raw materials at lowest cost but to reduce the cost of the final product. For ensuring this there are a large number of well known parameters such as right price, right quality, right contractual terms, right time, right source, right material, right place, right mode of transportation, right quantity and right attitude. All these have been considered jointly. A diagram indicating these is shown in Figure 2.1 (Purchase Parameters).

(*a*) **Right Price:** It is the primary concern of any manufacturing organisation to get an item at its right price. But right price need not be the lowest price. In this context it may be worth remembering John Ruskin's famous statement: ***"There is hardly anything in the world that some body cannot make a little cheaper and the man who considers price alone is a lawful prey."*** While it is very difficult to determine the right price, general guidance can be had from the cost structure of the product. The tender system of buying is normally used in public sector organisations, but the objective should be to identify the lowest "responsible" bidder and not the lowest bidder.

(*b*) **Right Quality:** Right quality implies that quality should be available, measurable and understandable as far as practicable. In order to determine the quality of a product sampling schemes, inspection etc. would be useful. The quality particulars are normally obtained from the indents and experience indicates that a substantial portion of the indents prepared by the user departments are invariable incomplete.

(*c*) **Right Time:** For determining the right time the purchase manager should have lead time information for all products and analyse its components for reducing the same. Lead time is the total time elapsed between the recognition of the need of an item till the item arrive and is provided for use. Obviously, this covers the entire duration of the material cycle and consists of precontractual administrative lead time, manufacturing and transporting lead time, and inspection lead time. Since the inventory increases with higher lead time, it is desirable to analyse each component of the lead time so as to reduce the first and third components which are controllable. While determining the purchases the buyer has to consider emergency situations like floods, strike etc.

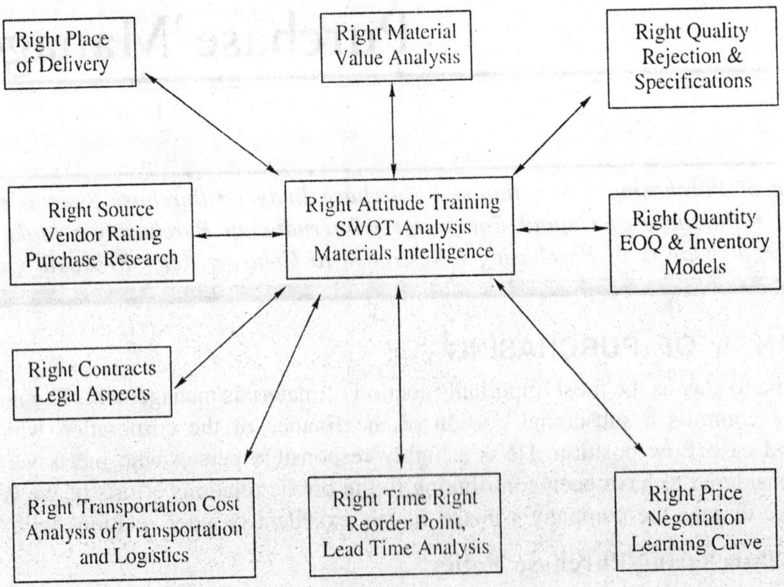

Figure 2.1 Purchase Parameters.

(*d*) **Right Source:** The source from which the material is procured should be dependable and capable of supplying items of uniform quality. The buyer has to decide which item should be directly obtained from the manufacturer. Techniques such as value analysis will enable the buyer to locate the right material. Right modes of transportation have to be identified as this forms a critical segment in the cost profile of an item. It is an established fact that the cost of shipping of ore, gravel, sand etc. is normally more than the cost of the item itself. Specifying the right place of delivery would often minimise the handling charges.

(*e*) **Right Quantity:** The right quantity is the most important parameter in buying. Concepts, such as economic order quantity, economic purchase quantity, fixed period and fixed quantity segments will serve as broad guidelines. But the buyer has to use his knowledge, experience and common sense to determine the quantity after considering factors such as price structure, discounts availability of the item, favourable reciprocal relations and make or buy considerations.

(*f*) **Right Attitude:** Developing the right attitude too is necessary as one often comes across such statements as "Purchasing knows the price of everything and value of nothing." "We buy price and not cost." "When will our order placers become purchase managers?" "Purchasing acts like a post bon." Purchasing should therefore, keep progress as its key activities and should be future oriented.

The buyer has to adopt separate policies and procedures for capital and consumer items. He should be able to distinguish between indigenous and international purchasing procedures. He should be aware of the legal and contractual aspects in an international practices.

2.2 NEGOTIATION & VENDOR SELECTION

The selection of the ultimate supplier (vendor) is based on the negotiation between the buyer and seller. Negotiation is a skill exercised by both buyer and seller.

Negotiations particularly for prices, have been accepted as a policy by some materials managers, since perfect competition does not exist in Indian situations and hence the concept of lowest bid does not always work. Negotiation is indeed a battle of wits and an art of embodying sophisticated tactics by both the buyer and the seller. Normally buyers should not opportunist and try to function as arbitrators between the factory and the supplier. The buyer must enable his suppliers to make a reasonable profit in the short run and survive as well as grow in the long run. He should remember that he is buying not only for today's price but tomorrows's cost as well. In this process the buyers help the suppliers towards finding more economical ways of working rather than squeezing out the profit margin. Selling at a loss will drive the supplier out of business reducing sources of supply. It is in this context that the art of negotiation is treated as a forum for exchange of views rather than cut throat buying. In negotiating both the buyer and the seller try to evaluate each other with regard to price and quality.

The parameters influencing the process of negotiation of an item are availability, number of sources, price, delivery, penalty, discounts package and transportation. The bargaining power will definitely be influenced by the preparedness of the buyer as well as place and time of negotiation.

The known techniques used for negotiations are price analysis, persuasions, discussion, interrogation, investigation, staging a walkout, prolonged silence, weighing pros and cons, offensive strategy, defensive strategy, blow hot and cold, suggesting formula and learning curve. A successful negotiator has to possess the qualities of patience, persistence, persuasiveness, clear thinking, logical analysis, optimism, knack of getting along with people, ability to plan and be "thick-skinned." While negotiating a buyer should hope for the best and at the same time be prepared for the worse.

2.3 PURCHASE BUDGET

Since purchasing activity accounts for a substantial portion of corporate finance it assumes great importance among various budgets such as sales budget, personnel budget and revenue budget. The purchasing budget indicates the purchase to be made for achieving the complete budget plans. These represents the requirements of direct and indirect material and purchased services as set out in the production cost and capital expenditure budgets. The budgets are adjusted in respect of any planned increase or reduction of inventories or raw materials or other supplies including stores and spare parts as well as purchase orders already placed. As far as possible, the requirements should be expressed in physical as well as fiscal terms.

The purchase budget enables the purchase department to plan its purchase and place long term contracts after considering all relevant factors. It also facilitates the planning of cash requirements. In the budgetary process, periodic statements should be prepared to enable the management to control and compare the budget with actual expenditure.

2.4 PURCHASE SYSTEMS & PROCEDURES

(*i*) **Introduction:** In organisations depending on the size and nature of operation, the quantum of purchase varies anywhere between few thousands of rupees and hundreds of crores of rupees. Naturally this necessiates formalised systems and procedures for case of operation and accountability. Formal procedures have been laid down in initiating purchase, selecting suppliers, placing purchase orders, follow up, receiving materials and so on. Here, we will discuss the various systems that are used in the purchase department.

We can classify the systems in the following manner:

(*a*) Pre-Purchase System

(*b*) Ordering System

(*c*) Post Purchase System

(*a*) Pre-Purchase System: Initiating the purchase through requisition requirement programmes, selection of suppliers, obtaining quotations and evaluating them are broadly the pre-purchase activities.

Table 2.1

MATERIAL REQUISITION FORM

Date:

From:

(*a*) Department Requiring The Material

(*b*) Requisition Reference Number

To Material Management Department.

Kindly procure the material mentioned below:

Description of the material	*Quantity Required*	*Suggested Supplier*	*Purpose*	*Approximate Date when The Material is required*

Requisitioned By: Authorised By:

(*i*) Requisitions: The department concerned, in need of a material, usually presents a completed requisition form. A typical requisition form is shown. A Requisitions may be made by anyone in the concerned department. However, generally it has to be countersigned by a senior official. (See the Material Requisition Form)

It is very important to note that capital equipments cannot be requisitioned in this manner. These decisions are taken normally at board level and they are treated differently for taxation and accounting purposes.

(*ii*) Travelling Requisitions: This document is widely used for requisitioning of items that are required frequently in bulk quantities over a long period. The travelling requisition is prepared, as shown in Table 2.2. It travels from the requisitioning department to the purchase department often. During each stage a purchase order is initiated. Factors, such as specifications and supplier details, are written permanently and provisions for entering date, quantity required names of requisitioner etc. This reduces paper work and eases the operation.

Enquiries: Many organisations often invite suppliers to quote for supply materials. For this purpose a standard formula is used which is similar to a purchase order in all respects, except that words such as "this is only a request for quotation", or "this is not a purchase order", are printed so as to ensure that the supplier does not construct the request for quotation as a firm order.

(*b*) Ordering System: Having selected the supplier and rates agreed, the buyer places purchase order on the supplier, expressing the terms and conditions. Purchase order once accepted becomes a binding contract. The details that are normally furnished in a purchase order are listed below:

(*i*) Purchase order reference number (which will be quoted in all subsequent follow up measures pertaining to that order).

(*ii*) Description of the materials and detailed specifications.

(*iii*) Quantity required and delivery schedule.

(*iv*) Location where the materials are to be supplied. (Usually the name and address of buyer).

(*v*) Signature of materials manager who can authorise the purchase order.

Table 2.2

TRAVELLING REQUISITION FORM

Date:

Material Description:

Part Number:

Annual usage:

Suppliers: *A*
B
C

Requisitioned					*Purchased*			*Received*		
Date	*Quantity on hand*	*Requisitioned*	*Requisitioned by*	*Approved by*	*Date*	*Qty.*	*Supplier*	*Price*	*Dt.*	*Qty.*

(*vi*) Detailed terms and conditions.

By and large, organisations send the supplier an acknowledgment copy alongwith the purchase order and thereby try to obtain a written acceptance from the supplier.

(*c*) Post Purchase Systems: This includes follow up procedures, receipt and checking of invoices.

(*i*) **Follow Up:** Follow up implies commitment of time and money and therefore has to be selective. Certain priorities could be established for follow up. Only critical items requires continuous follow up. Depending upon the movements, items can be classified into fast moving or slow moving. For fast moving items follow up can be initiated whenever stock level depletes to one month consumption. Similar norms can also be established.

(*ii*) **Receipt:** It is a schematic record of consignments received, carrier details and descriptions are to be maintained in chronological sequence to help in quick identification of materials, so that inspection can be arranged prior to acceptance. Many organisations have a separate central receiving section for this purpose.

(*iii*) **Invoice Checking:** The supplier normally sends an invoice for the materials supplied to the buyer for payment. It is important that this invoice is matched against the receipt details, quantity accepted and rejected so that payments can be made within the discount period and provisions be made which will help in funds planning.

(*d*) **Special Purchasing Systems:** There are several special systems adopted for purchasing as discussed below:

(*i*) **Forward Buying:** Forward buying committing an organisation far into the future usually for a year, is in vogue. Depending upon the availability of the item, the financial policies, the economic order quantity, the quantitative discounts and staggered delivery, the future commitment is decided. This type of forward buying is different from speculative buying where the motive is to make capital out of the price changes, by selling the purchased item.

(*ii*) **Tender Buying:** In public buying, all semblance of favourism, patronage and personal preferences should be avoided. As such it is common for government departments and public sector undertakings to purchase through tenders. Private sector organisations adopt tender buying only for high value items. The steps involved are to establish bidders list, solicit bids, evaluate bids by comparing quotations, and place order with the lowest bidder. However, care has to be taken that the lowest bidder is a responsible party and is capable of meeting the delivery schedule and quality requirement.

(*iii*) **Use of Standard deviation for Tendering:** This can be best explained by the use of the following example:

- **Blanket Orders:** Minimise the administrative expenses and is used for 'C' inventories. These provide a required quantity of specified items over a period of time, usually for one year, at an agreed price. Deliveries are made depending upon the buyers need. The system relieves the buyer from routine work, giving him more time for focusing attention on high value items.
- **Zero Stock:** Some firms try to operate on the basis of zero stock and the supplier holds the stock for these firms. Usually the firms of the buyer and seller are close to each other so that the raw material of one is the finished product of another, as for example, naptha in a fertilizer plant is one of the final products of a refinery. Alternatively, the system could work well if the seller holds the inventory and if the two parties work in close co-ordination.
- **Rate Contract:** The system of rate contract is prevalent in public sector organisations and government departments. It is common for suppliers to advertise that they are on rate contract with the DGS & D for the specific period. After negotiation, the seller and the buyer agree to the rates of items. Application of rate contracts has helped many organisations to cut down the internal administrative lead time as individual firms need not go through the central purchasing department and can place orders directly with the supplier.
- **Reciprocity:** Reciprocal buying means purchasing from one customer in preference to others. It is based on the principle, ***"If you kill my cat, I will kill your dog" and "Do unto your customers as you would have them do unto you."*** Other things like soundness from the ethics and economics point of view being equal, the principles of reciprocity can be practised. However, a purchasing executive should not indulge in reciprocity on his initiative when the terms and conditions are not equal with other suppliers. It is often found that less efficient manufacturers and distributors gain by this process, what they are unable to gain by price and quality. Since this tends to discourage competition and might lead to higher prices and few suppliers, reciprocity should be practised on a selective basis.
- **Systems Contract:** This is procedure intended to help the buyer and the seller to reduce administrative expenses and at the same time ensure suitable controls. In this system, the original indent, duly approved by competent authorities is shipped back with the items and

avoids the usual documents like purchase orders, material requisition, expediting letters, acknowledgments, goods inwards report etc. The contract is invariably simple, covering only delivery periods, price and invoicing procedure.

(e) Practices of Procurement:

(i) So far as ethical practices of procurement are concerned, the buyer-seller relationship and ethics are important. The buyer as well as the seller know very well that good relations are essential for the smooth running of the business. Yet there are many suppliers who frequently fail to meet the delivery schedule and fail in quality standards. Vendors on the other hand complain about delayed payment, cancellation of orders and increased rejection due to strict inspection. The buyers and sellers must recognise that they are partners in progress and as such, good relationship go a long way for a smooth business activity.

The primary objective of the relationship is to buy and sell for a profit. This should be recognised by the buyer as well as the seller. The supplier can assist the buyer through ideas of art reduction, new products and service even during a crisis. Such healthy relationships are possible only when both the parties are competent in their profession and respect the principles of human relations.

Suppliers expect fair and honest dealings, ethical practices and a minimum amount of rush orders. During negotiations they prefer to deal with buyers who have proper authority. The materials manager ensures that personal contacts are encouraged and he should periodically visit the vendors plants to assess their strengths and weakness.

(ii) Ethics in buying: Ethics, though closely related to personal values are obviously influenced by moral standards prevalent at the corporate level, industry level, national and international level. Ethics have more significance to a materials manager as he is dealing with many suppliers, evaluating them and awarding them contracts.

Since, a materials manager is empowered to spend large sum of money for buying, he is subjected to temptations day in and day out. Therefore, it is necessary for the materials manager to resist such temptations and be above board. Ethical practices can be fostered by devising procedures and systems for control purposes as well as by selecting buyers who have unquestionable integrity, character and high moral standards.

Policy decision pertaining to personal buying, acceptance of gifts, and entertainments can solve many problems. Besides being honest and refusing to accept favours from suppliers, an ethical buyer should be equitable in his dealings with suppliers.

Also, during the process of negotiations the buyer should not resort to unethical practices. Many organisations have developed a code of ethics which the buyers are expected to practice in their profession.

It is rather unfortunate that organisations adopt double standards-one for the acceptance of gifts by the buyers and another for their salesman using gifts for sales promotion. The code of ethics formulated in India for buying is based on the following principles and standards:

(i) To consider the interest of the company in all transactions.

(ii) To buy without prejudice, seeking to obtain the maximum ultimate value for each contract.

(iii) To subscribe and work for honesty and truth in buying and selling and to denounce all form and manifestations of commercial bribery.

(iv) To co-operate with all organisations and individuals engaged in activities designed to enhance the development and standards of buying.

The buyer should adopt separate policies and procedures for capital and consumer items. The materials manager should be able to distinguish between indigenous and international purchasing procedures and should be aware of the legal and contractual aspects in international practices.

(*iii*) Quality Approach in Ethical Procurement: Right quality implies that quality should be available, measurable and understandable as far as practicable. In order to determine the quality of a product, testing the representative sample for useful parameters is of prime importance. The quality particulars are normally obtained from indents, and experience indicates that a substantial portion of the indents prepared by the user departments are invariably incomplete. Such incomplete indents often cause unnecessary delays in procurement as the indentor has to be referred to and if not referred results in heavy rejection. Drawings are also attached to the indents, particularly for spare parts. Since the objective of purchasing is to ensure continuity of supply to the user departments, the time at which the material is provided to the user department assumes great importance.

If the suppliers consistently fail to meet the quality requirements, then the materials manager may decide to change them. It is essential to find out whether the exacting quality requirements are necessary at all. It may mean specialised procedures, tooling, skilled labour and rigid inspection standards. A buyer also has the option of changing the supplier if necessary.

2.5 VENDOR DEVELOPMENT

(*i*) **Meaning and Need for Vendor Development:** When a machine becomes obsolete in design and the manufacturer stops production of such machines, the users of the machines find it difficult to obtain necessary spare parts for the runability of the machines.

The user of an obsolete machine tries to locate a suitable supplier for critical spare parts and the process is known as vendor development.

Vendors development have become very necessary in case of jute and textile industries, where many machines have become obsolete due to rapid advances in design and development.

The user of an imported equipment finds it difficult to import critical spares for a long time due to high cost and long lead time and in course of time develop a vendor for supplying the necessary spares regularly. Such vendor development is the result of import substitution.

In addition to above cases a large industry like a steel plant an Automobile plant develops suitable vendors for regular supply of ancillary items.

(*ii*) **Procedure of Vendor Development & Evaluation:** Purchase department, design department and maintenance department are jointly involved for suitable vendor development.

The following steps are followed for vendor development:

1. Detailed drawings are prepared for the spare parts which is to be developed indigenously. Such drawings indicates detailed dimensions with tollerence, metallurgy including materials of construction and standards such as IS, BS or ASTM to be followed etc.
2. A specification sheet is prepared for the spare part showing reference drawing number, manufacturing process to be adopted, materials of construction hardness, surface finish etc. and also quantity of the item.
3. An enquiry is floated to prospective vendors inviting offers indicating price and delivery schedule and details of existing facilities for manufacturing of the item.
4. Offers are scrutinised and prospective vendors who satisfy the requirements are short listed.
5. Inspection of existing facilities for each vendor is carried out.

6. Annual balance sheet for 2/3 years for each vendor is scrutinised and fixed assets, current assets, liabilities, turnover and profit etc., are identified.
7. Post and present customers of each vendor are noted and some of these customers are contacted for knowing the performance of the vendors.
8. At least two suppliers are identified and necessary contract is issued for regular supply of the item.

9. Detailed Procedures–Vendor Development

(*i*) Technical:

(*a*) **Source determination:** Sources of materials are extremely important with regard to market conditions, price trends and the general industrial climate. Source determination helps in bringing about a fair competition among the suppliers and supply failures are kept at a minimum. Source development is important for import substitution, cost reduction and quality improvement. Source determination needs are dependent on factors such as make or buy decisions, amount of Sub-contracting, break-even points at manufacturing and plant capacity. Source determination activities are broadly classified as the following:

(*b*) **Searching:** The search process begins with the finalisation of specifications. It consists of identifying the sources of supply. Normally, comprehensive information can be obtained from the Indian Trade Journal, Newspaper advertisements, telephone directory, yellow pages, and publications of Government agencies like the Directorate General of Technical Developments, Directorate General of supply and Disposal and the Bureau of Indian Standards.

Trade shows, technical exhibitions and samples are other important sources that assist the search process.

(*ii*) Commercial:

(*a*) **Selection:** The search process provides a list of possible sources. In the selection process, more specific information on the supplier's financial strength, quality, facilities, efficiency, industrial relations, technical excellence and position in industry.

Such sources should be selected which would meet the delivery and quality requirements in the long run at competitive price levels.

(*b*) **Negotiations and Trial orders:** After preliminary screening and selection, the process of negotiation starts with the vendors for placing trial orders. Various aspects such as terms of delivery, price and quality are finalised during this stage.

(*c*) After the trial orders are executed, it becomes necessary to rate the vendors' performance in meeting the quality, delivery and price parameters in a systematic manner.

The vendor's representative, if necessary may be called for a trunk discussion to point out the areas of improvement.

Such a constructive approach, based on a rating system, will definitely help in improving the performance of the supplier.

(*iii*) Automobile Industry Vis-a-Vis Ancillary Units: A manufacturer of automobiles is in need of services of large number of suppliers for the regular supply of ancillary items such as Axels, differential box, bumpers, gear box, steering, spark plugs, seats, light systems, lubrication system and wheels etc. Reputed Ancillary industries such as TVS, Sundaram Fasteners, MICO, Sona Steering etc. are regular suppliers of various items required for final assembly of an automobile.

(*iv*) **Import Substitution and Vendor Development:** Critical spares for an imported equipment need to be developed indigenously in order to save precious foreign exchange to minimise lead time and inventory level.

"JUST IN TIME" method of manufacturing is possible only if indigenous reliable vendors for all necessary parts, which are to be procured are developed systematically in course of time.

Suitable vendor development helps in smooth flow of the production process and minimise the inventory level and thus helps in reducing unit cost of production and enhancing profitability of the organisation.

2.6 PURCHASING OF CAPITAL EQUIPMENT

(*i*) **Significant Differences:** The purchase of capital equipment usually occurs once in ten or fifteen years and significant differences in the purchase of major equipment from the purchase of consumption materials are:

(*a*) **Extent of Negotiations:** Purchase of major equipments a result of careful negotiations and analysis of various alternatives available to an organisation. The number of contacts and discussions with the vendors will be much greater as compared to consumption differences.

(*b*) **Lead time Requirement:** A unique feature in the purchase of capital equipment is the lead time required for its supply. Though very few equipments are standardised, most of the major equipments are custom built and require sufficient lead time for the suppliers to fabricate or manufacture and deliver.

(*c*) **Size of the Expenditure:** This is a major considerable as the organisation would have to invest large amounts over a long duration. Moreover the equipment directly influences the manufacturing operations of the organisation. It is natural that the purchasing of major equipments is a matter of significant concern to the top management.

(*d*) **Availability of Sources:** Since many of the requirements of a major equipment are specific and typical for different types of industry the number of suppliers available are also very few and the organisation has to decide carefully a number of factors.

(*ii*) **Consideration in Evaluation of Bids:** As the purchase of capital equipment involves huge expenditure, the evaluation of the bids of suppliers should be done in extensive manner based on the following considerations.

(*a*) **Operating characteristics and Engineering Features:** This is the most influential factor in selecting the supplier of major capital equipment. In almost all organisations, the initiation of capital equipment purchasing comes from the production department or the user department. Once the production or the user department establishes the need for the equipment and defines its functions, then the design and operating characteristics form the most important factors in the selection of the specific machine to be purchased.

The engineering features of the required equipments should be compatible with the existing process and the specific question that should always be asked is: **Does the equipment fit in with the existing operations and what are the modifications required in adapting a new equipment to the existing system?**

(*b*) **Economic Analysis of Investment:** Economic analysis of investment on purchase of a major capital equipment is to be done only after several acceptable prices of equipments are found. One of the most important considerations is not simply to compare the cost of the equipment that is involved at the time of purchase, but to consider also the cost of modifications or additional fittings required, the total operating cost involved, in the total plan of the equipments economic life, and an estimation of cost of maintenance. The specific mention of the cost of maintenance is due to the fact that cost of operation can be forecast definitely while forecasting maintenance cost is difficult and subjective.

Several methods of economic analysis are available for evaluating investments as follows:

1. **Pay Back Period Approach:** This approach is the simple and most widely used method for evaluating investment. It is the length of time required for the cash in flow resulting from an investment to equal the original outlay on the investment that is the time required to get back the initial investment on the equipment. This is mainly used in case of purchase of equipment that have short economic life and the organisation is of the view that the equipment should pay for itself. Hence the shorter the pay back period the better is the investment. The formula for pay back can be given as $t = c/i$ were "t" is the pay back period, 'c' is the initial capital outlay of the investment and "i" is the average annual cash in flow expected from the investment. It is important to note that in the estimation of cash in flow, "I" depreciation should be included, as depreciation by itself is a measure of capital recovery.

2. **Return On Investment Approach (ROI):** Return on investment is just the reciprocal of pay back period *i.e.*, $ROI = I/C$, where "I" is the average cash in flow after taxes, and "C" is the original cash outlay. Generally there are two ways of estimating the return on investment (*i*) Return On Original Investment (*ii*) Return On Average Investment.

   In the first the return is calculated on the actual value of the original investment and the salvage value expected at the end of economic life is taken instead of "C." In the methods the average annual carrying is taken to estimate the return of investment.

3. **Internal Rate of Return:** This method is understood under different names, discounted rate of return, yield of an investment etc. It can also be defined as the procedure to find a rate of interest that will make the present value of the cash proceeds expected from an investment equal to the present value of the investment. It is the rate of discount which when applied to the future cash flows will equate their sum to the original price of the investment.

   It is usually a trial and error method. Probably the method can be easily understood by the following formula.

$$C = \frac{R_1}{(1+r)} + \frac{R_2}{(1+r)} + \frac{R_3}{(1+r)} + \frac{R_n}{(1+r)} + \frac{S}{(1+r)n}$$

   where "C" is the initial capital investment, "r" is the discounted rate of return. "$R_1, R_2, R_3 \ldots R_n$" are the cash in flows (or net savings) over the years "1, 2, 3, ... n" (n being economic life of the equipment) and "S" is the salvage value of the equipment (investment) at the end of "n" years - the economic life.

4. **Discounted Cash Flow Method:** As against the above method the discounted cash flow (DCF) Method gives a true picture of return on investment as it takes care of differences in times at which revenues are generated from an investment. The DCF method uses the "present value concept in the evaluation of investment. If the total present value concept in the evaluation of investment. If the total present value of the future revenue is more than present investment then it is worth going in for the investment. "Present Value", in the simple terms means "a rupee earned today worth more than a rupee earned years later." Similarly a rupee earned a year later is same as Rs. 0.909 earned today.

(*iii*) **Purchase of used Equipment:** As a fundamental principle, any industry will prefer new equipment to used equipment. Used equipment, if available, is purchased in preference to new equipment, mainly because of economic considerations. The buyer under no circumstances is restricted to purchase of new equipments only.

In general the sources of used equipments are: (1) Directly from the owner, (2) used Equipment Dealers and (3) Brokers and auctioneers. The majority of the purchase of used equipment is done from used equipment dealers and it is essential that every purchase executive in an organisation develops a list of sources of used equipments. The first source of used equipment mentioned above-the original owner- is usually preferred by most prospective buyers as they feel that it is advantageous to buy the machine from the original owner as they can see the machine in operation at the source and also learn details about the usage history of the machine.

In most cases used equipments do not carry any warranty from the supplier. But in case where the purchase is from used equipment dealers, dealer guarantee can be obtained for the equipment purchased from them.

(*iv*) **Purchase versus Lease:** The question of leasing equipment arises because of (1) availability of funds, (2) duration for which equipment is required (3) necessity of the organisation to obtain the equipment immediately (whereas purchase of new equipment may involve a lot of procedural and policy delay) and (4) capital equipment is available on lease.

The major considerations of leasing as against purchasing capital equipments are:

1. It may be very economical to lease the equipment when it is needed for relatively short period. On the other hand since most leases are for definite terms and terminable on short notice, it may result in depriving the lease of a needed facility.
2. In the context of fast changing technology and obsolescence of equipment leasing could avoid the purchase of less efficient price of equipment.
3. In general, in a lease the leases bears the dismantling, loading and unloading charges and transportation expenses both ways, from the lessor's location to lessee's and return, whereas in purchase of new equipment, the equipment is generally sold at delivered price.
4. The rent of leased equipment is an item expense for tax purpose whereas the purchase price is an investment to be depreciated over a number of years. That is as long as lease payments exceeds the value of allowable depreciation, and additional tax benefit is occurred.
5. One of the most important disadvantages of leasing is that the lessor retains control of the equipment and not the lessee. The loss of ownership places certain restrictions in the manner in which the equipment is to be operated and it is obligatory on the part of the lessee that he allows the lessor access to the equipment for inspection at any point of time.

(*v*) **Role of the Purchasing Manager:** Unlike production materials, purchase of capital equipments is decided by a top management committee. The committee usually consists of members representing production, Design and Engineering, Finance and Purchase. The recommendations of this committee are then finally approved by the General Manager or the Chief Executive of the company before capital equipment is purchased.

The next important role of a purchase manager is to supply the qualitative information regarding the potential suppliers. He is in the best position to gather information regarding the image, the technical capabilities, the financial soundness and reliability of the supplier. He should also find out weather the supplier is capable of producing the technical know how mainly in regard to the installation, commissioning and after sales service. It is also his responsibility to check a suppliers locusstandi. A purchase manager has to get complete details regarding offers to potential supplies, tabulate them and supply them to the finance department so that they can make a through analysis. On the whole, the role of a purchase manager in the procurement of a capital equipment is that of a liason man.

2.7 INTERNATIONAL PURCHASING

(*i*) **Need:** For growing economy like India's achieving self sufficiency should be the goal but not at the cost of imports. Importing is an essential economic function which cannot be completely eliminated. Ricardo's principle of comparative advantage stages that it would be beneficial for an economy to concentrate on the production of items in which it specialises, export these items and import requirement of other items. The principle though not totally practical, cannot be dismissed. International trade is undoubtedly governed by political motives and as such, a country cannot totally rely on another country for its requirement of specific items. It would be equally fruitless to undertake import substitution at any cost. The Government of India from time to time reviews the import policies considering various aspects such as trade balance, raw material position etc. Recently the import policy has been liberalised as shortage of raw materials has led to under utilisation of the capacity. In some cases automatic licences will be issued to cut down procedural delays.

(*ii*) **Procedure:** If a company is importing for the first time the foremost step for it would be to check weather the item is allowed to be imported. This information will be available in the Red (Blue) book. If the item is banned for imports (on the ground that it is indigenously available) the starting point is to get a list of all local manufacturers and ask for quotations. If these manufacturers is not in a position to supply then a written statement to the effect may be obtained from them. These statements could be presented to the government to get the clearance for import.

In case the import clearance is obtained or item is not banned for imports, the company has to go through the following stages to accomplish the purchase.

(*a*) **Locating Foreign Source of Supply:** This has to be done by contacting the Ministry of Trade, Foreign Consulates and Embassies, Indian Consulates in foreign countries etc. A foreign consulate or embassy has a commercial attache who is well versed with the list of suppliers in his country.

(*b*) **Procurement of Item:** At this stage the importer will be involved with foreign source of supply, manufacturing unit of his company, engineering department and governmental institutions like DGTD, MMTC and STC.

(*c*) **Documentation:** Special documents used for indigenous purchases are required. The commonly used documents are:

(*a*) Bill of Ladding

(*b*) Invoices

(*c*) Certificate of origin

(*d*) Weight Certificate

(*e*) Insurance Policy

(*f*) Markings of Packages.

(*iii*) **Nature of Documents:** The following are the basic documents required for international purchasing.

(*a*) **Bill Of Ladding:** The bill of ladding is the most important document which accompanies bills of exchange drawn under letters of credit. It is the evidence of the fact that the goods have been despatched by the exporter and gives the importer title of the goods and enables him to claim them on arrival at destination.

A bill of ladding is a document signed by the Master of a ship or by the ship owners or the agents acknowledging the receipt of certain specified goods for carriage and embodying an undertaking that the goods will be delivered to the consignee or to his order assignee or merely to order. The bill specifies the part of shipment, the destination and the condition under which the goods are received for carriage. It is at the same time (*i*) Receipt of goods delivered to carrier for transportation (*ii*) a contract between the shipper and the carrier for transportation of the goods and then delivery to the consignee or his order and (*iii*) a document of title to the goods giving the holder title to the goods mentioned.

Bills of ladding are prepared by the shipper on forms supplied by the shipping company. Normally a bill of ladding shows the date and place of shipment, the port of destination, the number, contents and identification mark of the goods shipped and the amount of freight paid or to pay. The detailed particulars of the number of packages the mark they bear the contents and the amount of the freight on them are entered in the space provided for them.

Goods are released at the destination only against surrender of the bill, when one copy has been surrendered, the other copies becomes void.

(*b*) **Invoice And Certificates:** Among the documents that accompany bill of exchange drawn under letters of credit in foreign trade transactions are the commercial invoice, the consular invoice the certificate of origin and the packing list. There are in effect detailed descriptions of the goods shipped their prices and other charges, the country of origin of the goods and other particulars of the transaction which of these documents are included and in what form is a matter of contract between the buyer and the seller.

(*c*) **The Commercial Invoice:** The commercial invoice describes the merchandise, indicates the price and other details of the transaction. The name and the address of the buyer and the seller, vessel of shipment, part of discharge, shipment, export and import permit numbers, the number of contract and invoice. The financial terms of the sale, such as weather under letter of credit, sight drafts etc. are given. The number of packages and the identifying marks and number on them are clearly indicated. The goods contained in the packages are detailed and prices are given item by item, the trade discount is deducted from the gross aggregate price of the goods and a total net value is shown. Any other charges to be included, under the contract such as for packing, freight, insurance and the cost of preparing a consular invoice etc. are added to the total. The commercial invoice is not a document or a title, nor it is negotiable. It's main utility is a book keeping device for both seller and buyer.

(*d*) **Packing Lists:** A packing list serves to indicate the exact nature, quantity, and quality of the contents of each package in a shipment. The list helps the importer to identify the goods and check them against his own order. Banks may require such a list when they have financial interest in the merchandise. Clearance of goods through customs is also facilitated by packing list.

(*e*) **The Certificate of Origin:** The laws of some countries require certificate of origin of the imported goods to be produced before clearance of goods by customs and assessment of duties. An importer therefore may request the exporter to send a certificate of this kind along with other documents.

(*f*) **Nature of Insurance Policy:** Marine insurance policy is a contract between the insurer and the insured whereby the former in consideration of the payment of a premium by the latter, agrees to indemnify the latter against the loss incurred by him in respect of goods exposed to "perils of the sea", or to the particular perils insured against. For a policy to be valid the insured must have an insurable interest in the goods subject to insurance *i.e.,* he benefits from the existence of the goods and suffers a loss if the goods are damaged or lost. The insured need not have this interest at the time of insuring, but must have acquired it at the time of putting a claim under the policy for damage or loss of the goods.

(*g*) **Markings of Packages:** A packing list serves to indicate the exact nature, quantity and quality of the contents of each package in a shipment. The list helps the importer to identify the goods and check them against his own order. Banks may require such a list when they have a financial interest in the merchandise. Clearance of goods through customs is also faciliated by packing list. The packages should be suitable marked with address, dimensions, weight and other particulars. The packings should be seen correctly and in conformity with instructions in the order.

(*h*) **Payments:** The importer is involved with banks, ministry of finance and the reserve bank. The documents involved are: (*i*) letter of credit/drafts (*ii*) Terms of Payment (*iii*) Rate of exchange (*iv*) Payments under various credits and trade agreements.

- **Letter of Credit:** A letter of credit is an arrangement whereby the obligation to pay an exporter is undertaken by a bank. The bank's credit is available to an importer who is not known outside, and who otherwise would not be trusted with goods by a trader in another country. If a Letter of Credit is received from a bank the credit standing of the importer is of little consequence. What becomes important to the exporter is the credit standing of the bank issuing the L.C.

  The importer requests a bank in his country to issue a Letter of Credit in favour of the exporter. The bank cables or writes to the correspondent or some other bank in the exporters country that the credit has been opened in favour of the exporter and the latter bank informs the exporter about it. The advising bank informs the exporter that it will honour drafts drawn by the latter under terms and conditions laid down in the Letter of Credit.

(*iv*) **Trading Organisations:** To aid the import of certain basic raw materials like copper, zinc, tin, lead and nickel, the government has set up a trading organisation - Minerals and Metals Trading Corporation of India. It is possible for companies to arrange the procurement of basic metals through MMTC. The delivery arrangements could be staggered and hence the investment in inventories, can be brought down. For the imports of certain other materials like caprolactum, chemicals, raw cashew nuts etc. there is another government undertaking—The State Trading Corporation.

The above mentioned trading, organisations require to undertake long term contracts with international suppliers to safegaurd against fluctuating conditions in supply and price. Both MMTC and STC are important canalised agencies and account for about 50 percent of the imported value. With strict import procedures and heavy supply lead time scarce foreign exchange is locked up in the inventories. The government has realised the situation and is making attempts to cut down the time of clearance of imports to 3–4 months. It has also set up two trading organisations which provide help in the import of basic raw materials. The government of India is taking several measures like automatic licences for speeding up licencing procedures. The hope of import clearances being made faster and the measures taken for import substitution are healthy signs of a purchase executives.

2.8 MAKE OR BUY DECISIONS

Factory to be considered for make or buy decision are:

1. Quality Requirement.

2. Quantity Requirement.

3. Cost Aspect.
4. Technology for Production.
5. Item with high contribution (Sale Price less Variable cost) is favoured for production.

1. **Quality Requirement:** If the company's available resources fail to satisfy quality requirement, then the item should be bought from outside source, who may be a specialised producer of such item.
2. **Quantity Requirement:** Small quantity requirement may not be economical to make and therefore should be outsourced. Economical scale permits undertaking production of an item whose quantity requirement is very high.

   But, if the company's infrastructure does not permit production of an item, then even the high volume requirement is to be outsourced.
3. **Cost Aspects:** For production of an item in the promised both fixed and variable costs are to be considered. If the new capacity is to be installed then additional fixed cost will be incurred.

   If the high volume of an item is produced in the factory at the same or lower unit cost of production compared to the outside suppliers then it is justified to produce in the factory.
4. **Technology for Production:** If the specialised technology is required for producing an item, then depending on availability of technology and volume of item required, the company has to buy for low quantity requirement and may plan for production if the high volume requirement can justify import of technology to produce the item at competitive date.
5. **High Contribution Margin:** Marginal costing is very useful with regard to decisions involving make or buy production of high contribution margin article can recover the total fixed cost quickly and when the entire fixed costs are recovered, production of each additional item would produce profit equal to contribution amount for each item.

(*a*) Business process out sourcing (BPO) and Make or Buy decision. BPO is a management based corporate strategy through which a business firm can do the following courses of action.

(*i*) It can get some products from its product range manufactured by another party who acts as licensee.

(*ii*) It can get some components or parts manufactured by another party who acts as its licensee.

(*iii*) It can get some intermediate products manufactured by another party who acts as its licensee.

Example: Sona Stearing supplies stearing wheel for many car makers in India. TVS supplies many vital components to car makers in India.

Similarly, Siemens Ltd. (in India) gets components of A.C. drives made by small companies who act as its licensee.

Small companies belonging to SSI sector is exempted from paying Central excise duty and also eligible for other benefits of lower electrical power tariff, lower or no sales tax in some cases. Combinedly, all these benefits enable a small producer to supply an item to a large company at a lower market price than it would cost the company to produce it.

(*b*) Economics of Make or Buy Decision: The following graph explains the economics of Make or Buy decision.

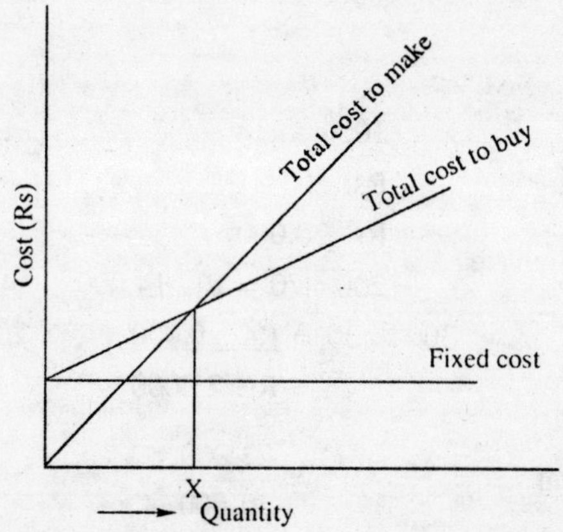

Figure 2.2 Make or Buy Decision.

For and upto quantity '*X*' of the product, it is economical for the company to buy and for quantities higher than *X*, it is economical to make.

(*c*) Competitive Advantage Principle: Make or Buy decision is guided by the competitive Advantage principle. A ceiling fan manufacturer can outsource most of components depending on cost and can only assemble and sell the products.

Competitive Advantage is derived due to:

1. Large Economy or Scale
2. Cost Leadership
3. Superior Technology (Rolls Royle's Millennium Fantom Luxury car)
4. High Productivity.

A firm while changing over from buying "to making" should adopt sound cost management system. For buying if it uses a telescope, for making it should use a microscope.

Problem: A factory can manufacture two products *A* and *B* by using two materials *P* and *Q*. Product *A* is expected to sell at Rs. 70/unit and *B* at Rs. 30 per unit. The operating data are as follows.

Output	With Material *P*	With Material *Q*
	A 200 units	*A* 400 units
	B 300 units	*B* 200 units
Quantity of raw material usage	1000 kgs	1000 kgs
Labour Usage	300 man-hours	250 man-hours
Electricity Consumption	1000 kwhrs	1500 kwhr
Cost of raw materials per kg.	Rs. 20	Rs. 30
Labour per man hour	Rs. 5	Rs. 5
Electric Energy per kwhr.	Rs. 1.50	Rs. 1.50

(*a*) Compare the Productivity of Material, Labour, Electric Energy in using materials *P* and *Q*.

(*b*) Comment on the relative advantages of using either of the materials.

Solution.

	P	*Q*
Quantity of material used	1000 kgs	1000 kgs
Cost of raw materials per kg.	Rs. 20	Rs. 30
(*i*) Total cost of materials used	Rs. 20,000	Rs. 30,000
(*ii*) Value of output	200× 70 = Rs. 14,000	400 × 70 = Rs. 28,000
	300 × 30 = Rs. 9,000	200 × 20 = Rs. 6,000
	= Rs. 23,000	= Rs. 34,000
Productivity of raw material	$= \frac{23,000}{20,000}$	$= \frac{34,000}{30,000}$
	= 1.15 (Higher)	= 1.13 (Lower)
(*iii*) Cost of labour	300 × 5 = Rs. 1500	250 × 5 = Rs. 1250 (Lower)
Productivity of Labour	$= \frac{23,000}{1,500}$	$= \frac{34,000}{1,250}$
	= 15.55	= 27.20 (Higher)
(*iv*) Cost of Electrical energy	= 1000 × 1.50	= 1500 × 1.50
	= Rs. 1500	= Rs. 2250
Productivity of energy	$= \frac{23,000}{1,500}$	$= \frac{34,000}{2,250}$
	= 15.55 (Higher)	= 15.01 (Lower)
(*v*) Total Cost	= (*i*) + (*iii*) + (*iv*)	= (*i*) + (*iii*) + (*iv*)
	= 20,000 + 1,500 + 1,500	= 30,000 + 1250 + 2,250
	= Rs. 23,000	= Rs. 33,500
(*vi*) Profit	= (*ii*) – (*v*)	= (*ii*) – (*v*)
	= 23,000 – 23,000	= 34,000 – 33,500
	= Nil	= Rs. 500

(*b*) Therefore, there is profit in using material *Q* than material *P*.

2.9 LEGAL ASPECTS OF PURCHASING

(*i*) **Law of Agency:** *i.e.,* the purchaser employs an agent for purchases on his behalf. An agreement is made between purchaser and the Agent.

(*ii*) **Law of Contract:** Purchase order between buyer and seller is a law of contract and is binding for both parties in the court of law.

It may be said that the purpose of Law of Contract is to ensure the realisation of reasonable expectation of the parties who enter into a contract. The law of contract may be defined as that branch of Law which determines the circumstances in which a promise shall be legally binding on persons making it. The Indian contract act of 1872 (Act IX 1872) lays down certain general rules regarding contracts. The act is not exhaustive.

Law of contract provides that an agreement enforceable by law', is a contract. The law of contract differs from other branches of law in an important aspect. It does not lay down a number of rights and duties which the law will enforce, it consists rather of a number of limiting principles to which the parties may create rights and duties for themselves which the law will uphold.

(*a*) **Definition of Contract:** A proposal or an offer when accepted is a promise. A promise and every set of promises forming the conditions for each other is an agreement. An agreement, if made with free consent of parties competent to contract, for a lawful consideration and with a lawful object is a contract. A contract has been defined as an agreement enforceable by law, or in other words a legally binding agreement between two or more persons by which rights are acquired by one or more to act or for bearence on the part of the other or others.

If we analyse these definitions, we find that a contract consists of two elements, **an agreement** and **its enforceability** by law. An agreement is the same as a promise. A promise is defined thus when the person to whom the proposal is made signifies his acceptance there to, the proposal is said to be accepted. A proposal when accepted becomes a promise. Hence in order to form an agreement there must be an offer or praposal by one party and the acceptance of proposal by the other. To sum up Agreement = offer + Acceptance.

An agreement cannotes that at least two parties expressed themselves with sufficient certainty and with terms which correspond on the object.

To conclude contract = Agreement + Enforceability at Law. All contracts are therefore agreements but all agreements are not contracts.

(*b*) **Essential Elements of a Valid Contract:** A contract in order to be made enforceable by law must have the following essential elements.

1. **Offer and Acceptance:** There must be a lawful proposal or offer by one party and a lawful acceptance of that praposal by other party thus resulting in an agreement. The terms of offer and acceptance must be definite.

2. **Legal Relationship:** The agreement must create legal relationship between the parties. If there is no intention to create legal relationship, there can be no contract between the parties.

3. **Lawful consideration:** The agreement to be enforceable by law, must be supported by a consideration. The term consideration in simple words means "**Something in return.**" The agreement is legally enforceable only when both the parties give something and get something in return. A promise to do something, getting nothing in return, is usually not enforceable by law.

4. **Capacity of Parties–Competency:** The parties to the agreement must be capable of entering into a valid contract. Every person is competent to enter into a contract if he is of sound mind, age of majority and not disqualified by contracting by any law to which he is a subject. Flaws in capacity to contract may arise from minority, luancy, idiocy, drunkenness and status.

5. **Free and Genuine Consent:** It is essential to the creation of every contract that there must be free and genuine consent of the parties to the agreement. The parties must agree upon the same thing in the same sense is they must be of the same mind on all material terms of the contract.

6. **Lawful Object:** The object of the agreement must be lawful. It is lawful unless it is forbidden by law or is of such a nature that if permitted would defeat any provisions of law.

7. **Agreement not Declared Void:** The agreement, though it might posses all the essential elements, must not have been expressly declared void by any law in force in the country.

8. **Certainty and Possibility of Performance:** The terms of agreement that must be certain and not vague or ambiguous. If the agreement is vauge and if it is not possible to ascertain the meaning of agreement, it cannot be enforced. The terms of agreement must enable performance. An agreement to do an act impossible in itself cannot be enforced.

9. **Legal Formalities:** The agreement may be oral or in writing. Where it is in writing it must comply with necessary legal formalities as to writing registration and attestation. If the agreement does not comply with these legal formalities it cannot be enforced by law.

(iii) **Breach of Contract:** The party which sustains a loss due to breach of contract will be so compensated with respect of damages that it will be placed in a position as if the contract has been performed. In commercial transactions the aggravated party can claim only the actual loss caused to him and not to others.

Damages arising out of a breach of contract in the usual course are recoverable. However, damages which arise owing to circumstances peculiar to the case and which would not have arisen during the normal course are not recoverable. Unless the circumstances are made known to the party which breaks the contract and such damages are contemplated by both the parties at the time of entering into the contract. The amount of compensation by way of repatriation of damages will be as far as possible, the amount which will place the aggrieved party in the same position as it would have been, had it not suffered the breach of contract which led to such damages. Very often parties wish to reduce the damages to a certainty. This they achieve by fixing a rate or sum at which damages are to be assessed. If such an amount is a genuine pre estimate of damages then it is known as liquidated damages. However, if the amount fixed is unconscionable with respect to the greatest loss that could have followed from the breach, it would be considered as a penalty. As per Indian contract act it is for the court to ascertain the actual loss and award the same.

1. **Patent Rights:** The buyer can protect his organisation by adding special patent infringement clauses to his purchase orders. However, when the buyer orders to his own specifications this does not apply. It is often the case that big buyers give financial and technical assistance to the supplier for developing new products and materials. It is advantageous in such cases, for the buyer to include a clause in the purchase order, covering the patent rights in inventions discovered by a supplier in the course of executing his purchase contracts.

2. **Settlement of Disputes:** Arbitration is used for settling disputes between buyers and sellers. It is less time consuming when compared with litigation. For this purpose the buyer must include an arbitration clause and the supplier has to agree to it. Once such a clause is stipulated, the court will not entertain any suit unless arbitration process is exhausted. Arbitrators have similar powers as the court and their award is binding and enforceable on the parties.

The sales of goods Act, 1930 came into force from 1st July, 1930. A contract of Sale of goods is a contract whereby the seller transfers or agrees to transfer the property in goods to the buyer for a price. It includes an actual sale as well as an agreement to sell.

The sale of goods act and its knowledge is of utmost importance to the people, who deal in purchase and sale.

Some vital points of Act are as follows.

1. Essentials of a contract sale:

(i) There must be two parties—a buyer and a seller.

(ii) There must be some goods. Transfer of ownership of goods from seller to buyer is essential.

(iii) The price in money must be paid on transfer of property on sale.

(*iv*) The subject matter of the contract of sale must be movable property.

(*v*) All the essentials of a valid contract must be present in the contract of sale.

2. Conditions and Warranty: The buyer and seller are at liberty to enter into contract on any term they like. The agreement for sale or goods may contain many term relating to the quality and quantity of goods time, place, mode of delivery, settlement of price etc.

The stipulations imposed on the two parties may be either a condition or a warranty. A condition is a stipulation which is essential to the main purpose of the contract. Whereas, warranty is collateral to the main purpose of the contract and in case of breach, the aggrieved party can claim damage only. Consumerism is an outcome of sufferings and exploitations of consumers, who aim to secure protection from commercial exploitation. The former President of USA Mr. John F. Kennedy had defined the basic consumer rights. "As the Right of Safety, the Right to be informed, the Right to choose and the Right to be heard."

The government of India has entacted certain laws to protect the well being of the consumers and to safe guard them.

Some important Acts are as follows.

(*a*) The prevention of Food Adulteration Act. 1954.

(*b*) The Essential Commodities Acts 1955.

(*c*) Weights and Measures Act, 1958.

(*d*) The Monopolies and Restrictive Trade Practices Act., 1969.

(*e*) Drugs and Cosmetics Act., 1940.

(*f*) Drugs Control Act., 1950.

(*g*) Dangerous Drug Act., 1930 etc.

The consumer movement should be strengthened in our country so that the tendency to push up prices could be curbed and the quality of services and products ensured.

Among consumers under Indian condition, the literacy level is low and purchasing power is poor. But one must be aware of one's rights and should not hesitate to exercise them in right direction. Consumer problems must be reduced by making them good buyers through education and implementing various Acts as mentioned above.

2.10 REFERENCE TO CONTRACT ACT, DRUGS CONTROL ACT, SALE OF GOODS ACT, IN RESPECT TO PURCHASE ACTIVITIES

1. The consumer rights constitute consumer bill of rights: In 1962, President John F. Kennedy, in his consumer message, summed up these rights consumers and paved the way for organised consumerism in the USA and all over the world.

The Right to Protection of Health and Safety: It is the right to be protected against Products and Services which are hazardous to health or life..

In the case of food and drugs, we need safety to consumers. Drugs control act, hold the manufacturer and seller responsible for any type of administration and spurious type drug which may cause partial disability or serious health hazards for consumers. In phase–I, the side effects of a drug is known. As per drug Acts, any drug should be put through 3 phases of tests after it is first tested on animals like rats and rabbits etc. In phase–I the drug is taken by healthy individual who may be willingly accept the drug against substantial money, in phase–II, the drug is given to a small number of sick patients to determine dosage level and in phase–III, the drug is given to large number of sick patients by doctors and hospitals to determine its efficacy.

For any drug, the package must contain the harmful side effects and the shelf life. No drug is to be used beyond its self life. Clear instructions on package should be written for safe storage condition. Some schedule drugs can only be sold by chemists against the physician's prescriptions.

2. **Law of contract:** From the material manager's point of view, the law of contract is an important branch of merchantile or commercial law because all commercial transactions start from an agreement between two parties. The object of law of contract is to introduce definiteness in commercial and other transactions.

2.11 PROBABLE QUESTIONS

1. What are the functions of Purchase organisation?
2. Explain the different methods of Purchasing.
3. Explain in detail the procedure of purchasing a Capital Equipment from a foreign supplier.
4. Distinguish between:
   (*a*) Purchase requisition and Purchase by tender.
   (*b*) Rate contract Purchasing and Running Contract Purchasing.
5. What is "Vendor Development"? Describe the procedure of Vendor Development.

3

Store Management

• *Store Management* • *Integrated Materials Management & Evaluation* • *Probable Questions.*

3.1 STORES MANAGEMENT

1. Objectives Functions and Importance of Store: Store is an important place having direct connection with many user departments in a manufacturing company.

The vital objective served by a store is to provide uninterrupted service for the production activities. A store is the most valuable building where many valued materials and spares are stored and thus large amount of money is locked up in a store.

The important functions of a store are as follows:

1. To receive, store and issue materials spares, tools, equipment and other item for uninterrupted production activities.
2. To minimise obsolescence, surplus and scrap through proper codification, preservation and handling.
3. To indicate stock accumulation discrepancies and abnormal consumption and effect control measures.
4. To ensure good house keeping so that material handling, material preservation stocking, receipt and issue are carried out smoothly and conveniently.
5. To provide assistance in verification and provide supporting information for effective purchase activities. Long periods of storage for various components spares from 4 to 18 months may be effected depending on the lead times, distant sources of supply.

2. Location and Layout of a Store: The location of a store is decided while preparing the general layout of the production unit. A store should be in the central location from all user departments. This minimises handling and ensures timely despatches.

For a Stores layout, the governing criteria are easy movement of material handling equipment and for employees engaged in stores activities. The stores layout should be such that optimum utilisation of storage space, judicious use of storage equipment *i.e.,* shelves, racks, etc. takes place.

Another important factors governing the location are the convenience of user departments, volume and varities of goods handled and the easy access of various material handling equipment like Forklift trucks, Pay-loaders, Trollies, Conveyors and Cranes etc.

In the case of warehouses stocking finished goods, factors such as proximity to party, railway lines, quality of roads, etc become quite important.

While designing a store, proper lighting, ventilation, safety and provisions for fire fighting are duly considered. As far as possible, natural light and ventilation benefits are utilised for a stores building. While deciding the storage space, due consideration should be given to the space required for the movement of material handling equipment. Every cubic-inch of store room costs to the organisation. For the economic use of the stores areas, vertical stacking and storing with shelves within the limits of ceiling are carried out.

3. **Stores Systems and Procedures Identification:** The main reasons why a large number of unnecessary items and spare parts or obsolete items are held in stores, are misleading nomenclature, faulty numbering and the use of suppliers' part numbers or trade names for describing the items. These cause account for the fact that often same item is identified by various user departments through the functions it performs.

   This aspect requires proper identification of item.

   Codification: Rationalised codification is essential in the case of items and spares for easy identification because the range and number of item and spares are very large. Many expensive spares such as bearings has considerable interchangeability even when manufactured by different firms and a common code could serve the purpose from a functional view point.

   Further, various items are slow moving and as well as highly specialised. Hence, identification by appearance is rather difficult and a proper codification will be helpful. The item and spares should be grouped through codification so that the user department can easily locate the item inside the store. Normally the major groups for codification consists of categories such as hard ware items, tools, machinery spares, electrical spares, mechanical spares and general spares etc. It is common to use 9 to 10 digit codes where the digits indicate respectively the broad categories described above and the metal such as steel, copper, etc. then the items such as bolts, nuts, and the dimensional characteristics.

   The following benefits are obtained through codification:

   1. It helps to identify the item easily.
   2. Systematic grouping of similar items is facilitated by codification.
   3. Codification facilitates use of standardisation.
   4. Ordering becomes more economical as like items are ordered together.
   5. Location problems of items in bins are reduced by codification.
   6. Through codification service levels can be improved for the same level of investment.
   7. Servicing time is less due to easy identification.
   8. Stock levels are less as duplication has been eliminated by codification.
   9. Obsolescence is less as the number of items is less due to codification and easy identification.
   10. Codification facilitates computerisation.
   11. Logical grouping of items facilitates variety reduction easily.
   12. The simplicity of codification enables even unskilled workers to distinguish one item from another and locate it in the store.
   13. Codification introduces discipline and reduces inventory by removing non stock items and reducing items on temporary codes.
   14. Codification aims at maximum benefit to user departments.

4. **Storing and Handling Equipment:** Uses of modern material handling equipment provide reduction in the cost storage and handling and also provide safety and speed in handling and storing.

   "Parkomat" the fully automated car handling and storing for parking of automobiles station in the Park street junction in Kolkata is an example of modern parking unit. Material handling equipment which are usually used in a general store are as follows. Trolleys, Pallets, Wheel barrongh, Forklift-

Trucks, Pay-loaders, Gantry Cranes, Mobile Cranes, Bridge Cranes, Monorails with electric hoists, Chain pulley blocks, Conveyors and Chutes.

Platform weigh scales and Road weigh-bridge, Road Cum Railway bridge etc. are used in stores and yard for verification of weight of various materials in stores.

5. **Issue of Materials:** The materials stored in the store are issued to various jobs or production departments against the authorised material requisition (MR). The issues are recorded in the store ledger and the respective jobs or production departments are debited with the price of material issued. As the time of purchase and the time of issues are mostly different and the market price of materials tends to vary, the problem of pricing the materials issued neccessitates certain policy formation. This is also important for costing and pricing policies.

   The fundamental consideration is whether to price the issues on historical price *i.e.,* the original purchase price, or at the replacement price *i.e.,* prevailing market price at the time of issue or at some other price.

6. **Verification of Materials:** This is physical verification of proper stock records kept in the bin-card as well as the stores ledgers. When the materials received or issued, they are properly recorded and the new balance is struck at the end of every transaction. The bin should contain the quantity which is shown in "Balance" column of the bin-card.

   In case of pilferage above systems will not tally. For some low temperature boiling liquids like Alcohal, Petrol etc. the "Balance" discrepancy may come due to evaporation loss.

(*a*) **Under Periodic Inventory Verification:** All items of the store are verified through counting, weighing and measuring etc. at the beginning of every month and also on the last day of the financial year. But under perpetual Inventory verification, the verification function becomes a continuous function rather than periodical.

All the items are verified on the continuous basis. Generally, those items which have reached a minimum level are selected for the verification. This policy reduced the burden of verification.

The verification work is arranged in such a way that every item is verified twice or thrice during the year on rotation basis. This system does not require the employment of any special staff for verification. The store-keeper carries out the verification work according to his/her convenience.

7. **Store Accounting and Record keeping:** Proper record keeping in Store is useful for accounting and costing purposes. Up-to-date stores records help in determining the quantity of respective material items on particular point of time which provides the guidelines for fresh purchase or disposal of the materials.

   The store records can broadly be classified into two:

   (*a*) The Bin card

   (*b*) The Stores Ledger

   (*c*) Issue of Materials.

   (*a*) **The Bin Card:** Bin or Stock Card

Bin Card

Bin No. .... Max Qnty. ....

Material Code No. .... Ordering Level ....

Stores Ledger Folio .... Minimum Qnty. ....

Date	Qnty. Received	Qnty. issued	Balance	Remarks

The bin card is attached to each bin, shelf or other form of containers. The bin cards for coal, steel items etc. stored in open yard are kept at the desk of the store-keeper.

The bin card is used as basis for verifying the physical stock and the stores ledger accounts.

(*b*) **The Stores Ledger:** The stores ledger keeps the proper record of materials specifying their quantities as well as money value. It is a record which charges the respective department or the job at the price of materials issued to them.

The stores ledger card specifies the account number location, description of the materials, unit measurement, maximum, minimum and recorder level, debit, credit and the balance columns under the description of receipt, issue, and balance specifying both quantity and rupee value.

When the store-keeper issues material to any department or job against material requisition, a copy of material requisition is sent to the stores ledger clerk. He makes entry in the "Issue" section of the card, specifying the date, requisition number, the deptt. or job, the quantity, the unit cost and total cost. Finally, the balance is calculated and entered in the balance column.

(*c*) **Issue of Materials:** The materials are issued from store against receipt of a material requisition (MR) specifying the deptt., date, material required with code number, quantity and signed and approved by proper authorities of the deptt. requiring the item.

The issue is made on the basis of First in First Out (FIFO) method or Last in First Out (LIFO) method. FIFO method is followed for materials with low shelf life. Generally, all issues from store are done during specified working hours.

8. Disposal of Surplus and Scrap: The surplus and scrap consist of the following:

(*a*) Spoiled materials

(*b*) Rejected Items

(*c*) Defective parts

(*d*) Obsolete materials *i.e.*, outdated quality for items

(*e*) Wastes from production departments like metals, scraps, pieces etc.

(*f*) Non-returnable containers and packing cases.

Such surplus and scraps involve some commercial value. These should be disposed or periodically and proper credit of the amount realised should be taken in the books of accounts. Such disposal also releases the space in the stores. Further discussions are continued under point 15 next in this chapter.

9. Stores Receipts: Receiving concerns control on quantity and quality of materials from the time they are received until they are accepted and taken into stock.

The importance of receipt function is high-lighted as follows:

(*a*) Errors in purchase transaction can be detected more easily at time of receiving of material rather than afterwards.

(*b*) Correctly performed receiving function can prevent malpractices.

(*c*) Receiving section of store can assist purchase department in improving effectiveness of vendors.

(*d*) Verification of correctness of paperwork and appropriateness of supply before accepting the goods is helpful.

(*e*) Preparing necessary documents such as discrepancy note, goods inward note, etc. is done.

(*f*) Important documents used in receiving goods in store are as under:

- Delivery challan in duplicate. The original is retained and the duplicate is returned to the supplier duty signed on acknowledgment of receipt.
- Railway Receipt (RR) or Lorry Receipt (LR) is the document which acts as an authorisation slip for getting the delivery of goods.
- Bill of Entry is the document received from the clearing agent against imports.

10. Inspection, Quality Control and Storage (Custody) in Stores: After the materials are unpacked and verified for quantity, it is offered to quality control department for quality certification. Most commonly used approach is to forward the complete set of GRR.

The task of inspection of material may require the following activities to be performed.

(*a*) Physically send the material to inspection department.

(*b*) Indicate the location where material is kept in store.

(*c*) Provide copy of the drawing (or sketch) of component to be inspected.

Inspection department on receipt of GRR carries out the neccessary inspection and either accepts the material or enters the discrepancies in the GRR. Some companies use a separate rejection note to inform the inspection results.

Accepted materials are sent to the receiving store and rejected/defective items are sent back to the supplier, usually on "freight to pay" basis.

Storage and preservation measures are for the following:

(*a*) To keep materials safe from damages and spoilage.

(*b*) To maintain materials at their original value and quality.

(*c*) To reduce storage losses and consequently to reduce production costs.

The store should safe against theft, pilferage, fire and rodent menace. Normal pest-control measures are adopted in store. The store should inform the user department about the expiry date of any item well in advance.

11. Valuation of Stock in Store: The factors that are to be included in building up the cost of materials received at store are price, freight charges, insurance and taxes.

Duty drawback statements are prepared for availing of the duty exemption in respect of goods to be exported.

(*a*) First in First Out (FIFO), Last in First Out (LIFO) Average cost, Standard cost, Market price at the time of issue, latest purchase price, replacement or current cost are some of the methods in the valuation of stock issued to production.

(*b*) In FIFO method, the value of stock is the amount that has been paid. Under LIFO, the latest market price is charged to the issue.

(*c*) Under Average cost method, the issues to Production department are split into equal batches from each shipment at stock. It is a realistic method reflecting the price levels and stabilising the cost figures.

(*d*) Market value is known as replacement rate costing is the market price prevailing the time of issue.

(*e*) Standard cost: A standard rate is determined based on detailed analyses of market prices and trends. This standard rate is kept fixed for a definite period of six months or more.

For costing during this period, this rate is used.

(*f*) In evaluating the cost of stock at the close, a provision is kept to account for any obsolescence. This is based on the past experience and is usually worked out as a percentage of the total stock value.

12. **Principles of efficient layout of store:** The following aspects should be considered for designing the layout of a store for a manufacturing organisation.

(*a*) The floor area should be adequate and should suit to the specific characteristics of the materials stored e.g. liquid, inflammable and fragile etc.

(*b*) The gangways should be wide enough for easy movement of necessary material handling equipment such as Trolleys, Fork Lift Trucks etc.

(*c*) The materials which are used most frequently should be located near the issuing point.

(*d*) The vertical height of store should be utilised for shelves and racks for storing various light weight items using handling equipment.

(*e*) Use of suitable material handling equipment such as Cranes, Lifts, Hoists, Forklift Trucks etc. will benefit stores operation.

(*f*) Provisions of safety for working personnel and security for materials stored should be ensured.

(*g*) Use of natural light should be encouraged. Also sufficient lighting and ventilation are to be arranged.

13. **(*a*) Stores Organisation:** The stores manager or stores incharge assisted by a store keeper is responsible for stores operation and reports to Commercial Manger or Materials Manager.

(*b*) Merits of centralised storing:

1. Facilitates codification & computerisation of stores items.
2. Possibility of standardisation of materials reducing the variety of item stored.
3. Requirement of stores operating personnel, cost of arranging safety and security are minimised.

14. **Replacement of Materials:** Receiving and issuing of inventories are the common and recurring phenomena in manufacturing organisation. When the inventories fact below a particular level, they are replenished by the fresh purchases. The reorder (ROL) level is an important technique of inventory control. It fundamentally deals with "when to order" to replenish the inventories.

When the existing stock of inventories reaches the point of ROL, the purchase action is initiated to replenish them. ROL is mentioned in the bin-card of each inventory item. Generally, size of the order is determined on the basis of economic ordering quantity (EOQ), which is also an important technique of inventory control.

ROL for each item is worked out on the basis of parameters like Lead time, Average consumption level, and Safety Stock.

Thus ROL = Lead time × average daily consumption + safety stock

(*a*) ROL is controlled through the following technique:

(*i*) **Two-Bin System:** Under this system, the inventory item is divided into two parts. One part is active from which issues are made and the other part is kept reserved and touched only when the active part is exhausted. It is also known as the bin reserve system.

When the reserve part is touched a fresh order is placed to replenish the stock. The reserve part becomes active and the earlier active part which is exhausted is replenished with the fresh stock.

The fresh order is placed for the fixed quantity. The quantity in the reserve part serves as a reordering level.

This method is applicable to low-cost, high volume items which have consistent usage. This method avoids any record keeping.

15. **Disposal of Surplus and Scrap in Store:** (Continued from Point 8 in this chapter)

Production control generating the scrap should be associated with the disposal action. Two basic questions have to be answered in this context before disposal action is contemplated.

(*i*) Does the scrap generated have any value?

(*ii*) Is the value significant enough to warrant process classification?

For example, copper scrap has a high market value. Hence, it is economically sound to segregate this scrap and prevent its contamination. It is also essential to keep a proper account of scrap generated in different departments. Disposal follows when scrap and waste can not be utilised within the plant. Before disposal is initiated, the feasibility of use by sister organisations, returning to the vendors, selling to outside companies or perhaps donating to a charitable organisation may be explored. When the scrap is mixed, the price will be lower than the lowest element in the mixture. When costly scrap such as copper, aluminium and tungsten etc are involved, it is absolutely essential to segregate the scrap and waste, according to various grades. Since scrap is generated process wise, it comes out in a segregated condition and there should be no difficulty in sorting.

Disposal of scrap is indeed a tricky business. One hand, the warehouse incharge has to deal with a set of hard bargainers, and at the same time, he has to face audit queries with regard to pricing. It must be mentioned that scrap market is very erratic. Hence one has to do adequate preparation and planning, before initiating disposal action, many methods are used for disposal. Two methods frequently used are open auction and tender, periodically, once in three months or so. Clearance depends upon the size of scrap yard and accumulation of waste. Parties in both cases are normally required to inspect the scrap in the yard and deposit earnest money.

Very often the company, based on its experience, insists on a basic price, depending upon the category of scrap. In some cases, the disposal section enters into a long-term contract with industrial end users like foundries or mini steel plants. The contract procedure and legal formalities adopted in purchasing are applicable in the sales of scrap/waste also.

Many companies have found to their dismay, components scrapped by them appearing in the market and competing with their products. Automobile spare parts and bearings are prone to such dangers. This is the price which organisation pay for not dismantling and disfiguring the scrap before disposal. For this purpose, a few organisation, go to the extent of requesting vehicle users to demolish filters and spark plugs before scrapping them. Thus, disposing, salvaging and utilisation of scrap amount to an art, no amount of theoretical inputs can substitute man's intelligence which has the knack of converting waste into money

3.2 INTEGRATED MATERIALS MANAGEMENT & EVALUATION

MIS for materials management computers and materials management criteria for evaluation Inventory Turnover Ratio

1. **Management Information System:** In a business organisation, every transaction generates some kind of data. When necessary data is collected and a meaningful pattern is derived from it, it is called information. Management converts information into decisions. The management information system is used for strategic planning and for exercising managerial control on all functional activities. The determinants in management information system include the opportunities, risks, available technology, available information sources, corporate strategy, corporate structure, manpower and style of leadership.

Thus, management information system can be defined as an organised network of information flow aimed at supporting management by furnishing relevant, reliable and timely information. Use of personal computers and electronic data processing system has provided material managers with the tools to handle information floors with unbelievable speed facility and accuracy. The increasing use of computers in many organisation has kindled new awareness of information needs and materials intelligence.

2. **MIS for materials Management:** The terms, materials intelligence, purchase intelligence, creative purchasing, purchase information system, materials research, materials information system etc signify one and the same system which helps the materials manager to know where the required item is materials research becomes important accounting for the bulk of cash outflow in the company. Materials research includes the steps involved in systematic investigation for locating alternative supply sources.

   The materials manager depends on an up-to-date and accurate exchange of information from other departments in the company as well as from external sources. Integrated MIS helps him to handle most quantities of information quickly.

   Materials intelligence is the process of applying different scientific principles for the purpose of developing a system in sufficient details to realise materials management objectives.

(a) Objectives of Material Intelligence:

1. Attain high efficiency in all activities of materials management.
2. Find alternative sources of supply.
3. Standardise, simplify and indigenously substitute the items.
4. Avoid stock outs and excessive stock-in.
5. Reduce paper work in purchase stores and inventory control.
6. Optimise inventory levels.
7. Optimise materials handling cost.
8. Optimise transportation cost.
9. Reduce packaging charges.
10. Develop better communication within the department, organisation and with suppliers, transporters, bankers and relevant government departments.

(b) MIS & Internal Information: Materials intelligence can be collected from sources within the organisation, as well as from outside sources. The internal sources include the data generated by the materials department and the information relevant to an individual organisation are as under.

1. Material Planning-short term and long-term.
2. MRP, BOM and ERP.
3. Sales forecast-quantity and price, for all major items.
4. Accounting information costs, stock valuation, pricing of issues.
5. Policy criterion on make-buy lease replacement and project buying.
6. Quality specification and challenging engineering designs.
7. Production scheduling and purchase planning.
8. Inventory control, reserve, safety, buffer minimum, maximum, stock out of raw materials, spare parts, semi-finished and finished goods.
9. Received item & quality control rejects.

10. New product development and new materials requirement.
11. Lead time and its components, fluctuation and follow-up.
12. Consumption norms and fluctuations in consumption.
13. Credit, discounts and bill payment term.
14. Shelf-life, preservatives, storage space and issue methods.
15. Source development, buyer-seller relations vendor rating and ethics.
16. Obsolete items, surplus, slow-moving and non-moving item, insurance spares and scrap disposal.
17. Stock verification codification, value analyses.
18. Customs, excise, & sales tax procedures and claims.

(c) MIS & External Information

1. Information on general market condition can be obtained from suppliers sales force, trade publications, bulletins and economic dailies.
2. Total demand and supply at macro level can be obtained from planning commission documents and association documents.
3. A constant updating of information on prices, supply, demand, competitions etc.
4. Information on possible sources of supply can be had from suppliers salesperson, advertising media, exhibition, trade-shows and trade journals.
5. Information on prices, discounts, sales tax and other aspects.
6. The types, availability and cost of transportation which influence input costs.
7. Governments monetary policy and policies on taxation, dual pricing subsidies etc which have direct bearing on price and availability.
8. The balance of payment situation, volume of imports and exports generally govern the import trade control policy.
9. RBI's bulletin and weekly statistical supplement give a picture of currency and finance in a concise manner.
10. DGS & D & DGTD, BIS—are also helpful.

(d) Intelligence Techniques: The following methods are available to convert the data into material intelligence.

1. General/Market/Demand/Supply analyses
2. SWOT Analysis
3. Vendor rating and supplier analysis
4. Transport/freight charges analysis
5. Price/Cost Analysis
6. Purchase Systems & Procedures
7. Cost reduction techniques.
8. Examine the relevance of fiscal and economic information in the formation of materials intelligence.

3.3 COMPUTERS AND MATERIALS MANAGEMENT

With the emergence of large scale integrated chips, thousands of electronic gates, constituting entire submits, can be built into a single chip resulting in fourth generation computers. These fourth generation super computers have started their operations in India. Because of the speed at which computer does mathematical operations, sorting and printing, it is used for work which would be prohibitively expensive if done manually.

Lot of corporate secret information is stored in the computer memory or in floppy disc and data security has become an important issue for materials management. The inputs to the computer system and the outputs to be generated from the system should be identified.

The various tasks, that have to be performed on the computer to achieve the desired outputs are conceptualised, through flow charts. Codification, input and output formats are decided upon. Detailed program specifications to carry out the necessary jobs are also developed at this state.

Programming the computer in a language it understands is to be done for proper use. The specifications developed from the basis on which programs are written with systematic date to check the logic and performance of the entire system. Testing is done with the entire system and then it is introduced to run in parallel with the manual system.

This enables to check the accuracy and stabilise the functioning of the system. For computerisation, the coding structure required for different attributes in the system such as item code, supplier code, limit of issue, limit of order, unit of sales, job order numbers, cost centres code, Purchase order numbers, etc., must be finalised. This is the best method of unique identification in a computer.

Computer master file is a directory of permanent and semi-permanent information on a set of related items. Creation of the master file is a time consuming process and this has to be done in parallel with programming, so that by the time all programs are ready the files are also ready.

In the computer system the processing involved is as follows. The monthly/weekly/daily transactions are fed to the computer. Based on these and the data available in the master files, the computer produces the desired output reports and simultaneously updates the contents of the master file. The different output reports are then produced at different stages in the system.

The computer is useful in generating a large number of reports in all areas of materials management including activities of purchase department, general stores, finished product warehouse inventory control, transportation, field warehousing and order processing etc. The application areas fall into two categories—periodic or on time and daily or continuous.

The one-time application which is done annually or monthly are *ABC* analysis, obsolete items, lead time analysis EOQ, safety stock, Buffer stock consumption norms, stock statements, inventory valuation, service level/stock outs customer complaints etc.

3. (*a*) Computer Application in Materials Management is discussed below:

1. **Forecasting Requirements:** Sales forecasting is an estimate of future customer needs. For the very survival of a company, it must be able to forecast its customers' needs fairly accurately and meet the customer needs as quickly as its competitors. These sales forecasts form the basis for production plans and production budgets which in turn form the basis for materials plans and materials budgets. Since forecasting techniques need vast amounts of past sales data and also data regarding economic indicators, population, market characteristics data etc., storage and analysis of these data is facilitated by computer hardware and software.
2. **Materials Planning:** Sales forecast is the major to materials planning. The sales forecast is converted into forecast for finished goods. The bill of materials is used to estimate the requirement of materials for producing the finished goods as per the sales forecast. The bill of materials data (product explosion based on product design documents such as product design documents such as product structure tree, part lists etc.) and the master production schedule (estimate of finished products to be produced for time period such as quarter or month or week) are stored in the computer and based on these data, the materials requirements for the production program are arrived at.

3. Purchasing: The various aspects of computer application in purchasing are:

(*a*) **Creation of supplier data base:** Information about suppliers such as company name and address, name of contact person and his/her designation, telephone numbers, fax numbers, e-mail address, website details, quality systems used, payment terms etc.

(*b*) **Sourcing evaluation:** Supplier ratings such as financial data, quality system, capabilities, track record, strength and weaknesses etc.

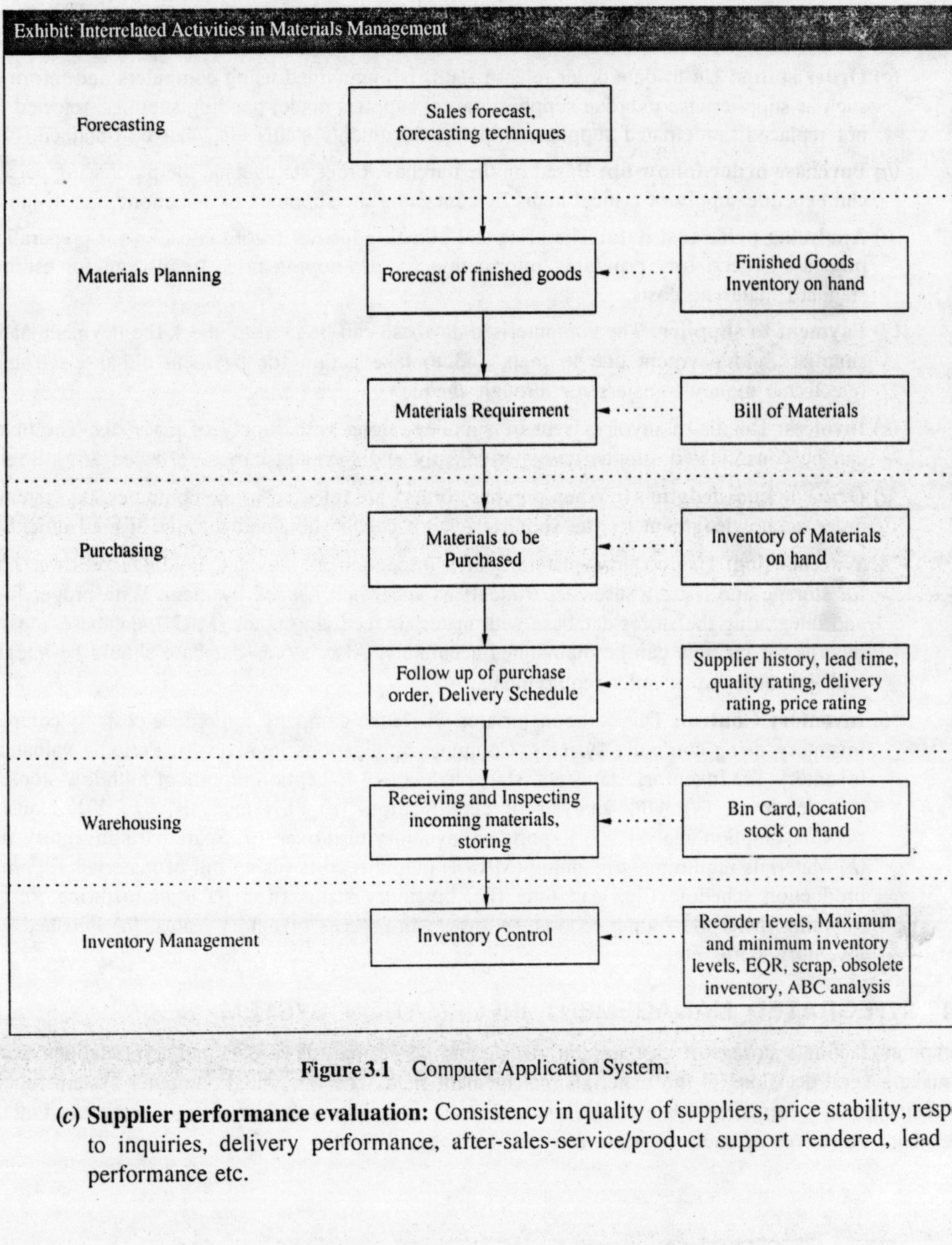

Figure 3.1 Computer Application System.

(*c*) **Supplier performance evaluation:** Consistency in quality of suppliers, price stability, response to inquiries, delivery performance, after-sales-service/product support rendered, lead time performance etc.

(*d*) **Supplier performance history:** Quality supplied, quantity accepted, delivery as per promise or delivery delayed etc.

(*e*) **Maintenance of product specification:** Company standards, national and international standards.

(*f*) **Purchase order release:** Filling the purchase order format through computer and printing of purchase orders or sending the purchase order to the supplier through internet, by E-mail or by fax using fax modem of the computer. Electronic Data Interchange (EDI) can be used if the company's computer system is linked with the supplier's computer system. EDI provides faster information transfer between the buyer and the seller.

(*g*) **Order status:** Up-to-date order release status is maintained using computers and information such as supplierwise overdue supplies, partial supplies made, pending supplies, rejected items not replaced, anticipated supplies, shipping documents status etc., can be obtained.

(*h*) **Purchase order follow up:** Based on the purchase order status data, the purchasing personnel can expedite supply of critical items by contacting the suppliers by telephone, fax, E-mail etc.

(*i*) **Analysing price cost data:** The price and purchase history record is useful for preparation of purchase orders, for providing information for developing price trends and for estimating standard materials costs.

(*j*) **Payment to supplier:** The computerised database can be used to check the payment status to suppliers and payment due to them and to take action for payment either electronically (electronic money transfers) or through cheque.

(*k*) **Invoices:** Details of invoices sent by suppliers along with supply of materials. The invoices can be consolidated supplierwise–periodically and payment can be effected accordingly.

(*l*) **Order acknowledgment:** When purchase orders are released in the computerised system, the order acknowledgment by the supplier in turn can be obtained through E-mail quickly.

4. **Warehousing:** The incoming materials, after inspection are moved to holding stores/warehouses for storage and issue to user departments as and when needed by them. With proper linking and integrating the stores database with materials receiving notes (MRN), database, the stores records for receipts can be maintained accurately. Also, stores database should be integrated with job order/work order requirements.

5. **Inventory Control:** This is the major area where the company can reduce costs by controlling inventory using computer systems. Computer applications involve: (*a*) Periodic valuation of inventory, (*b*) Inventory status and stores ledger, (*c*) Exception reports of high/low stocks and re-order level, (*d*) *ABC* analysis or classification. (*e*) FSN analysis, (*f*) *X-Y-Z* analysis, (*h*) Consumption analysis, (*i*) Reports on inventory turn over, (*j*) Spare parts inventory status, (*k*) Materials requirement planning (MRP I) output reports (using bill of materials file, master production schedule file, lead time file, inventory status file), (*l*) Manufacturing Resource Planning (MRP II)–output reports, (*m*) Work-in-process inventory status, (*n*) Finished goods inventory status etc.

3.4 INTEGRATED MANAGEMENT INFORMATION SYSTEM

Computers facilitate storage of vast amount of data and faster analysis of data and computations required to make several decisions in the materials management field. The integrated computer system functions as an integrated information system which would result in the smooth operation of materials functions. The major objectives of such a system are:

(*i*) Accuracy in reporting demand and inventory.

(*ii*) Ensuring fast response to changes in environment such as changes either in supply or price of materials, changes in customer taste and so on.

(*iii*) Measuring performance of functions such as purchasing, sourcing, vendor rating and inventory control.

The normal flow of information regarding materials in an organisation is discussed below with detailed explanation of activities:

A computer system obtains input data/information from production planning, product design, maintenance department, sales and purchase departments. It can provide output data/information regarding inventory records to production planning department, remind purchase department about supply status and for follow up and send purchase orders directly to suppliers for standard repeat purchase items.

Integrated Management Information System using computer encompass the following areas:

(*i*) Long-term and short term sales forecasting and production schedules.

(*ii*) Materials manual.

(*iii*) Information regarding lead time, supply status (shortages, if any) price trends, anticipated price changes etc.

(*iv*) Materials requisition from production planning to stores.

(*v*) Materials issued from stores to production department.

(*vi*) Information regarding incoming materials and inwards inspection (rejected items report).

(*vii*) Due dates of supply from purchase department.

(*viii*) Information to purchase department for follow up of suppliers.

(*ix*) Purchase requisitions to purchase department.

(*x*) Printing of purchase orders.

(*xi*) Materials supplied by suppliers to receiving stores.

(*xii*) Previous year's consumption data.

3.5 EVALUATION OF INTEGRATED MATERIALS MANAGEMENT

Materials function provides an excellent scope for the computer application. Applications of computers in materials management can be classified under three groups: Operating systems, reporting system and decision support systems. To keep track of various operations going on in materials department, different types of reports are required. The computer can produce all these reports at very high speed and accuracy.

Typical and useful reports are as follows vendor delivery record, purchase material price variance, Materials consumption for the period. Expenditures due to materials used by various departments, inventory transactions and stock status, accounts payable. "*We live by sales but make our profits from materials*"– *is the central theme behind the evaluation of the materials management function.*

3.6 INVENTORY TURNOVER RATIO

It is the figure that indicates the number of times the inventory is rotated in a year, e.g. inventory equal to one month's consumption means a turnover of 12 times and inventory equal to 6 months consumption means an inventory turnover of 2 times. The turnover ratio indicates how best the capital tied up in inventory is utilised.

Example: Opening Inventory Rs. 7 Lac
Closing Inventory Rs. 5 Lac
Average Inventory Rs. 6 Lac
Consumption during the year Rs. 24 lac

$\therefore$ Inventory turnover ratio $= \frac{24}{6} = 4$ *i.e.*, 4 times a year

(*a*) Significance of Inventory turnover ratio: Inventory turnover greatly affects the profitability of a company. Let us consider the example as given on next page.

	Company X	*Company Y*	*Company Z*
1. Cost of Sales (Rs. Lac)	50	50	50
2. Gross Profit 15% (Rs. Lac)	7.5	7.5	7.5
3 Material Consumed (Rs. Lac)	25	25	25
4. Inventory held as month's consumption	1 month	6 months	12 months
5. Inventory turnover ratio	12	2	1
6. Value of inventory held (Rs. Lac)	2.1	12.5	25
7. Inventory Carrying Cost @ 25% (Rs. Lac)	0.525	3.13	6.25
8. Net Profit (Rs. Lac)	6.98	4.37	1.25

In one of these companies, there was a sales turnover of Rs. 200 lac in a year and it earned a profit of Rs. 20 lac and the capital employed was Rs. 100 lac.

1. Purcentage of Profit on Sales $= \frac{20 \text{ lac} \times 100}{200} = 10\%$

2. Turnover of Investment $= \frac{20 \text{ lac}}{100} = 2$

3. Percentage return on investment $10 \times 2 = 20\%$

In the next year, this company reduced its inventories by Rs. 20 lac. The other thing *i.e.*, sales turnover and profits remained the same.

4. $\therefore$ Capital employed Rs. 80 lac

5. Turnover investment $= \frac{\text{Rs. } 200 \text{ lac}}{\text{Rs. } 80 \text{ lac}} = 2.5$

A large part of capital is tied up to inventries and hence reduction in inventory may improve the return on assets, though profits on sales remain the same. Consider the following: Our earning are sales revenue minus costs of materials, labour, sales cost and administrative costs etc. Our capital employed is worth our inventories, cash, fixed assets, plant and meaning etc.

$\therefore$ Percentage of Profits on Sale $= \frac{\text{Earning} \times 10}{\text{Sales Revenue}}$ ...(*A*)

and Turn over of investment $= \frac{\text{Sales revenue}}{\text{Capita employed}}$ ...(*B*)

Percentage Return on Investments $= A \times B$

= Percentage of Profit on Sales × Turnover of investments

6. Percentage Return on Investment $= 10 \times 2.5 = 25\%$

Therefore, it is clear that a reduction in inventory increases the returns *i.e.*, profits.

3.7 PROBABLE QUESTIONS

1. Describe the objectives and function of a store.
2. How are location and layout of a store decided?
3. Describe the inspection and quality control and storage procedures for a store.
4. How is valuation of stock is worked out?
5. Write about the importance of *MIS* for materials management.
6. What is Inventry turnover ratio? Write about its significance.

Case Study 1

LOCATION FACTORS FOR CALL CENTERS

Call centers are frequently mistaken for telemarketing operations, when in fact they are not. Most are "in bound" facilities that take reservations and orders or provide customer service. The industry has boomed during the past decade as more and more firms decided to outsource such customer service processes, so that they could concentrate on core competencies.

India is one of the favoured destinations for companies wanting to outsource their operations. The reasons why companies prefer India are:

- Highly skilled, English-speaking workforce.
- Cheaper workforce than their Western counterparts. According to Nasscom, the wage difference is as high as 70–80 percent when compared to their Western counterparts. If a bank shifts work of a 1000 people from US to India it can save about $ 18 million a year due to lower costs in India. According to Mckinsey, giant US pharma firms can reduce the cost of developing a new drug, currently estimated as between $600 million and $900 million by as much as $200 million if development work is outsourced to India.
- Lower attrition rates than in the West. The attrition rate in India is 12–35 percent while in USA it is 70–120 percent in call centres.
- Dedicated workforce aiming at making a long-term career in the field.
- Round-the-clock advantage for Western companies due to the huge time difference.
- Lower response time with efficient and effective service.
- Internet has driven marginal cost of transferring data to zero and telecom costs are falling.
- Mature process expertise and six sigma culture.

The portfolio becomes even more attractive because of its Network Readiness World Economic Forum's network. Readiness Index ranks India 45th out of a total of 102 countries for 2003-2004. The index studies degree of preparation of participate in and benefit from information and communication technology developments.

Indian economy has also benefitted from the boom in the outsourcing industry. On hiring front, the industry absorbed about 2,45,100 people by March 31, 2004 experiencing a growth rate of 40–45 percent. This in turn has motivated foreign companies to invest in this industry, thereby leading to more influx of FDI. Indian revenue from the outsourcing industry has grown from 107 to $583 million.

Motivated by the positive role of the outsourcing industry in economic growth, Indian government gives incentives to make India more attractive by reducing cost of entry. This, in turn, increases attractiveness of variable like labor cost and supply, time zone, telecommunication structures, financial structure etc.

Sources: Knowledge Base, October 4, 2004, ***http:/www. bpoindia. org/knowledge base/# Indian-market-size****: Prasuna, D.G. (2003, January), BPO: Advantage India, Chartered Financial Analyst, India, pp. 19–26; World Economic Forum, The Global information Technology Report: Towards an Equitable Information Society. Oxford University Press. New York, 2003-2004, pp. 3–20, 152: Attrition in India BPO Industry, October 4, 2004,* ***http://www. bpoindia. org/research/ attrition. shtml****; Knowledge Base, October 4, 2004,* ***http:// www. bpoindia. org/knowledge Base/# indian-market-size****: Ehr Mark, Indian Outsourcers make big Gains, October 23, 2004* ***http://www.nwfusion. com/newsletters/asp/2004/ 1018out:.html****; NASSCOM, India Tech Boom, October 23, 2004, NASSCOM Web site:* ***www. nasscom. org/artdisplay.asp? Ar id = 234****.*

Proximity of Suppliers and Resource

Firms dependent on inputs of bulky, perishable, or heavy raw materials emphasize proximity to suppliers and resources. In such cases, *inbound* transportation costs become a dominant factor, encouraging such firms to locate facilities near suppliers. For example, locating paper mills near forests, and food processing facilities near farms is practical. Another advantage of locating near suppliers is the ability to maintain lower inventories.

Proximity to the Parent Company's Facilities

In many companies, plants supply parts to other facilities or rely on other facilities for management and staff support. These ties require frequent coordination and communication, which can become more difficult as distance increases.

Utilities, Taxes, and Real Estate Costs

Other important factors that may emerge include utility costs (telephone, energy, and water), local and state taxes, financing incentives offered by local or state governments, relocation costs, and land costs.

Case Study 2

TOYOTA PRODUCTION SYSTEM

If you were to select one company that is exemplary of excellence in automobile manufacturing, it should probably be Toyota (**www.toyota.com**). Worldwide in its presence, it has a total investment of $13.1 billion in 12 manufacturing plants that employ 32,500 associates in North America alone. Toyota was at the forefront of firms developing lean systems for manufacturing, and today the Toyota Production System (TPS) is one of the most admired lean manufacturing systems in existence. Replicating the system, however, is fraught with difficulties. What makes the system tick, and why could Toyota employ the system in so many different plants when others have difficulty?

Most outsiders see the TPS as a set of tools and procedures that are readily visible during a plant tour. While they are important for the success of the TPS, they are not the keys to the heart of the system. What most people overlook is that Toyota has built a learning organization over the course of 50 years. Lean systems require constant improvements to increase efficiency and reduce waste. Toyota has created a system that stimulates employees to experiment with their environment by seeking better ways whenever things go wrong. Toyota sets up all operations as experiments and teaches employees at all levels how to use the scientific method of problem solving.

A Toyota Motor Corporation employee works on the assembly line at the Tsutsumi plant in Tokyo. The TPS stimulates employees to experiment with their environment by seeking better ways when things go worng.

There are four underlying principles of the TPS. First, all work must be completely specified as to content, sequence, timing, and outcome. Detail is important, otherwise there is no foundation for improvements. Second, every customer-supplier connection must be direct, unambiguously specifying the people involved, the form and quantity of the services or goods to be provided, the way the requests are made by each customer, and the expected time in which the requests will be met. Customer–supplier connections can be internal–employee to employee–or external–company to company.

Third, the pathway for every service and product must be simple and direct. That is, services and goods do not flow to the next available person or machine, but to a specific person or machine. With this principle, employees can determine, for example, that there is a capacity problem at a particular workstation and then analyze ways to resolve it.

The first three principles define the system in detail by specifying how employees do work, interact with each other, and design work flows. These specifications actually are "hypotheses" about the way the system should work. For example, if something goes wrong at a workstation enough times, the hypothesis about the methods the employee uses to do work is rejected. The fourth principle, then, is that any improvement to the system must be made in accordance with the scientific method, under the guidance of a teacher, at the lowest possible organizational level. The scientific method involves clearly stating a verifiable hypothesis of the form, "If we make the following specific changes, we expect to achieve this specific outcome." The hypothesis must then be tested under a variety of conditions. Working with a teacher, who is often the employees' supervisor, is a key to becoming a learning organization. Employees learn the scientific method and eventually become teachers of others. Finally, making improvements at the lowest level of the organization means that the employees who are actually doing the work are actively involved in making improvements.

These four principles are deceptively simple; however, they are difficult to replicate. Nonetheless, those organizations that have successfully implemented them have enjoyed the benefits of a lean system that adapts to change.

Source: Spear, and H. Kent Bowen, "Decoding the DNA of the Toyota Production System." Harvard Business Review (September-October 1999). pp 97–106. Updated March 2003.

Case Study 3

CUSTOMER DEMAND PLANING AT UNILEVER

One of the critical drivers in managing value chains is effective customer demand planning (CDP), which begins with accurate forecasts. CDP is a business planning process that enables sales teams (and customers) to develop demand forecasts as input to service planning processes, production and inventory planning, and revenue planning. *Forecasting* is generally seen as the process of developing the most probable view of what future demand will be, given a set of assumptions about technology, competitors, pricing, marketing, expenditures, and sales effort. Planning, on the other hand, is the process of making management decisions on how to deploy resources to best respond to the demand forecasts. Forecasts must generally precede plans: It is not possible to make decisions on staffing levels, purchasing commitments, and inventory levels until forecasts are developed that give reasonably accurate views of demand over the forecasting time horizon.

Unilever (**www.unilever.com**), the fast-moving consumer products supplier, has a state-of-the-art CDP system. Using software from Manugistics (**www.manugistics.com**), the current system blends historical shipment data with promotional data, allowing information sharing and collaboration with important customers. The system begins with shipment history and current order information, the foundation upon which Unilever's system is built. This baseline forecast depends solely on past and present information, so reliable data is a critical requirement. Because data frequently is collected from disparate legacy systems, it may contain errors and may not necessarily lead to the best forecast. Moreover, statistical information is not useful in forecasting the outcomes of certain events, promotions, rollouts, and special packages, which are very common in the industry. To overcome this problem, at unilever must adjust the statistical forecasts with planned promotion predictions conducted by special sales teams. For each promotion, the sales-planning system predicts the "lift," or projected increase in sales, and routes it to the demand-planning system, which applies it to appropriate *stock-keeping units* (SKUs) and distribution centers each week. In turn, these forecasts are reviewed and adjusted if needed.

Lipton tea is one of many Unilever products, and its demand must be forecast for around the world. Here tourists walk past a souvenir and food stall in Beijing, China, which offers cups of Lipton tea. For centuries, globalism's story traveled with merchants who shepherded spice along Eurasian trade routes. Now it travels over wires and radio waves, satillites, airplanes, and gigabytes

Furthermore, Unilever conducts external market research and internal sales projections that are analyzed, combined with the retail customer promotions, and fed into the demand-planning system. To further improve the accuracy of its forecasts and reduce inventory lead times, Unilever–the purveyor of Dove, Lipton, Hellmann's, and hundreds of other brands–compares point-of-sale (POS) data with its own forecasts. Unfortunately, not all customers provide POS data. Moreover, integrating the data is not easy because it comes in different formats, which forces the company to build interfaces in order to manage it. Because creating these interfaces is expensive and time consuming, most companies, including Unilever, only collect POS data from its largest customers. Ultimately, planners at Unilever negotiate the final numbers each week and feed these forecasts into the demand-planning system.

Overall, the current system has been a success. Unilever has reduced its inventory and improved its customer service. However, if collaboration and the usage of POS data were to increase, Unilever would likely reap even larger benefits from its more accurate forecasts. The next step for Unilever is to collaborate with its customers and suppliers, a process by which forecasts, promotion plans, and other data are shared among these firms to determine the final forecast. This process is known *as collaborative planning, forecasting, and replenishment. (CPFR).*

*Source: Mitchell, Robert L. "Case Study: Unilever Crosses the Data Streams" Computer world (December 17, 2001): **www.computerworld.com/softwaretopics/erp/story/0,10801, 66754,00, html;** Mitchell, Robert L. "Tech Check Getting Demand Planning Right." Computerworld (December 17, 2001): **www.computerworld.com/softwaretopics/erp/story/0,10001,66576,00.html**: Schoenberger, Chana R. "The Weakest Link." Forbes (October 1,2001) www. forbes, com/forbes/2001/1001/114_print. html.*

Case Study 4

AGGREGATE PLANING AT MEMORIAL HOSPITAL

A 265-bed regional health care facility is located in the mountains in Dehradun. The mission of the hospital is to provide quality health care to the people. To accomplish this mission, three objectives have been outlined by the CEO of the hospital:

1. maximize customer service to increase customer satisfaction,
2. minimize costs to remain competitive, and
3. minimize fluctuations in workforce levels to help stabilize area employment.

The hospital's operations are segmented into eight major wards for the purposes of planning and scheduling the nursing staff. These wards are listed in Table. I along with the number of beds, targeted patient-to-nurse ratios, and average patient census for each ward. The overall demand for hospital services has remained relatively constant over the past few years even though the population of the seven countries served has increased. This stable demand can be attributed to increased competition from other hospitals in the area and the rise in alternative health care delivery systems, such as health maintenance organizations (HMOs). However, demand for Memorial Hospital's services does vary considerably by type of ward and time of year. Table 2 provides an historical monthly breakdown of the average daily patient census per ward.

The director of nursing for the Memorial Hospital confronts one of the most challenging aspects of her job: planning the nurse-staffing levels for the next calendar year. Although the average demand for nurses has remained relatively stable over the past couple of years, the staffing plan usually changes because of changing work policies, changing pay structures, and temporary nurse availability and cost. The Director has begun to collect information to plan next year's staffing levels.

The nurses at the hospital work a regular schedule of four 10-hour days per week. The average regular-time pay across all nursing grades is Rs 80 per hour. Overtime may be scheduled when necessary. However, because of the intensity of the demands placed on nurses, only a limited amount of overtime is permitted per week. Nurses may be scheduled for as many as 12 hours per day, for a maximum of five days per week. Overtime is compensated at a rate of Rs 100 per hour. In periods of extremely high demand, temporary part-time nurse may be hired for a limited period of time. Temporary nurses are paid Rs 90 per hour. The hospital has a policy that limits the proportion of temporary nurses to 15 percent of the total nursing staff.

TABLE -1
WARD CAPACITY DATA

Ward	Number of Beds	Patients per Nurse	Patient Census*
Intensive care	20	2	10
Cardiac	25	4	15
Maternity	30	4	10
Pediatric	40	4	22
Surgery	5	†	†
Post-Op	15	5	8 (T–F daily equivalent)‡
Emergency	10	3	5 (daily equivalent)‡
General	120	8	98

·Yearly average per day.

† The hospital employs 20 surgical nurses. Routine surgery is scheduled on Tuesdays and Fridays; five surgeries can be scheduled per day operating room (bed) on these days. Emergency surgery is scheduled as needed.

† Daily equivalents are used to schedule because patients flow through these wards in relatively short periods of time. A daily equivalent of 5 indicates that throughout a typical day, an average of five patients are treated in the ward.

TABLE -2
AVERAGE DAILY CENSUS PER MONTH

Ward	J	F	M	A	M	J	J	A	S	O	N	D
Intensive care	13	10	8	7	7	6	11	13	9	10	12	14
Cardiac	18	16	15	13	14	12	13	12	13	15	18	20
Maternity	8	8	12	13	10	8	13	13	14	10	8	7
Pediatric	22	23	24	24	25	21	22	20	18	20	21	19
Surgery*	20	18	18	17	16	16	22	21	17	18	20	22
Post- Op†	10	8	7	7	6	6	10	10	7	8	9	10
Emergency†	6	4	4	7	8	5	5	4	4	3	4	6
General	110	108	100	98	95 .	90	88	92	98	102	107	94

*Average sugeries per day.

† Daily equivalents.

Finding, hiring, and retaining qualified nurses is a problem that hospitals have been facing for years. One reason is that various forms of private practice are luring many nurses away from hospitals with higher pay and greater flexibility. This situation has caused Hospital to guarantee its full-time staff nurses pay for a minimum of 30 hours per week, regardless of the demand placed on nursing services. In addition, each nurse receives a four-week paid vacation each year. However, vacation scheduling may be somewhat restricted by the projected demand for nurses during particular times of the year.

At present, the hospital employs 130 nurses, including 20 surgical nurses. The other 110 nurses are assigned to the remaining seven major areas of the hospital. The personnel department has limited average cost to the hospital for hiring a new full-time nurse to $400 and for laying off or firing a nurse is $150.

QUESTIONS

1. Explain the alternatives available to the Director while developing a nurse-staffing plan for Memorial Hospital. How does each meet the objectives stated by the CEO?
2. Based on the data presented, develop a nurse staffing plan for Memorial Hospital. Explain your rationale for this plan.

Source: This case was prepared by Dr. Brooke Saladin, Wake Forest University, as a basis for classroom discussion.

Case Study 5

IMPLEMENTING A PERIODIC REVIEW INVENTORY SYSTEM AT HEWLETT-PACKARD

Hewlett-Packard (www.hp.com). manufactures computers, accessories, and a wide variety of instrumentation devices in more than 100 separate businesses, each responsible for its own product designing, marketing, and manufacturing processes as well as the required inventories to service its customers. At most HP businesses, inventory-driven costs (which include currency devaluation, obsolescence, price protection, and financing) are now the biggest control lever that the manufacturing organization has on business performance, measured in terms of return on assets or economic value added. Inventory is a major cost driver and the most variable element on the balance sheet.

Most of HP's business units were inefficient, carrying more inventory than needed in order to achieve a desired level of product delivery performance. They often used simplified approaches, such as ABC analysis, to determine their safety stocks for independent demand items, ignoring supply or demand uncertainty, part commonality, desired part availability, or cost. The solution was to develop a periodic review system that used part availability targets and included as many uncertainties as possible. The system, although in principle similar to the *P* system discussed in this chapter, uses complex equations to determine the review interval and target inventory parameters. The complexity arises from considering uncertainties in supply as well as demand in the determination of the safety stocks.

Even though the system could be shown to reduce inventories and improve customer service, no benefits would be realized until the planning and procurement staff actually used it. Since each business unit had some unique characteristics, the results had to be easily understandable and credible, and the system had to be easily configurable to each situation. Consequently, HP developed a software wizard that allows the user to enter product data and costs in a friendly environment, develops the equations for the periodic review system, and then translates the results to the user's format requirements. The wizard is programmed in Excel, which allows users access to all of Excel's functionality for conducting their own analyses.

The periodic review system and the software wizard have been very successful. At HP's Integrated Circuit Manufacturing Division, for example, planners cut inventories by $1.6 million while simultaneously improving on-time delivery performance from 93 percent to 97 percent. Other benefits included less expediting, fewer disagreements about operating policy, and more control of the production system. The system is used across a wide variety of product lines and geographies wordwide. HP believes that, without exception, the product lines how have more efficient operations.

Source: Cargille, Brian, Steve Kakouros, and Robert hall. "Part Tool, Part Process: Inventory Optimization at Hewlett-Packard Co." OR/MS/TO DAY (October 1999), pp. 18-24.

Case Study 6

IBM'S ROCHESTER PLANT USES MRP 11 TO EXECUTIVE ITS FAST TURNAROUND STARATEGY

IBM's Rochester, Minnesota, plant (www.research.ibm.com) is responsible for the final assembly of IBM's AS/400 midrange computers. The complex includes a printed circuit board assembly and testing facility that provides subassemblies to the final assembly lines. Each AS/400 computer is assembled to customer order, which the plant does more than 50,000 times per year. There are more than 10,000 different configurations. The plant must manage over 57,000 parts and assemblies no matter where they might be in the 3.6 million square feet of space the facility occupies, a daunting task without the help of modern systems. To remain competitive in this industry, IBM must promise delivery of complete computers within 96 hours of receiving the order. In addition, because of the short lead times, the plant must procure materials before firm customer orders are received, which requires careful management of inventory levels and shortages.

The IBM eServer 1825 has a revolutionary on–off capacity on–demand feature that allows smaller customers to turn on extra processing power when needed. The Rochester, Minnesota plant produces the As/400 iServer midrange computers

A core element of the plant's fast turnaround strategy is a mapics MRP II system (www. mapics. com), which took 18 months to install. In addition, IBM developed an application called Production Resource Manager (PRM), which interfaces with a firm's MRP II or ERP systems. In addition to typical inputs to an MRP II system, PRM requires *bills of capacity*, production, suppliers and inventory constraints, and optimization objectives, such as maximizing profits, minimizing costs, or minimizing inventories. The bills of capacity are analogous to bills of material, except they contain the amounts of specific capacities that are needed by a particular configuration of the final product and when they are needed. PRM takes the MRP II plan for component and purchased material replenishment orders and modifies it as needed to account for supply and component availability, capacity constraints, and objectives. The many outputs include a master production schedule, an optimal component production schedule, a revised shipment schedule, and a critical parts list.

The system has enabled the Rochester plant to improve its inventory accuracy. to 99 percent and reduce safety stocks by 15 to 25 percent. The system also includes a cost accounting module, which makes costing information that used to take more than a week to obtain immediately available. In addition, planners can simulate "what-if" scenarios quickly to see the impacts of various events on the production schedule. MRP II and the PRM application have enabled IBM's Rochester plant to execute its fast turn around strategy.

Sources: "Success Stories: IBM Rochester, Minnesota. USA" MAPICS, Inc. (2000): Weaver, Russ. " PRM in Action at Rochester, MN" IBM Corporation (1996); Weaver, Russ."Production Resource Manager." IBM Corporation (1996).

Airlines:

Whenever an airline schedules a flight, there are requirements for facilitating goods (meals, beverages, and fuel), staff (pilots, flight attendants, and airports services), and equipment (plane and airport gate). Forecasts of customer patronage of each flight help determine the amount of facilitating goods and the type of plane needed. A master schedule of flights based on the forecasts can be exploded to determine the resources needed to support the schedule.

Hospitals:

With the exception of the emergency room, appointments, which are a form of master schedule for specific services, generally drive the short-term need for health care resources in hospitals. Forecasts of requests for various services provided by the hospital drive.

PRODUCTION MANAGEMENT QUESTION BANK

Group A– Multiple Choice Question

Choose the correct alternatives from the following.

1. For an Integrated steel plant, the plant location decision will be chiefly influenced by the consideration of

(a) proximity to the market

(b) proximity to the raw material

(c) availability of good-transportation system

(d) all of these

2. Line balancing is a technique for

(a) job assignment (b) work place lay out

(c) method study

3. ISO9001 is a system for

(a) quality management

(b) operational planning

(c) productivity improvement

4. Condition monitoring is method for

(a) preventive maintenance

(b) upgradation of facilities

(c) asset utilisation

5. Which of the following is not a type of control chart?

(a) standard deviation chart or sigma chart

(b) mean chart or $\overline{X}$ chart

(c) range chart or $\overline{R}$ chart

(d) type and enter or chart

6. When do you resort to "Breakdown" maintenance.

(a) when you assemble a new machine for installation

(b) when a machine in operation comes to "breakdown".

(c) when you apply a brake to stop running machine

(d) when the machine becomes obsolete and has to be replaced by a new machine

7. Mass production system is adopted when
   (a) volume is very large and variety is less
   (b) volume is small and variety is large
   (c) both volume and variety are medium
   (d) none of these

8. Which of the following is a material handling equipment that could be used in a plant?
   (a) Fork lift truck (b) P–4 computer
   (c) Mercedes-benz car (d) air conditioners

9. Statistical quality control is done to
   (a) prevent any defective product from giving out of factory
   (b) observe the trend of product quality
   (c) initiate corrective action if quality trend shows an adverse pattern.
   (d) none of these

10. Preventive maintenance refers to
   (a) a system of scheduled and planned maintenance to minimize problem of breakdown.
   (b) the repair work undertaken after the failure of machine or equipment.
   (c) the maintenance undertaken on the prediction of any fault in the machinery
   (d) none of these

11. Work study formerly known as
   (a) method study
   (b) work measurement
   (c) time and motion study
   (d) none of these

12. "Cost of Quality" is the
   (a) cost of creating a quality product
   (b) cost of maintaining quality instruments
   (c) cost of not creating a quality product
   (d) all of these

13. Production planning and control is difficult for
   (a) mass production (b) jobbing work
   (c) batch production (d) none of these

14. Project works follow
   (a) product type layout
   (b) process type layout
   (c) fixed position layout
   (d) cell type layout

15. For continuous process of material handling is to use
   (a) cranes (b) fork lifters
   (c) conveyers (d) lifts

16. Day-to-day planning of operation is called
(a) scheduling (b) dispatching
(c) despatching (d) inspection

17. High variety and low volume are characteristics associated with
(a) batch production
(b) mass production
(c) job shop production
(d) continuous production

18. Materials Requirement Planning (MRP) is associated with which of the following stage of Production Planning and Control?
(a) planning stage (b) action phase
(c) control phase (d) all of these

19. The system of holding reservoirs of materials for feeding into the production system is known as
(a) push system
(b) pull system
(c) pond-draining system
(d) synchronous manufacturing system.

20. The periodic monitoring and analysis of equipment conditions to predict future equipment performance is practiced under
(a) proactive maintenance
(b) preventive maintenance
(c) corrective maintenance
(d) none of these

21. The work done by hand and body movements could be classified according to Gilbreth into fundamental motions and are termed as
(a) line balancing
(b) Therbligs
(c) controlled movements
(d) cycle time

22. A ship building industry will be best fitted for
(a) process layout
(b) product layout
(c) fixed position layout
(d) flexible manufacturing system layout

23. The Process Control Measure in a situation where member of defects is the criteria for acceptance or rejection, a special control chart used is called
(a) cusum chart (b) p-chart
(c) c-chart (d) r-chart

24. TQM stands for
   (a) total quality monitoring
   (b) total quality management
   (c) total quality maintenance
   (d) none of these

25. Fitness for use is known as
   (a) quality (b) quality circle
   (c) TQM (d) kaizen

26. Which of the following ratios is used as assess the efficiency of the PPC department?
   (a) total assets turnover ratio
   (b) interest coverage ratio
   (c) debt-equity ratio
   (d) employee turn over ratio

27. Which one of the following is not a fixed cost?
   (a) rent (b) insurance
   (c) manager's salaries (d) material

28. Statistical quality control is done to
   (a) prevent any defective product from going out of the factory
   (b) observe the trend of product quality
   (c) initiate corrective action if quality trend shows an adverse pattern
   (d) none of these

29. Continuous improvement is the concept of
   (a) quality (b) quality circle
   (c) TQM (d) kaizen

30. Time allowed to an operator to carry out as specified task under specified condition and at the defined level of performance is called
   (a) observed time (b) normal time
   (c) standard time (d) none of these

31. PDCA stands for
   (a) plan, do, check and act
   (b) prepare, do, continue and action
   (c) progress, do, check and act
   (d) none of these

32. PERT stands for
   (a) program evaluation review technique
   (b) program evaluation renew technique
   (c) project evaluation review technique
   (d) none of these

33. The control chart which is used in a situation where fraction defectives are the criteria for acceptance or rejection is called

(a) $\overline{X}$-chart (b) R-chart

(c) P-chart (d) C-chart

34. Standard time is equal to

(a) normal time

(b) average time

(c) normal time + allowance

(d) average time + allowance

35. Which one among the following is a fixed type of material handling system?

(a) trolleys (b) conveyors

(c) industrial trucks (d) wheet barrow

36. PPC department helps the marketing department in relation to

(a) getting a new customer

(b) formulating the delivery schedule of the order

(c) convincing an old customer

(d) correcting the dealings of the marketing department

37. Line balancing is a technique for

(a) job assignment (b) work place layout

(c) method study (d) material handling

38. For continuous process of material handling are used

(a) cranes (b) fork-lifters

(c) conveyers (d) lifts

Group–B Short Answer Type Questions

1. What factors would you consider for selection of material handling equipment?
2. What is "preventive maintenance"? Write the advantages and disadvantages of preventive maintenance.
3. What is the relationship between observed time, normal time and standard time.
4. Discuss the significance of statistical quality control.
5. Distinguish between quality control and inspection.
6. How is preventive maintenance different from Breakdown maintenance?
7. State the objectives of a sound maintenance system in an industrial unit.
8. What is ISO and what is its objectives? What is the different between ISO 9001 and ISO 9002?
9. Explain about the revisions made on ISO since its first approval.
10. State the advantages of a good plant layout.
11. State the difference between specification limit and control limit.
12. Write notes on

(a) performance rating (b) kaizen philosophy
(c) different types of inspection

13. Explain why material handling equipments are essential in a factory.
14. Define production planning and control function and their utility in a factory.
15. What are the objectives of scientific management as explained by F.W. Taylor.
16. Define cycle graphs and chrono cycle graphs.
17. What are the difference between hoists and cranes? Differentiate between gravity and power conveyors.
18. What do you mean by "work sampling"? Point out the advantages and limitations of "work Samplings"
19. What do you mean by work study and method study? Discuss.
20. Write notes on
    (a) Quality assurance (b) six sigma
    (c) therbligs (d) kaizen philosophy
    (e) motion study
21. Define the concept of aggregate planning
22. How do you explain performance rating.
23. State the difference between product and process layout.
24. Write a note on kaizen philosophy.
25. Discuss the significance of statistical quality control.

Group–C Long Answer Type Questions

1. Discuss with the help of flow diagram various production management functions and their inter-relationships with each other. Briefly enumerate the role of production management in a changing business world.

2. (a) Describe the main features of drawing nearness diagram (relationship chart). Explain how it helps in developing plant layout.

(b) XYZ manufacturing co. makes various products with the help of six departments as per the sequences given. Draw a nearness diagram on the basis of data as under:

Deptt No	Sequences		Product
1	1–4–5–6	→	A
2	2–4–5	→	B
3	1–4–6–3	→	C
4	6 – 2– 4–5	→	D
5	4 – 1 – 5	→	E
6	1– 4 – 5 – 6	→	F

3. (a) Discuss various inventory analysis techniques with special reference to selective control.

(b) Compute ABC classification and draw the diagram from the data given below on the basis of values of consumption

Item No	Annual Consumption (units)	Value units (Rs)
1	100	400
2	500	60
3	200	70
4	30	200
5	30	100
6	75	20
7	50	30
8	50	40
9	40	30
10	40	20

4. (a) Briefly explain main features of time study. What are the aspects do you consider while compiting work content?

(b) Work out the total work content from the following data. Rest and contingency allowances are proviled as 13% and 2% respectively.

Elements	Observed time	Rating	Frequency
A	0.20	90	1
B	0.05	80	1
C	0.03	100	1
D	0.78	100	1
E	0.06	100	1
F	0.05	100	1
G	0.20	85	$\frac{1}{5}$
H	0.06	80	1
I	0.10	90	1
J	0.40	90	$\frac{1}{20}$

5. Write short notes on:

(i) ABC analysis

(ii) Capacity planning and its objectives

(iii) Deming's approach to quality

(iv) Material handling

(v) Statistical process control (SPC)

(vi) Productivity and its types.

6. What do you mean by Production Planning and Control (PPC)? Discuss briefly the objectives of PPC. How can the efficiency of PPC function be measured?

7. How can the production system be classified? State briefly the features of mass, batch and project production systems.
8. What is statistical quality control (SQC)? Discuss the different tools or techniques of SQC.
9. What are the objectives of "Material Handling system?" Discuss the factors to be considered for selection of the material handling equipment.
10. What is meant by work measurement? Discuss the steps in work measurement. Point out its benefits.
11. Discuss the various steps in time study procedure. Show how is the standard time of a job calculated.
12. (a) What is a control chart and state of control?

    (b) Describe the various types of control chart.
13. What do you mean by production? What do you mean by production systems? Discuss in details how production systems can be classified.
14. What are the different factors influencing plant layout? What do you mean by product layout and process layout? Tabulate the various merits and demerits of the above mentioned layouts.
15. What do you mean plant maintenance? What are the benefits from preventive maintenance? Discuss in details the different materials handling equipments.
16. What do you mean by work study? Enumerate the steps involved in a stopwatch times study. Explain the significance of the work sampling as a technique for work study.
17. What do you mean by statistical process control? Discuss the different charts used in SPC. What is a quality circle?
18. (a) What are the objectives of " Method study"?

    (b) Discuss the various steps in method study procedure.

    (c) Point out its advantages.
19. Considering the following data, apply rate of return (ROR) method to select the best site for a plant

Factors	Site 1 Rs	Site 2 Rs	Site 3 Rs
Land	50,000	75,000	1,00, 000
Building	1,50, 000	1,25,000	1,00,000
Inbound logistics	18,000	22,000	18,000
Outbound logistics	22,000	18,000	25,000
Raw material	60,000	80,000	55,000
Electricity	10,000	15,000	10,000
Water	30,000	25,000	35,000
Salary	45,000	50,000	40,000
Expected sales	2,50,000	3,00,000	2,50,000

20. What is work sampling? What are its merits? A group of 10 workmen working 8 hours perday (one shift) on a group of engine lathes produced 320 pieces of a component. During the study, it was observed that workmen were idle for 20% of the total available time and 80% of the time they worked at an average performance of 75%. Calculate standard time for the job assuming

(i) the operation to be completely manual

(ii) the workmen are entitled to 20% allowance for this type of work.

21. (a) Define "Cost of quality".

(b) Explain the three categories of cost of quality

(c) Write a short note on 150 9000 series of standards on quality management systems.

22. (a) What are objectives of materials handling systems?

(b) Discuss the factors to be considered for selection of the material handling equipment.

23. What is time study? Enumerate the steps in conducting time study. What is meant by standard time? Discuss the different types of allowances considered in setting the standard time.

24. Define ideal plant location. State the steps in choosing a plant location.

25. A company is to decide on the location of a new plant. It has narrowed down the choice to three location A, B and C. Data in respect of which are given below:

Locations

Factors	A	B	C
1. Wage & salaries	20,000	20,000	20,000
2. Power & water supply	20,000	30,000	25,000
3. Raw material	80,000	75,000	60,000
4. Total initial investment	2,00,000	3,00,000	2,50,000
5. Distribution expenses	50,000	40,000	60,000
6. Miscellaneous expenses	40,000	25,000	30,000
7. Expected sales per year	2,25,000	2,50,000	2,25,000

Use a suitable criteria and advise the company on the best choice.

26. (a) Define production system

(b) What are the different production system?

(c) Explain any two production systems with examples.

27. (a) Mention the objectives of material handling system. What factors should be considered for selection of material handling equipment?

(b) Discuss in detail the different material handling equipment.

28. (a) Define production planning and control (PPC). What are the objectives of PPC?

(b) How in the efficiency of PPC function measured?

29. Write notes on

(a) Inspection

(b) motion study

(c) work measurement

(d) maintenance.

MATERIALS MANAGEMENT QUESTION BANK

Group A–Multiple Choice Question

Choose the correct alternatives from the following:

1. Which one of the following in not included in the 5R in purchasing?
(a) quality (b) quantity
(c) price (d) none of these

2. Which of the following is not a function of purchasing management?
(a) selecting the source
(b) placement of purchase order
(c) physical control of material
(d) none of these

3. The purchase order form is designed by
(a) materials manager (b) purchase manager
(c) marketing manager (d) none of these

4. ABC analysis is method of
(a) stock classification (b) stock codification
(c) both (a) & (b) (d) none of these

5. The objectives of forward purchasing are
(a) to guard against interruption in supply
(b) to economic the use of storage space
(c) to guard against the future rise in price
(d) all of these

6. PERT stands for
(a) program evaluation review technique
(b) program evaluation renew technique
(c) program elimination review technique
(d) none of these

7. Which of the following is not a method of valuation of materials?
   (a) LIFO method
   (b) FIFO method
   (c) ABC method
   (d) standard price method

8. JIT contributed to the
   (a) reduced inventories and WIP
   (b) reduced supplies
   (c) reduced information flow
   (d) reduced manpower planning

9. Safety or buffer stock represents
   (a) the inventory level beyond which materials should not fall in any case
   (b) the extra inventory stock maintained to meet the demand
   (c) the stock which must be maintained in hand all the times
   (d) the quantity of material which a firm should not exceed

10. Reciprocity is
   (a) selecting one's own suppliers
   (b) selecting one's own customers
   (c) selecting one's own customers as suppliers
   (d) selecting one's own suppliers as customers

11. Value analysis is a technique of
   (a) calculating the inventory level
   (b) finding out the unnecessary cost associated with the production
   (c) appraising the investment proposals
   (d) routing and scheduling

12. "Hedging" technique is used
   (a) when there is an organised commodity market
   (b) when large quantities of a particular commodity are bought and sold
   (c) both (a) and (b)
   (d) none of these

13. Purchase budget has an impact on
   (a) profitability of the company
   (b) materials budget of the company
   (c) bill of materials
   (d) all of these

14. Right quality means
   (a) over specifying the quality standards for purchasers
   (b) under specifying the quality for purchasing
   (c) buying standard items
   (d) buying quality which suits the needs without incurring extra cost to the company

15. Purchase order is a legal binding contract only if it is
(a) accepted by the supplier
(b) acknowledged by the supplier
(c) posted by the buyer
(d) none of these

16. JIT is a concept which means
(a) Japanese language
(b) making a plan from time to time
(c) getting the items just when they are needed for production
(d) raising purchase order just before delivery

17. FSN analysis classifies goods on the basis of
(a) function, size and number
(b) fast, slow and non-moving
(c) foreign made, small scale and non-standard
(d) frequently required, sometimes required and never required

18. The type of purchasing where the purchaser tries to protect himself by entering into two transactions a purchase and a sale contracts in two markets whose prices fluctuate is known as
(a) speculative buying (b) Forward buying
(c) Hedging (d) Blanket order

19. A list of all items incorporated into a finished product with specifications and quantity requirements of each item of materials is generally known as
(a) master production schedules
(b) bill of materials
(c) purchase budget
(d) materials budget

20. The time interval between placing an order and the actual replenishment is known as
(a) delivery time (b) order time
(c) lead time (d) none of these

21. The record of movement of materials against each kind of stock in respect of daily transactions, which is attached to each bin or shelf or any other form of container in known as
(a) stores ledger
(b) stock identification card
(c) materials receipt note
(d) bin card

22. The method by which a limited number of items, selected at random or on a preplanned basis, are checked everyday at specific time intervals in known as
(a) physical verification
(b) periodic verification
(c) continuous verification
(d) materials audit

23. **The system of purchasing from one's customer preferred to others is known as**
(a) forward buying (b) tender buying
(c) reciprocal buying (d) blanket order

24. **The classification of inventory based on annual consumption and annual value is known as**
(a) ABC classification (b) VED classification
(c) PSN classification (d) HML classification

25. **Fixed order quantity system of inventory management is also known as**
(a) Max-min system
(b) Q-system
(c) re-order point system
(d) all of these

26. **The document prepared on receipt of materials in store is known as**
(a) MRN (b) GRN
(c) challan (d) bill of materials

27. **Which of the following cost in not taken into consideration for make or buy decision**
(a) fixed cost (b) variable cost
(c) semi-variable cost (d) none of these

28. **The key benefit of codification is**
(a) to prevent duplication
(b) to have accurate identification
(c) both (a) & (b)
(d) none of these

29. **A device to move materials along a definite path and used for moving bulk materials over long distances is known as**
(a) for-lift trucks (b) elevator
(c) hoists (d) conveyors

30. Work-in-progress is a
(a) procedure
(b) method
(c) value addition process
(d) none of these

31. The criteria of VED analysis is
(a) unit price of materials
(b) annual value consumption
(c) critical nature of item
(d) none of these

32. Follow-up cost and set-up cost are examples of
(a) ordering cost (b) carrying cost
(c) under-stocking cost (d) overstocking cost

33. Materials which are processed from wastage are called
(a) obsolete (b) scrap
(c) surplus (d) waste

34. The oldest stock is depleted first in
(a) FIFO method
(b) LIFO method
(c) average stock method
(d) standard and cost method

35. In the period of rising price, the most effective method of pricing inventory is
(a) FIFO method
(b) LIFO method
(c) average cost method
(d) standard cost method

36. A stipulation in a contract of sale pertaining to goods which is essential to the main purpose of the contract is called
(a) rejection (b) warranty
(c) acceptance (d) condition

37. When the contract of agency is in writing it is called
(a) law of agency (b) Quifacit peractuam facit
(c) power of attorney (d) none of these

38. An arrangement whereby the obligation to pay an exporter is undertaken by a bank is called
(a) Bill of ladding (b) letter of credit
(c) international credit (d) hundi

39. The type of buying must suitable for C category of items of inventory is
(a) forward buying (b) tender buying
(c) blanket order (d) systems contract

40. The system of codification which uses 7 digits and is applied in 3 phases is called
(a) kodak system (b) brisch system
(c) none of these (d) all of these

41. Which of the following is false for ABC analysis?
(a) always better control is the other name for ABC analysis
(b) ABC analysis is based on principle of critical few and trivial many
(c) ABC analysis is also called pareto analysis
(d) all of the statements are true

Group–B Short Answer Type Questions.

1. What do you understand by materials management? What are the broad function of materials management?
2. Name and discuss in short about five laws that have indirect impact on purchase activities.
3. What are the basic factors in choosing "materials handling equipment"?

4. What is 'Q' system of inventory. In a "Q" system of inventory what is called to be ROP.? How is it calculated?
5. Explain entire purchasing procedure with the help of a block diagram.
6. State the different methods of stock verification.
7. (a) Explain briefly what you understand by MRPI and MRP2. Discuss briefly.
   (b) Explain briefly the concept of supply chain management.
8. State objectives of materials management.
9. State the factors to be taken into account in arriving at make or buy decision.
10. Define the terms "obsolescence", "surplus", "defective" and "scrap" in storage control. Briefly state their disposal procedure.
11. Differentiates between P-system and Q-system of inventory management.
12. Distinguish between Bin card and store ledger.
13. Medical Aids Co. manufactures a special product A. The following particulars are collected for the year 2008.
   (a) monthly demand of A 1000 units
   (b) cost of placing an order Rs. 100
   (c) annual carrying cost per unit Rs 15
   (d) normal usage 50 units per week
   (e) minimum usage 25 units per week
   (f) maximum usage 75 units per week
   (g) Re-order period 4 to 6 week

   Compute from the above
   (i) Re-order level (ii) Re-order quantity
   (iii) minimum level (iv) maximum level
   (v) average stock level
14. Differentiates between forward buying and speculative buying.
15. What is economic order quantity? How is it calculated?
16. What are the benefits of scientific store keeping?
17. Define materials management. "Management of materials is very significant in a Firm" – Discuss.
18. Define make or buy decision. What are the different factors that influence the "make or buy decision", except cost factor.

Group–C Long Answer Type Questions.

1. Give a general picture of the vendor development and explain the scope of vendor rating system in Indian industry. Explain the benefits of vendor rating system.
2. What is material requirement planning? What are the inputs of MRP? Discuss the steps involved in materials requirement planning.

3. State the latest concept of Just-in-time technique of purchasing. Explain its scope in Indian situation. Give a comparative analysis between JIT and Traditional purchasing.
4. (a) Explain the concept of EOQ graphically and analytically.
   (b) An organisation purchases 20,000 cardboard boxes per year each costing. Rs 100, cost of ordering is Rs 400 per order, and cost of carrying is 30% of average inventory value.
      (i) Determine EOQ
      (ii) Two vendors have quoted for the same with the following terms and conditions.

   Vendor A has quoted 10% discount for order quantity of 10,000 and vendor B has quitted 20% discount for supplying entire total at a time. Which is the most economic offer? Will you lay any conditions while accepting the offer?
5. (a) Explain briefly the following selective control systems stating their application and use. ABC analysis, VED analysis, SDE analysis and FSN analysis.
   (b) Draw "Pareto" curve.
6. Discuss about the various legal aspects that the purchase manager has to deal with.
7. State the latest concept of just-in-time technique of purchasing. Explain its scope in Indian situation. Give comparative analysis between JIT and Traditional purchasing.
8. Explain the different buying methods of purchasing. What are the centralized and decentralized system of purchasing?
9. (a) What do you understand by MRPI ? How is it used in planning materials?
   (b) What is MRPII? How is it different from MRPI?
10. (a) What is EOQ. Explain the concept of EOQ mathematically.
    (b) A shopkeeper has an annual demand of an item of 600 units. He buys from a supplier at a cost of Rs 6/ per item and the cost of ordering is Rs. 10/= each time. If the stock holding costs are 20% per year of stock value, how frequently should he replenish his stock?

    Suppose the supplier offers a 5% discount on orders between 200 and 999 items and a 10% discount on orders exceeding or equal to 1000, can the shopkeeper reduce his cost by taking advantage of either of these discounts?
11. (a) What is vendor rating? On what major parameters are vendors rated?
    (b) Give on quantitative technique by which vendor rating can be performed?
12. Write short notes on following.
    (a) ABC analysis (b) VED analysis
    (c) Legal aspects of purchasing (d) FSN analysis
    (e) perpetual inventory system.
13. (a) Describe the various methods of valuation of stock.
    (b) Prepare a ABC plan from the following data of "metro works".

Item	1	2	3	4	5	6	7
Unit	1,800	500	1,500	1,2000	2,000	1,000	2000
Cost p.u.	33.5	300	10	34	5	200	12.5

14. (a) Briefly discuss the various methods of purchasing practised by various organisation.

(b) Discuss the purchase procedure of materials departments with the help of a diagram.

15. (a) The following information is available in respect of material X and Co. Ltd. Re-order quantity 12,000 unit, lead time 4 to 8 weeks, Maximum consumption 4000 units per week. Normal consumption 3000 unit per week, Maximum consumption 1550 units per week. Ascertain

(i) Re-order level (ii) Minimum stock level

(iii) maximum stock level.

16. Product A consists of three B types subassemblies and one C type sub assembly. The sub-assembly B consists of one D, one E sub assembles and one F. The subassembly E consists of a D and a F.

(i) Prepare a product tree

(ii) Prepare the numbers of each subassembly/components required to produce fifty units of item A.

17. Discuss the advantages and disadvantages of centralized and decentralized purchasing. Suppose you are working in a steel plant. It has several units like ore mines, coal mines, very big township, hospital etc. All such units are various types of materials. Many items are common. Explain how you would organise your purchase department.

18. (a) What is materials requirement planning?

(b) Discuss the inputs, processing and output of MRP system.

(c) Classify the following items into A, B and C category.

Sl.no	Item	Annual usage	price/unit Rs.
1	Graphite	4000 kgs	10/kg
2	Toluene	800 kgs.	5/kg
3	Wax	600 kgs	10/kg
4	Cap	2000 kgs	6/kg
5	Drums	1000 kgs	18 each
6	Oil	150 kgs	9/kg
7	Caston	3000 kgs	0.2 each
8	Powder	200 kgs	0.5/kg
9	Spirit	400 kgs	1/kg
10	Hydrochloric Acid	2500 kgs	6/kg
11	Carbon	700 kgs	15/kg
12	Nail	5000 kgs	0.10 each.

19. State the key elements of JIT system. Explain the salient features of JIT system. Explain the difference between JIT and MRP approach. What are the advantages of JIT system?

20. What is vendor rating and evaluation? Discuss the methods of vendor rating.

21. An auto parts supplier sells Hardly-brand batteries to car dealers and auto mechanics. The annual demand is approximately 1200 batteries. The supplier pays \$28 for each battery and estimates that the annual holding cost is 30 per cent of the battery value. It costs approximately \$ 20 to place an order (managerial and clerical costs). The supplier currently orders 100 batteries per month.

(a) Determine the ordering, holding and total inventory costs for the current order quantity.

(b) Determine EOQ

(c) How many orders will be placed per year using EOQ.

(d) Determine the ordering, holding and total inventory costs for the EOQ. How have ordering cost, holding cost, total inventory cost changed?

22. (a) What is ABC classification? Why is it necessary? Explain as to how the items can be classified into ABC categories.

(b) Discuss the use of ABC analysis in deciding the safety stock of various items.

23. (a) What do you understand by scientific store keeping? State the main objectives of it.

(b) Name the different types of store and explain briefly the function of each store.

24. (a) Briefly discuss the various methods of purchasing practised by various organisation.

(b) Discuss the purchase procedure of materials department with the help of a diagram.

25. Explain the purpose of the following files.

(a) order files.

(b) Item master file

(c) Product structure file

(d) Inventory transaction file

(e) Machine utilisation card file